Charles Popham Miles

**Correspondence on the French Revolution, 1789-1817**

Charles Popham Miles

**Correspondence on the French Revolution, 1789-1817**

ISBN/EAN: 9783337229856

Printed in Europe, USA, Canada, Australia, Japan

Cover: Foto ©ninafisch / pixelio.de

More available books at **www.hansebooks.com**

# THE CORRESPONDENCE

OF

# WILLIAM AUGUSTUS MILES

ON THE

# FRENCH REVOLUTION

1789–1817

EDITED BY THE

REV. CHARLES POPHAM MILES, M.A., F.L.S.

HONORARY CANON OF DURHAM
MEMBRE DE LA SOCIÉTÉ D'HISTOIRE DIPLOMATIQUE

*IN TWO VOLUMES — VOL. II.*

LONDON
LONGMANS, GREEN, AND CO.
AND NEW YORK: 15 EAST 16th STREET
1890

# CONTENTS

OF

# THE SECOND VOLUME

*Mr. Miles to Mr. Long. January 6, 1793.*
Treaty of Commerce null—Le Brun complains to the National Convention on the prohibition of corn, &c.—The Alien Bill—Chauvelin and Pitt—Advance of the Prussians—Dumouriez in Paris—The Austrians in Piedmont . . . . 1

*Minutes by Mr. Miles.*
Interview with Pitt on behalf of Chauvelin—English Cabinet pledged—Executive Council *means* war—Condorcet and Sieyès hostile—Le Brun actuated by private pique—Pitt a convert to war—Mischievous coalitions—War imminent—Instructions to Chauvelin—The 'Childers' fired into—Ill-humour of the English Cabinet—War party in England . . . . . 2

*Mr. Miles to General Dampierre. January 8.*
Abuses in France demanded a revolution—Mistake in calling the *people* to become legislators—Lafayette and his enemies—Tyranny supersedes liberty . . . . . 6

*Mr. Miles to the Editor of the 'True Briton.' Dec. 1792.*
Shock of the French Revolution—The mist of error must be dispelled—Anarchy worse than despotism . . . 9

*M. Fabry to Mr. Miles. Liège, December 28, 1792.*
England on the eve of war—Difficulties in Liège—The domains, &c., under sequestration—Prussia and Austria—Liège drifting towards France—Union with Belgium not practicable . . 10

*M. Maret to Mr. Miles.  Paris, January 5, 1793.*

   Opinion in Paris deluded—Insults of the British Parliament—Chauvelin—Visit of Maret to England—Le Brun would welcome co-operation with Miles . . . . . . . 12

*M. Mourgue to Mr. Miles.  Montpellier, January 1.*

   Critical events in Paris—Tranquillity in the south of France—Dangers due to legislative bodies—Union of 'proud Albion' with the Coalesced Powers—Evils of the Revolution—Why should England be troubled about the Scheldt?—England and France injure each other . . . . . . . 13

*M. Reinhard to Mr. Miles, January 10.*

   No courier from Paris—Resolution of Chauvelin—Reinhard desires an interview with Miles . . . . . 17

*Mr. Miles to M. Fabry.  January 11.*

   Joseph II.—Austrian Netherlands, Liège, Holland—Duke of Leeds in 1790—French straying from right principles—Despotism strengthened—*Levelling* leads to universal *ruin*—Le Brun at Hervé—Secret agents in London—Intercourse with French Government discouraged—Liège again under tyranny—Executive Power responsible for war—*Equality* ridiculous—Some *bridle* necessary—The clergy should not be robbed—Flanders, Brabant, Liège, may yet succeed . . . . . 17

*Mr. Miles to M. Maret.  January 11.*

   France must retreat or fight—War may endanger Liège—Nothing demanded from the Executive Council that would humiliate—The orders issued to the French generals—Conquests still retained—Decrees of November and December justify fears—Treaties guarantee the Scheldt—Maret may come to England without fear . . . . . . . 22

*Mr. Miles to M. Le Brun.  January 11.*

   Projects against England—Misconception of the first interview between Pitt and Maret—France dazzled—*Equality* impracticable—English people not in revolt—Decrees of November 19 and December 15—Burke—The Revolution too violent—Le Brun must be moderate . . . . . . . 26

*M. Reinhard to Mr. Miles.  January 12.*

   Courier arrived—Chauvelin requests interview with Grenville—Reinhard desires interview with Miles . . . . 28

*Minute by Mr. Miles.*
    Conduct of Grenville mischievous—Despatch of Le Brun to Chauvelin—Despatch received by Miles . . . . 28

*M. Maret to Mr. Miles. Paris, January 7.*
    Activity of armaments and language in British Parliament contradict pacific assurances—Haughtiness of English Ministers—France prepared for war, but desires peace—Promises not to make conquests are consistent with repelling aggression—Indemnification for war expenses justifiable—The Scheldt insufficient cause for war—Dutch should come to an understanding with Belgians—Plot of Pilnitz—The Republic an important factor—Intervention discouraged by hostile laws—Alien Bill—Decree of November 19 will be explained—England must cease to menace—The first blow will be struck in Holland—Chauvelin will present his credentials, or Barthélemy may be proposed . 28

*Mr. Miles to Mr. Pitt. January 12.*
    Important despatch received—Requests an interview . . 87

*Mr. Miles to M. Maret. January 12.*
    Must postpone answer to letter—Convention should adopt conciliatory measures—Loquacity of Burke not to be regarded—Reason, not resentment, must trace the course—The Republic must not exact recognition as a *preliminary* step—Let the Convention promise not to incorporate Belgium . . . 37

*Mr. Miles to Mr. Pitt. January 13.*
    Letter received from Le Brun—Requests an interview with the Minister . . . . . . . 89

*Mr. Miles to Mr. Aust. January 13.*
    The Cabinet may have peace on honourable terms—An interview with Grenville desired . . . . . 39

*Mr. Aust to Mr. Miles. January 13.*
    No commands received from Grenville . . . . 40

*Mr. Pitt to Mr. Miles. January 13.*
    Wishes to see the papers received from Paris . . . 40

*Mr. Miles to Mr. Pitt. January 13.*
    Promises to be with the Minister . . . 40

*M. Reinhard to Mr. Miles. January 13.*
Request from Chauvelin—Rupture of treaty—Grenville will receive Chauvelin . . . . . . . . 41

*Minute by Mr. Miles on interview with Mr. Pitt* . . 42

*Mr. Miles to M. Maret. January 13.*
Attempt to ward off war has brought annoyance—Correspondence must cease . . . . . . . . 43

*Minute by Mr. Miles.*
Message from Lord Grenville—Ministers willing to receive information from France . . . . . . 43

*Mr. Joseph Smith to Mr. Miles. January 14.*
The letter from Le Brun mislaid . . . . 44

*Mr. Miles to Lord Fortescue. January 15.*
The late intelligence from Paris—Instructions received by Chauvelin—Pacific declarations of the Convention—Interview of Miles with Pitt—Republic acknowledged by Sweden and Naples—Neutrality of Spain—Decline of confidence in Mr. Pitt . 44

*M. Maret to Mr. Miles. Paris, January 11.*
Inaccuracies in the report of Le Brun—French Minister deceived—Expected judgment on Louis XVI.—Explanation desired about Barthélemy and Chauvelin—Hope of peace not abandoned—Uncertainty may lead to the incorporation of the Liégeois . . . . . . . . . 46

*Mr. Miles to M. Le Brun. January 18.*
Neither prudence nor justice in Le Brun—Attempt to prevent war thwarted—Responsibility rests with the French minister . 47

*M. Noël to Mr. Miles. Paris, January 19.*
Preparations for war—Enthusiasm in France—Chauvelin culpable—Dampierre inquires after Miles—Noël named Chargé d'Affaires at the Hague—Duc d'Aumont in error . . 48

*M. Reinhard to Mr. Miles. January 19.*
Reply of Lord Grenville—Misunderstanding—New causes of offence—Chauvelin . . . . . . . 50

*M. Reinhard to Mr. Miles. January 25.*
Order for the departure of Chauvelin . . . . 50

*M. Reinhard to Mr. Miles. January 26.*
    Departure of Chauvelin—Reinhard leaves . . . 51

*M. Reinhard to Mr. Miles. January 27.*
    Forwards letter from Maret—Desires an interview . . 51

*M. Maret to Mr. Miles. Paris, January 23.*
    Departure of Maret for England . . . . 51

*Mr. Long to Mr. Miles. January 28.*
    Pitt wishes Miles not to answer Maret . . . . 52

*Minute by Mr. Miles on the Crisis .* . . . . 52

*M. Maret to Mr. Miles. London, January 30.*
    Desires an immediate interview with Miles . . . 54

*Minutes by Mr. Miles on interviews with M. Maret* . . 55

*Mr. Miles to Mr. Aust. February 4.*
    Efforts in favour of peace not acceptable—Exaggerated statements by Chauvelin—Conduct of Maret in London . . 57

*Mr. Aust to Mr. Miles. February 4.*
    Order issued for Maret and Mourgue to leave . . . 59

*Minute by Mr. Miles on the Crisis .* . . . . 59

*Mr. Miles to Mr. Aust. February 5.*
    Maret hopes that war may be avoided—No letters received by him since he left Paris—Regrets that Chauvelin had not been recalled—Lord Stanhope—Dumouriez and Holland . . 59

*M. Maret to Mr. Miles. February 5.*
    Departure in a few hours . . . . . 61

*M. Maret to Mr. Miles. February 6.*
    Leaves London—Has written to Lord Grenville . . 61

*Mr. Miles to Mr. Pitt. February 6.*
    Reports interviews with Maret—Intentions of the Executive Council—Declined to become the channel of communication—Maret demurs about writing to the Minister until instructions

arrive from Paris—Treatment of Chauvelin—Executive Council wish to avoid war—Would abandon conquests and the Scheldt—Dumouriez proposed to negotiate with Pitt—Maret intends to wait at Calais in hope of being recalled to London . . 61

*Minute by Mr. Miles on the Crisis* . . . . . 64

*M. Maret to Mr. Miles. Dover, February* 7.
Detained for want of packet-boat—Sailors averse to cross the Channel—No letters pass between France and England—Fate of the two nations thereby influenced . . . . 65

*M. Scipion Mourgue to Mr. Miles. Calais, February* 8.
War has been declared—Claims continued friendship of Miles 65

*M. Mourgue to Mr. Miles. Montpellier, January* 23.
Delirium of liberty in the southern provinces—Astonishment at England joining with tyrants—Both nations will suffer from war —The colonies—Contest on behalf of the Scheldt ridiculous— Mischief from misunderstandings—Distinct ideas of *principles* and *interests* are confounded—Ministers too much ministers of kings—France and England formed to esteem each other— Austria, left to itself, would receive a severe lesson from France 66

*M. Maret to Mr. Miles. Calais, February* 8.
Attacked by privateers—Cured of sea-sickness—First intimation that war had been declared—Appointment as General Agent in Belgium . . . . . . . . . 69

*Mr. Miles to M. Maret. February* 12.
Acknowledges packet received—Correspondence must be restrained—Chauvelin, Walckiers, Le Brun . . . 70

*Mr. Miles to Mr. Devaynes. February* 12.
Suggests a relief fund on behalf of widows and orphans—The measure would be popular . . . . . . 71

*M. de La Colombe to Mr. Miles. March* 11.
Proposal to raise an army in the South of France against the Convention—Release of Lafayette desired—Limited monarchy —No aid required from England . . . . . 72
' Declaration on the part of the Inhabitants of the Cevennes, Auvergne, Dauphiny, &c.,' presented by M. de La Colombe . 74

*Minute on the Flight of Louis XVI. and Lafayette* . . 75

*From a Lady to Mr. Miles. Paris, March* 12.
Austrians at Valenciennes—Paris in a convulsion—Tribunal révolutionnaire decreed—Speech of Robespierre—Santerre—Crisis anticipated—Difficulty in leaving Paris—Le Brun—Beurnonville—Misery and turpitude . . . . . 76

*Mr. Miles to Sir Edward Newenham. April* 1.
Communication with France interrupted—French army a banditti—King of Prussia and Empress of Russia—Dumouriez, victorious or defeated—Appropriation of Poland—Constitution of England—Ineffectual advance towards peace—Large account to settle with Pitt . . . . . . . 78

*Handbill distributed by the Coalesced Powers* . . . 81

*Mr. Miles to Mr. Pitt. July* 10.
War could not have been avoided without personal offence to the King—Auvergne and the Cevennes . . . . 83

*Proposal of M. de La Colombe* . . . . . 84

*M. Noël to Mr. Miles. Paris, August* 16.
Efforts to avoid the war fruitless—Madness and imprudence occasioned the war—Maret and Sémonville arrested . . 85

*Madame de Montgeroult to Mr. Miles. Baden, August* 24.
Appeals for help on behalf of her captured husband—The arrest of Maret and Sémonville . . . . . 86

*Mr. Miles to Madame de Montgeroult. September* 10.
The arrest at Novale—Difficult for the English Government to interfere—The insult communicated to Mr. Pitt . . . 90

*Mr. Miles to M. Noël. September* 10.
Noël reproached by Le Brun—Disposition of England misrepresented—State of France due to the nobility and clergy—Marat, Danton, Robespierre—France has kept the *tigers*—Despotism formerly supported by Le Brun—Mistaken ideas of Paine—Insurrection in Great Britain was expected in Paris—Sieyès in favour of war—His phlegmatic character—The enormities committed cause tears of blood—Posterity should learn a valuable lesson . . . . . . . 91

*Mr. Miles to Captain Ball. September* 12.

The Bishop of Saint-Pol-de-Léon complains of articles against the Emigrants—The direful change in France produced by the highest orders—Court of Versailles—Impossible to foresee the issue—All Europe involved in convulsions . . . 97

*Mr. Miles to Mr. John Lovedon. September* 15.

The Duke of York—Military experience necessary—Parliament should recall his Royal Highness . . . 100

*Mr. Miles to Mr. Pitt. September* 16.

Distribution of Lord Hood's proclamation at Toulon suggested—A numerous party in Paris favour monarchy . . . 101

*Mr. Miles to M. Noël. September* 17.

Effect of Lord Hood's proclamation—Monarchists became republicans after August 10, 1792—The repose of Europe depends on rational government in France . . . 102

*M. Noël to Mr. Miles. Venice, September* 27.

Events do not indicate *rapprochement*—Death of M. de Montgeroult—Friends dead or in fetters—Brissot, Pétion, Biron, Dumouriez, Le Brun—France will never receive the law from a foreigner—Sieyès lost sight of . . . 104

*Mr. Miles to Mr. Long. October* 28.

Report of Noël on the effect produced by Lord Hood's proclamation—New publication by Mr. Miles . . . 105

*Mr. Miles to Mr. Pitt. November* 28.

Rumour that the Minister had plunged England into war . 107

*The Duke of Leeds to Mr. Miles. December* 5.

Acknowledges the recent publication—' *Conduct of France towards Great Britain Examined* ' . . . 108

*Mr. Miles to M. Noël. December* 6.

Attempts to initiate proposals for peace—Effect of the battle of J mmapes—The Low Countries deprived of liberty—Depraved morals in France—Better order of things will arise in the future 108

*Mr. Long to Mr. Miles. December* 7.

The recent publication of Mr. Miles will be useful . . 110

CONTENTS OF THE SECOND VOLUME xiii

PAGE

*Mr. Miles to Mr. Long. December 7.*
Acceptance by Fox of a subscription—The position of Pitt thereby improved—No dependence on Emigrants—Blunders in the conduct of the war—The Netherlands, Toulon, Lord Hood, Duke of York—Pitt hampered—Stands high in public opinion . 110

*Mr. Miles to Mr. Pitt. December 16.*
Renewed offer of M. de La Colombe—Lyons might have been saved—Violated promise of the King of Sardinia . . . 112

*M. Noël to Mr. Miles. Venice, December 26.*
Difficulties debar negotiations for peace—French couriers waylaid—Sir Richard Worsley—Projects for assassination—D'Hancarville, D'Entraygues—Noël willing to co-operate with Miles—Jemmapes, Dumouriez—Moral character of Danton—Morals of the English—Their love of gold—The French nation frank—Rousseau on morals—Le Brun—Capture of Toulon . . 113

*Mr. Miles to Mr. Aust. December 30.*
The Black Sea—Mines of wealth in Spain and Turkey—Prohibition of British manufactures . . . . . 118

*Mr. Miles to Sir Edward Newenham. December 30.*
Services rendered to the Minister—Would not pledge his pen in favour of any Administration—No desire for employment in Ireland—Dreads the issue of the war . . . . 118

*Mr. Miles to Mr. Long. December 31.*
Evacuation of Toulon—Pitt forewarned—Offer to create a diversion in the South of France neglected—Lyons and Toulon—The failure at Corsica—Lord Hood—Lord Grenville—Limited monarchy—Red hot royalists—English Government misled . 119

*Minute on the proposal of M. de La Colombe* . . . 122

*Mr. Miles to M. Noël. January 5, 1794.*
Advises moderation to Danton and Robespierre—The Low Countries, Liège—France may yet rise—Pitt will not continue the war if Danton intimates that France desires peace—Robespierre incorrupt, but vindictive—Mirabeau had no character—His firmness at Versailles—Lafayette more to be depended on . 122

*Mr. Miles to Sir Edward Newenham. January 6.*
Will not pledge himself to write for any Minister—Clamour for Reform—The time not yet arrived—Toulon and Lyons—The war badly conducted—Obstinacy of the English Court . . 125

*Mr. Penrose to Mr. Miles.  Florence.*

    Campaign opened in Italy—The Spanish fleet—Langaro—French fleet . . . . . . . 127

*Mrs. Ware to Mr. Miles.  Ghent, January 6.*

    Intense cold—Officers sick of the war—Dunkirk expedition—Prince Cobourg, Duke of York—Maubeuge—Sickness in the army—Bad bread—Flemish hotel—English convent at Bruges—Bishop of Bruges—Hanoverian sick soldiers—French everywhere triumphant . . . . . . . 129

*Sir Edward Newenham to Mr. Miles.  Dublin, January 11.*

    Overwhelmed by the bad news—Toulon, Dunkirk, Mentz, Trèves—Retreat of Wurmser—Luxemburg—Turin—France will dictate to Europe—Russia might change affairs—Expedition of Lord Moira—The unfortunate Royalists—O'Hara—Confidence in Pitt—Jourdan's army—The Dutch . . . 131

*Mr. Miles to Mr. Long.  January 12.*

    Lyons and Toulon—Alps of France in favour of limited monarchy—King of Sardinia—Lord Hood—Lord Moira not received in Brittany—Motion by Duke of Grafton—No confidence in factions . . . . . . . . 134

*Mr. Long to Mr. Miles.  January 13.*

    Income of the Duke of Grafton affected by the war . . 137

*Mr. Miles to M. Noël.  January 14.*

    Cessation of hostilities may become a necessity for France—Aggression by her—Opinion in England—Danton and Robespierre could terminate disorder . . . . . 137

*Mr. Miles to Mr. Pitt.  January 16.*

    Measures suggested to Danton and Robespierre—The evacuation of Toulon favourable to success—Duke of Grafton's motion 140

*The Duke of Leeds to Mr. Miles.  January 20.*

    Wishes success to his desire to proceed to Bâle on a mission of peace . . . . . . . . 140

*M. Noël to Mr. Miles.  Venice, January 23.*

    Neutrality of Venice—Worsley—France has a terrible account to settle—Negotiations difficult—France converted into a camp—The Coalition ought to speak first . . . . 141

## CONTENTS OF THE SECOND VOLUME XV

*Mr. Miles to M. Noël. January 24.*

House of Commons in favour of Pitt—Ministers not obstinately resolved on war—Decree of the Convention pronouncing penalty of death—England dreads the subversion of old governments—Pacific offers from Paris would receive attention—General O'Hara . . . . . . . . 143

*Mrs. Ware to Mr. Miles. Ghent, January 31.*

Austrians and Prussians overpowered—Duke of York—Prince of Cobourg—Desertion among English troops—Wretched condition of the sick—Captain Nicholson—Sir William Erskine popular—Dumouriez alarmed—Duke de FitzJames—Computed force of the Allies—French cavalry—War converts men into savages—Our success overstated in the House of Commons . 145

*Sir Edward Newenham to Mr. Miles. Dublin, February 1.*

Victories in the Indies—The Brest fleet—Admiral Hood—Italy—Brunswick and Wurmser too weak—Russia—Lord Moira may be *burgoyned*—Probable attempt on the English coast—French may land in Ireland—Confidence in Pitt—His hopeful speech—Crisis for Great Britain—Sir L. Parson's notice . 148

*Mr. Miles to Sir Edward Newenham. February 8.*

A gloomy prospect—Lyons lost through the King of Sardinia—Dissatisfaction of the army under the Duke of York—Responsibility of the Minister—Hostilities could not have been avoided after August 10, 1792—Lusignan, M. de Grave—Pitt's speech in the House of Commons—Fallacy of his predictions—Conversation with Charles Long—Correspondence of Miles discouraged—Cabinet without authentic information—Lord Buckingham—Lord Cornwallis chased into Torbay . . . . 151

*M. Noël to Mr. Miles. Venice, February 9.*

Danton and Barère written to—No answer received—Danton and Robespierre may lose their influence—Falsehoods of the *Émigrés*—France might make the first overtures—The conduct of England raises difficulties—Pitt unacceptable—Every Frenchman has become a soldier—Danger of disbanding troops—House of Austria—Poland—Russia—Turkey—Development of force in France—Death of Le Brun . . . . . 156

*Mr. Miles to Sir Edward Newenham. February 12.*

Perfidy of the National Convention—Six thousand victims seized—Freedom destroyed—France inflamed by the Allies—*Dernier ressort* . . . . . . . . . 159

*Mr. Miles to M. Noël. February 21.*

Peace less visible in 1794 than in 1793—Object of the Revolution defeated by general depravity—France the aggressor in respect to England—Conduct of Dumouriez—King of Hungary—Opinion in England—Paris distracted—Barère violent—Collot d'Herbois aims at supremacy—Rescue of Louis XVI.—Non-interference of Pitt . . . . . . . 161

*M. Noël to Mr. Miles. Venice, March 14.*

No replies from Paris—Correspondence useless—Proposal of Miles forwarded to Danton—Report of Barère on peace—Non-interference with old governments promised—Negotiations must be with the Convention—Rumours about General O'Hara a *ruse*. 164

*Mr. Miles to Mr. Long. March 30.*

Lord Grenville and the South of France—His responsibility—Publication against Burke . . . . . . 166

*Mr. Miles to M. Noël. April 11.*

Danton — His death — Not incorruptible — Robespierre — A speedy issue to the war hopeless . . . . . 167

*M. Noël to Mr. Miles. Venice, April 30.*

Noël accused in Paris—The 'Moniteur' can travel only *viâ* Geneva . . . . . . . . . 169

*M. Noël to Mr. Miles. Venice, May 22.*

Dangerous position of Noël—Friends in Paris dead—Contemplates flight—Desires a passport—Would warn the factions in England . . . . . . . . 170

*Minute by Mr. Miles on the Position of Noël* . . . 172

*Mr. Miles to Mr. Aust. June 18.*

Aspect of affairs—Ministers imposed upon—Grenville . . 173

*Mr. Miles to Mr. Sheridan. June 18.*

Pitt could not have avoided hostilities—The *conduct* and the *object* of the war a different question—Carlton House . . 174

*Mr. Miles to Mr. Nicholls. June 22.*

Robespierre above the influence of money—Statesmen *perdent la tête*—Force of public opinion—Danger of physical force—Robespierre and the aristocracy—Jacobins—National Assembly —Horne Tooke . . . . . . . 175

|  | PAGE |
|---|---|

*Mr. Miles to Sir Edward Newenham. June 25.*

American Minister in London—Invitation to Newenham—David Hartley—Washington—Lafayette transferred to Olmütz—Sympathy from America—Burke—Pitt—The Allies—Duke of York. . . . . . . . . . 178

*Imprisonment of Lafayette* . . . . . . 181

*Mr. Miles to Mr. Pitt. June 28.*

The Auvergne would have supported limited monarchy—Lyons and Toulon—Lord Grenville—Offer to sound opinion in Paris . . . . . . . . 182

*Minute by Mr. Miles on the above Letter* . . . . 183

*Sir Edward Newenham to Mr. Miles. July 19.*

The Allies—Cobourg must yield to Robespierre—Hanover, Berlin, and Holland exposed—The Spanish fleet—Corsica—Sardinia—The gallery at Florence, Citizen David—Sir Sidney Smith—Salvation depends on Pitt—King of Prussia—Windham, Fitzwilliam, and Portland—Miles must not drop his pen. . 184

*Mr. Miles to Sir Edward Newenham. July 29.*

Disasters to the Allies—Royalty endangered—Perfidy of Courts—Our ancestors in 1688—Changes were inevitable—The common herd of mankind reason badly—Statesmen fail to observe with accuracy—Opinions take root rapidly . . . . 186

*Mr. Penrose to Mr. Miles. Florence, August 3.*

Progress of the French—The Jacobins—Mr. Jenkinson—Constitution of Corsica—French fleet—Lord Hood—French in English pay. . . . . . . . . 188

*Mr. Nicholls to Mr. Miles. August 5.*

Need not separate from Pitt—Position of the Cabinet—Feeling in England—The Stadtholder—Auckland, Malmesbury, St. Helens—The government in Holland must be modelled to the wishes of the people—The *joyeuse entrée*—Lord Thurlow . 189

*Mr. Miles to Sir Edward Newenham. August 9.*

The Stadtholder demands succour—Prince of Orange and a hostile party—Danes and Swedes—Neutrality of the Baltic—The French may descend on Ireland—Personal respect for Pitt . 190

*Mr. Miles to Mr. Woodfall. September 8.*

No one in the political vineyard has tasted less of the grape—Statesmen should be honest—Europe threatened—Pamphlet entitled, '*Rassurez-vous*'—Pitt could not have avoided hostilities—Chauvelin—Republicans and Royalists impatient for war—Marat and Robespierre . . . . . . 192

*Mr. Miles to Sir Edward Newenham. September 25.*

Pitt preferred to Fox—Pitt in 1784 and in 1794—Conduct of the war faulty—Lloyd's Coffee House—Lord Chatham—Merchant ships unprotected—One million sterling in losses—Duke of York—Vigour demanded, not lucrative contracts—French are brave—English Cabinet weak—The Jenkinsons—Pitt overruled . . 193

*Sir Edward Newenham to Mr. Miles. October 5.*

Asks for early news—Alarming rumours . . . 196

*Mr. Miles to Sir Edward Newenham. October 13.*

The Cabinet should have been explicit—Friends of limited monarchy have disappeared—The French not to be dragooned—The Dutch desire peace—Lord Spencer—King of Prussia—Bellegarde taken—Spain alarmed—Letter from Madrid . 197

*Mr. Miles to Mr. Rose. October 16.*

Excesses have dishonoured the Revolution—The whole world affected by the poison—Insular position of England—Explicit declarations might have averted difficulties—The friends of *limited monarchy* would have overthrown the Convention—Offers were neglected . . . . . . 198

*Mr. Miles to Mr. Sturt. October 19.*

Danger from either peace or war—Alliance with France advocated since 1780—Royalists in Paris indefatigable in their efforts for war—The poison re-acts under the Republic—Venom diffused by the *émigrés*—War could not have been avoided—France like a man in his cups—Arrogance of German despots—Cologne and Bonn fallen . . . . . . . 200

*Mr. Miles to Sir Edward Newenham. October 27.*

Situation deplorable—Bargain of Malmesbury—Illness of Burke—King of Prussia—Mission fails at Vienna—The Dutch—Duke of York, Brunswick—French at Coblentz—Extracts of letters from abroad . . . . . . 203

*A French Emigré to Mr. Miles. November 1.*

France and Prussia—The *intrigants* in 1789—Count de Ségur—Popular policy in France—Berlin and Vienna—Le Brun piqued by the refusal of pension in 1787—Chauvelin—English Court glad of pretext for entering the Confederacy—Indifference of the Dutch to the Scheldt—The *émigrés*—Imprudence of Pitt . 205

*Mr. Miles to Mr. Nicholls. November 4.*

Pitt could not have avoided war after 1791—He desired peace—His dereliction from Whig principles—No power to treat with in France is absurd. . . . . . . 207

*Count de —— to Mr. Miles. The Hague, November 18.*

Loss of Nymwegen and of Dutch affections—Intrigues of Vergennes in Holland not so injurious as the present conduct of England—The Dutch may unite with France—English Ambassador at the Hague—Lacombe at Bois-le-Duc—France would detach the Allies from England—Imbecility of the English Cabinet—Daendels—Dutch Commissioners gone to Paris . 207

*Mr. Penrose to Mr. Miles. Florence, November 22.*

Italian politics—Escape of the French fleet—Admiral Hotham—Mutiny on board the 'Windsor Castle'—Retreat of Prussia—English policy paying *en avance*—The *émigrés*—France and Corsica . . . . . . . . 211

*Count de —— to Mr. Miles. The Hague, November 26.*

Mission of the Greffier to the English Cabinet—Determination of England to continue the war—Information demanded from Holland of all that passes—Attitude of the Convention towards England might have been discovered—The policy of France—Tuscany desires peace—*Hauteur* of the English—Wyndham at Florence—The French in Piedmont—English fleet in the Mediterranean—Prince Galitzin . . . . . 212

*M. Barthélemy to Mr. Miles. Bâle, December 17.*

End of the war desired—Profession of faith by the National Convention—Merlin de Douai—Madame de Montgeroult—Sémonville and Maret . . . . . . 215

*Count de —— to Mr. Miles. The Hague, December 26.*

Lacombe—Pacific disposition of France—Hostility of English Ministers—Holland implored to continue the war—English Ambassador at the Hague—Mission of Mr. Eliot—Instructions

|  | PAGE |
|---|---|
| to Lord St. Helens—Contradictory despatches of Lord Grenville—Thugut kept in good humour—English guineas valued by the Germans—Ministers subsidised—*Emigrés* in the pay of England . . . . . . . | 216 |

*From* —— *to Mr. Miles. Madrid, January* 1, 1795.

Spanish Government alarmed—Diet of Ratisbon—Duke of Alcudia on the situation—Austria and Prussia—Spain may refuse to hazard her own safety . . . . . . 219

*Mr. Miles to Sir Edward Newenham. January* 15.

France determined to possess Holland—No longer a prediction—Spain desires a separate peace—France enraged against England—Irish affairs depress—Conversation with the Reverend Dr. Jackson—Duke of Leeds and Mr. Pitt . . . 221

*Mr. Miles to M. Barthélemy. January* 20.

Maret—Bad faith of Le Brun—Hope for the dawn of peace—Hatred between the two nations impolitic—The crimes committed in France are an advantage to her enemies—Let the Republic announce her readiness to negotiate . . . . 223

*Mr. Miles to Mr. Pitt. January* 22.

Readiness of the Convention to receive propositions for peace consistent with the interests of France . . . . 225

*Mr. Miles to the Duke of Leeds. January* 22.

Declaration of his Grace in Parliament on the war—Copy of letter to Pitt enclosed . . . . . . 226

*Mr. Miles to Lord Buckingham. January* 23.

The Cabinet can stop the effusion of blood—Offer to proceed to the Continent to obtain information—Appointment of Mr. Wickham as Chargé d'Affaires at Berne—Mistaken expectation of the Duke of Portland and Lord Grenville . . . 226

*Duke of Leeds to Mr. Miles. January* 23.

Approval of the course pursued by Mr. Miles . . . 228

*Mr. Miles to the Duke of Leeds. January* 24.

Mr. Pitt in 1792—Ministers should know their resources before they embark on war—Unequal to the task—Prospect of affairs not encouraging—Offer of La Colombe neglected—Lafayette—King of Sardinia—Lyons and Toulon sacrificed—Displeasure of the Minister incurred by the effort to preserve peace—Negotiations with France could now be opened . . . . . 229

*Mr. Miles to Lord Lauderdale. January 23.*

Publication by his Lordship—Error corrected—The part taken by Mr. Miles to prevent war gave offence—Le Brun could have maintained peace—The infant liberties of France might have defied the English Cabinet—In both countries there were men impatient for war . . . . . . . 231

*Mr. Sturt to Mr. Miles. January 24.*

Willing to state in the House of Commons his sentiments on peace or war—Declaration of Lacombe at Bois-le-Duc—Opinion of Mr. Fox on the situation . . . . . . 233

*Mr. Miles to Mr. Sturt. January 27.*

The present Government in France no impediment to negotiations—Assurance of the Convention—Barthélemy—Conference of Maret with Pitt in 1792—Want of principle a disqualification for Ministers . . . . . . . 234

*Mr. Miles to Sir Edward Newenham. February 14.*

Lord Buckingham opposed to Pitt—Ministers should be driven from office—Scramble for plunder—The French and the West Indies—Prussia negotiating for peace—Pitt incapable . . 235

*Mr. Miles to M. Barthélemy. February 14.*

Detention of mails by the ice—Steps taken to open negotiations—Switzerland the centre of intrigue—Pitt renounces the project of restoring the *ancien régime* in France—He will advance towards peace on the Convention being willing to treat—Wish of the English people—France should not be dazzled . 236

*Mr. Miles to Captain Beaulieu. February 27.*

The speech of Johannot—Rouzet—The Convention—Peace favoured—It might soon be secured—The Opposition—The English Cabinet . . . . . . 238

*Captain Beaulieu to Mr. Miles. March 11.*

Voyage across the Channel of eight days—Friendship vowed towards Mr. Miles—France in favour of peace—Gratitude towards Captain Hicks, R.N. . . . . . 240

*Mr. Miles to M. Barthélemy. April 27.*

Regrets that his power is too limited to secure peace—The course of events must decide—Union between France and England preached to the Marquis de Bouillé and Vicomte Damas in 1780—Introduces Mr. Flint . . . . . 241

*Mr. Duncombe to Mr. Miles. Copgrove, August 2.*

Acknowledges receipt of the 'Letter to the Prince of Wales on a Second Application to Parliament to discharge Debts wantonly contracted since May 1787'—Alarming state of affairs—Recognition of the Republic in France desirable—Pitt overruled in the Cabinet—Army of the Prince of Condé—King of Great Britain answerable—The venal Chapel at St. Stephen's—Volunteer corps . . . . . . . . . 243

*Mr. Miles to Mr. Long. August 6.*

Article in the 'Times' on France and Spain—Court of Madrid —Pitt forewarned that Spain would join France—He might have anticipated it—Equivocal excuses of Don Langaro . . 245

*Mr. Miles to Lord Fortescue. August 10.*

The only nail, *notre unique espoir*, has failed—Spain has followed Prussia—Not suspected by the English Cabinet—No apology admissible—Pitt forewarned—Correspondence with Barthélemy—Obstinacy of the Cabinet—Revival of the Family Compact—Mission to Paris in 1790—Ministers would desire peace if they realised their position—Fatality attends men in power—Pitt uninformed—Dominant wish of George III.— Chauvelin, Maret, Noël, Reinhard—La Colombe—Mr. Fox— Lord Bute . . . . . . . . 246

*Mr. Sturt to Mr. Miles. August 22.*

Not an enthusiast for Mr. Fox—His sterling advantages—The Coalition—French navy—Large war-ships a mistake—Light privateers more useful—Expedition of Puisaye—*Emigrés* at Southampton . . . . . . . 250

*Mr. Duncombe to Mr. Miles. September 3.*

Public affairs not consolatory—Importance of present events —Good opinion of Pitt tottering—Influence of the King over the Cabinet—Expedition of Lord Moira—Waste of public money . 252

*Mr. Penrose to Mr. Miles. Florence, September 10.*

Riviéra de Gênes—Retreat of the Austrians—Inactivity of the Imperial army—Politics of the Court of Vienna—French squadron joins the Spanish fleet—English Admirals, Hotham and Mann—The *émigrés* under Prince de Condé—Their character— M. de Puisaye—Noël has left Venice . . . . 253

*Mr. Miles to Mr. Long. November 10.*

Rupture with France opposed in 1790-1792—Pitt warned that he could not stop the Revolution—Opportunities for observing events in Paris—Proposal to rescue the Queen—Decision of the Cabinet to support the resolutions of Pilnitz—Pitt again forewarned—Burke—The Cabinet misinformed—Former wars with the Court of Versailles controlled by money payments—Not so now—Opportunities to restore peace neglected—Spain and Holland might have been preserved—Genius of the French—Ministers sin against experience . . . . . 255

*Mr. Miles to Mr. Hugh Elliot. November 29.*

General talk in favour of peace—Court of Vienna—Thugut—Opportunities lost—Pitt—Motion of Mr. Grey—Austrian Netherlands—Duke of Leeds better poet than statesman—Example of America—French and Genoese—Sardinia—The spirit of avarice in England—No further direct intercourse with Pitt—Burke—High opinion of Mr. Elliot—Spain will soon join France . 258

*Mr. Miles to Mr. Sturt. December 8.*

Weary of all parties—No expectation to find men angels—Until the war Pitt an able Minister—The Coalition—India Bill—Commercial Treaty—The Opposition lack public confidence—Sieyès and Rewbell—Return of the Stadtholder a favourable moment—France not yet wise enough to come to terms . . 261

*Mr. Miles to Sir Edward Newenham. Froyle, December 20.*

London the arena of political incapacity—Retirement and mental inactivity—Independence of Ireland—The Opposition—Fox—Pitt—Political corruption—Lord Malmesbury—Hazy horizon—Fall of Pitt—Failure to seize the Spanish fleet—Spain and France—England embarrassed by mismanagement . . 263

*Mr. Miles to Lord Buckingham. Froyle, December 25.*

Improvident counsels—Deplorable state of England—Impolitic to expose blunders at present—The Family Compact—Alliance with France—Duc d'Aiguillon—French as friends or enemies—The Constitutionalists neglected—Parliamentary reform—Pamphlet entitled ' *Que deviendra de nous ?* '. . . . 267

*M. Maret to Mr. Miles. Bâle, December 26.*

Announces release from imprisonment . . . . 273

*Mr. Miles to the Duke of Leeds. Froyle, December 30.*

Refrains from giving public contradiction to personal attack—Incapacity of the King's servants—Belgium and Liège in 1787—Mission of Mr. Miles to Paris in 1790—Failures in the administration of Pitt—His security delusive . . . . 274

*Mr. Miles to Mr. Pitt. Froyle, December 30.*

Stupendous results anticipated from the assembling of the States-General at Versailles—Resistance of the higher orders injurious—Destined gigantic stature of France—A dark and dismal night before us—Detachment of France from Spain desired by Pitt—Mission of Mr. Miles to Paris—Family Compact—Insult at Nootka—Courts of Madrid and Versailles—Opinion in Paris —Unpopularity of the Treaty of Commerce—Cabals of Emigrants impatient for war—Armaments in England suspected—Assistance given by France to America—Spanish Minister in Paris—Family Compact, the League of Despots—Mirabeau and the Family Compact—Alliance with England preferred to union with Spain —Full information forwarded by Mr. Miles from Paris—Every obstacle to the wish of Mr. Pitt removed—The project to detach France from Spain unaccountably abandoned—An open avowal of neutrality neglected—Distrust of England inspired by the aristocrats—Convention of Pilnitz—France needed pacific assurances from the English Cabinet—Efforts of Mr. Miles in 1792 to preserve peace—Misrepresentations by Mr. Burke—Liberty, not anarchy, desired—Revolutions serious things—Pontiffs of Rome —Philip II. and the Spanish yoke—Republic of Batavia--Independence of America—Court of Versailles—Authority of history —Error of statesmen . . . . . . 276

*Mr. Miles to M. Maret. Froyle, January 28, 1796.*

Congratulations on the liberation of Maret—Proposes to visit Switzerland—Rewbell, Mourgue, Guyot, Le Brun . . 285

*Mr. Miles to Mr. Erskine. Froyle, December 10.*

Motion by Fox for liberation of Lafayette—General Fitzpatrick's motion—Falsehood of charges against Lafayette—Flight of Louis XVI.—Murder of Foulon—Part taken by Miles against Fox—House of Commons degraded . . . . 286

*Mr. Erskine to Mr. Miles. London, February 18, 1797.*

Pamphlet by Erskine—Publications by Miles—Lamentable state of England . . . . . . . 288

*Mr. Erskine to Mr. Miles. March 12.*

The coalition between Mr. Fox and Lord North—Fox a man of integrity—Pitt has endangered the Constitution—Our duty is to promote happiness—Robert Adair—Keppel—Newspaper calumnies—The King and his Ministers—Danger of the country 289

PAGE

*From —— to Mr. Miles. Paris, June 5.*
Signs of peace—Visit to Froyle—Election of Barthélemy—His capacity for duty . . . . . . . 291

*Mr. Miles to the Marquis de Lafayette. September 27.*
Congratulations on the liberation of Lafayette—Foul treatment during his captivity—Mr. Burke—Slanders contradicted . 291

*Mr. Miles to Mr. Nicholls. Froyle, April 10, 1798.*
Accommodation with France impracticable at present—The Republic and the Monarchy—England abandoned—Alliance between France and Ireland—M. de Vergennes—Separation of Ireland from England encouraged at Versailles—Hope of the Directory—Irish insurgents the dupes of France—'United Irishman'—Views of the Irish point to independence—Parliamentary reform . . . . . . . . 292

*The Marquis de Lafayette to Mr. Miles. Widmold, August 2.*
Expresses obligation for friendship under adversity—Correspondence of Mr. Miles in the Ministerial papers—Object of attack by Mr. Burke—The governments of the future . . . 294

*Mr. Miles to Mr. Flint. Froyle, May 19, 1799.*
Arrest of French envoys by Austrian hussars—Roberjot and Bonnier—Cut down—Horrors sanctioned—Mr. Miles in childhood—Not intimidated from love of right . . . . 296

*M. Barthélemy to Mr. Miles. London, July 30.*
Invitation to Froyle—Injuries received from his countrymen —Returns to the Continent . . . . . 297

*Mr. Miles to M. Barthélemy. Froyle, August 2.*
Congratulations on escape from exile—France and England should be united . . . . . . . 298

*Mr. Miles to Captain Ball. Froyle, September 20, 1799.*
Communication from Ball forwarded to Pitt—Our diplomacy —Parliamentary corruption—Governorship of Malta—Wish of the inhabitants—Malta Congress—Sicily and its monster King— France and the Porte—Cession of Malta to the Emperor Paul— Northern Confederacy—English commerce—Opinion of Pitt changed—His unacquaintance with foreign politics—Causes assigned—Russia and Constantinople—Fall of Mantua—Court of Vienna—Bonaparte and the Grand Seigneur—England filched

—*Emigrés*—Aboukir—Count not men above their worth—Macnamara Russell, and Barthélemy—Pickmore—Sir Peter Parker—Captain Irwin—George Ball . . . . . 299

*Mr. Miles to Mr. Butler.   January 17, 1801.*
Information desired by Herbert Marsh not available—Origin of our hapless contest—Perfidy of the Court of Vienna—England drawn into the vortex—Mr. Belsham—Letter of Le Brun to the British Court—Pitt advised in the infancy of the Revolution—Cleared of the guilt of aggression—Fox on the mission of Maret—Pitt misled by Burke . . . . . . 304

*Lord Buckingham to Mr. Miles.   Stowe, January 26.*
Politics of France levelled against England—Brabant corn shipment for England . . . . . . 306

*Mr. Miles to Lord Buckingham.   January 28.*
Conduct of France towards England—Pichegru—Holland—Private intelligence neglected by Pitt—His great abilities—An infant in foreign politics—Duke of York—Folly in subsidising—France strengthened by the Revolution—The war against England not a *bellum internecinum*—Emperor of Russia—King of Prussia in 1786 . . . . . . . 307

*Mr. Miles to Lord Buckingham.   January 28.*
Pamphlet on Russia by Miles at the request of Pitt—Russia and France—Aim of Prussia—Peace possible—Pitt compelled against his judgment . . . . . . 310

*Lord Buckingham to Mr. Miles.   Stowe, January 30.*
The *bellum internecinum*—France strikes at Great Britain—Negotiation for corn . . . . . 312

*Mr. Miles to Lord Buckingham.   February 3.*
The blows of France levelled against England—Abbé Sieyès—Inference from Lord Buckingham's words—Mandate of George III. for war. . . . . . . . 312

*Mr. Miles to Lord Lansdowne.   February 4.*
Mistaken idea of the English Cabinet—France not intent on a *bellum internecinum*—Overtures of the First Consul—Arrogance of England—Exportation of grain from the Low Countries prohibited . . . . . . . 313

*Mr. Miles to Mr. Erskine. March* 1.
Mr. Fox and the exigencies of our times—Pitt and Fox in the same Administration—Whig principles of Pitt abandoned . 815

*Mr. Miles to Lord Buckingham. March* 29.
Employment under Mr. Addington—Catholic question . 316

*Lord Wycombe to Mr. Miles. Dublin, October* 9.
Surprise on hearing of peace—Glorious for France—Expenditure of 250 millions—Foundation of a military Republic—A Consul on a footing with an Emperor—Bonaparte in Etruria—Poverty of the new King—Duke of Portland—Mr. Garland—Charles Sturt . . . . . . . 316

*Mr. Miles to the Marquis de Lafayette. London, October* 22.
English can now correspond with French—Friendship should be consolidated—Necessity for the Revolution . . . 818

*Lord Wycombe to Mr. Miles. Dublin, November* 3.
Parties in England—Scramble for booty—Pitt and Addington—Burke—Irish and English interests—Injustice of the Union—The treaty with France a respite only—South of Ireland in need of civilisation . . . . . . . 319

*The Newfoundland Fishery* . . . . . 320

*Mr. Miles to Lord Hawkesbury. December* 4.
Newfoundland cod fishery—Petition of the merchants of St. Malo—Projet de décret (*Archives Parlementaires, xxiii,* 712) . 322

*The Deputies from Malta,* 1802 . . . . . 323

*Mr. Miles to Sir Alexander Ball. April* 24, 1802.
Escort of Malta deputies—Civilities shown by France should be adopted—Manners of the English—Maltese entitled to respect . . . . . . . . 327

*Sir Alexander Ball to Mr. Miles. London, May* 29.
The Listons—Attendance at public offices—Lord Hawkesbury, Mr. Hammond, Mr. Rolleston—Arduous task in Malta—*Saint Ball*—All the powers arming—The Turks . . . 329

*Sir Alexander Ball to Mr. Miles. Malta, December* 10.
State of the Maltese—Hope and fear—Situation of Ball—Maltese Republicans and France—Paper war—Bonaparte in

Italy—Naples, Sardinia—Death of the Duke of Parma—French orders to the Duchess—French Minister at Florence—Apathy of the English—Oranges, Barbary dates, climate of Malta . . 330

*Mr. Miles to Mr. Rolleston. June* 10, 1803.

Importance of Egypt pointed out to Pitt in 1786—Baron de Tott—Savary and Volney—Wheat on the shores of the Euxine—Sir Sidney Smith—Treaty of Amiens—Malta—Canning—'A feverish repose'—The Ministers and Malta—Addington and Hawkesbury—Memorial presented to Lord Hobart—Non-surrender of Malta—Fable of Calypso . . . . 332

*Sir Alexander Ball to Mr. Miles. Malta, November* 2.

Circulation of the Malta 'Gazette'—'Moniteur'—Ambition of Bonaparte—Capture of London—French gasconade—Contentment of the Maltese—General Veal unsuccessful in Malta—The Order—Infamous reports against Ball—Lord Nelson in favour of Sardinia or Minorca—Escape of the Toulon fleet—Malta preferred . . . . . . . . 334

*Mr. Liston to Mr. Miles. Pall Mall, May* 10, 1805.

Unable to visit Brownsea—The contending parties—Political criminality—Friendly advice . . . . . 336

*Mr. Miles to Mr. Jekyll. Brownsea, January* 9, 1806.

Prospect before us—Situation critical—Achievement of Nelson—Giant strides of Napoleon—Valour of our tars—We take ships, France takes cities—Foreign politics not the *forte* of Pitt—Map of Europe in 1793 and in 1806—Pitt drove Addington out of office—Mischievous counsels . . . . . 338

*Mr. Miles to Lord Buckingham. Brownsea, January* 21.

Offer of his literary exertions—Alliance of France—Splendid nonsense of Burke—France would 'rise a phœnix from her ashes'—The demands of Mr. Pitt and Lord North entombed . 340

*Mr. Flint to Mr. Miles. London, January* 23.

Death of Mr. Pitt—His star set in clouds—Lord Sidmouth may form an Administration—Union of parties . . . 341

*Mr. Miles to Mr. Flint. Brownsea, January* 26.

The errors of Pitt may be entombed—He might have been able to 'ride in the whirlwind and direct the storm'—Mr. Burke—Pitt conjured to cultivate French confidence—Neutrality of

England impossible—Pitt yielded to Burke—The *émigrés*—Mr. Miles marked as *un patriote enragé*—France recovered from delirium—Opportunities for peace lost—Lord Lansdowne after Aboukir—Napoleon as Emperor—Pitt should have controlled the King—Sterling talents more important than union of parties—Pitt and Fox—Lord Sidmouth—Administration under Fox preferred—Opposition brought into contempt—Lord North—The Coalition and Pitt—Napoleon . . . . . 342

*Mr. Donovan to Mr. Miles. St. James's, January* 23.
Attendance at a public office—Death of Pitt—Talk of a Regency—The Opposition—Lord Hardwicke—Mr. Miles urged to exert his pen . . . . . . . 345

*Captain Pickmore to Mr. Miles. Ramillies, January* 26.
Squadron escaped from Brest—Death of Pitt—Lord St. Vincent—Lord Lansdowne—Verses on Nelson—Importance of the navy—Treatment of the heroes of Trafalgar . . . 346

*Mr. Miles to Lord Moira. December* 1.
The winds waft only disastrous intelligence—Unavailing prediction to Mr. Pitt—The Cabinet ignorant of the character of the Revolution—Mission of Mr. Miles to Paris in 1790—Mr. Hugh Elliot—The French now at Hamburg—Prediction neglected—Russia and France—Exclusion from the Baltic—Sweden—The diadem of its sovereign suspended like the sword of Damocles—Bonaparte—Danger of England . . . . 347

*Mr. Miles to Baron de Nolcken. February* 18, 1807.
Dinner invitation—Recall of Mr. Liston from his embassy—Lord Hawkesbury—Copenhagen—Lord Folkestone, Sir John Gifford . . . . . . . . 349

*Mr. Miles to Lord Moira. Foley Place, July* 17.
An endeavour to obtain peace the wiser course—An understanding with France recommended to Pitt and Addington—Russia, Austria, King of Sweden—Denmark not a secondary power—Her neutrality worth obtaining—Secret mission for Mr. Miles in the Baltic—Mr. Canning—Admirals Essington and Gambier—Sir Home Popham—Opinion of Baron Nolcken—Bonaparte—Russia—Cession of Malta and the Cape—Hanover—M. Maret—Appointment at Carlton House—Proposal to go to Memel—Lord Hutchinson . . . . . 351

PAGE

*Sir Alexander Ball to Mr. Miles. Malta, August 2, 1807.*

Publications on Malta by Mr. Eton and Mr. Dillon—Attempt to injure Ball—Administration of Malta under the Duke of Sussex—Alleged discontent of the Maltese—Consiglio Popolare—Ball made President—An impudent falsehood—The French blockaded in La Valetta—Lord Nelson—Maltese in arms—Split into parties—Plunder—Ball requested to land—Government—Maltese never thought of an Assembly—Ball the first to suggest a Congress—Becomes its President—Mutiny in Malta—Froberg's regiment—Attachment of Maltese to the British Government—Proofs of their zeal in favour of England . . . . 353

*Lord Moira to Mr. Miles. Donington, August 23.*

Advantageous to learn the disposition of the French—Operations at Copenhagen—The King in an odd situation—Bonaparte. 355

*Lord Moira to Mr. Miles. Loudoun Castle, September 19.*

Copenhagen—Our cruisers in the Baltic—Danes not hostile to us—Holstein—The French watched—Horror of bombardment . . . . . . . . 856

*Lord Moira to Mr. Miles. Newcastle, October 24.*

Procedure against the Danes—No ground of presumption against them—Subscription for the sufferers . . . 856

*Lord Moira to Mr. Miles. Donington, November 15.*

Our procedure against Denmark—Pretext for the abandonment of arguments with us—Wish for peace—Our improvident conduct—Employment of Mr. Miles desired . . . 857

*Mr. Miles to Mr. Long. November 19.*

From the Bosphorus to the North Cape hostile to us—England detested everywhere—Bonaparte strikes at our maritime code—Culpability on our part—Peace with France preferable to an alliance with Austria, Russia, or Prussia—Mr. Addington—Our sincerity at the peace of Amiens distrusted by the French—New coalitions feared—Mission of Mr. Miles to sound M. Maret contemplated—Practicability of reaching Paris . . . 358

*Lord Moira to Mr. Miles. February 5, 1808.*

Employment of Mr. Miles would gratify the Prince—Message from Moira to Canning—Fermentation on the Continent—Desirable that Miles should obtain intelligence for the Government—King of Sweden—Inveteracy of Denmark since the mad enterprise against Copenhagen . . . . . 360

*Lord Moira to Mr. Miles. Donington, September* 20.

Acknowledgment of personal civility—The convention in Portugal a mortification—Ministers—Sir Hew Dalrymple—Command of the army—Sir Arthur Wellesley—The game not over in Spain—Napoleon bound to great exertions—The patriots—Surrender of Dupont—The French ought to fail, but a rough contest still . . . . . . . . . 361

*Lord Moira to Mr. Miles. Bridlington, September* 27.

The retreat of Junot facilitated—Resources of England inefficaciously applied—Decisive influence in Spain a necessity—Bonaparte will fail—France must be overcome . . . 362

*Lord Moira to Mr. Miles. Donington, April* 3, 1811.

Difficulties of the political position at home—The present Government injurious—Dissolution of Parliament inpracticable—The friends of the Prince left unrewarded—Admiral Pickmore. 363

*Mr. Miles to Lord Moira. July* 12.

Lord King and his tenantry—Copyhold possessed by Mr. Miles—Indecision of Lord Eldon—Bank-notes a legal tender—Mirabeau—First issue of assignats—Object of Mirabeau—Counter-revolutionary measures then plotting—'National domains'—Exchange of assignats for money—Palais Royal—Peregaux—Measures of Government towards America—Possible loss of Canada—France and Ireland—Dangerous position of the Prince and the country . . . . . . 364

*Lord Moira to Mr. Miles. London, August* 13.

Mr. Liston—His accuracy—Affairs on a declivity—Recent proclamation in Ireland—The Prince misled—No employment possible for Mr. Miles under present Ministry . . . 366

*Mr. Miles to his Wife. London, February* 17, 1812.

Lord Grenville and Lord Grey thrown out—Lord Moira—The Regent—Employment assured under a new Ministry . . 366

*Colonel McMahon to Mr. Miles. Pall Mall, February* 20.

The Regent informed that Mr. Miles has called at Carlton House . . . . . . . . . 367

*Mr. Miles to his Wife. London, February* 20.

Injudicious conduct of the Prince—Domestic happiness a counterpoise to political vexations—Desires to see his Royal

Highness rise in public opinion—His position now more rickety
—Manly conduct of Lord Moira—Mr. Miles abandons hope of
employment—Crooked turn of public affairs—The Prince pledged
to Lord Moira—Faith broken—Lord Powis goes to Ireland—
Lord Wellesley—Intrigues at Carlton House—The present
triumph due to the absence of public virtue in the Opposition—
The Listons and the Constantinople embassy . . . 368

*Mr. Miles to Lord Moira. February 21.*

Difficulties encountered by his Lordship—Hopes of the country
disappointed—Injudicious conduct of the Prince—The confidence
of Lord Moira appreciated . . . . . . 370

*Mr. Miles to his Wife. London, February 27.*

Lord Moira and the Administration—The Prince—Catholic
Emancipation—Mr. Perceval—Disappointment of the country—
Strength of the Opposition—The Ministers and Mr. Miles—Possible mission to the Continent—Colonel McMahon—Vote in the
House of Commons . . . . . . 371

*Lord Moira to Sir Home Popham. April 23.*

Employment for Mr. Miles on the Continent expedient—Lord
Melville—Copenhagen—Bonaparte . . . . 373

*Mr. Miles to Sir Home Popham. April 30.*

Expected appointment to Corcyra under Fox—Brilliant prospect in the Peninsula—Acrimony of the King of Denmark—
Successor to Mr. Heathcote at Cologne—Mission to Paris in 1790
—Mr. Hugh Elliot . . . . . . . 374

*Lord Melville to Colonel McMahon. May 2.*

Appointment for Mr. Miles to see his Lordship at the Admiralty . . . . . . . . 375

*Mr. Miles to Lord Melville. Southampton, May 3.*

Explains his absence from London—Readiness to proceed to
the Baltic . . . . . . . . 375

*Mr. Miles to Sir Home Popham. Hythe, May 13.*

Death of Mr. Perceval—Regarded as *good news*—Feverish
state of the country—Ill-advisers of the Prince—Private character
of Perceval—Lord Liverpool—Lord Moira should form the
Administration . . . . . . . 375

*Lord Melville to Colonel McMahon. May* 14.
Arrangements with Mr. Miles suspended by the death of Perceval . . . . . . . . 377

*Colonel McMahon to Mr. Miles. Carlton House, May* 14.
. The death of Perceval suspends consideration of the mission of Mr. Miles . . . . . . . 377

*Sir Home Popham to Mr. Miles. May* 14.
Blank in politics—Indecision of the Prince—Castlereagh and Canning—Lord Wellesley and Lord Moira . . . 877

*Mr. Rice to Mr. Miles. May* 16.
Result of the Cabinet Council—Lord Wellesley sent for—Canning and Castlereagh—Schemes of Wellesley—Huskisson—Lords Camden and Westmorland—Lords Holland and Moira—Intemperance of Opposition—Entanglement with the Grenvilles—Lord Grey—Lord Ellenborough—Determination of the Prince—Execution of Bellingham . . . . . 378

*Mr. Miles to Lord Moira. Hythe, May* 20.
Dislocated state of Government—Unpopularity of the Regent—Lord Moira might restore calm . . . . . 380

*Sir Charles Flint to Mr. Miles. May* 26.
Opposition and Administration—Catholic concession—War in the Peninsula—The Cabinet and Lord Wellesley—Lord Liverpool—Opinions laid before the Prince—Installation of the Knights . : . . . . . . 381

*Lord Moira to Mr. Miles. November* 3.
Supposed influence of his Lordship with the Prince—All going on ill—Ministers buoyant—Expected fall of Napoleon—Appointment to India—Hopes to see Mr. Miles employed . . 382

*Mr. Miles to Lord Moira. Hythe, November* 3.
Lord Moira appointed Governor-General of India—Promise of the Prince Regent to Mr. Miles not fulfilled—All thoughts of a foreign mission relinquished—Politics of Mr. Miles and the Administration—His manuscripts—Personal sacrifices for the public welfare . . . . . . . 383

*Mrs. Liston to Mr. Miles. Pera, July* 15, 1812.

Shock on hearing of Perceval's death—Report of Lord Moira going to Ireland—Sighing after news from England—Literary work more permanent than the patronage of Ministers—Pera the suburb of Constantinople—Report of plague—Desire for home news . . . . . . . . . 384

*Mrs. Liston to Mrs. Miles. Pera, January* 11, 1813.

Sir Robert Wilson sent to Petersburg—Lord Cathcart—Kept in a bustle of news—Dependence on the British Ambassador—Public news sent to Bagdad and India—Lord Moira—Violence of the plague . . . . . . . 386

*Mr. Miles to the Marquis de Lafayette. Hythe, December* 28.

Contemplates writing on the Revolution of 1789—Voluminous correspondence preserved—Asks for authentic materials . . 388

*Mr. Miles to the Marquis de Lafayette. Hythe, June* 12, 1814.

Death of Madame de Lafayette—A tempestuous night—Love of liberty—Lafayette and America—Prince Bishop of Liège in 1787—Pitt the champion of Parliamentary reform—Alliance with France—Mission of Miles and Hugh Elliot to Paris in 1790—English Cabinet accurately informed—Pitt implored not to quarrel with France—Edmund Burke . . . . 389

*Mrs. Liston to Mr. Miles. Constantinople, October* 25.

Delirium of joy—Congress—Bonaparte and Turkey—Anecdote—The Regent—A certain great personage—Mr. Robert Elliot—Mr. Rolleston—Constantinople . . . . . 391

*The Marquis de Lafayette to Mr. Miles. Paris, Aug.* 28, 1815.

Situation of France—The Allies—A cloud of uneasiness—Freedom as the ultimate result—Opinion of Bonaparte—His hurtful career—Might have escaped—No right to injure him—Death of Mr. Whitbread . . . . . . 393

*The Marquis de Lafayette to Mr. Miles. Lagrange, Jan.* 5. 1816.

Forwards documents to assist Mr. Miles in writing a Memoir of the French Revolution . . . . . . 395

*Mr. Miles to Sir Matthew Wood. Paris, February* 20, 1817.

Demand for Parliamentary reform—Danger of refusing—An enemy to mobs—Annual Parliaments—Corrupt House of Commons—Ill-qualified legislators—Hunt, Cartwright, Cobbett—

Turrents of blood may flow—Leaders of a revolution among the first victims—Anarchy may place England in the situation of France when under Robespierre—It may be the turn of England to suffer—British Cabinet responsible for the desolation of Europe—The King charged as the author of the war—Opinion of Lord Moira—Message to Mr. Pitt—'*Must war with France or resign*'—Lord Liverpool—Pitt's avarice of power—Meeting at Spa Fields—Liberators of the people aspire to be sovereigns—Elective franchise—Hedge Lane, Chick Lane—The masses as returning officers—Country in danger—The bulk of the people must be guided—Popular ferment alarming—Fences of the Constitution—Ministers must concede. . . . . 896

# INDEX TO THE CORRESPONDENCE

|   |   | PAGES |
|---|---|---|
| I. From Miles *to* Aust | . . . . | 39, 57, 59, 118, 173 |
| ,, | Ball . . . . | . 97, 299, 327 |
| ,, | Barthélemy . . . | 223, 236, 241, 298 |
| ,, | Beaulieu . . . . | . 238 |
| ,, | Buckingham . | 226, 267, 307, 310, 312, 316, 340 |
| ,, | Butler . . . . . | . 304 |
| ,, | Dampierre . . . . | . 6 |
| ,, | Devaynes . . . . | . 71 |
| ,, | Elliot . . . . . | . 258 |
| ,, | Erskine. . . . . | . 286, 315 |
| ,, | Fabry . . . . . | . 17 |
| ,, | Flint . . . . . | . 296, 342 |
| ,, | Fortescue . . . . | . 44, 246 |
| ,, | Hawkesbury . . . . | . 322 |
| ,, | Jekyll . . . . . | . 338 |
| ,, | Lafayette . . . | 291, 318, 388, 389 |
| ,, | Lansdowne . . . . | . 313 |
| ,, | Lauderdale . . . . | . 231 |
| ,, | Le Brun . . . . | . 26, 47 |
| ,, | Leeds . . . . . | 226, 229, 274 |
| ,, | Long . | 1, 105, 110, 119, 134, 166, 245, 255, 358 |
| ,, | Lovedon . . . . | . 100 |
| ,, | Maret . . . . | 22, 37, 43, 70, 285 |
| ,, | Melville . . . . | . 375 |
| ,, | Miles, Mrs. . . . | . 366, 368, 371 |
| ,, | Moira . . . | 347, 351, 364, 370, 380, 383 |
| ,, | Montgeroult . . . . | . 90 |
| ,, | Newenham | 78, 118, 125, 151, 159, 178, 186, 190 193, 197, 203, 221, 235, 263 |
| ,, | Nicholls . . . | 175, 207, 292 |
| ,, | Noël . | . 91, 102, 108, 122, 137, 143, 161, 167 |
| ,, | Nolcken . . . . | . 349 |
| ,, | Pitt . | 37, 39, 40, 61, 83, 101, 107, 112, 140, 182, 225, 276 |

|   |   | PAGES |
|---|---|---|
| I. From Miles *to* Popham | . | 374, 875 |
| ,, Rolleston | . | 332 |
| ,, Rose | . | 198 |
| ,, Sheridan | . | 174 |
| ,, Sturt | . | 200, 234, 261 |
| ,, 'True Briton' | . | 9 |
| ,, Woodfall | . | 192 |
| ,, Wood | . | 396 |
| II. To Miles *from* Aust | . | 40, 59 |
| ,, Ball | . | 329, 330, 334, 353 |
| ,, Barthélemy | . | 215, 297 |
| ,, Beaulieu | . | 240 |
| ,, Buckingham | . | 306, 312 |
| ,, Count de —— | . | 207, 212, 216 |
| ,, Donovan | . | 345 |
| ,, Duncombe | . | 243, 252 |
| ,, Emigré | . | 205 |
| ,, Erskine | . | 288, 289 |
| ,, Fabry | . | 10 |
| ,, Flint | . | 341, 381 |
| ,, Lady | . | 76 |
| ,, Lafayette | . | 294, 393, 395 |
| ,, Leeds | . | 108, 140, 228 |
| ,, Liston | . | 336, 384, 386, 391 |
| ,, Long | . | 52, 110, 137 |
| ,, McMahon | . | 367, 377 |
| ,, Maret | . | 12, 28, 46, 51, 54, 61, 65, 69, 273 |
| ,, Moira | . | 355, 356, 357, 360, 361, 362, 363, 366, 382 |
| ,, Monsieur —— | . | 219, 291 |
| ,, Montgeroult | . | 86 |
| ,, Mourgue | . | 13, 65, 66 |
| ,, Newenham | . | 131, 148, 184, 196 |
| ,, Nicholls | . | 189 |
| ,, Noël | . | 48, 85, 104, 113, 141, 156, 164, 169, 170 |
| ,, Penrose | . | 127, 188, 211, 258 |
| ,, Pickmore | . | 346 |
| ,, Pitt | . | 40 |
| ,, Popham | . | 377 |
| ,, Reinhard | . | 17, 28, 41, 50, 51 |
| ,, Rice | . | 378 |
| ,, Smith | . | 44 |
| ,, Sturt | . | 233, 250 |
| ,, Ware | . | 129, 145 |
| ,, Wycombe | . | 316, 319 |
| To McMahon *from* Melville | . | 375, 377 |
| ,, Popham ,, Moira | . | 373 |

The long intervals between the dates of letters, as shown towards the close of the 'Correspondence,' arise from the necessity of restricting these volumes to reasonable limits.

In the spelling of proper names, autographic signatures have been copied, whenever available, from original letters or documents. Thus the Tables of Contents show *Le Brun*, instead of *Lebrun*, which latter form is by far the most common in use. The autograph of Bonne-Carrère appears among Mr. Miles's papers as *Bonnecarrere*, and without any accent. Hence it is occasionally so spelt in these volumes. *See* Baron Ernouf's 'Maret, Duc de Bassano,' p. 58. For Rochefoucault, Vol. I. p. 398, *read* Rochefoucauld.

# CORRESPONDENCE

### MR. MILES TO MR. LONG

Sunday, January 6, 1793

IT is now midnight. M. Reinhard has just left me, and before the pen drops from my hand, for I am more than half asleep, I hasten to tell you that the Treaty of Commerce is the same as declared null, and that Le Brun makes two more complaints this very day to the National Convention, on the prohibition of exporting corn and on the Assignat Bill. M. Chauvelin is instructed to demand of Lord Grenville whether the Alien Bill includes Frenchmen, and, if our Minister answers in the affirmative, he has orders to say that the Treaty of Commerce is at an end. Reinhard was the bearer of a note to me from M. Chauvelin. I inclose a copy; you will do with it as you please, but it is Chauvelin's expressed wish that it should be communicated to Mr. Pitt. It is as follows: 'Si M. Pitt désire s'expliquer sur les affaires politiques, ou s'il a quelque chose à communiquer au pouvoir exécutif à Paris, M. Chauvelin prendra sur lui de le voir en particulier.'[1]

---

[1] On December 26, Chauvelin had himself made a direct application to Mr. Pitt for a private audience, and received on the same day the following reply: 'Monsieur,—J'ai reçu votre honorée du 26. Dans ma première conversation avec M. Maret j'avais exprimé l'espérance que j'avais, que le mode d'explication particulière *qu'il suggérait* pourrait être utile.

A large body of Prussians is moving towards Dumouriez's army. Dumouriez himself is at Paris with 800 men in his pay, resolved, if possible, to save the King's life; and these 800 will be joined by 3,000 Fédérés. The Austrians have passed from Milan into Piedmont. You see I communicate to you a mixture of news.

*Minute: January* 7.—On hearing from Mr. Long that he declined to 'convey any message to Mr. Pitt respecting M. Chauvelin,' I called upon the Minister at his own house, saw him, and had the mortification to receive a positive refusal from him to see either M. Chauvelin or any other agent of the French Government at present in London. This obstinacy and other circumstances dispose me to think that our Cabinet is too far pledged with the powers on the Continent to avoid taking part in the war, and, what is still more to be lamented, the French furnish the Minister with excuses in abundance, and even justification for hostilities, since the Executive Council *means* war, and only amuses us until matters are ready. Noël, Reinhard, Maret, and the Mourgues, father and son, are for peace. Chauvelin disapproves of Le Brun's report made on the 20th December to the Convention, and requested me, through Reinhard, to say as much to Mr. Pitt. Condorcet and Sieyès, I know, are decidedly for war. Le Brun, I fear, is further actuated by private pique for having been refused, in 1787–88, an annual allowance of 50*l.* from

Mais, quand je l'ai revu, j'ai appris qu'on n'était pas disposé à un tel mode de communication. Votre lettre n'exprime pas avec quel caractère vous vous adressez à moi en ce moment, et, après ce qui s'est passé, je ne pense pas qu'il y ait aucune convenance ou utilité à ce que, dans les circonstances présentes, je converse avec vous. Je suis obligé, en conséquence, de vous prier de permettre que j'évite l'honneur de vous voir.'

' Cette lettre était en anglais. Nous reproduisons la traduction envoyée par Chauvelin à Lebrun.'—Ernouf, p. 106.

the Treasury, which I solicited for him in return for some civilities which, at my request, he had shown the British Government when he edited the 'Journal Politique et Général de l'Europe' at Hervé.[1]

Le Brun has the vanity to wish for the declaration of war against Great Britain under the Ministry of Mr. Pitt; and the criminal design is only too well seconded by certain classes afraid of losing their tinsel greatness in the progress of the Revolution. Mr. Pitt, decidedly a friend of peace in 1790, when he sent me to Paris, is, I am afraid, a convert to war. May I live to see the day when England, regulating her diplomatic relations by maxims of justice and enlightenment, will spurn mischievous coalitions with foreign courts, and, avoiding all baneful aspirations, cherish the virtue of forbearance and peace! But from all the circumstances, and from the want of real liberty and good faith on the other side of the Channel, I much fear that war will break out. On the other hand, from the notes in my possession, I think that, if France will be prudent and sincere, the British Cabinet will preserve a peaceful attitude; but if otherwise, I shall hold myself bound in honour to separate from Mr. Pitt and take part against him. I have assured the Executive Council ' que si on suivrait mes conseils et serait de bonne foi, je défierois le Ministre anglais de faire la guerre à la France.' But there is neither wisdom, nor sincerity, nor gratitude in Le Brun, and the curse of war is apparently inevitable. O peace, peace! I would sacrifice my life for the preservation of peace! Nor is it the Revolution which, in the just sense of the word, the

[1] 'Le Brun, the Foreign Minister, hated Austria, because it had enslaved his second home, Liège; and England, because, when he was supporting himself by journalism, it had refused him a pension.'—Von Sybel, ii. 214. Sybel refers to the *Authentic Correspondence with M Le Brun* as his authority.

advocates for war in this country apprehend, but the reform of abuses, which, although they are sapping the dearest rights of Englishmen, it is the object of faction to preserve and augment. Hence the cause of that terrible alarm now sounded throughout the kingdom, and which, by means of mercenary writers, will not cease to sound. O God! when will our nation be just to itself, and withdraw its confidence from men who have so long abused their liberty and power?

> But th' age of virtuous politics is past,
> And we are deep in that of cold pretence.[1]

Reinhard yesterday brought me some papers, and reported the instructions transmitted by the Executive Council to Chauvelin, 'That he should demand of Lord Grenville if the French were included in the Alien Bill, and to say that, if they are included, the Treaty of Commerce is at an end.' These instructions arrived in Portman Square yesterday, and they appeared in the public prints several hours before they were officially communicated to the Foreign Office, which, as Aust tells me, was not till noon this day; the purport of this delay being in accordance with the French principle lately established in revenge for our haughtiness, that, in the first instance, the *people* should be parties in the cause and be influenced to quarrel with the Government. Chauvelin received from Lord Grenville an answer to his note at half-past four o'clock. It merely stated that, 'as the character of M. Chauvelin was null in this country, his paper was inadmissible.' He was outrageous at this laconic reply, and despatched it this evening to Paris by a courier.[2]

[1] Cowper.

[2] *Extract from Note of M. Chauvelin to Lord Grenville.*—'The undersigned has received orders to demand of Lord Grenville to inform him by a clear, speedy, and categorical answer, if, under the general

*Minute: January* 8.—Reinhard called upon me again. He laments the warmth with which the two Governments conduct themselves. After inquiring if the English Minister was much incensed at the firing into the 'Childers,' sloop of war, last week from one of the forts that defend Brest,[1] he asked if I thought there remained any possibility of preventing the war by opening a negotiation. I told him that the only means left to France to avoid the war would be for the National Convention to declare explicitly that Savoy would be restored, that the opening of the Scheldt would be renounced, and that it should be agreed to treat with Vienna for a general peace. Reinhard replied that such an arrangement, he believed, might take place if it was not exacted. I took care to impress upon him that I

---

denomination of foreigners in the Bill preparing by Parliament upon the proposition of a member of the Administration, the Government of Great Britain mean likewise to include France.'

*Reply of Lord Grenville to M. Chauvelin.*—' January 7.—After the formal notification which the undersigned has had the honour of making to M. Chauvelin, he finds himself obliged to send back to him the paper which he received this morning, and which he cannot consider otherwise than as totally inadmissible, M. Chauvelin assuming in it a character which is not acknowledged.'—*Annual Register, State Papers,* 1793, pp. 122-125. An abstract of the 'Act for establishing Regulations respecting Aliens arriving in this Kingdom,' &c., is given in the *Annual Register,* 1792, Appendix to *Chronicle,* p. 110.

[1] 'Plymouth, le 5 Janvier.—Le " Childers," étant à croiser vendredi à deux heures de l'après-midi devant Brest, s'avança à trois quarts de mille des batteries de ce port. Il était sans couleurs. Une des batteries lui tira un coup à boulet, qui passa heureusement par-dessus, sans lui causer aucun dommage. Le " Childers " alors arbora pavillon anglais. Mais le fort arbora aussitôt les couleurs nationales, avec un pendant rouge sur l'enseigne. Les autres forts suivirent son exemple. Pendant ce tems-là le " Childers " avait été entraîné par la marée à un demi-mille environ de ces forts, et obligé à cause du calme d'avoir recours aux rames, pour ne pas arriver trop près. Tout à coup, les batteries, à un signal qui fut fait, commencèrent sur lui un feu croisé, qui l'eût criblé, si un vent frais, qui s'éleva, ne l'eût mis à même de se dégager.'—*Moniteur,* 23 Janvier, 1793. See Herbert Marsh, i. 220.

was not authorised to announce the above conditions, but I touched on these points, which *I knew* to be the cause of the ill-humour of my own Government, and which would be the pretext for hostilities in the event of the war party in England bringing Mr. Pitt to renounce his pacific views. There is a party among us who breathe nothing but war. Still, I believe that, if the Convention would demonstrate its desire for peace by declarations so equitable and prudent, the British Cabinet would agree to a discussion that would tend to restore harmony between the two countries. The Executive Council may be pacific, but the National Convention appears to me to be insane, and its follies will embitter the war.[1]—W. A. M.

### MR. MILES TO GENERAL DAMPIERRE [2]

January 8, 1793

You do me wrong, my dear General, unless the distinction I have made between liberty and licentiousness can be called a desertion of principles. I am still the advocate of the Revolution in 1789, but not of its consequences. The abuses in your government certainly required reform; and, I am willing to admit that no efficacious and substantial remedy short of a revolution could have availed, because there were too many men interested in the preservation of those abuses which beggared and oppressed your nation. The misfortune

---

[1] 'Gouverneur Morris, who observed events in Paris very closely, was convinced in December that it would be impossible for England to avoid war. He describes how the French politicians "affect to wish Britain would declare against them, and actually menace the Government with an appeal to the nation;" but he added, "in spite of that blustering they will do much to avoid a war with Great Britain *if the people will let them*. But the truth is that the populace of Paris influence in a great degree the public councils."'—Lecky, vi. 114.

[2] Au service de la République française.

is that, having been afraid to trust yourselves with the important task, you called the *people* from their labour and from their means of livelihood to assist in the new government, whereby their habits of industry were destroyed, and, what will long be felt and lamented, you converted your mechanics and handicraftmen into legislators; forgetting that it is not every man who handles a spade that is qualified to use the pruning-knife. You will remember what I repeatedly said to the hapless Lafayette, as also to you, and to all with whom I conversed at Paris—that a revolution in your government, without a revolution in your morals, would be of no avail; that the popularity which our friend enjoyed—for it was enjoyment to him—was delusive, and would terminate either in his assassination or exile. I am sure that, if ever my name has occurred to him in his confinement, Lafayette will have recollected my prediction, and, particularly, what passed between us on the three days during which the National Guards and the municipal officers filed before his door, in proof of his momentary triumph over the intrigues of Monsieur d'Orléans. You dined with us each day. Think of the professions, even of loyalty as well as of affection, which M. de Lafayette received from the military and corporate bodies at Paris, and then recollect that, at the distance of a year, he was obliged to save himself by flight from the fury of those very people who pretended to idolise him! At the present time, when perfect liberty and equality are professed by everybody, and promised to every people, the most inexorable tyranny is exercised; the freedom of speech, and almost of thought, is proscribed by the terror that reigns, and an entire submission to vague and contradictory opinions is exacted with savage barbarity.

Believe me, my dear General, it is not in the nature of things that a Government vicious in the extreme should produce good citizens. Its corruptions, extending even to private life, must destroy all reverence for virtue; all private, all public faith; and, although the duration of such a Government will continue no longer than the terror it inspires, yet its subversion, without a revolution in the morals of the people, will only substitute in its place an anarchy still more frightful and deplorable than the despotism it has banished. This is my confession of faith; and, being equally an enemy to tyranny and to anarchy, I will neither flatter the one nor countenance the other. With respect to the letter mentioned by you as having been directed against your revolution, it is herewith inclosed. It was most certainly written by me, as you conclude, and, what you in your enthusiasm may consider as a proof of incivism, it was sent for publication in a journal called in this country a 'Ministerial paper,' with some others on the same subject. Your perusal of this letter will, I hope, remove your erroneous impression, and convince you that I have not renounced a cause supported by me through life, and which I never will abandon. But my love of liberty is not to engage me to go all the lengths which madmen, or bad men, would wish in order to gratify their whims or their interest. Examine, I beseech you, and judge for yourself; and remember that it is only in the silence of the passions that the voice of reason can be heard. On this subject I maintain convictions cherished from my infancy, and, trust me, I will not in the decline of life descend an apostate to the grave. The war that you announced I have long foreseen. Heaven send us a good deliverance! Adieu!

*To the Editor of the 'True Briton'*[1]

December, 1792

Sir,—The French Revolution, like the shock of a tremendous earthquake, has been felt from one extremity of the globe to the other. It has opened to the intellectual world a new train of ideas, not less bold and hazardous than novel and extraordinary, and which must eventually produce throughout the vast continent of Europe an entire change in the manners, opinions, and customs of men. As a friend to civil and religious liberty, I am not displeased to behold questions which relate to the freedom and happiness of mankind brought forward and discussed in those nations where the human mind has been kept in bondage; where it has been shackled with an affinity of useless and disgraceful prejudices, and forbidden by the despotism of illiterate and profligate Governments to rise to the dignity of thought. It is full time, Sir, that the mist of error should be dispelled, and the reign of injustice cease. Those who have exercised a brutal tyranny over their degraded and uninformed subjects may well tremble at an investigation that tends to dissolve the charm by which their ill-acquired power was maintained. If such consequences alone were to result from the French Revolution, no good man could repine at an event so salutary and beneficial; but, on the contrary, he would rejoice at whatever tends to rescue the wretched exile from the bleak and gloomy deserts of Siberia, and which, restoring the sweets of friendship and of freedom, grants to him a portion of that light and heat which

---

[1] Published also in *The Conduct of France towards Great Britain*, p. 187. It is to this letter that General Dampierre refers, December 24, 1792.

cheers and animates the mind and heart of every Englishman. Let the sacred sun of liberty blaze forth in meridian glory; let its splendour illumine and enliven the various nations of the earth as yet unhappily plunged in darkness and ignorance; but do not let its scattered rays be collected into a focus to destroy what they ought to vivify and preserve; do not let the greatest blessing we can possess be polluted and degraded to answer the foul and unnatural purposes of the most depraved licentiousness, nor suffer the popular and seductive cry of 'Liberty' to estrange us from the rational enjoyment of our civil and political rights. It is here, Sir, that the line must be drawn, or else an anarchy still more deplorable, if possible, than the severest despotism will ensue, and expose us to all the mischiefs and to all the excesses of which a sanguinary, profligate, and ungovernable rabble is capable.

### M. FABRY TO MR. MILES

Liège: December 28, 1792 [1]

I received, my dear friend, your letter of the 4th instant only a few days ago. I know not whither it has been wandering, nor if my reply will find you still in London. You are not aware of it perhaps, *but, in fact, you are on the eve of a war*, and, in this case, you will not surely come to Liège. You have no idea, my friend, of the embarrassment with which I am overwhelmed. I have had only one happy moment since my return; it was when my fellow-citizens received me with an attachment that penetrated my soul. At this instant nothing happens as I could wish, and I am by no means assured as to the future. The Austrian brigands and all our cowardly tyrants have ravaged my

[1] Received January 9, 1793.

country, and the French finish what the Austrians commenced. The Generals cannot put a stop to the indiscipline, and, instead of going as far as the Rhine, they take up their winter quarters here. Dumouriez has left for Paris. It is said that he will not return. The combined despots are going to make fresh efforts, and the spring will perhaps bring about our destruction. The French put under sequestration all our ecclesiastical property, the domains, and those of our emigrants, in pursuance of the decree of the Convention of the 15th December. As to our future, provided they do not abandon us, we shall endure it all.

In 1790 I wished very much to follow your good advice and throw off the yoke of the Empire, but it was not then possible to manifest the intention. I have since declared it as my own in the face of all Europe, nor will I ever capitulate with tyranny. I declare eternal war against Prussia, who has in a cowardly way deceived us, against perfidious Austria and infamous Wetzlar.

Liège has already named its representatives to our future Convention, but the rest of the country is not yet organised for this election. Bassenge, Lesoinne, Honcart, myself, my son, and some other true patriots, to the number of twenty, represent the arrondissement of Liège.

You ask for news of the estimable Regnier. Alas! we have lost him, as also the virtuous burgomaster Doncéel. They are dead, and their loss is irreparable.

Chestret remained on the territory of Prussia and Holland during the whole time of our bondage; he has reappeared within these few days.

I foresee that we shall ask to be an 85th department of the French Republic, but it will be in spite of me.

Our union with the Belgians appears scarcely possible at present; we differ too much in principle, and your noble project is destroyed. I hope, however, that they will follow a project of my own, which is to bring into our arrondissement Stavelot, Limbourg, and all the territories on the right bank of the Meuse from the frontiers of France, &c. If they had listened to me, if they had marched at the time straight on Liège, I venture to think that they would be masters of Cologne, and of Bonn and Coblentz.

The Abbé Noël had the kindness to search for me, but, not being successful, he offered in a note to take charge of a letter for you. He leaves the day after to-morrow. I wrote to him this evening begging him to say a thousand things to you from me, but they have returned my letter, not having been able to find him. Adieu, my dear friend! *Je vous embrasse, et suis pour la vie tout à vous.*

### M. MARET TO MR. MILES.

Paris: January 5, 1793[1]

I am very sorry, my dear Miles, to be still unable to write, but my position will exonerate me. You know with what an amount of work I must be overwhelmed after an absence of two months. You have written to Mourgue with a little too much sharpness on the first report of Le Brun. I believe that if I had arrived before it had been issued the Minister would have consented to some essential alterations. But how can it be helped? I was *en route*, and public opinion was deluded by the numerous accounts that were abroad. Since my return I have spoken boldly and frankly, but I have encountered great obstacles. The insults of the

[1] Received January 9.

British Parliament, the national pride of the French, their courage and the immensity of their resources—here are the reasons and the facts, to which the enthusiasm of liberty and victory give an energy which can neither be modified nor restrained! Do you really think that Chauvelin can remain? If I come and embrace you, and pass a few moments with you, would I be under the shelter of your new laws? Would it not be possible to obtain through Mr. Pitt a safe-conduct, without which I would never set foot in England?

Le Brun desires me to express his regret that he is still obliged to defer the pleasure of writing to you. He begs you not to doubt his esteem. If, supposing an impossibility, our nations could draw near to each other and come to a mutual understanding, he would hail with great joy the opportunity of communicating with you, and of labouring together in this salutary and peaceful work. Assuredly your Government could not choose any person, under any circumstances, with whom Le Brun would have more satisfaction in speaking on public affairs.

*M. MOURGUE TO MR. MILES*

Montpellier: January 1, 1793

It is long since I had the pleasure of conversing with you. My son, when in London, often spoke of your kindness. I cannot better commence this year than in expressing my sincere gratitude for all that you have done for him. Continue a friendship which will always be so precious to us.

The critical events in Paris persuaded my wife and myself to repair to Montpellier, as our native place, early in October; and we find in the surrounding tranquillity an enjoyment which can alone fill the void occasioned

by the absence of our dear children. We behold a sky
of which I had almost lost the remembrance. Since
the 15th November there has not been a cloud on the
horizon, and the sun is so hot that we close our blinds at
the appearance of noon. The local political horizon is
as yet almost as pure, as serene—nothing here disturbs
the peace; but, on the contrary, whatever concerns
the production of the soil, or tends to promote commerce, obtains a firm hold in these agricultural and
industrial regions. Fortunes have doubled within three
or four years, prosperity in other directions has followed
in the same progression, and the people attribute to the
Revolution these perceptible advantages. The privileged classes, who have been regarded as burdensome
to the people—the persons, for example, with fixed
rents—are, however, in a different and much more
grievous condition; they have lost their former ease,
and hence you will understand what are *their* ideas on
the Revolution.

A singular metamorphosis has taken place. We see
men formerly in the profession of the law, and others
now occupied in commerce, establishing manufactories
and promoting trade; and, if events which we cannot foresee do not disturb these southern parts of France, there
will be an immense increase in population and in augmen-
tation of wealth; but alas! events are influenced by so
many causes that it is difficult to foresee the results.
I much wish that we could be near each other, as at the
beginning of the Revolution. You remember that we
were in accord on great principles; and yet, how we
trembled at the means employed to assert and maintain
them, and how we predicted the fatal consequences that
have ensued. We had seen only too well—and I lament
that our prescience has been verified—the way in

which people reasoned, or rather falsely reasoned, on consequences; the false views, too metaphysical, or perhaps too interested, of our first National Assembly, then of our second legislative body, and, may we not add, of the National Convention, have conducted us to the point where we now are. The precipice is such as to terrify the faint-hearted; but we must contemplate it with courage, and even with hope.

I confess that, amidst all my ideas between hope and fear, I had never imagined that a nation calling itself free, and glorying in its liberty—the proud Albion—would join the forces of tyrants combined to enchain anew a people who have felt the weight of their political and social bondage. Are the words *liberty* and *humanity* vain sounds in the ears of your Ministers? I acknowledge that our efforts to liberate ourselves have been accompanied by culpable errors, extravagances, and even horrors. Some of our principal agents have been devoid of purity of heart and mind; we do not attempt to conceal it; but nevertheless, ought free men to stifle, on account of our lamentable moral failures, great principles, and exterminate those who developed them?

What are the motives of your Government in the quarrel which she seeks against us? What has England to gain or lose whether the Scheldt is opened or closed to the inhabitants on its banks? Why should it trouble England that a nation has recovered liberty and rights for which she herself sacrificed money and blood nearly three centuries ago? Or what does it signify to England that the despots of Vienna and Berlin should be obliged to give more or less freedom to those whom they call their people? Does your nation wish to throw down the gauntlet, and constitute herself the champion of all the tyrants of the world? Will her fleet cease to cover the seas when the Imperial eagle no longer hovers over this side of the Rhine? Or will the sugar, the coffee, the cotton, of your islands be less in demand when the German nations, more free, shall have become more industrious and more wealthy?

Your nation also committed some excesses in your Revolution; but your liberty remains—your prosperity is the magnificent result. You remember only the names of the violent men who sullied your moments of transition. It will be the same with us. The war against North America is a blot on the history of England in this century. Will not enlightened statesmen profit by your experience? It would not be difficult to prove that England and France would have everything to gain by conduct diametrically opposite to the course which at present each pursues: all your misfortunes, all your debts, all your fiscal laws for centuries past, have arisen from your quarrels with France, and all our misfortunes, all our debts, and even the bondage from which we desire to escape, have arisen from our quarrels with England! If, then, we conclude that both nations are so insane that an amicable union based on principle is an impossibility, the two peoples must be content to witness further misfortunes and miseries, and to see the oppressors of the human race triumph in their machinations. I much fear that your Government, including both your King and his Ministers, are more afraid of French opinions on liberty and equality than of any political power which France may ever acquire.

The decree against the emigrants has given me much pain, since it may interrupt the education of my children now in England, and may for the moment confound them with that contemptible class, who, by their principles and actions, would stir up enemies against their country; although a distinction must be made between emigrants armed in hostility to their fellow-citizens and many Frenchmen good at heart, but whom the horrors of the time have compelled to fly to a foreign land.

You can write to me at my usual address in Paris. Your letters will be forwarded to me here if I have not left. Adieu, my dear Sir! *Je vous embrasse de tout mon cœur.*

### M. REINHARD TO MR. MILES
January 10, 1793

I thank you, Sir, for your kindness. We have not had a courier, and the resolution of M. Chauvelin will depend probably on the decision taken at Paris.

I count positively on having the honour of seeing you to-morrow between two and four o'clock. I have many things to say to you. I salute you with all my heart.

### MR. MILES TO M. FABRY
January 11, 1793

It was an agreeable surprise, my dear Fabry, to receive on the 9th instant your letter dated the 28th of December. In despair at seeing you made the sport of the Court of Berlin and at last banished from your country by the Austrians, I thought of retiring in the meantime from any further interference with your politics; but there is a fate which unwittingly directs us, and against which we cannot flatter ourselves to advance. Always in love with liberty—a liberty, however, which is rational and regulated by general consent —I saw with very sincere joy the Belgians chase their tyrants beyond the Rhine, and the Liégeois, equally oppressed, follow the same noble example. On my arrival in England in January 1790 I had a long conversation with the Minister of Foreign Affairs—the Duke of Leeds—and I explained to him your old *régime*, and the infamous conduct of Joseph II. towards his subjects in the Netherlands; but, as your grievances in particular did not constitute a sufficiently strong motive for England to quarrel outright with the House of Austria, I adopted other means for engaging our Government to guarantee your independence, means both just and prudent, and, if his Grace had listened to me, we should not at present have any dispute with France—the Scheldt would not have been opened; there would be no French troops to-day in Liège, or Brabant, or Austrian Flanders; Holland would not be menaced, nor would England be on the point of seeing herself despoiled of the peace that is so necessary for her welfare. The United Provinces would thus have possessed a barrier against France, and all cause of discord between that nation and England would probably have been dispelled. My project, you know, was to convert the Principality of Liège and the Austrian Netherlands into a republic independent of the empire; and, having explained to the Minister in detail the political and commercial advantages that would have resulted, I felt that I had only done my duty, and, at the same time, had indicated to the Foreign Office its duty also, in anticipation of an approaching and inevitable crisis. After profound silence, the Minister replied *that it would be going very far*. It is thus that the *future* does not always enter into the thoughts of statesmen to whom chance may intrust the fate of their fellow-citizens. It is a misfortune, but what is to be done? You might have enjoyed political liberty these three years past; the French would have been without pretence for invading Brabant; and my country would not have been, as you affirm it now is, on the very eve of war with France.[1] What may be the result of this war no one can foresee ; but it may prove disastrous to France herself, who, since the Revolution of 1789, has committed follies often mingled with atrocities. You may judge, you who know the sincerity of my heart and my zeal for true liberty, how I must be afflicted to witness a whole nation straying, as the French are straying at this moment, from right principles, and, in pursuing a course at once *bizarre* and unjust, are strengthening the despotism which it pretends to overthrow and destroy. If France had been well directed, as I often said to the unfortunate Lafayette, all the tyrants of Europe from Constantinople to St. Petersburg would have been crushed before the end of the century—we should have seen the base wickedness of the North and all the kinglets of Germany extinguished ; but, the embankment which restrained the vices of the *ancien régime* within the regal enclosure of Versailles being broken down by the Revolution, and there being no sufficient authority substituted in its place, a frightful and general outbreak has supervened, and the whole country finds itself inundated with crimes and intrigues which, unhappily, the *levelling* and *narrow-minded* populace convert into instruments of universal ruin. I venture to assure you that, were it not for this spirit of intrigue and manifestation of crime, France would already have taken a strong and firm position among the nations of Europe, instead of being compelled to seek for safety

[1] 'The confidential relations of Fabry with Dumouriez and Le Brun—the latter of whom was under the greatest obligations to him—afford a strong presumption that he had good authority for what he communicated. It is most probable that, when he asserts *that this country was on the eve of a war*, he knew that it was the resolution of the Executive Council to hold no longer any measures with Great Britain.'—W. A. M. *Conduct of France towards Great Britain Examined*, p. 74.

and to preserve her political existence in a total and general *bouleversement* of all the other Governments of the world! This unheard-of and inexplicable conduct is worse than the thousand blunders committed by the unfortunate Van Eupen and Vandernoot in 1789–90. I said at the time that never had so good a cause been lost by so bad an advocate.

You know, my dear friend, how earnestly I have desired to see your country free, and with what ardour I have toiled while there existed yet a gleam of hope for success. The same principles—the same philanthropy—have influenced me in the effort to preserve to France the fruit of all her labour during the last consecutive three years. You are not ignorant of my behaviour towards Le Brun when he fled from Hervé to Vienna. I command the right to expect from him frank and honourable conduct. He has attained his present position by the most extraordinary chance, which proves that human life is often but a game. Now, although I have written and pointed out the course he should pursue—if he sincerely desires to maintain amity with England—and have assured him of my continued effort to avert a war between the two countries, he has assumed a haughty tone, and insists that the English Minister shall acknowledge the Republic, and treat officially with M. Chauvelin, who is not recognised here. During four months he has had secret agents in London. The Executive Power recedes, and refuses to negotiate in the only way at present possible. Mr. Pitt, indignant at the proceedings in Paris as compromising the honour of the English nation, discourages me from holding further intercourse with the French Government; and thus the narrow bridge of communication now in use may soon be broken. I will fully

instruct you as to what I have said to Le Brun and
Noël, also to Maret, and to many others here, both
French and English; and, if the Executive Power, as I
have reason to know, had followed my advice at the
beginning, when it was a question of introducing Maret
to Mr. Pitt, the independence of Liège and the Netherlands would have been acknowledged, and the impending war might have been averted. I cannot tell you more
in a letter which perhaps may never reach you; but, in
a word, if war does break out, it will be the fault not
of the Cabinet of St. James, but of the Executive Power
in Paris; and, in this case, I fear that you will fall
under the tyranny of Wetzlar and the Tartuffes.
England has exacted nothing from France but the surrender of Savoy—that is to say, the renunciation of all
conquests—of the Scheldt, and to consent to treat with
the Court of Vienna for a general peace. The Secretary
of the French Legation remarked to me that these conditions were very humiliating. I replied that it ought
not to be a question of pride but of justice. Behold,
then, in brief, my dear Fabry, the history of my labours.
I have not yet finished. I will oppose with all my
power any movement that would tend to give Liège
back to the Tartuffes. Write and tell me all that happens in your neighbourhood. If fate wills that you
should again quit your home, come and seek an asylum
in England. A thousand kind remembrances to all
your family, to Chestret, and to all my friends. Assure
them that I shall be happy when Liège is free. Do not
fear the size of your packets while inclosing them to
Mr. Aust at the Foreign Office, Whitehall. *Je vous
embrasse mille fois, mon cher cher Fabry.* Adieu!

P.S.—I pray you to send to me some of your newspapers, those which best express the general sentiments

of your fellow-citizens. I am curious to know the names of those whom Hoensbruck put to death on his re-entry into Liège. The good and virtuous Doncéel died, I suppose, from chagrin, as also Regnier. It is a great misfortune, for I always found in these two men honesty and unity of purpose. According to the gazettes, the French cause trouble at Bruxelles; they do harm there, and, what is still worse, in the Low Countries also. If Bonnecarrère is at Liège, I pray you to recall me to his remembrance, also to that of General Dampierre. Poor Charles de Geloes, I hear, was drowned at Liège. When I saw him in 1790 he reminded me of the history of Cardinal de Retz; with this difference, that he had neither his intelligence nor his influence, only a hearty desire to play the *first rôle* in the Revolution. The ridiculous system of *equality*, as popularly understood, can never be established. Some kind of *culte* is necessary—a bridle; but this bridle must be bridled, and the bridle must be *good laws*. Give, then, a fair rent to the monks and the *religieuses*—it is their right; and, in order that religion may not be degraded, increase the salaries of your parochial clergy—the curates and vicars, whose burdens are heavy, and in succouring them you will attach them to your interests. If you are faithful to each other, and are determined—no matter what part France may take, provided that she does not join your enemies—Flanders, Brabant, and Liège will make headway against Prussia and Austria. Adieu!

### *Mr. Miles to M. Maret*

January 11, 1793

The despatch sent by M. Chauvelin on Monday, December 31st, must certainly have reached you, although you have not acknowledged its receipt. You tell me of the ardour of the French people and of their immense resources. Alas! my dear Maret, it is no longer a question of either the one or the other. After the grievances detailed by Lord Grenville in his reply to M. Chauvelin's note, what other part could France take but to retreat or to fight? I know of no other. You will perhaps tell me that what has been exacted is too humiliating; but, my dear friend, it is not a question of pride, but of justice. I have begged you to impress on Le Brun how much more glorious it would be for France to consent to a general peace, after having freed the Netherlands and the country of Liège, than to continue a war which, although we cannot foresee its results, will endanger the liberty recently acquired by the Liégeois and the Belgians, as well as the new order of things in France. The Executive Power would then enjoy the praise of having consolidated the French Revolution, you would possess leisure to restore your dilapidated finances, and at the same time reorganise the machinery of government and revive a commerce at present almost destroyed. Public tranquillity, as well as the fortune and glory of those who at this moment hold in their hands the destiny of France, would be reassured by peace. And what is the price demanded for all this? Nothing but what is dictated by justice. If the National Assembly, in a moment of intoxication, commits mistakes or injustice, it behoves its members to correct the one and to repair the other. Allow me to repeat, what you have already seen in the reply of Lord Grenville, that the order given to your generals to follow the enemy on neutral ground is an attack upon the independence of the Powers not at war with France, the resolution of the Council on the opening of the Scheldt is an infraction of treaties, and the appropriation of Savoy is contrary to your own principles. You have renounced all conquests. And yet you make and retain them! How can a nation be trusted which respects neither its treaties nor its oaths? The decree of the 19th November, as well as that of the 15th December, being conceived in general terms, and inviting, so to say, the people of all countries to revolt against their respective Governments, promising them substantial help, are grievances too evident and too serious not to make the British Government indignant. These decrees justify its fears, and especially since the National Assembly received, with an eagerness as unbecoming as impolitic, the addresses of some factious clubs in England which are known not to dissimulate their intention of subverting the established order of things among ourselves. See, then, my dear Maret, where we are! If you can engage the Executive Council to retrace its steps relative to the above points, war will not take place. You must admit that England cannot but feel herself included in the decrees which offer what you call '*fraternity*' to all the people of the world! It is also evident that our political existence will by no means allow the encroachments of France, nor can you deny that the treaty of 1788 obliges us to guarantee the closing of the Scheldt, and that France is in like manner bound by the treaty of 1786. It is also true that political engagements, so long as they exist, ought to be respected.

Answer my letter, I beseech you, as soon as possible, and in person, if you will, for *that* would infinitely please me. Fear nothing from the new law; I can assure you that foreigners may travel in England as freely now as formerly. But there must be no intrigues, nor any intercourse with factious men who would compromise public tranquillity. I believe you to be too honest to meddle with any such business; and, besides, I hope you will be charged with an *olive branch*, and, in this case, you will be received with open arms. Come, then, without fear; alight at my house, and consider my home as your own. Adieu![1]

[1] 'The attitude of Chauvelin was so hostile, and his connection with disaffected Englishmen so notorious, that the English Government would hold no confidential communication with him; but through the instrumentality of Miles some correspondence was still kept with Maret, who had now become Chef du Département at the Foreign Office under Lebrun, and even with Lebrun himself. In a very earnest, though very amicable letter, dated January 11, Miles had warned Maret that, unless the French Convention could be induced to recede from its present policy, war was absolutely inevitable.'—Lecky, vi. 112.

'It is clear that France had no right to expect a cessation of the warlike preparations on the part of Britain, unless the former would condescend to accept of conditions which were indispensably necessary for the preservation of the latter. This matter was represented very perspicuously by Mr. Miles on January 11, 1793, in a letter addressed to his friend M. Maret, who was then become *Chef du Département pour les Affaires Étrangères*, and, consequently, the principal person in that department after the Minister himself. Mr. Miles pointed out the impossibility that the British Government should remain tranquil unless the Executive Council would consent to fulfil what was required in the proposed conditions; and, at the same time, he positively assured M. Maret that, *if the Executive Council would comply with them, a war would not take place.* To the French Minister for Foreign Affairs himself Mr. Miles had already written on the 2nd January on the same subject, and had assured him *that the fate of Britain and France depended on the decision of the Executive Council.* The words of the original are: " C'est au pouvoir exécutif à décider;" and, a few lines after, " Vous êtes maître de leur destin." If this Council, then, had been really desirous of peace, it would have decided in favour of the acceptance of the proposed conditions, especially as they contained nothing more than the proposal that France should remain true to the principles which, from the commencement of the Revolution, it has uniformly professed.'—Herbert Marsh, ii. 99. See also *Authentic Correspondence*, Appendix, p. 106.

Marsh observes: 'As this letter was written to a man in an official capacity, and is a document of some importance, it is necessary to quote from the original.' Accordingly he produces nearly the entire letter as written in the original French. From the words—' descendez chez moi et considérez ma maison comme la vôtre,' Marsh drew the inference that Maret was the guest of Mr. Miles during his second visit to London. But on that occasion he alighted at the French Embassy in Portman Square.

### Mr. Miles to M. Le Brun

January 11, 1793

I am mortified by what I have been told respecting your inconsiderate projects against England, by the inexact interpretation which you gave to the National Convention on the interview of M. Maret with Mr. Pitt, and by the subsequent adverse events, which engender the apprehension that all my efforts to preserve peace will result in the declaration of war! I believe that if you had been better informed you would have adopted a different course. Nor must you be vexed at the temper I have shown when under the conviction that you had exceeded your duty; but, on the contrary, you should reflect on the horrors inseparable from war, and which it has been my object to avert. In all my proceedings I have acted towards you with the greatest loyalty; my sole aim has been to maintain good feeling between our two countries, and I had even flattered myself with the hope of seeing laid the foundation of a permanent alliance. But France, led astray by her recent victories and dazzled by her success, imagines that all the world is prepared to adopt the impracticable principles of *equality* without modification or reserve. You still believe that the English people are ready to revolt against their Government, and under this erroneous impression you deem it possible to accomplish our national ruin by the promulgation of the two decrees of November 19 and December 15.

I have come to the front at this very critical moment to unite two nations formed to love, not to murder each other. On this question I am neither English nor French but a citizen of the world, desiring peace, hating tyranny even more than war, and ready to shed my blood if thereby both war and tyranny could be abolished from the human race. My efforts have exceeded the bounds of prudence. No personal interest has influenced me. On the contrary, I have brought myself into antagonism with friends both in France and in England.

You attach too much importance to the Parliamentary speeches of Messrs. Burke and Windham. The former appears ready to sell himself to the highest political bidder, whilst the latter is the slave of prejudices imbibed from his youth. Burke is indeed a man of great talents; he is well informed; he is eloquent, but his speeches in the House of Commons fail to *convert* men to his views; nor, indeed, was he more successful in his attempt to change the opinion of the Opposition even when all the charms of his intellect were displayed in favour of liberty, and when the dictates of reason concurred with his efforts to put an end to the brutal and tyrannical war on which the Minister of that day had embarked with America. He is under the influence of a cabal, and delivers the sentiments and the wishes of his masters, whose only object is to supplant the Minister and establish themselves in his place. You need not, then, allow the speeches of Mr. Burke to alarm you. But, on the other hand, you must show deference even to the prejudices of our people. Your Revolution is altogether a new epoch in the annals of the world; its progress is too violent to inspire any other sentiment than fear and horror. Le Brun, be prudent, and, above all, be just and moderate. You know me. Do not despise my advice. Do not harass either your country or mine by a war which may end in the ruin of the one or the other, and perhaps in the misery and destruction of both. Adieu!

*M. REINHARD TO MR. MILES*

Portman Square: January 12, 1793

It is only half an hour since the courier so long expected has arrived.[1] M. Chauvelin has already written to Lord Grenville to request an interview. I am charged with two letters for you. I wait for you to fix the hour when I may have the honour of seeing you.

*Minute: January* 12.—The note of M. Chauvelin was written at 3 P.M. on this Saturday afternoon, the instant that the courier arrived. The servant took it to the Foreign Office. Lord Grenville kept him waiting two hours and sent him away without any answer. This conduct, since it is mischievous, shows little wisdom in the management of the momentous concerns of the nation. I have received important papers from the Executive Council in Paris. The despatch transmitted from Le Brun to Chauvelin contains word for word what he is to repeat to Lord Grenville, and from which the former is not to depart; the purport of which is to desire his Lordship would name the day on which he will present M. Chauvelin as Minister from the Republic. His credentials are *en route*. If personally disagreeable, another will be named. The despatch I have received was sent by order of Le Brun.

*M. MARET TO MR. MILES*

Foreign Office, Paris: January 7, 1793

I take a large sheet of paper, my dear Miles, as I wish to write a long letter—if time and business will permit; for there can be no want of matter in the

---

[1] 'A cette époque il était sans courrier de France depuis douze jours.'
—Ernouf, p. 116.

correspondence between two men, friends of humanity and liberty, and who take an equal interest in the prosperity of their country.

What, then, has become, my dear Miles, of those benevolent and pacific dispositions which you had led me to expect? Can I find them in the activity of your armaments, in the reproachful language adopted by even the wisest men in your Parliament towards everything that concerns France, in the veritable hostile acts of which Frenchmen, both in their persons and in their commercial interests, have become the object since the re-assembling of your Legislature, or in the haughtiness truly insulting which your Ministers do not cease to oppose to the wise and moderate conduct of the Republic? No, *mon cher*, it is not thus that we can be drawn together. The two nations in alliance would assure reciprocal prosperity, and, living on good terms, it would not be long before they enjoyed the beneficial and honourable advantage of being the arbitrators of the various interests of all the powers of the world. But, at least, if they arm themselves one against the other, they ought to contend without ceasing to maintain mutual esteem. Our Government does not fear war; it is aware of its resources, and of the extent of your means; it knows who would be its friends and who your enemies. Its active foresight has placed it in a position to defend itself, or even to attack with vigour; and our calculations, established on sure bases, hold out sufficient chances of success to induce the belief that the good fortune which until this day has crowned all its enterprises will not abandon our standards should you force us to direct our victorious arms against you. Nevertheless, it still desires peace—it would prefer it to the most successful war—it is ready, in order to obtain it, to make every sacrifice which the dignity of the Republic and the interests of our country could permit.

In your letter of the 22nd December you establish the bases of pacification, on which I am about to enter with you into a cordial and detailed explanation.

You demand, first, that France should renounce all projects of aggrandisement, and you support yourself by the principles which the Constituent Assembly had declared. It will not be unprofitable, my dear Miles, to rectify your ideas on this very modern epoch of our history. The representatives of the French nation declared to all the powers that France will never undertake any war with the view of making conquests. You thence conclude that all the powers can make war against France without running any other risk than the depopulation of their country and without fearing a permanent invasion of their land. You conclude that, in the event of an unjust aggression, France, after having exhausted her treasures in self-defence, would never be able to seek a legitimate indemnification in the possession of some part of her enemy's territory, or in the employment of means to make it repent for having troubled a nation whose generous principles would assure the peace of Europe. France, according to you, would be a vast domain which all the kings could divide amongst themselves, while their own States, favoured by a ridiculous inviolability, would be to us the sacred Ark on which we could not lay a sacrilegious hand. If then, *mon cher*, you desire that in the future France should renounce all projects of aggrandisement, you must exact at the same time that all the powers should for ever renounce attacking her. Prudence desires to weaken her enemy, justice authorises

self-indemnification for the expenses of a war in which
the enemy is the aggressor. If Savoy, if Nice, if
Mayence, remain in our hands on the conclusion of
peace, do you suppose that there would result from the
possession of these countries an exact compensation for
the enormous expenses which the kings have occasioned by attacking us within our boundaries? France
will not be really aggrandised if she retains some portions of territory as a slight compensation for the
capital expended, and which would also be one of the
bases of her grandeur and power. Nor will she have
been wanting to her principles, for she is pledged not
to undertake war for the purpose of aggrandisement.
It is not France who undertook the war against the
kings of the North. They armed themselves against
her liberty; they have dragged other kings into their
unjust enterprise, they have been vanquished, they
ought to pay the expenses of their folly, and we should
retain the fruits of the victory.

However, my dear Miles—and as a loyal and frank
man this observation will not have escaped you—we
have ceded claims which European policy has always
regarded as incontestable to rights which our philosophy
will never contest. We have subordinated these legitimate indemnifications to the will of the conquered
people; and, after having possessed ourselves of their
territory, we have left them the liberty of living independent under our gratuitous protection, or of uniting
themselves to us. We have reserved to ourselves the
right of declining their union, but, whenever we judge it
convenient or have occasion, we will avail ourselves of
the option. For example, great victories have made us
masters of Belgium. We willingly consent to assure for
her a free and independent existence, although a consider-

able portion of her richest provinces are well disposed to become part of the French Republic. Thirty-one communes of the country of Liège have already expressed this wish—the Council has rejected it; and its opinion on this point is conformable to that of the principal members of the National Convention. Judge, my dear Miles, if the projects of aggrandisement on the part of a nation whose principles are so strict and whose conduct is so in accordance with these principles can inspire England with just fear.

You next demand that we should renounce the opening of the Scheldt. Tell me, I pray you, if this trivial object can become a veritable subject for war. By this act, in conformity with all the principles of the right of nature and of nations, have we made any attack on the interests of your country? Are even the rights of Holland very sensibly injured? Does she not possess the most important arms of the Scheldt, which, traversing her territory, are entirely within her dependency? Would it be equitable to demand the sacrifice of the sacred rights of the Belgian people because the exercise of these rights promises them a prosperity which excites the jealousy of a neighbouring people? But this new means of prosperity for Belgium is not so important as they wish to believe. The Belgians were in part indemnified for this privation by the establishment of their interior canals. This question, discussed sufficiently in detail in the note of Chauvelin to Lord Grenville,[1] examined by other reports in all our public papers, decided beforehand by principles which do not admit of any compromise, does not exact a more ample discussion with a man who, like you, possesses a rational and philosophic mind, and who has the principles of

[1] *Annual Register*, 1793: *State Papers*, p. 114.

patriotism in his heart. I am sure, my dear Miles, that a friend of humanity like yourself is the enemy of all insidious pretext for an unjust war, and I will not add more than a word on this subject. The Belgians have entered upon all their rights; they are free to preserve them all, or to sacrifice a part. Let the Dutch come to an understanding with them on the affair of the Scheldt; we will be peaceable spectators of that negotiation, whatever may be its result.

You propose, in your letter, as a third basis of negotiation, peace between the Republic and the Court of Vienna. You desire that we should consent to treat with that power—our principal enemy. And, first, where have you seen that we refused to treat with her? Where are the propositions she would make to us? What does she offer as the reparation which she owes to us? We have been the object of her insults, and we have despised them; she has sent against us her armies, and we have beaten them; she has desired to invade the land of liberty, and in return we have conquered a part of her territory to deliver it from bondage. You see, my dear Miles, when Austria addressed us, we did not delay our reply; and, I must tell you frankly, I do not believe it would be possible for us soon to adopt further communications with her. She desired to raise all Europe against us—she had almost succeeded—when the *éclat* of our victories and the importance of our success detached some threads from the plot of Pilnitz. Austria hoped for the subjection of the whole of France; it is a war to the death that she has presumed to wage against us; it is a combat to the death in which she has engaged us against her. By what right and for what advantage would England wish that we should abandon a sentiment which, in order to be just, must be implacable? It is, you say, according to all appearances, the philanthropic gift of a general peace which people desire that we should make to humanity, and this general peace would be one of the bases on which they would recognise the Republic. But if a general peace can depend upon us, we are then an important factor in the political scale—we must hold in Europe a very imposing position; and yet you have the pretension to subject us to conditions in order that our existence may be recognised. We have notified our existence to Austria, and to Prussia, and to Sardinia by great victories; Spain and Naples cease to contest it; Holland will, perhaps, very soon ask leave of us to recognise it; Sweden has never denied it; the Porte, misled by contemptible intrigues, has doubtless already discovered the snare which her natural enemies and ours have spread for her. You alone, adhering to unjust pretexts, appear unwilling to renounce prejudices of form—diplomatic difficulties which our dignity repels, and which your loyalty disavows. You pretend, perhaps, to the glorious *rôle* of mediator; but it is reason, justice, liberty, victory, which should, in your estimation, rise as mediatrices between our enemies and ourselves. When, in the month of September, the combined armies advanced towards the capital of this great kingdom, which they thought to cover with ruin and carnage—the *chef-lieu* of this immense society of 25,000,000 of men, to whom, surrounded by every sort of hatred and revenge, they would bring bondage, opprobrium, and death [1]—did you then speak of mediation in order to spare great disasters to humanity? What, then, is this pacific intervention which you appear to offer in the

[1] This parenthesis does not occur in the copy preserved at the Foreign Office, Paris.

midst of the activity of your arsenals and of your dockyards, in the midst of all your menacing dispositions and your hostile laws? Abroad you arm against us, at home you invest your Government with a persecuting power, evidently directed against our brethren, of whom several are perhaps already the victims; and, as if you would not leave us the least doubt as to your intentions, your Council forbids to load in your ports any cargo of foreign wheat, without giving security that it will not be unloaded in France. It is war that you wish when you speak to us of peace; it is peace that we wish when we question you about war. Are you thinking of that sort of intervention which people call armed mediation? It could be accepted only from weakness; it is nothing else than political violence, which the Republic is not disposed to allow. Renounce it, my dear Miles, since we can no more renounce honour and glory than the consciousness of our strength. We wish to be just before as after victory, and we know ourselves to be still victorious.

You should have recognised our moderation in our declarations to Lord Grenville, for, although several things in his reply have appeared to us as insults, we still consent to reply to him. Chauvelin will present a note which leaves at the same time as this letter. In it will be seen, if it is made public, the new development of our declarations relative to the decree of the 19th of November; it is also therein shown that the Council, in order fully to reassure you, is disposed to ratify its principles by an explanatory decree of the Convention. You will remember that I had given Mr. Pitt a glimpse of the possibility of this step.

We need not recur to your disquietudes about Holland, for it appears that at length this principal cause of division between our two nations is removed.

I ought, however, my dear Miles, to tell you in frankness and confidence that, if England does not cease to menace and insult us, prudence and the rights of a legitimate defence will compel us to take rigorous measures. We are ready—our armies are there—liberty summons them; and it is in Holland that we shall strike the first blow against England. It behoves that you quickly make your decision. Procrastination, which would be useful to you, will be injurious to us, and we ought not to allow it.

At the same time that he delivers the note which we send to him, Chauvelin will present his credentials; and if, as you confidentially tell me, he is not at all acceptable to your Ministry—if the refusals which he may experience are due, as I am led to believe, rather to his personality than to the character with which he is invested, let them say so. I am certain that we will not put into the scale the interests and the *amour-propre* of a man against the great interests of which he is the agent. I am even authorised to say to you that we would not be averse to recall him, and to send as his successor some one who would be agreeable to your Ministry—M. Barthélemy, for example, who appears to me to have conciliated the esteem of all your countrymen.[1]

Adieu, my dear Miles!

HUGUES BERNARD MARET,
Premier Chef du Département des Affaires Étrangères.

P.S.—I finish this very long letter without having even mentioned my friendship for you; but you would

[1] 'Barthélemy (celui-là même qui fut dans la suite membre du Directoire et proscrit en Fructidor) avait occupé le poste de Londres avant Chauvelin. C'était un homme aussi peu républicain qu'on pouvait l'être en occupant un emploi sous la République. Cette proposition semble indiquer que la démarche de Maret aurait été un peu antérieure à l'arrangement concerté avec Dumouriez.'—Ernouf, p. 115.

not be just to me if you required that I should repeat the assurance of it. The Minister, who is at the Council, wrote to you a letter which we cannot find at the Bureau of the Couriers. It had been sent there. It shall be despatched to-morrow by post.[1]

*MR. MILES TO MR. PITT*

January 12, 1793

I have this instant received by the courier arrived from Paris this day an official despatch, which you will not be displeased to have communicated to you, for it puts it in your power to preserve the blessing of peace. I beg the favour to know when I may be permitted to wait on you.

*MR. MILES TO M. MARET*[2]

January 12, 1793

Mr. Pitt being in the country, I have not been able to obtain as yet an answer to the demand you have forwarded to me; but whilst waiting until I can see the Minister or receive his orders, I will reply to some passages in your friendly letter, in the hope that you will listen to me with your wonted kindness and employ your good offices with the Executive Council and the Convention to persuade them to adopt conciliatory measures. I am sorry that time will not permit me to enter into any details. The courier leaves this afternoon, and I have only a moment in which to write to you.

With respect to the absurd language in which they indulge in the House of Commons, and the loquacity of Mr. Burke, who has made himself ridiculous by the

---

[1] This postscript does not occur in the copy preserved at the Foreign Office, Paris.

[2] 'Il n'existe aucune trace de la réponse de Miles, mais on va voir que cette réponse était parvenue, et qu'elle laissait quelque espérance.'— Ernouf, p. 122.

abuse of his talents and by his apostasy from principles, I pray you to pay no attention to such things; besides which, liberty of speech must not be forbidden; and, at his age, he is allowed to talk with all the greater freedom—and even to use insulting words without any one being offended. If the insults which he has uttered were raked up, and if Parliament had declared by an express law that every Frenchman is a scoundrel, you would have the right to complain bitterly, and even to demand that we should retract such injustice. But, as it is, you ought not to attach any importance to what is said by individuals; let us leave the firebrands to themselves, and let us reason, for it is reason, and not resentment, that must trace the route which we have to follow.

I see with inexpressible joy the possibility of a *rapprochement* between the two countries. There is, however, one point so tenaciously held by you that, if you do not abandon it, the *rapprochement* can never take place—it is a position which you have assumed and of which you make great account. You still exact that the Court of London should recognise the French Republic as a step preliminary to any explanations; and you promise that the Convention will then give satisfactory assurances as to the decree of November 19th, and that the Executive Council will postpone the affair of the Scheldt. But rather, my dear friend, I would ask you to re-assert, as a preliminary measure, the statement which you once had the goodness to make to me, and say that *the Convention does not by any means intend to incorporate the Belgic provinces or your other conquests with France.* You will then find that, when the object of jealousy and apprehension has been removed, there will no longer be any pretext for a declaration of war.

But I have a thousand fears. I am sick at heart. I am disconsolate at seeing everything go wrong. Still, whatever may occur, dear Maret, I will continue to cherish friendship for you, and I pray God to preserve liberty, and make the human species worthy to enjoy it. Remember me to Le Brun and Mourgue. I foresee the moment when every bond between France and England will be broken. Adieu! I embrace you with all my heart.

*MR. MILES TO MR. PITT*

January 13, 1793

This is merely to inform you that the 'instructions' transmitted to M. Chauvelin by the same express that brought my despatch from M. Maret are communicated to me in a letter which I have received from Le Brun, and I am authorised to make to you a statement with which M. Chauvelin is not acquainted. I beg to know when I may have the honour of laying before you the communication sent to me from Paris.[1]

*MR. MILES TO MR. AUST*

January 13, 1793

When I wrote to you last night I had not entirely read the despatch which I received from Paris. The

---

[1] 'Il [Chauvelin] venait d'expédier la déclaration, quand arriva, trop tard de quelques heures, le courrier parti le 8 de Paris, porteur du projet de réponse à la note anglaise du 31 Décembre précédent. Cette réponse reproduisait en partie les explications du Mémoire confidentiel envoyé en même temps à Miles. Elle a été publiée depuis, mais sans l'instruction particulière dont elle était accompagnée, et dont la minute, conservée aux Archives, est de la main de Maret. On y prescrivait à Chauvelin la plus grande réserve dans ses démarches comme dans son langage. S'il parvenait à obtenir de Grenville un nouvel entretien particulier, il devait surtout s'attacher "à faire ressortir le contraste des mesures violentes récemment adoptées par le ministère britannique, avec la modération dont nous faisions preuve vis-à-vis de certains sujets anglais qui avaient tenu en France une conduite compromettante," comme le lieutenant de vaisseau Blackwood, qui venait d'être mis en liberté, bien qu'il eût été trouvé porteur de correspondance d'émigrés.'—Ernouf, p. 116.

'instructions' sent to M. Chauvelin are contained in it; but I am authorised to say to the Minister what he cannot say, and indeed what he does not know.[1] I shall only add for the present that the Cabinet, if it is not resolved upon war, may have peace on terms honourable to the country. As I do not suppose that Lord Grenville will make any difficulty in seeing me on a subject of so much importance, I shall beg the favour of you to solicit in my name an interview with his Lordship.

### Mr. Aust to Mr. Miles

Foreign Office: January 13, 1793

I am still without any commands from Lord Grenville on the subject of your communication; and, indeed, his Lordship has been so very busy that it has been impossible for me to speak to him on that head since his return from Windsor. I shall not fail to give him the further information you have sent, and I will forward your letter immediately to Mr. Pitt.

### Mr. Pitt to Mr. Miles

January 13, 1793

I have just received your two letters. I can have no objection to see any information respecting the sentiments of persons in France. I therefore wish you either to bring or send to me immediately the paper to which you refer, but I think it right to apprise you beforehand that it will be impossible for me to have any communication with you respecting its contents.

### Mr. Miles to Mr. Pitt

January 13, 1793

I am this instant honoured with your commands, and will wait on you in less than half an hour. With

---

[1] See Letter to Lord Fortescue, January 15. Also Letter to Mr. Pitt, February 6.

respect to any communication as to the contents of the papers received by me from France, *that*, Sir, is a matter for your determination, not mine, and on which I will offer no opinion.

### *M. REINHARD TO MR. MILES*

January 13, 1793

M. Chauvelin requests that you will not communicate the contents of your Paris letters to Lord Grenville until after the conference which he has demanded of him. But this is left to your own discretion.

The departure of our courier will depend on the arrival of an answer from Lord Grenville; at all events, send your letters before midnight, and if we do not despatch a courier I will forward them to my friend, who leaves to-morrow morning direct for Paris. The suggestion that I have just made at the express desire of M. Chauvelin is only that you should *delay* the communication of your letter. I will certainly see you to-day.

Mr. Aust, with a note somewhat curt, has just returned the declaration of the rupture of the treaty, and a quarter of an hour afterwards there arrived a letter from Lord Grenville inviting M. Chauvelin to go at once to the Foreign Office.[1] If you say nothing to the contrary, I will be with you at eight o'clock.

---

[1] 'Rien n'était plus sensé que de prescrire à Chauvelin une attitude conciliante, un complet détachement des fauteurs d'anarchie; mais ce rôle cadrait mal avec ses antécédents. Le ministre Grenville consentit pourtant à l'écouter. Chauvelin eut avec lui, le 13, trois conférences dont il envoya la relation par courrier extraordinaire. On déclina la réception des lettres de créance; on consentit néanmoins à recevoir, à titre purement officieux, la dernière réponse française; enfin, sans en être pleinement satisfait, on paraissait disposé à recevoir des communications ultérieures.'—Ernouf, p. 117.

*Minute:* Sunday, January 13.—Previous to my interview with the Minister this day, I wrote on the margin of the despatch received from M. Maret the following observations: 'Acquainted as Mr. Miles is with some of the members of the Executive Council, and assured of their confidence in his judgment and integrity, he has not hesitated to employ every means in his power to dissuade them from giving offence to this country or to her allies. He has carried some points on which they appeared obstinate; and he has no doubt but the Scheldt will be renounced, and all the offensive matter in the two decrees of November 19th and December 15th removed by the National Convention *preliminary* to the British Cabinet acknowledging the Republic. He is even induced to believe that an agent will be sent over to treat with Mr. Pitt, confidentially, in the event of the Minister expressing such a wish. The object steadily kept in view by Mr. Miles has been to render a service to his country and its Government, and to prevent a rupture which he is convinced must lead to fatal consequences.'

The Cabinet was sitting when I arrived. Mr. Pitt came out, and received from me the despatch, or *exposé*, of Maret with great good-humour, and of course the marginal notes exactly as I had scribbled them. I requested that he would return it to me. He took it in to the Cabinet, and in about an hour he came out furious, freighted with the bile of the whole Cabinet, aggravated by that of Mr. Burke, who, although not in the Ministry, attended on this occasion.[1] Would to God he had been asleep in the bosom of Abraham, for he has done us a

---

[1] 'Ce parti, dont je n'ai pas besoin de dire que j'excepte l'infâme Burke admis et consulté au Conseil privé,' &c.—Chauvelin to Le Brun, December 8, 1792.

world of mischief! Burke, I know, is highly enraged at what I have said against him. On handing back Maret's despatch, which had been directed to me by the order of Le Brun, the Minister expressed his desire that I should no longer correspond with the French Executive Council on the subject of peace or war. On taking leave I said: 'Remember, Sir, if you go to war with France you will ruin your country.' I went away chagrined, and returned to Cleveland Row disconsolate and depressed.—W. A. M.

*Mr. Miles to M. Maret*
January 13, 1793

For having wished, my dear Maret, to ward off the most terrible scourge that can possibly afflict the human race, and to preserve peace between our two countries, I have drawn upon myself much annoyance. They expressly forbid me to carry on with you, or with the Executive Power, any further correspondence on the subject of peace or war. As I certainly have not the right to interfere with the affairs of the Cabinet, and still less to dictate the course it ought to pursue, I feel that I must suspend for the moment all communication with you on public affairs; but, whilst abandoning our correspondence, I do not renounce your friendship, nor the love of liberty and justice. Whenever circumstances permit us to renew our epistolary intercourse, do not forget to enclose your letters under cover to my bankers, Messrs. Biddulph, Cocks, and Co., London.

*Minute: January* 14.—After the Cabinet broke up yesterday, Lord Grenville desired Mr. Aust to tell me that I was not absolutely enjoined to drop all correspondence with the French Government, but, on the contrary, Ministers would be much obliged for any information it might be in my power to give them. Thus reassured, I continue my intercourse with the Executive in Paris, and will make communications from time to time to his Majesty's Ministers.[1]

### MR. JOSEPH SMITH TO MR. MILES
January 14, 1793

Mr. Pitt had given the letter you mention to Mr. Long, whom I shall see either this evening or to-morrow. I will remind him to forward it to you.

*Minute.*—It was never returned. It is the letter which I received from Le Brun. It is an important paper. So also is that of Maret.—W. A. M.

### MR. MILES TO LORD FORTESCUE
January 15, 1793

I fully intended to have communicated to your Lordship by Saturday's post some very important intelligence received from France by an express, which brought M. Chauvelin positive instructions to require of Lord Grenville to fix a day on which he would present him at St. James's as Minister from the Republic. I had also a letter from the French Minister. It authorised me to declare to Mr. Pitt that the Scheldt would be as good as given up; that the Convention would do away by a revision of its law all the offensive matter contained in the decree of the 19th November, and that the Executive Council had rejected the offers of Liège and of some of the Belgic provinces to incorporate themselves with France. These are points which I have

---

[1] 'But without effect, as the present situation of the British Empire can best explain.'—Note by Mr. Miles attached to this Minute, and dated March 1, 1804.

not ceased to enforce in all my correspondence with the reigning party in Paris, and the letter I received by the courier was of such importance that I apprised Mr. Pitt of my wish to lay it before him. He accordingly desired my attendance on Sunday. The Cabinet was sitting; he received my papers very cordially, and was extremely civil. But on his return in about an hour I found him altogether the reverse; he assumed a tone which much displeased me; but, as his requisition that I should discontinue all correspondence with people in France on the subject of negotiation for peace or war was perfectly just, I made no scruple to comply with it, feeling that I have neither the right nor the power to take the business out of the hands of the Cabinet and venture on deciding the fate of our country. It is some consolation that I have moderated the wildness and excitement of the French Executive Council, and have thereby engaged them to observe such terms of accommodation that the British Ministry will risk something more than their popularity and their places if they should now precipitate the country into a war. Sweden acknowledges the Republic. Naples sends its Minister now in London to Paris for the same purpose, and to atone for the insult offered by the Neapolitan Minister at Constantinople to the French Government and nation. The Treaty of Neutrality which France has proposed to Spain, and which it is still thought the latter will sign, I notified to the Minister in the middle of last November, but he was incredulous as to the correctness of my information. On the 12th instant I wrote to M. Maret, and pressed the Executive Council to make the concessions they offer *preliminary* to our acknowledging the Republic. If this is done, Ministers will not venture on war, and my zeal, which has been so offensive to them, will yet prove beneficial both to our country and to a considerable portion of mankind, for whom a declaration of war would be a sentence of death. So late as this morning Lord Grenville had not sent an answer to M. Chauvelin relative to the recent letter from Le Brun.[1] Circumstances will soon determine how much longer I shall exert myself to support Mr. Pitt and his Administration.

### M. MARET TO MR. MILES

Paris : January 11,[2] 1793

Tell me then frankly, my dear Miles, what are the grounds of your complaint. Is it on account of the inaccuracies which appeared in the report that Le Brun made before my return? I agree with you that his statement of the conferences with our secret agents is not exact. I was not a secret agent : I had no authority to treat, nor had I any mission ; and in declaring this to Mr. Pitt and to yourself I acknowledged nothing but the truth. The Minister deceived himself, but I neither deceived you nor Mr. Pitt. If my friendship is dear to you, God preserve you from harbouring such an opinion; for I feel very sensibly that it could not survive a suspicion so injurious, which would equally wound my delicacy and my sincerity. Banish, then, my dear Miles, those painful ideas, and let us think only of the interest which we mutually feel to continue in friendship with each other.

*January* 15.—The courier who will take this letter has been delayed until this moment for the judgment on

---

[1] See Introduction, p. 75. The answer of Lord Grenville, dated January 18, is given in the *Annual Register*, 1793 : *State Papers*, p. 125; also in *Parliamentary History*, xxx. 206, and by Marsh, ii. 89–93.

[2] Received in London January 18.

the King. The Assembly will pronounce it this day. I will add a word to inform you of the decision.¹ I received with great pleasure your letter of the 11th instant. I await your reply to mine of the 7th. I wish you to explain about Barthélemy; you told me confidentially that Chauvelin would not be received, and yet, I am informed, you have expressed your readiness to see him, and he hopes to obtain through you an amicable reception from Mr. Pitt. I want a solution of this question.²

I hope that, after the measures which will be taken by our Government and by yours, some degree of harmony may be re-established; but I much fear lest the long-continued uncertainty may in the meantime pledge us to the Liégeois, who desire to be united to France, and even to the Belgians, whose finest provinces —the two Flanders, Hainaut, and Namur—are ready to express the same wish. With the well-founded hope of peace we should not hesitate to reject any such appeal; but, with the persuasion that we cannot avoid war, we should probably determine to abandon our present caution and unite them. We are, however, trying to avoid a determination which we do not think necessary for ourselves, and which would not enter into the views of your Government. Adieu, my dear Miles! Always devotedly yours.

### Mr. Miles to M. Le Brun

January 18, 1793

An event has lately happened which deprives me of the pleasing hope of being useful to the cause of

¹ On Thursday, January 17, the sentence of death was voted. On the following Sunday it was fixed that the decree should be carried out within twenty-four hours. The execution took place on Monday, January 21, and the news of the death of Louis XVI. reached London on the afternoon of January 23.

² See Minutes, January 3 and 4.

humanity. I wished to prevent the war, that terrible scourge to mankind; but an ill-fated vanity prevents your attending either to prudence or justice. I find myself thwarted and harassed on every side. For many years you have known my principles: my conduct has ever been dictated by the love of truth and liberty, not by such an extravagant and unbridled liberty as yours, but by a liberty well understood and well conducted, which would make this world a terrestrial paradise. But what is to be done? Enthusiasm blinds you; and you are insensible alike to justice and to prudence. When the Commercial Treaty was in agitation I expressed my wish in a letter to Mr. Pitt that it might become the basis of an alliance between the two nations, who had it in their power to insure an eternal peace to Europe and the world. But, instead of peace, I see war on the point of being declared—a war that will engulf both nations. Le Brun, you will become responsible for all its horrors! Reflect upon it, I beseech you; there is yet time, you can yet repair all. My heart is full and oppressed by dark and melancholy prospects. Life weighs heavily upon me. Adieu![1]

### M. Noël to Mr. Miles

Paris: January 19, 1793

I have not forgotten the engagement I contracted before I left London. It was too favourable an op-

---

[1] 'On the 18th of January Mr. Miles closed his correspondence with the French Minister Le Brun. . . . But this last warning was of no more avail than the preceding; the resolution once formed was not altered; and Le Brun's obstinacy, of which Mr. Miles had already complained in a letter to Maret of the 4th of January, rendered him insensible to the calamities in which he and his colleagues were wantonly involving Great Britain and France.'—Herbert Marsh, ii. 104. See *Authentic Correspondence*, Appendix, pp. 113, 115, &c.

portunity to acknowledge my gratitude not to avail myself of it.

On returning to France I found my countrymen prepared for war, which they declared to be inevitable. An incredible ardour prevails in our ports—sailors enlisting in crowds, even children eager to enter on board, and seamen envious of the glory with which our soldiers are covered. In travelling through Flanders and Brabant I found everywhere the same enthusiasm among our troops; but all this ardour is a poor consolation to me for the evils which we are about to experience. Chauvelin is culpable without doubt; but he is not the only cause of the lamentable *contretemps* by which all my efforts to preserve peace have been destroyed. I should have esteemed myself only too happy in co-operating towards this great work, and I shall never forget that it is not due to you that I have failed to secure the glory so much to be regretted. It is a pleasure to render to your philanthropy and generous solicitude the acknowledgment they deserve.

Your friend Dampierre prays you not to be so indolent; it is an age since he received news from you. I am appointed Chargé d'Affaires at the Hague. My journey from Brabant here was somewhat difficult. I am still in a frightful vortex; it is no longer the same Paris as when you saw it in 1791. I often recall your reply to the Duc d'Aumont. I have thought of it a thousand times, and events fully prove that you were right.[1] I am completely sobered in respect to the affair of the 10th of August, but I have become wise too late.

---

[1] 'This unfortunate nobleman, who had equally to complain of the cruelty of a worthless father and the despotism of the old Government, was boasting one day at M. de Lafayette's that in six months the *New*

### M. REINHARD TO MR. MILES

Portman Square: January 19, 1793

I hold you in esteem as a man of your word, and who dreads war because it is at once the shame and the scourge of the human race. The reply of Lord Grenville has arrived. It appears to render impossible all means for coming to an arrangement. The English Government misunderstands us, and hence I still entertain some hope. I have not had time to wait upon you. It is Saturday—three o'clock in the morning. I write with my hands stiff from cold and my heart boiling with indignation. The despatch of the 8th has not been satisfactory on any point. If its notification had been made in a regular and official form, he would have replied that the declaration of the rupture of the Treaty of Commerce, and the manner in which they have answered on the Scheldt, were new causes for offence. He added that it would be useless to converse with M. Chauvelin on particular points, but that he would be ready to hear him again, under the same unofficial form, if he should have anything to propose that would embrace the general system of affairs relative to the present crisis, and which concerns at the same time England and her allies and the general security of Europe. *M. Chauvelin leaves!*

### M. REINHARD TO MR. MILES

January 25, 1793

M. Chauvelin leaves to-day on an order from the Government which enjoins that he should depart on

*Constitution* would be finished and public order restored. I sat next to him, and, asking him "*In what time?*" he repeated, "*In six months.*" "Say rather," I answered, "in *six years*, and you will be nearer the truth." This was in January 1791.'—W. A. M. See *Conduct of France towards Great Britain,* p. 152.

or before the 1st of February next. They have been infinitely polite! Are you in town? I wish very much to see you.[1]

#### M. REINHARD TO MR. MILES
*Portman Square: January 26, 1793*

I wish to tell you, my dear Sir, that M. and Madame Chauvelin left yesterday; that I have just been with Mr. Aust to demand security for the persons whom M. Chauvelin leaves behind, and for the papers of the Legation; that all I could draw from Mr. Aust is that he would speak to Lord Grenville about my request; that I am to depart on the 30th instant; that I must not leave without seeing you, and that it is very desirable that I should carry with me the certainty of your continued friendship.

#### M. REINHARD TO MR. MILES
*January 27, 1793*

The enclosed letter from M. Maret just received is for you, my dear Sir. I propose seeing you to-morrow evening after seven o'clock. Let me know if that hour is convenient to you. The engagement which you have made ought not to be so understood as to interdict you from writing a word in reply to a man who, although he has the misfortune to be charged with the affairs of France, believes himself to be not unworthy of your friendship.

#### M. MARET TO MR. MILES
*Paris: January 23, 1793*

You will learn with some surprise that I depart very soon for London. You shall be informed of my arrival the very moment that I set my foot in your city. If you have anything to communicate, write to me, *poste restante*, Dover, and I will pick up your letter in passing.

[1] See Introduction, p. 76.

I hope they will not forbid me to see you; assuredly they will never prevent me from loving you.

### Mr. Long to Mr. Miles

January 28, 1793

I am desired by Mr. Pitt to say to you, in answer to your note accompanying a letter from M. Maret, that he thinks you should not answer M. Maret, and he wishes you to decline making yourself the channel of any verbal or written communication from him on the subject of French affairs. Mr. Pitt desires me to return his thanks to you for the communication you have made. The fate of the King is, indeed, a melancholy subject to dwell upon, and his will must, I think, melt every heart.[1] Your verses I read on Saturday morning. They are excellent.

*Minute: Monday.*—Wrote at once to Long on the receipt of his note. I remarked that, although I had previously resolved not to answer Maret, I am the more confirmed in my intention by knowing the sentiments of Mr. Pitt; that, in conformity with his desire, I would decline to be the channel of communication on French affairs, but that, in my opinion, Maret would bring ample concessions; that war would be a hazardous measure, and certain to embarrass Ministers, and that the massacre of Louis XVI. could never be a pretext for hostilities after the repeated assurances given by Mr. Pitt that he would never interfere with the interior government of France.

I find a general aversion bordering on horror to war with France.[2] An unpopular war is to be dreaded.

---

[1] A copy of the will of Louis XVI. is given in the *Annual Register*, 1793: *State Papers*, p. 133.

[2] 'Les négociants de la Cité, plus calculateurs qu'enthousiastes, désirent la paix, et pour me servir des expressions d'un de nos obser-

Every man deplores the melancholy fate of Louis XVI., but the inestimable blessings of peace and the tide of national prosperity ought not to be interrupted under the vain and illusory pretext of revenging the death of an individual whose existence or dissolution had ceased to be an object of national importance long before he fell on the scaffold. If war were demanded to resist invasion, or to counteract any such increase of territory on the part of France as might be incompatible with our security, the wisdom of Ministers could not be too much applauded—the entire vigour and energy of the people ought to support them; but, if France will give to Great Britain and to her allies pacific assurances, can Mr. Pitt venture, nay, will he dare to precipitate this country into an unprofitable and ruinous war? The question is serious. For what purpose are we going to war? Is it for the mutilated body of the King? Surely not. Is it to extricate the unhappy, persecuted, and deserted Queen from the labyrinth of her prison—from the merciless power of the assassins of her husband? Surely not. Any such attempt on the part of an individual would, morally speaking, be laudable, and prove, if successful, that the age of chivalry was not extinguished. But *nations* are not to turn *knight-errants*, and run wild in pursuit of adventure. What would be heroic in a man might be vicious and unpardonable in a State; kingdoms have one policy, irresponsible individuals another.

vateurs, mon arrivée a produit dans la Cité *un changement de dispositions qui nous est favorable.* Le bruit seul de mon voyage avait fait en un jour remonter les effets publics de trois pour cent. Les propriétaires (country gentlemen) ne sont pas moins opposés à des mesures hostiles. . . . Le Ministère anglais parait encore divisé en deux partis fort distincts. Le parti purement Royaliste veut une guerre de contre-révolution et ne connait pas d'autres intérêts. Depuis la mort de Louis il la veut plus ardemment que jamais, et ses moyens d'y déterminer et de la faire se sont accrus.'—Maret to Le Brun, January 31, 1793.

The latter exposes only himself and family, and may be permitted an act of extravagance without incurring any extraordinary censure; but the former is charged with the happiness of millions, and, instead of risking any serious or irremediable calamity, is solemnly bound to consult and provide for the security and independence of the nation. If, indeed, the present order of things is likely to be reversed—if the Convention is to share the fate of preceding Assemblies and be annihilated—if there is to be another *ad interim* constitution—it would be imprudent and unsafe to treat with a people whose fluctuating opinions on the *form* of their Legislature would demonstrate that their *policy* would also be devoid of unity or stability of purpose. The dignity of England would be exposed and its independence hazarded were we to negotiate with France whilst still in an unsettled state; but, on the other hand, when the permanency of the Government has been assured and pledges given of goodwill towards this country, no reasonable cause or pretext for hostilities ought to be recognised.

The secretary of M. Noël has arrived and brought me a letter from the Hague. Noël says that the Dutch are averse to war; the peasants are resolved not to inundate the country, and there is no dependence upon the troops. Noël has had two interviews with the Pensionary.—W. A. M.

### M. Maret to Mr. Miles

Portman Square: January 30, 1793

I have only this moment arrived, my dear Miles. I desire to see you as soon as possible. Let me know the hour at which I may find you at home this evening.[1]

---

[1] See Introduction, pp. 79-84; and Lecky, vi. 125, 126.

*Minute: Wednesday.*—Maret arrived this afternoon, and sought an interview with me immediately. He came in the evening, with Reinhard and Mourgue, and remained until eleven o'clock. He declined *for the moment* to enter into particulars; but he assured me in general terms that his mission was pacific.

The Queen is to be taken before a common tribunal to be tried, but there is nothing against her. The Prince Royal is to be under the care of the nation. The debates in the English House of Commons and the mobs at Rouen accelerated the death of Louis XVI.

*Minute: January* 31.—Went to Maret, and remained with him from nine until near eleven o'clock. He told me in confidence that France would relinquish the Scheldt in a manner perfectly satisfactory to this country. France will also give up Nice and Mayence, renounce the Belgic provinces, and fall upon a method that will release Savoy from being any longer a portion of French territory; she will also withdraw her troops from Belgium, and consent to a general peace, provided that the confederated powers defray in part the expenses of the war. Maret asked if I thought Dumouriez would be well received here; that it was proposed he should offer himself as the negotiator, in the first instance to arrange the terms, and that, when he had settled these with the British Ministry, he would receive full powers to sign and exchange; that the object was peace with England. Dumouriez is to be assured of personal safety. Lord Auckland desired an interview with M. de Maulde before he left the Hague. The French Minister replied that, having no longer any public character, he could no longer see him. His Lordship then expressed the hope that he would come and chat with him and the Grand

Pensionary. He came. It was proposed to M. de Maulde that, if the French vessels would descend and pass out of the Scheldt, no notice would be taken of them by the English ships under the command of Captain Murray. In order to avoid any act of hostility, the smaller vessels came through the canals to Ostend. Dumouriez has gone to Antwerp to arrange a convenient spot for an interview with Lord Auckland and the Grand Pensionary. In case the propositions which Maret has brought over should not be accepted, Holland is to be instantly invaded. Maret, not knowing what effect the dismissal of Chauvelin may have in France, is resolved not to demand an interview with Mr. Pitt until fresh instructions arrive from Paris; he expects to hear on Saturday or Sunday.

It thus appears that Maret has come to London authorised to offer propositions conformable to the advice I gave him in my letter of the 12th of last month, but with what truth on the part of the Executive Council I know not; all is trick, I am afraid, on both sides, and war is no less the wish of party in England than of party in France. I am sick at heart. Maret writes this day to Le Brun.

After my conversation with Maret I saw Mr. Long, and pressed him on the subject of peace and on the conditions required to preserve it. In reply to my special question as to whether the British Cabinet would consent to the Austrian Netherlands and Liège being erected into an independent republic, he said that no objections would be made to such an arrangement, 'but we cannot allow them to be annexed to France as a part of its republic or territory.' If the Cabinet had been wise from *choice* in January 1790, instead of discerning their policy from *necessity* in January 1793, this country would have escaped the condition of soliciting as an act

of forbearance on the part of France what she might
have granted as a favour to the Liégeois and the Austrian
Netherlands, and, by so doing, the question of opening
the Scheldt—*the source of our present controversy*—would
have been avoided. The French, in that case, would
not have meddled with the navigation of the Scheldt—
they would not even have thought of it—and, while
respecting the independence of a people become free,
they would have had no pretence for marching to the
very gates of Holland. As to the nonsense of offending
the Emperor, it scarce deserves notice; he deserved to
lose the provinces. If, then, according to the suggestions which I had made, the freedom of the Netherlands
and of the Pays de Liège can be obtained; if France
will relinquish the opening of the Scheldt to those whom
it most concerns, and if she will resign her conquests
and agree to a general peace, all will go well; but, on
the other hand, if France is unjust or England is
obstinate, war is inevitable.[1]—W. A. M.

## Mr. Miles to Mr. Aust

February 4, 1793

I take it for granted that I am under the ban of the
Empire by your not answering the question I proposed
to you, and I am confirmed in this idea from a hint
thrown out to me yesterday by a noble peer, who, from
motives of friendship, communicated to me the opinion
of certain persons on the subject of my efforts in favour
of peace. So delicate were my sentiments on this
question, that I discontinued all correspondence with
the Executive Council ever since the 13th of last month,
and in making this sacrifice from the respect due to
Mr. Pitt I thought I did all that could be expected. It
is my determination not to become the channel of com-

[1] See *Conduct of France towards Great Britain*, p. 110.

munication with France until authorised; but the strong and insatiate desire for knowledge that I possess, and the intimacy that has subsisted between myself and those with whom I associate, will not permit me to give up friendships, and I do not despair that the information derived from these intimacies may, without committing any breach of confidence, be of material service to Government. If the French cede everything—and I have no positive reason to doubt but that their concessions will be ample—I shall have had some share in effecting this great and important national good; and, conscious of the purity of my intentions in the interests of humanity, I am really indifferent as to all the rest.

I dine with Maret this day in Portman Square; he expects a courier every minute, and I am to see him the instant he arrives. If anything occurs, you shall know it immediately. If the violent and exaggerated accounts of Chauvelin do not provoke the French into some act of folly or madness, all may yet go well. Maret has commercial advantages to offer which appear plausible and beneficial. The *Suisse* in Portman Square has orders not to admit Lord Lauderdale, Mr. Parke, Mr. Perry of the 'Morning Chronicle,' the Rev. Mr. Sablotanière of Sloane Street, and many others. Maret was yesterday at Madame de Flahaut's; she told him that she expected Lord Lansdowne and Mr. Windham every minute, whereupon Maret left the house. He has forbidden all people who are obnoxious to Government, and means to observe the utmost circumspection. Vandernoot called on him yesterday. Lord Lauderdale called in Portman Square on Saturday—I saw him there—when Maret entreated him to cease from calling.[1]

[1] 'Aust, I was told, apprehensive of giving offence to Lord Grenville, consulted his Lordship on receiving an invitation from me. Lord Grenville objected. It was to meet Maret at dinner at my house last evening.'—W. A. M.

*Mr. Aust to Mr. Miles*

February 4, 1793

Many thanks for your Irish news. In return I can now inform you that I have just seen an order issued in the usual form from the Home Department for Messrs. Maret and Mourgue to quit the kingdom in three days.

*Minute.*—I was with Maret when a letter came to him from Lord Grenville informing him that such an order would be sent. Maret showed me the letter. It notified to him that he would have an Order in Council to depart in three days, since 'the circumstances of the times rendered it improper that his stay in this country should be prolonged.' Maret thanked his Lordship for the obliging manner in which he had made this communication, and requested passports for himself and suite and papers. I remained with Maret until midnight. My heart forebodes that this war will be one of extermination. O France! O England! why are you so furious against each other?—W. A. M.

*Mr. Miles to Mr. Aust*

February 5, 1793

Maret, on receiving Lord Grenville's notification, resolved not to delay his departure a moment longer than was necessary after the arrival of the Order in Council. It had not reached him last night. He still hopes that war may be avoided, and that he will return to England very soon. He is much astonished at not having had a line from Paris since he left it; nor has he received any newspapers of later date than the 28th of last month. He laments, and I believe with unaffected sincerity, that the concessions which I recommended to Le Brun early in December, *and which he is now authorised to make*, were not agreed to at the time;

that the Executive Council did not act upon my advice to allow Maret to remain in this country, and recall Chauvelin, to whose despicable intrigues the delay, and the subsequent mischiefs arising from that delay, may be attributed. I am extremely averse to war from an innate repugnance to the shedding of blood. Besides, war multiplies crimes. The earth, if it were endowed with moral faculties, would sink beneath the pressure of those which already exist. It is to this strong sentiment that must be attributed the zeal I have shown, somewhat officiously I confess, to preserve peace between the two nations; and, since I have not succeeded, I do not care how soon I retire from the tumultuous scenes of life into obscurity and repose.

Lord Stanhope was announced to Maret last night about half-past eight. I was in close conversation with him at the time, and, as he was on the eve of his departure, he made no difficulty in receiving his Lordship. I was much pressed to stay; but, as it is my unalterable resolution, under present circumstances, to have no communication on public matters with any members of the Opposition, nor even to be present at any such conversation, I withdrew at the same instant that Lord Stanhope entered the room. It is a justice due to Maret to declare that he has been extremely anxious to prevent the war. He was the principal cause why Dumouriez did not march directly into Holland after the battle of Jemmapes. The matter was several times proposed and warmly insisted upon. His objections, which I have had in my possession, prove a vigorous and reflecting mind, less under the influence of enthusiasm than of reason, and combining, as far as the false and crooked politics of nations will admit, integrity, interest, and convenience.

*M. Maret to Mr. Miles*

Portman Square: February 5, 1793

We leave in a few hours. Come and see us, my dear Miles, so that we may once more have the pleasure of embracing you.

*M. Maret to Mr. Miles*

February 6, 1793

I have this moment sent to Lord Grenville the letter about which I wrote to you, and I regret that I have not been able to communicate to you its contents.[1] Adieu, my dear Miles! We part. I embrace you with all my heart.

*Mr. Miles to Mr. Pitt*

February 6, 1793

M. Maret has left London, and, as I have been much with him during his short stay, it is due to you, as also to myself, that I should explain the conduct I observed, and forward to you a faithful report.

M. Maret alighted in Portman Square on Wednesday last, January 30th, and applied at once by letter to ascertain whether I would receive him. My answer was in the affirmative. He then called upon me, and, after mutual civilities, assured me that I might inform you of the intentions of the Executive Council towards this country, which intentions the National Convention were disposed to ratify, and which were so perfectly pacific that he did not doubt you would listen with pleasure to the propositions he had to offer. I answered that it was impossible that I should be the channel of communication, and I recommended him to transmit the propositions to you without delay. To this he demurred until he received fresh instructions from

[1] 'Maret had asked my advice about his writing to Lord Grenville, and told me what he intended to say.'—W. A. M.

Paris, for, since the departure of M. Chauvelin was not known in the metropolis when he left, he was apprehensive that the circumstance of the late Ambassador having been ordered to quit the kingdom, and the manner in which he would represent the matter, might change the position and precipitate a rupture, which, he added, it was the *ardent* and *unanimous* wish of the Executive Council to avoid; and that, under these circumstances, he would content himself with apprising Lord Grenville of his arrival, and wait for instructions before he applied for the honour of an interview with you. He showed me his credentials as Chargé d'Affaires. I remarked that, although I could not take upon me to be the channel of communication, I felt too sincere an interest in the welfare of both countries to dissemble my indifference as to the object of his mission, and that I should be thankful on my own account for any information he would impart.

M. Maret opened himself to me without reserve. He reprobated the atrocious murder of the King, and lamented the event as a calamity no less dishonourable than afflicting to the nation; he stated that M. Chauvelin had shamefully deceived the Executive Council, and that nothing but misrepresentations and falsehoods had marked his despatches since he lost all hope of remaining in this country; and that, if the British Cabinet were disposed to peace, instead of being inclined to war, peace might be obtained in a manner satisfactory to your wishes. France, he assured me, would give up Nice, Mayence, Worms, and all its conquests on the Rhine, also the Scheldt; she would renounce Liège and the Low Countries on condition that their independence should be guaranteed, and she would contrive the means for detaching Savoy from her jurisdiction.

He further observed that, if you are disposed to listen to this offer, he had instructions to propose M. Dumouriez to negotiate with you; that this latter person would come over to England on being assured of protection; that he would be invested with authority to sign and exchange, and that the National Convention would ratify whatever was mutually arranged.

Such, Sir, is the substance of the information communicated by M. Maret to me. He is not aware that I am imparting it to you, and I pray you to consider it as for your own private use. I forward it from a sincere and unaffected desire to procure for you every possible light at this awful and eventful moment.

M. Maret left London early this morning. It is his intention to transmit to you, if he meets the courier at Calais, the instructions with which he was charged, and, in the hope of yet avoiding war, he will wait at that seaport for your answer with the expectation that you will authorise his return. If he does not find orders awaiting him at Calais, he will despatch a courier to Dumouriez, and entreat him not to enter Holland nor to commit any act of hostility against the Dutch. He would then pursue his route to Paris, whence, he trusted, the Minister Le Brun, on the part of the Executive Council, would direct to you a letter containing the specific propositions.

In apprising you of the above particulars, I beg you to believe that I am influenced by personal regard for yourself, as well as for the success of your administration, and by the ardent desire to see peace preserved and our country rendered happy. I repeat that neither M. Maret nor any other person is aware of this communication. He wrote to Lord Grenville previous to his departure.

*Minute: Wednesday, February* 6.—This morning I made a communication to the Minister in the hope that he would change the fatal resolution and desire an interview with Maret. In a subsequent note I stated to Mr. Pitt the specific commercial advantages which were offered by the Executive Council. Maret has wished as ardently as myself to preserve peace between the two nations; but there are men in high credit in this country who rejoice at the horrible excesses of the French in the hope that they will force us into the war. If these men live to see the progress of the contest, they will change their opinion before it is over. They calculate ill: we are now going to war for the first time with France; we have often been in conflict with her Court, but never before with the nation, and this consideration should make us pause.[1]

Last night I took leave of Maret at eleven o'clock, and at seven this morning Mourgue and he left Portman Square on their return to Paris. Now the sword is drawn between France and England, it will never be sheathed until one or the other falls. This war is not like any other. It is all France against England. I tried to prevent it and have failed.

The 'True Briton' has published certain paragraphs which assert that Maret was not provided with credentials as Chargé d'Affaires. The assertion is untrue. I write to Heriot, the editor, to deny the charge. I suspect Bland Burgess is the author of this false statement. The representation that Maret came over for stock-jobbing purposes has come from the same source.

---

[1] 'Non, monsieur, on ne calcule pas assez que peuvent des millions d'hommes armés, dont le courage est échauffé par un enthousiasme qui double la force et centuple les bras. On peut vaincre la France, mais on ne peut la subjuguer.'—The Abbé Noël to Mr. Miles.

I am told that he has been violent in his abuse of Maret, which abuse has been necessarily at haphazard.[1]

### M. MARET TO MR. MILES

Dover: February 7, 1793

I am still here, my dear Miles. The Custom House would not allow the departure of the pacquet-boat on which I had taken my passage. The pacquet-boat with the mail delays its departure as long as it can. The sailors have a great aversion to cross over to Calais, where, by a strange violation of established rights and of the respect due from one nation to another, they have retained six pacquet-boats; among others, those which took over Reinhard and Chauvelin's servants. I know no motive that can authorise any such proceeding; and I intend, whatever may be the consequence, to protest against this incredible conduct, which, no doubt, public opinion disapproves.

Since Friday no letters from France have arrived here, no letters from England have passed to France, and hence occurs, *mon cher*, the absolute failure which I experience of any orders from the Government. *We are afflicted by this circumstance, which, more than people believe, has influenced the fate of the two nations.* Adieu, my dear Miles! Accept the cordial assurances of inviolable attachment.

### M. SCIPION MOURGUE TO MR. MILES

Calais: February 8,[2] 1793

Herewith I forward to you, dear friend, a long letter from my father. It has just arrived. We are on the point of starting for Paris, and I have only a

---

[1] See *Auckland Correspondence*, ii. 493.   [2] Received February 11.

moment to say that I am wretched on hearing that war has been declared—that it has become necessary to fight. Instructions will be sent for my brothers and sister to return to France immediately. I commend them to your friendship on their way through London. I thank you for all your kind attentions. Adieu! Although our countries may be at war, I hope you will not forget the ties that have formerly bound me to you. I feel that I have new claims on your esteem and friendship. Pray let me hear from you. May I write as usual under cover to Mr. Aust? Once more, adieu!

### M. MOURGUE TO MR. MILES

Montpellier: January 23, 1793

A fortnight ago, my dear Sir, I renewed in my solitude the pleasure of communicating to you my thoughts on the general politics of the day. Events succeed each other with such astonishing rapidity, that, cut off as I am from all intellectual resources, I realise the need of maintaining our correspondence and of benefiting by an exchange of ideas. In these southern provinces we hear only of liberty—a veritable delirium of liberty has seized the population; every one speaks of fraternity, and all express the firm resolve to maintain it against all opposition, whether at home or from abroad. But universal astonishment is felt that England, the land of a free people whom we desire to esteem, should join with tyrants in a war with us. This sentiment has excited indignation. The other day, when present at a military ceremony, I overheard two veteran soldiers speak with admiration of your foreign defences. Among the crowd were some young men who regretted that the brave English should unite with the Continental armies—mere animal machines forced, even as cattle driven by a stick, into a combat on behalf of a worthless cause. All people here are anxious to be *au courant* with events. There is a general disposition to rush to arms. These reflections sadden me; they also lead me to consider the end of all this! Cato never ceased to say, *Respice finem*; but I believe that your statesmen and ours, blinded by the illusions of the moment, have neglected to pay attention to this wise counsel. What will be the certain issue of this war for England? And what for France? Assume the most favourable chances on behalf of your nation, and still additional taxes will be imposed upon you—your national debt will be augmented; and, whilst you risk the loss of your West Indian colonies, you will experience a fearful sacrifice both in men and money. Then as to France, what will be the result of all the injury that you may inflict upon her? An enormous circulation of assignats, a terrible expenditure of her men, and the calamity of bending beneath the weight of all the despots of Europe! This is all that you could expect, and I fail to see in our humiliation and grief any advantage that would accrue to your nation. We may be beaten, or broken, in the conflict, but by means of our climate, soil, and national spirit, a few years will repair our misfortunes, our principles would survive, and better security would be provided for the future. Should you disturb our West Indian possessions, you might possibly expedite the disruption of your own. This statement may appear paradoxical. Colonies, however, are to the metropolis what fruit is to the tree. The fruit when mature readily detaches itself; but a smart blow accelerates its separation. Such has been the case with your North American colonies. And your suc-

cess over our Antilles may hasten the loss of your own
islands. I would again ask what will be the issue of
this contest, as ridiculous as it is atrocious, on behalf
of the Scheldt? What fruit could be gathered from
your victory and our ruin? I must repeat the assertion that your Ministers have not considered the result
of a war which they would wage against us.

How much I desire to converse with you on an
infinite number of affairs! We should discuss the advantages of a policy entirely different from that which
now prevails—a policy which, instead of injuring, would
enrich both our nations. It is an extensive field over
which to roam, but I would rather talk over its cultiva-
tion with you *de vive voix* than by letter; and, moreover, I should be greatly refreshed by the pleasure of
your society. In the meantime I cannot refrain from
communicating my reflections. I follow with keen interest the differences that exist between our respective
Cabinets, and I perceive that they do not understand
one another, or, if you will allow me to speak frankly,
I think that your Government is very subtle, and,
although well informed, does not wish to come to an
understanding. *We* speak of national rights as a principle; *you* speak of the interests of nations as a convenience. Oh, that we could or would understand each
other! If only they would deal with principles when it
is a question of principles, and speak only of interest
when it is a question of interest, we might very soon
arrange our difficulty, as it appears to me, for, as a
matter of principle, the rights of nations are evident,
whereas, with respect to our mutual interests, we can
arrive at an understanding only by concerted agreement. Our respective Governments destroy this hope
when they confound these two distinct ideas. Ah! my

dear friend, how much Ministers are still ministers of kings and not the ministers of nations! I think it is one of the embarrassments which your Minister has to overcome in dealing with your King. What a topic have we here for moral reflection!

If, contrary to my wishes—if, contrary to our reciprocal advantages—war should be declared, I commend my poor dear children to your care. They are too young to know anything of political events. It is my wish that they should continue to profit by an education which my own experience has shown to be so valuable. May they see some day the reunion of two nations, which are formed to assist and esteem each other, and which so many causes, both physical and moral, should induce to live in amity! I am in an awful humour (*une humeur de diable*) against the House of Austria. If only you would keep out of the affair, what a severe lesson it would receive from us! If you would support our views, how we would humiliate its pride and curb the authority of Russia! How we would reduce these two colossal powers to their proper dimensions in the political scale!

I hope to be in Paris as soon as affairs become quieter. Address your letters to Rue de Grammont No. 17. They will be forwarded wherever I may be Can I send my letters as formerly free of postage? I salute you and embrace you with all my heart.

### M. MARET TO MR. MILES.

Calais: February 8, 1793

Within sight of port, the pacquet-boat which took me over was attacked by two privateers. I was sick at the time; the shots cured me, and I learned that war was declared. Adieu, then, my dear Miles, to all your philanthropic hopes! One thought consoles me—this war cannot last long; the courage of the two nations will insure reciprocal esteem, which, perhaps, will compensate by happy results the evils which are preparing. Then, my friend, we shall see each other again, and we shall enjoy our mutual attachment in peace. Adieu! Write to me.

P.S.—I found here letters appointing me Agent-General of the French Republic in Belgium. I know not whether I shall accept it. I have need for rest and to live alone for a short time.[1]

### MR. MILES TO M. MARET

February 12, 1793

Your packet, my dear Maret, arrived last evening, and I placed it faithfully this morning in the hands of your friend Vioffi himself, whom I had summoned for the purpose to my house. You are too honourable to keep up a correspondence with the factions in this country—I believe you to be incapable of it—or with

---

[1] 'Déjà les communications étaient interrompues ; des corsaires français rôdaient dans la Manche. Maret parvint à inspirer confiance dans son inviolabilité à un capitaine anglais, qui consentit à risquer le passage par un très-gros temps. Maret était couché dans sa cabine, souffrant horriblement du mal de mer, quand plusieurs détonations frappèrent ses oreilles. Au même instant le capitaine accourut à lui tout effaré. Il venait d'être abordé par un corsaire qui répondait à toutes les explications par des coups de feu. Maret, qui plus tard aimait à raconter cet épisode à ses enfants, assurait que cette émotion l'avait guéri comme par enchantement du mal de mer. Il monta sur le pont, déclina sa qualité diplomatique, parla si haut et si ferme, qu'il finit par se faire écouter. Le corsaire était lui-même un Anglais, donnant la chasse à ses compatriotes pour le compte d'une société d'armateurs. Pour le décider tout-à-fait à lâcher sa capture, Maret lui promit de prendre un intérêt dans sa commandite, et, finalement, arriva à Calais sous l'escorte de cet honnête industriel, qui fut tué quelques jours après dans une autre rencontre.'—Ernouf, p. 130. See *Conduct of France towards Great Britain*, pp. 155, 162.

the secret agents of the Executive Power, if there are any such here; but I should fail equally in the frankness of my character and in my loyalty as a good citizen, as also in the friendship which I have always testified towards you, if I did not pray you no longer to forward letters under cover to me—no matter to whom they may be addressed. It will, however, be a real pleasure to receive news from you, although you must not expect a regular and continuous correspondence from me, for, like yourself, I feel the need for retirement. Tranquillity has become a physical necessity, and I intend to seek it in the country, whence it would be impossible for me to write to you on the affairs which distract the two nations. I should not be grieved, however, to learn that Chauvelin and Walckiers were driven out of France, and that Le Brun had departed to resume his former business as a journalist at Hervé. I must aver that a nation is most unfortunate when its interests are committed to such hands.

Remember me to Mourgue. I cannot write to him. I will take care of his brothers and sister when they pass through London. Adieu !

### Mr. Miles to Mr. Devaynes[1]

February 12, 1793

As the die is cast, and the French have declared hostilities which the National Convention have long premeditated as an event contingent on the internal commotions they expected to excite in different parts of the kingdom, I take the liberty to suggest to you the propriety of a subscription for the purpose of affording relief to the widows and orphans of seamen and soldiers who may fall in the defence of their country. Such a measure

[1] Chairman of the East India Company.

may operate as a stimulus to the former, and render the dangerous expedient of *press-warrants* unnecessary. It may also counteract the arts of the enemy, who will practise every possible method to seduce our sailors into their service. Should this suggestion be adopted, I have no doubt from the loyalty of the times but it will produce a fund adequate to a comfortable provision for those who may become the objects of the charity. If you coincide with me, I shall beg leave to subscribe twenty guineas.

### M. DE LA COLOMBE[1] TO MR. MILES

March 11, 1793

You have requested a memorandum on the political situation of France, and on the means which might still be in her power for making a diversion. The unfolding of all my ideas, under any hypothetical form of government which the powers may have adopted and of which I am ignorant, would be too diffuse and too long to enable me to offer you an explanatory memoir. But if, as I believe, the European powers have no other views than to compel the French to re-enter their own territory, and to re-establish order under a limited monarchical Government; if they can measure the reality of the project according to that given basis, I shall have the honour of presenting to you a plan in all possible exactitude, and on the execution of which I would be responsible with my life. I am able to hold this language with all the more reason inasmuch as, notwithstanding my exile from France, I have still a considerable number of partisans, principally in the army, and in our mountains, where my father and part

---

[1] Lately, Major-Général au service de France, et Premier Aide-de-Camp de M. de Lafayette.

of my family habitually reside. I have induced them to act successfully for the maintenance of order during the course of our unfortunate Revolution; they have honoured me with their confidence, and wish me to be amongst them, because I have never belied my character, and have boldly declared myself the enemy of intriguers and of anarchists. Yes, Sir, all landowners and honest people who remain in France honour me with their esteem; they groan to-day beneath the poniard, and sigh only for a diversion which would dispel from around them the infernal doctrine of the present rulers. But I can assure you that they will not make a single attempt so long as they know that M. de Lafayette is in chains. If, on the other hand, the powers will be responsible for his deliverance, I will answer with my life, and with the life of all my friends, to bring about a diversion which, in a short time, would persuade the intelligence of France to adopt such a form of government as the general welfare of our people and the interests of Europe could possibly desire. This offer, which emanates only from the love of my country and of order, may be misunderstood by your Government; but, as I am neither a visionary nor an adventurer, as I ask nothing from any person and had indeed resolved to depart for America a month hence, I repeat to you in writing what I said to you *vivâ voce*, that, in case the powers would restrict themselves to re-establish a limited monarchy in France, and would accord liberty to M. de Lafayette and his companions in misfortune, I will be responsible for a general rising in the Cevennes and Auvergne in favour of that *régime*, and, as soon as I shall receive this positive assurance, I will proceed at once and at my own expense.

Declaration on the part of the inhabitants of the Cevennes, Auvergne, Dauphiny, and the adjacent country, given to me by M. De La Colombe, and, at his request, transmitted to the Secretary of State for Foreign Affairs, accompanied by a letter from M. De La Colombe himself, dated March 11, 1793.—W. A. M.

'The inhabitants of the Cevennes, Auvergne, Dauphiny, and the adjacent country, are ready to arm and march to Paris, and proclaim Louis XVII. King of France, provided they can be assured that the combined powers will be satisfied with the restoration of a monarchy, not such as was proposed in 1789, but a limited monarchy, in which the Ministers of the Crown shall be responsible to the nation. The inhabitants of the above districts, including the whole five departments, engage to furnish and to equip an army at their own expense of from 24,000 to 30,000 effective men, with artillery and ammunition; and all that is expected from the combined powers is an assurance that they will be satisfied with the establishment of a limited monarchy in France, and, in proof of their sincerity, release Monsieur de Lafayette and his unfortunate companions. These departments are called the Alps of France, and are invulnerable to an invading enemy. The utmost tranquillity reigns in them; and the priests who have not taken the oaths say Mass in as perfect security and as publicly as they did before the Revolution. Anxious, however, as these departments are for a limited monarchy, they are resolved to prefer a republic rather than suffer the return of the old Government.

'LA COLOMBE.'

*Minute: March* 1793.—Facts from Major-General De La Colombe, who was taken with Lafayette, and who afterwards made his escape from the citadel of Antwerp :—

Lafayette knew nothing of the flight of Louis XVI. from Paris in June 1791. La Colombe went into his room in the early morning of that day, ignorant of what had happened till Lafayette informed him. He answered that in half an hour they would both be hanged, and, convinced of it, they embraced each other for the last time. Lafayette went to the Maison-de-Ville, and ordered the alarm cannon to be fired. La Colombe ran to engage the members of the Assembly not to dispute, but to unite. Alexander Lameth had made up his quarrel four days before with Lafayette, and on this occasion served him. The populace were for hanging La Colombe and Lafayette. On the return of the King, La Colombe refused to guard the château of the Tuileries, but took charge of the Dauphin on being earnestly pressed to do so. The Queen offered to give an account of her flight, but La Porte advised her not, saying that, if a single variation was detected from the fact—and it was possible she might deceive herself—she would be sacrificed. Lafayette resolved to quit the army, when he reflected that by fighting against the Austrians while the factions were acting against the monarchy he would sanction their enormities. When he called out his troops the whole army cried 'Vive Lafayette!' and not above 100 'Vive le Roi!' If he had gone against the public enemy, they would have followed him to death; not 10,000 would have marched to Paris. When Kersaint, the Commissioner from the National Assembly, was arrested and put in prison at Sedan, La Colombe went to him. He told Colombe that he had orders from the Assembly to assure Lafayette that, if he would join them, they would place him at the head of the Republic. Kersaint, who then voted for the dethronement of the King, now revolts at his death, and quits the Convention.

Several officers were on the point of leaving France when they heard of Lafayette being arrested. They then resolved to stay, preferring to die in the field than to perish in a dungeon. Felix Wimpffen threw himself into Thionville and ensured the defeat of the despot who, in an ill-written manifesto, threatened to put the whole country to the sword. M. de Maubourg was the first of Lafayette's party that fell in with the enemy on neutral ground, and demanded if they could pass safely; he was answered in the affirmative, and under that assurance they came within the enemy's lines and were captured.—W. A. M.

### FROM A LADY[1] TO MR. MILES

Paris: March 12, 1793

I conceive, my dear friend, that at this time you must have more certain intelligence than I can send you. The Austrians are said to be at Valenciennes, and Paris seems to be in a convulsion of despair. Troops are concentrating in the departments with all despatch possible, but not with enthusiasm or even willingness, at least I have reason to believe so. The report of the day is that Dumouriez has emigrated, but I do not believe it. The *Tribunal révolutionnaire* just decreed is the object of much terror, and if the barriers of Paris be shut I dread the consequences. In a speech of Robespierre yesterday is this remarkable passage: 'Il ne suffit pas de rassembler des troupes nombreuses pour combattre nos ennemis au dehors; il faut encore

---

[1] This letter was written under the *disguise* of an *English lady* on account of the danger to which the writer was exposed.

un régulateur fidèle pour conduire nos affaires intérieures.' Hear also Santerre's account given at the bar of the Convention: 'Santerre fait lecture des ordres qu'il a donnés pour maintenir la tranquillité dans la capitale; il ne croit point aux mouvemens qu'on semble redouter; ceux qui les annoncent, dit-il, n'ont d'autre dessein que de faire naître quelques propos séditieux qui ont, il est vrai, donné des inquiétudes. On répandait qu'il falloit un roi, et l'on désignoit le Citoyen Égalité; on appeloit son fils à la place de Commandant-Général de Paris, mais tous ces propos n'ont d'autre but que celui de diviser les esprits et de nous conduire à l'anarchie.' Compare this with Robespierre's speech, and make your reflections. Every one seems much agitated and prepared for a crisis, but I cannot well express all I imagine. I expect letters to-morrow, and if there is anything new will add it. If one were certain of being in safety, I am not displeased to watch the progress of the storm, and it is impossible not to feel all the powers of one's mind interested in the event. I do not willingly think of being obliged to relinquish my property which still remains at the Hôtel-de-Ville. But a moment of danger may arrive, and I have no passport. I must therefore request, my good friend, that you will be so obliging as to obtain one, which would serve me at any time. I shall not, however, leave France except on absolute necessity, but I shall be uneasy till I have the means of doing so.

Le Brun, I imagine, will not be long in office. Beurnonville [1] has already resigned, but the displacing even of bad Ministers at present only adds to the general confusion. The misery of Paris will soon be equal to its turpitude. I need say no more. Pray

[1] Minister of War.

excuse the incoherence of this letter. I write this at an hotel, within hearing of a dozen drums and the noise at the *table d'hôte* of the full chorus of the 'Marseillaise.' You say nothing of yourself or your family. I therefore venture to conclude you are well. I shall be anxious till I receive a passport. The idea of not being able to go is worse than the reality of remaining here. I have had letters to-day, but they contain nothing but what you will find in the inclosed. Adieu!

### Mr. Miles to Sir Edward Newenham

London: April 1, 1793

All communication between this country and France being stopped by the French, I learn with difficulty what is being transacted at Paris or in Brittany. Dumouriez is by this time out of the Austrian Netherlands. He was at Notre Dame de Halle, four leagues from Bruxelles, on the road to Mons and Valenciennes, on the 27th of last month. What the projects of the confederated powers may be I know not. That the French banditti are a race of remorseless miscreants whose extermination would be of use to justice and social order I am convinced, but, atrocious as they are, I am not disposed to think more favourably of the banditti that are opposed to them, or that the King of Prussia and the Empress of Russia are more amicable or less guilty than Dumouriez. My idea is that they are alike infamous, and that there is no moral difference between the regal scoundrel that triumphs at Dantzic and the democratic knave that retreats from Brabant. England, Prussia, and Austria would have treated with Dumouriez had he been victorious; and, in that case, he would have been called a hero, and crowned with laurels, whilst the despots of the earth would have hailed him as their good brother and cousin : victorious, all the virtues would have been attributed to him ; defeated, he is a rebel, a regicide, an assassin, and a plunderer ! Thus it is, my dear Newenham, that the *result* of our actions stamps them as criminal or laudable ; and thus Dumouriez may be crowned or hanged as he is successful or unfortunate. The question is whether, considering the short duration of human life, it is worth the trouble of any man who has the means of living otherwise to embark on such perilous enterprises—expose his existence, sacrifice his peace and reputation, and travel through dangers and inquietudes post haste to that spot where he will arrive sooner or later without any fatigue at all. Give me the silence of obscurity and the tranquillity of a mind free from guilt. I have no ambition to fight for sceptres and diadems, which when won are not, in my estimation, worth the trouble of wearing. I am so disgusted with public affairs and public men—I find so much fraud, trick, favour, and contention—so much dependent on chance and so little upon reason, that really I do not think that politics are worthy the pursuit of a wise and good man, so long as public men consist, with very few exceptions, of little else than knaves and fools.

There is a vice and profligacy in the Courts of Petersburg and Berlin which fully equals all that France under the wild dominion of a sanguinary low-born rabble displays at this instant. The scandalous appropriation of Poland to the territories of Russia and Prussia is another melancholy proof that morals are of small account in Courts, and that politics know no other rule but that of convenience. The usurpations of which I complain have been followed by private injuries and assassinations ; forfeitures and proscriptions are to consolidate and confirm the ill-acquired power of the northern despots. I know of no female in modern history so depraved as the Empress of Russia. Our country, while it preserves its happy constitution, can neither be dishonoured nor injured by monarchy. Our kings are bound by laws the limits of which they cannot pass without greater mischief to themselves than to us, and we have happily the means of correcting even a vicious tendency in them; while the millions who groan beneath the iron rod of tyranny in the rest of Europe have neither the spirit to resent nor the means of avenging the wrongs and insults they daily receive from licentious despotism; they bow in submission to the yoke, and acknowledge its equity and generosity so long as it does not absolutely curb them to the ground. My last letter contained a comparison between Lafayette and Dumouriez, or rather remarks on their different fates, with some strong but well-warranted reflections on the King of Prussia. I wish much to know if you received such a letter, for it was for your perusal and not for that of the world.[1]

The Convention and Executive Council in France, feeling the approach of danger, have made an ineffectual advance to open a negotiation for a separate peace with us; but they have a large account to settle, and they little know Mr. Pitt if they imagine he is to be tempted by fallacious assurances—dictated by fear, not contrition, and in the moment of adversity—to give up the game which their madness has in some sort thrown into his hands, provided it is well played—not cunningly and basely, but nobly, without which he will hazard the dignity and safety of the Empire. I will answer for his wisdom and fairness being well rewarded,

[1] There is no copy of this letter among Mr. Miles's papers.

and the peace will be honourable and advantageous if the war does not give rise to other projects than the strict legitimate ends of unprovoked contest.

### Handbill distributed by the Coalesced Powers

'SOLDATS FRANÇAIS!

'On vous trompe indignement depuis cinq ans; à force de promesses, de calomnies, de musique, d'espérances et de fausses nouvelles, on vous conduit à être les champions et les défenseurs de quelques scélérats, qui bouleversent et déshonorent votre patrie. Ils se servent de vous pour être les instruments de leur ambition et de leurs crimes; ils nomment liberté le plus dur et le plus avilissant esclavage; ils nomment liberté une contrainte terrible qui ne permet pas de proférer un mot ou d'avoir une idée contraire à leurs intérêts, sans verser son sang sur l'échafaud; ils nomment liberté cette tyrannie affreuse qui enlève à l'agriculture, à leurs familles, à leurs affaires une quantité innombrable de pauvres paysans au désespoir; ils nomment liberté le vol atroce de toutes les propriétés, le supplice de tous les honnêtes gens, les rapines, l'impiété, les plus horribles attentats, des forfaits et des brigandages dont l'idée seule fait frémir. Ils vous disent que vous êtes partout vainqueurs. Détrompez-vous: de vils régicides ne sont pas faits pour conduire à la victoire des soldats français. Ils vous disent que la France est tranquille. Détrompez-vous encore: elle est malheureuse et bouleversée. Ils nomment brigands de braves Français qui viennent arracher leurs frères à la honte et à l'esclavage, et qui, sous les étendards de la patrie et de l'honneur, font tous les jours de plus rapides progrès. Déjà ils approchent de Paris, et donnent la main aux infortunés qui de toutes parts s'arment contre vos oppresseurs. Les armées des puissances en guerre contre la France ont des succès constants; elles viennent encore dans cet instant de prendre Fort Louis. De tous les côtés la cause du crime et de l'esclavage—car c'est là votre liberté—succombe sous la justice et la valeur; vos gazettes sont remplies d'absurdités et de mensonges; on ne permet pas à la vérité de percer jusqu'à vous, parce qu'on craint le réveil du peuple et de l'armée. On vous dit entre autres que ceux de vous qui, indignés de tant de fureurs, de bassesses et de folies, quittent une armée sans réputation, des généraux qui vont des tripots de Paris au généralat et du généralat à l'échafaud, qui quittent ces hordes méprisables pour venir chercher chez nous des honnêtes gens et des soldats, sont mal reçus, maltraités, forcés de servir contre leur patrie, etc. Malheureux Français! Comme on vous trompe! Voici la pure, l'exacte vérité. Tous les déserteurs sont bien accueillis, on leur achète leurs chevaux au prix qu'ils y mettent s'ils veulent les vendre; on ne leur fait pas le moindre mal, ni la moindre insulte; on ne les oblige nullement à prendre service; on leur donne des passeports, ils vont où ils veulent; on les traite comme des amis et des frères. Tous ceux qui sont passés étaient heureux de se trouver avec nous. Soldats français! vous avez juré la haine de la tyrannie, et vous servez en esclaves les plus vils des tyrans! Vous avez juré de sauver votre patrie, et vous en faites par votre funeste opiniâtreté un séjour affreux de sang, de carnage, et de malheurs. Soldats français! quatorze siècles vous combattîtes sous les bannières de la gloire; comment pouvez-vous servir sous celles du déshonneur? Rougissez! venez, tous les militaires du monde sont frères; même les armes à la main, ils s'estiment; ils s'embrassent en les posant, il n'y a que les Français d'aujourd'hui qu'on rougit de nommer des camarades et des soldats. Sauvez votre réputation, votre honneur, votre patrie. Venez!—Avril 1793.'

*Minute.*—This is one of the thousand miserable expedients by which the coalesced powers carried on the war against a nation of enthusiasts, fighting, as they believe, for their liberty.

This handbill was distributed in great profusion at Tournay, but the printers alone reaped benefit from it. To what clodpoles the destiny of nations is confided! I cannot reflect on the carnage which a war of this description must occasion without horror, and I tremble for my ill-governed country, whose tide of prosperity is interrupted by the contest, and whose power may be annihilated as the result.—W. A. M.

### Mr. Miles to Mr. Pitt

July 10, 1793

The interest I take in the happy conclusion of the war, which, as appears from what has come to my knowledge, it was impossible you could have avoided without a personal offence to the King, and the strong desire I feel that the contest may be terminated speedily in a manner honourable to yourself and advantageous to your country, and ultimately lead to eternal peace, are my motives for submitting the inclosed offer to your consideration. It is from a near relative of M. de Lafayette, and he has authorised me to say that a dozen of his friends in London are ready to set off for Auvergne and the Cevennes, where they are certain of collecting an army of 24,000 men immediately on their arrival. What degree of credit is to be given to their assurances I am unable to determine, and how far such a measure may accord with your arrangements does not become me to inquire. I conceive it to be my duty to transmit the inclosed to you, but I do not mean to take any further part in it than you may think proper to direct, however anxious I may feel for the return of peace and order.

### 'THE OFFER OF MONSIEUR DE LA COLOMBE.

' La résistance de l'armée française dans le cours de cette campagne doit commencer à convaincre les puissances alliées que leurs efforts combinés n'ont servi qu'à exalter de plus en plus l'enthousiasme d'une liberté mal entendue, qu'à aveugler le peuple sur les crimes de ses gouvernants en portant toute son attention à la frontière —et qu'enfin, ni le rétablissement de la monarchie, ni le retour de l'ordre, ne peuvent s'opérer par la force des armes étrangères. L'intérieur peut seul, par un mouvement bien dirigé, abattre l'anarchie et releverle trône; par un mouvement bien dirigé on doit entendre, amené par des chefs dont la vie politique ait été telle jusqu'ici, qu'ils puissent, sans être suspects, rassurer le peuple sur les vengeances personnelles, garantir des propriétés à tous les Français jetés jusqu'à présent dans les différents partis, l'oubli du passé, et pour l'avenir liberté, sûreté, et protection devant la loi. Les amis de M. Lafayette, que son arrestation au moment où il venait de se sacrifier pour la monarchie, que sa détention prolongée ne rendent que plus cher aux Français en effaçant l'impression de trahison qu'on avait cherché à jeter sur sa fuite, sont peut-être ceux qui peuvent travailler le plus utilement au rétablissement d'une monarchie en France, et, par conséquent, à la tranquillité de l'Europe. Je n'entre point dans le développement de la question politique, si les fers de M. de Lafayette n'ont

pas été un obstacle au succès des armes des Alliés, et
si les Français, en songeant aux cachots de Magdebourg,
et à la manière dont lui et ses compagnons y ont été
jetés, ont pu ou dû se fier à des manifestes qui leur pro-
mettaient amnistie et protection quand ces cachots
restaient toujours fermés ; mais on doit concevoir que
tant que cette contradiction entre les promesses des
puissances et leur conduite subsistera, les amis de M. de
Lafayette ne pourront obtenir que de faibles succès,
tandis que, s'il était libre, si l'on avait cette preuve
non équivoque à donner des intentions pacifiques des
puissances, je réponds alors, et sur ma tête, d'opérer
dans les montagnes d'Auvergne, dont lui et moi sommes
originaires, les Cévennes, le Vélay, le Gévaudan, et le
Languedoc, une diversion telle que bientôt on verrait
le gouvernement reprendre en France une nouvelle force,
et les efforts des anarchistes anéantis pour jamais. Je puis
répondre de cette diversion avec d'autant plus de sûreté
que dix personnes les plus attachées à M. de Lafayette,
et qui ont dans les différentes provinces dont je viens de
parler, soit par leurs propriétés personnelles, soit par
celles de leurs parents, des relations considérables, offrent
de partir pour y agir de concert avec moi.

'(Signé)    LA COLOMBE.'[1]

*M. NOËL TO MR. MILES*

Paris: August 16, 1793

I know not whether fate will permit me to see you
again. Pressing events, and the situation of my unhappy country, for which I have dreamt of liberty and
prosperity, allow me neither to project plans nor to
make calculations for the future. You have seen the
efforts I made to avoid this horrible war. Madness and

[1] See March 11.

imprudence have brought it about. You know the
fate of the unfortunate Maret, and of his companion
Sémonville. Whatever mine may be, I shall never
forget your obliging conduct, and I beg you to accept
the expression of my sincere gratitude. If you honour
me with a reply, which I only ask in case it will not in
any way compromise you, I beg you to address your
letter to Venice.

### Madame de Montgeroult to Mr. Miles

Baden en Suisse : August 24, 1793

Although I have not the honour, Sir, of being personally known to you, yet my husband is so connected
with the misfortunes of M. Maret, whom you esteem,
that without doubt his name will be familiar to you.
My husband and I had left for Naples with M. Maret.
M. de Montgeroult—who has been for ten years a
retired general officer in the French army, and who
has nothing to do with the political interests that have
led to the crime committed against two French Ambassadors—was arrested at Novale on the 25th July. He
was provided with a Swiss passport. He has been
bound and pinioned, and, in company with our Ministers, led to the fatal boat which has deprived me of
repose and of the happiness of my life. On that day,
Sir, I was in the depth of despair—remaining alone in
the midst of some thirty assassins, without support,
without help, without any resource ; and, being obliged
to fly from that horrid place where I was not safe, I
rode eight leagues on horseback at full speed in those
dangerous Alpine tracts, constantly under the fear that
I might be pursued by the Austrian satellites. I arrived
at night in the midst of a kind family. Since then I
thought it right to go to M. Barthélemy, the French

Ambassador, with whom I have spent some days, and where the cruelty of my position was mitigated by the arrival of letters from the unfortunate prisoners, who, as they tell me, were together and treated with consideration. Yesterday, however, after fifteen days' silence, a letter arrived from M. Maret, dated the 7th August. With a trembling hand I opened it, and read that he is separated from M. de Montgeroult; that since their arrival at Mantua each has been placed in close confinement under bolts and triple fastenings, and there they meditate day and night. This tomb is their world! They cannot communicate with each other; they are permitted to breathe only the atmosphere of their dismal habitation, in that warm and unhealthy country. In short, Sir, these most worthy and respectable men are treated as the worst of criminals. I cannot tell you what I felt on reading this doleful letter. My heart has failed, and, almost bereft of my senses, I sigh for the moment which would deliver me from an existence no longer supportable. The excess of my despair is such that my husband's fate, if not changed, will be the cause of my death. At the age of sixty, weak and infirm, after having steadily refused every kind of employment, because, as a man of peace, he could not conscientiously take part in the agitations of the Revolution, he had resolved to leave France, and circumstances gave to our journey a direction that separated us from the emigrants. M. de Weldseck, the Emperor's Minister at Milan, ought to have seen on examining our papers that M. de Montgeroult had neither ministerial instructions nor any correspondence connected with public affairs. Why, then, this severity? I wrote to him yesterday, assured him on my oath that my husband in going to Naples went there without any mission.¹ I have offered to go to Milan as a hostage for the truth of what I asserted; I have asked to share the captivity of my husband, who never could have anticipated such a dreadful fate. I wait for his reply. Should it be a refusal, the excess of my despair will make me capable of anything! I have sent to Lord Lansdowne an account of the abduction of the Ambassadors. Should you desire it, I shall have the honour of addressing a copy of the same narrative to you. It is important that English loyalty should know all the details of a complicated conspiracy, which required for its accomplishment a chain of perfidy and treachery such as no man of honour can consider without indignation, even though the right of war should authorise such atrocious measures. When the violation of neutral territory is proved, the removal by armed force of two men whose public character was known will surely not be inhumanly sanctioned by continuing to treat with barbarity individuals against whom they can bring no private reproach. What do they desire in arresting the envoys of France? Why do they prevent M. de Sémonville from proceeding to Constantinople? Is it necessary to plunge his wife and children in despair? Must they treat M. Maret as a scoundrel, to whom liberty would be dangerous? Ah, you know, Sir—you know that there never was a man more virtuous or more loyal. With what do they reproach him? Never has he approved of any excess—never has his name been connected, directly or indirectly, with those scenes of blood which have sullied the Revolution. He has always desired the general good; and I have seen the time when his most ardent wish was to tighten the

---

[1] Ernouf, in his narrative of this affair, says: 'Montgeroult, ex-officier général, *chargé d'une mission particulière* pour Naples' (p. 167).

bonds which should unite two philosophic and powerful people. I do not doubt that the justice of your King will disapprove an attack which, whilst it is a useless severity, plunges in despair good and innocent families. If you saw my unhappy condition you would be moved. I say nothing of the fainting state in which these brigands left me after depriving me of all that I possessed—*that is my last thought*;[1] but who can ever compensate the grief in which the bereaved families are now involved? In one moment the happy wife and children of M. de Sémonville are overwhelmed with grief! In the name of humanity, in the name of justice, in the name of the liberty of the people, interest yourself, Sir, on their behalf, by an appeal to the sympathy of your nation and to the probity of the Ministers of your King! They cannot, no, they cannot approve this crime. It violates every right, every principle, every treaty, everything, in fact, which constitutes order in the world and exercises a restraint on the wicked. Let your Government demand the release of our Ministers. What do they want with them? They have read all their secret papers. Even if they are replaced on neutral territory, they will scarcely attempt to reach their posts, for almost all the roads have become impracticable. Or, if they will not be just, let them at least be humane—let them soften their captivity by transferring them to a place less unhealthy than Mantua; let them allow their families to go and weep in their prison; and let them at once release M. de Montgeroult, who in no respect should be the victim of this cruel and deliberate political conspiracy. At the moment when fifty assassins broke into the inn at Novale, and, firing shots,

[1] 'Les bagages, les effets furent pillés, les diamants de Madame de Sémonville séquestrés : on la laissa sur la route sans aucune ressource, avec ses deux enfants et Madame de Montgeroult.'—Ernouf, p. 169.

dispersed the women and children, who demanded with loud cries the release of their father and of their husbands, M. Maret was heard to say, 'We are betrayed; but what consoles me is, that this violation of the right of people and of nations will excite the indignation of the whole of Europe, and will be for the happiness of my country.' Shortly after, he re-appeared —his hands bound, his chest covered by the muskets and poniards of these monsters. He maintained that dignified and tranquil manner which you know belongs to him; he approached and bade me a last adieu.

He was still speaking when they led him away to the fatal boat. His letter of yesterday is full of philosophy—the mildness and serenity of a great and pure mind. I wish I could send it to you. Ah! that your friendship for him may kindle your zeal! Every service rendered to him will do honour to those from whom it emanates. In helping him you will befriend M. de Montgeroult, and I shall owe you eternal gratitude. I shall expect your reply with impatience.

My address is at M. Barthélemy's, Ambassador of France, Baden en Suisse.

Receive, Sir, the assurance of the perfect consideration with which I am, &c.

HÉLÈNE DE MONTGEROULT.[1]

*MR. MILES TO MADAME DE MONTGEROULT*

London: September 10, 1793

I hasten, Madam, to reply to the letter with which you have honoured me. It was with infinite regret that I heard of the disasters which befell you on your journey; but, unfortunately, I can only sympathise with you in

---

[1] 'On arrêta, on mit aux fers après les avoir soigneusement fouillés et dévalisés, Maret, Sémonville, Montgeroult, secrétaires, courriers, en tout huit personnes.'—Ernouf, p. 169.

your trouble, and lament the sad fate of your husband and of M. Maret and M. de Sémonville. I believe that the right to put in a demand on behalf of travellers arrested on neutral territory belongs in this case solely to the canton in which the violation has been made; and, besides, Madam, you will agree with me on reflection that those foreign Courts which have not recognised the French Republic would feel some embarrassment from the inconsistency of any attempted interference on behalf of her ambassadors. This is exactly the unfortunate position in which the Court of London finds itself. However, I will take care that Mr. Pitt shall be made acquainted with the insult offered to the Ministers of France. I have not seen Lord Lansdowne for many years, and therefore, not having had the opportunity of seeing the memorial which you have forwarded to him, I willingly accept your kind offer to supply me with a copy.[1] I beg you, Madam, to remember me to the sufferers. When you have a moment to spare I shall be very grateful if you will give me news of M. Le Brun, of whom we no longer hear.

I have the honour to be, with the greatest consideration, &c. &c.

*MR. MILES TO M. NOËL*

September 10, 1793

Your letter, my dear Sir, dated the 16th of last month, was an acceptable token of remembrance and claims my immediate acknowledgment. Your talents and probity interested me in your favour at a very early period of our acquaintance, and I beheld your departure from this country with regret, not only on account of the war, which you foresaw and declared was inevitable,

[1] The *Mémoire* was received, but, although full of interest, is too long for insertion in this work. Mr. Miles pressed this case on the attention of both Mr. Pitt and Lord Grenville.

but because you were among the very few sent here by
the Executive Council whose conduct appeared perfectly irreproachable, in whom I found an unaffected
frankness and a proper conception of the relative
interests of the two nations. Acquainted as I am with
the expectation of those who sent them over, and
recollecting the representations you frequently made to
Le Brun, which drew from him nothing but reproaches
and ill-humour, I do not hesitate to declare that, if the
emissaries he employed had adhered to the truth in the
different reports which they transmitted relative to the
temper and disposition of the people in this country,
and if they had attended to your wholesome admonitions, the war in which all Europe is at present engaged
would probably have been avoided. But it was the
misfortune of your country, and of mine, to have a man
at the head of the Foreign Department in Paris who
was too corrupt to be influenced by considerations of
justice, and who, dazzled by the splendour of his situation, had become too vain and too insolent to listen to
the suggestions of prudence. The present deplorable
condition of France, however, is not to be entirely attributed to the avarice, ambition, or ignorance of those
whom a revolution the most wonderful in its nature and
the most terrible in its effects had called from penury
and obscurity. I am sufficiently read in French history
to know that the tremendous change that has happened
is to be placed in a great measure to the scandalous
rapacity and profligate manners of that pestilential and
contemptible banditti of legalised plunderers—your
nobility and the clergy of the highest class. They are,
in fact, the original cause of the Revolution. Had
the former been less rapacious, and the latter exemplary, as ecclesiastics ought to be, the abuses which

brought forward bad men and enabled them to obtain
credit by their clamour for reform would have been
diminished, and the old system, meliorated, would
have rendered a revolution not only unnecessary, but
impracticable. Your Marats, your Dantons, and your
Robespierres are the offspring of the accumulated
corruption of your bishops and of an upstart *noblesse*,
who had obtained wealth by rapine and titles by
purchase or intrigue. The vices, the profusion, and the
arrogance of these men engendered and vivified the
vermin that have desolated your once flourishing and
happy country; and, however much we may execrate the
present men in power, it would be unfair to saddle them
with the entire infamy of the mischiefs which the Revolution has produced. They are entitled only to a share
of it, but that share is more than sufficient to render
them the scorn and detestation of all good men. Vol-
taire says ' que les Français sont ou singes ou tigres;'
and, if he says true, I may venture to assert from the
samples among us that the *tigers* have kept possession
of France and made England a present of the *monkeys*.
I condole with you most sincerely on the melancholy
and deplorable state in which you describe your country
to be. Those who have had the direction of public
affairs since 1789 seem to have proceeded rapidly
from bad to worse; they have done little else than
vibrate between blunders and crimes; and the lust of
dominion and wealth, as you very justly observe, has
rendered them insensible to their real interests and duty.
I will forbear to recapitulate the criminal efforts of your
countrymen to introduce anarchy and all its attendant
horrors into this kingdom, neither will I recall to your
memory the impudent menace of Le Brun to appeal
from the British Cabinet to the British nation with a

view to separate them, and, if possible, induce the latter to unite with your Executive Council against the former. Vain and preposterous as was the idea, your Convention adopted it with one accord. From such ministers, and from such legislators, what good can possibly result? It was a menace not less atrocious than indecent and impolitic. It meant insult to the Cabinet and fraud to the nation; and what rendered it more remarkable was that it came from a man who, in 1787, supported in a journal that scarcely maintained him the despotism of Joseph II., and who was actually in treaty with the Court of Bruxelles, in March 1791, to return and establish a paper in Brabant in favour of the late Emperor! If, however, it had been merely the threat of an individual, it would have deserved no notice, but it received the sanction of your Legislature. The two decrees which the Convention passed in November and December, offering fraternity to the people of all nations who would revolt from their respective Governments, and declaring that the French would never make peace with those who adhered to monarchy, were written in the same spirit, and for the same purport. It then became evident that this country had little to expect from the justice of those who had usurped the sovereign authority in France, and that the mistaken idea of Mr. Paine, '*that all Europe in insurrection could alone preserve your infant liberties,*' was to be supported at all hazards, regardless of everything that is dignified in politics and equitable in morals, and at the expense of public faith and private virtue. It was this proceeding, so unmanly in itself, that disgusted the British nation, and decided the people to come instantly forward in support of the Crown. It was not merely the Minister, and those who are in the habit of supporting his measures, but those also that opposed him, who perceived and acknowledged that mischief was intended. They added their strength to that of the Government, and, making common cause with the Administration, secured the internal peace of the country and baffled the designs of the Executive Council. Surely, my dear Sir, the emissaries from France, and particularly M. Chauvelin, of whose guilt and incapacity you and I have but one opinion, have much to answer for should a day of reckoning ever arrive. If they had not represented to their employers that the people of England were ripe for revolt, I do not believe that Le Brun would have acted as he did, or that the Convention would have been so precipitate with their declaration of war; not that I mean to palliate their conduct, but to state the gross and impudent manner in which this country was calumniated and belied, and yours imposed upon, by men in whom truth was at that moment more a duty, if possible, than at any other. We have so often canvassed this subject together, and you have so often lamented the little credit given to your more faithful representations of the temper of the people in England, that I risk nothing of your friendship by the asperity with which I treat your Convention and Executive Council, and especially when I remind you that they both firmly believed that the declaration of hostilities at Paris would be the signal of a general insurrection in Great Britain. Events have proved how egregiously they were deceived.[1]

There is another man who has had a considerable share in bringing on the present contest with this country, but who, by keeping most artfully behind the

[1] 'Le Brun was zealously employed in gathering up all the threads of opposition and discontent which existed in the British Empire into his own hands, with the intention of overthrowing the existing constitution by a sudden move. The focus of these intrigues was the French Embassy in London itself.'—Sybel, *History of Europe*, ii. 247.

curtain, has escaped the animadversions he merits. I allude to the Abbé Sieyès, whom I knew at Paris, and who, even in 1790, insisted on the necessity of, and undertook to demonstrate the advantages that would result from, a rupture between France and England. It was not mere common-place declamation, but serious arguments that he urged, and urged them with as much vehemence as a man of his dark, undermining, and phlegmatic character is capable. I well remember with what cool and deliberate malice his opinions on almost every subject were given, and I prophesied at the time that sentiments of humanity would never be a bar to the projects he suggested. The diversified classes of the nobility among you were so numerous, and their privileges and exemptions were so incompatible with the general interests of society, that the humiliation of the one and the abolition of the other were sacrifices due to justice, as well as to the people who had felt the insolence and oppression of both. But the Abbé did not think that humiliation and deprivation were sufficient; his resentment extended to life as well as to fortune, and the privileged classes were to be punished with death. When it was first proposed to make a general sweep of all the titles throughout the kingdom and destroy all distinctions, he added, 'Ce n'est pas la noblesse, mais les nobles, qu'il faut détruire.'[1] The hint has not been thrown away. Thousands have since perished, not for their follies or even for their crimes, but for the vices of the Government, for the accident of birth, and for the errors of their education. Really, my dear Sir, in retracing these enormities my heart weeps tears of blood! I have recurred to these events because they strike most forcibly on minds which, candid and benevolent like yours, cannot descend to the baseness of justi-

---

[1] See *Mémoires de Lafayette*, iv. 37.

fying guilt by the consideration of benefits to be derived from crime. The four last years of French history would be a valuable lesson to posterity if it was in the nature of man to profit by the experience of others; but, unhappily, every individual must purchase the knowledge that is to improve and conduct him through life, and the purchase is frequently made at a period so late, and on terms so very disadvantageous, that it is more fit to serve as an example to his children than as an acquisition of importance to himself. Be assured, it will give me great pleasure at all times to hear from you.

### MR. MILES TO CAPTAIN BALL[1]

September 12, 1793

A French bishop, whose name I forbear to mention in compassion to his misfortunes, required our Government to punish the author of some paragraphs which, in a daily paper, lamented the dangerous increase of the emigrants, and condemned in general terms the conduct of a class of men who, instead of flying in all directions on the first alarm, ought to have stayed at home, as Englishmen would have done under similar circumstances, and have defended their acres and wives and children. I will not comment on the folly which imagined that Ministers, who are daily exposed to the most severe animadversions in the public prints, could prevent the appearance of similar strictures on the conduct of French refugees; but the application made by the Bishop suggests a strong presumption that these gentlemen felt the justice of the reproach.[2] If ever the pre-

---

[1] Captain of H.M.S. 'Cleopatra,' better known at a later date as Admiral Sir Alexander Ball, First Commissioner of Malta.

[2] The paragraphs here alluded to were written by Mr. Miles, and appeared in the *True Briton*, July 5, 1793. The complaint against the editor was made by the Bishop of Saint-Pol-de-Léon.

tensions of this worst description of emigrants to our hospitality be examined, it will be found that the confidence they received has been abused; that these people sit in vindictive judgment on such of their hapless countrymen as were anxious to preserve a medium between despotism and anarchy, but who have failed in the laudable attempt and have become outcasts; that they would now exact from the valour of England, in defiance of the principles of justice, the full restoration of tyranny and superstition on the shores they have abandoned; and that, at this moment, they fondly believe that the sole object of the war is to reinstate them in the power they have forfeited and in the possessions they have dishonoured. Ministers, when awakened from their dream, will ultimately execrate, as I do, the conduct of the blind and infatuated persons who have contributed fatally to mislead them.[1]

I aver it as a fact, founded on history, and confirmed by the knowledge of every candid and well-informed mind, that the Revolution is to be attributed to the French nobility, laity and clergy, and to the unexampled profligacy in which several of them lived. It is to those who rendered this dreadful expedient, this terrible

[1] 'In all this business I am incessantly reminded of the old fable of the fox who had lost his tail, and proposed to all the others to cut off theirs. The leading Democrats in Paris wish us to become Democrats. The unfortunate emigrants speculate with complacency on the troubles extending themselves to England, though England is their only place of refuge; and the partisans of the allied powers engaged in a disastrous war are impatient also to see us share their calamity. Our line is plain, and, unless God Almighty intends for some unknown purpose to send all mankind back to a state of barbarism, I still hope that the storm may be weathered; but I think it blows too hard to talk at present of retirement and "pensions" with so much philosophy as you do in your last letter. I am plagued to death, and put to expense also, by these unfortunate troops of emigrants.'—Lord Auckland to Sir Morton Eden, Hague, November 27, 1792. See *Auckland Correspondence*, ii. 470.

remedy, a measure of necessity by their prodigality and vexations, that the responsibility for all the mischiefs and all the horrors that have ensued must be assigned. These men, in fact, are the authors of the Revolution; not the blind misguided rabble, or even the factious and unprincipled anarchists who headed that rabble in 1789. The direful change in France has been produced by the highest orders in society, by those who, with their families and dependents, lived in splendour and pomp on the plunder of their country, whose dissolute manners were a scandal to religion and morals, and who, having basked in the sunshine of the Court of Versailles, sharing its profusion, have been partakers of its crimes. Revolutions originate in vicious and corrupt Governments. The huge and terrific mass, which cannot now be contemplated without horror, would have remained passive and inert under judicious legislation and moderate restraint. It is now in motion with a force that appears irresistible, and with an irregularity that defies prescience to ascertain its direction. Hence the abhorrence in which I hold the Court of Versailles, whose bankruptcy has produced calamities of an extent and duration unparalleled in history, and which, after having deluged France with blood, has now plunged our country in a war, the issue of which it is impossible to foresee. But for the wanton abuse of power by that Court, with its scandalous profusion, rapacity, and profligacy, the monarchy of France would still be in existence; whilst Europe, preserved from the dreadful convulsions which agitate it from one extremity to the other, would most probably have continued in the full enjoyment of peace, order, and security. It is to those who love the cause of humanity, upon whose virtuous minds the happiness and freedom of mankind have an honourable and permanent hold, and in whose estimation the *people* count for something, that I would appeal to pardon the warmth, or, it may be, the intemperance with which I deprecate the fatal consequences of guilt, ignorance, and folly; but I make no apology to the cold-blooded few who, by the arbitrary expression of their will, consign millions to death, as caprice, or interest, or ambition may dictate. Ever, dear Ball, in affection yours.

### MR. MILES TO MR. JOHN LOVEDON[1]

September 15, 1793

I mean no disrespect to the Duke of York when I say that the nomination of his Royal Highness to the command-in-chief of an army on whose operations the welfare of this country and, in some sort, the fate of Europe may depend, is extremely injudicious. The friends of Government say that it will have a good effect to place a Prince of the Blood at the head of the army, the plain English of which is, that he is to act as a talisman on his enemies, who, at the very mention of his name, are to lay down their arms and shrink into so many nonentities. The very sight of a Prince of the Blood is to intimidate and awe the legions of France—fighting under what they call and believe to be the banners of Liberty—into a surrender of their zeal, prejudices, and arms! This is bad reasoning. It is not high birth, but splendid talents and great military experience that are necessary to conduct an army in the field against France—provided it is meant to win the battle. It does not become me to pronounce on the former, but I feel no difficulty in saying that the inexperience of his Royal Highness, combined with

[1] M.P. for Abingdon.

other no less weighty reasons, form insuperable objections to his having such a command. In saying this, I say little more than what all know and feel to be just, though all have not sufficient virtue to publicly avow what they feel and know to be right. Weigh these observations well in your own mind, reflect well upon them in conjunction with all the various circumstances connected with them, and then say if you will not feel bold enough to do in Parliament what you acknowledge out of it ought to be done. Set an example at once of firmness, consistency, and patriotism, by moving for the recall of his Royal Highness, and follow that motion up by leave for a Bill to prevent any of the royal family from henceforward commanding in chief by sea or land. You own it ought to be so, and you curse the folly of having sent the Duke of York to Flanders. If so, why not act as you think? Be assured that I will support out of doors what you may propose within.[1]

### Mr. Miles to Mr. Pitt

September 16, 1793

It occurs to me that much advantage may be derived from my transmitting Lord Hood's proclamation on the 28th of last month to Madame de Montgeroult, with some observations of my own on the equity of the British Cabinet in directing that possession of Toulon should only be taken in trust for the son of the late King, and to be surrendered whenever monarchy, as it was accepted by Louis XVI. in 1789,

[1] 'When the intelligence reached St. Petersburg, in 1793, that the Duke of York was appointed commander-in-chief of the army to be employed on the Continent, Catherine exclaimed, "Je vois bien que Monsieur Pitt aime mieux sa place que sa patrie." '—*Letter to the Prince of Wales*, 1808, p. 83, by W. A. Miles.

should be re-established in France. The lady above mentioned has very extensive connections in Paris, and has been much engaged in political intrigue since the Revolution. She is decidedly in favour of monarchy; she is besides active, enterprising, and indefatigable; and I feel assured, from what I know of the sentiments of a numerous party at Paris, and of her zeal and capacity, that some thousands of Lord Hood's proclamation translated into French, with a very short address to the people, would have an almost instantaneous and happy effect in that metropolis.[1]

### *MR. MILES TO M. NOËL*

London: September 17, 1793

I wrote to you, my dear Sir, on the 10th instant, under cover, as you desired, in answer to your letter of the 16th of last month, and my resuming the pen so early is merely to inquire what effect you think the proclamation of Lord Hood at Toulon, on the 28th of last month, will have upon the minds of your countrymen. It is there expressly said that nothing more is required than the re-establishment of monarchy in France, as it was accepted by Louis XVI. in 1789, and that Toulon will only be kept in trust until the son of the late King is restored to the throne. You will perceive from hence that it is the wish of the British

---

[1] 'Considering that the sections of Toulon, by the Commissioners whom they have sent to me, have made a solemn declaration in favour of Louis XVII. and a monarchical Government, and that they will use their utmost efforts to break the chains which fetter their country, and re-establish the constitution as it was accepted by their defunct sovereign in 1789, I repeat, by this present declaration, that I take possession of Toulon, and shall keep it solely as a deposit for Louis XVII., and that only till peace is re-established in France, which I trust is not far distant.'
—Proclamation, August 28, 1793. Quoted by Alison, *History of Europe*, iv. 78.

Cabinet to restore order, not despotism, to your distracted country; and, unless a total revolution has taken place in men's minds, I should suppose that the declaration of his Lordship will have a happy effect in France, and stimulate the friends of limited monarchy to unite and declare for the infant Prince. I know many who conformed to circumstances, and became Republicans after the 10th of August. The necessity of the times required this submission. The scaffold or concession was their only alternative. The question for present consideration is whether it be not better for France to return to the form of government the first adopted, and terminate by that means a calamitous war, than persevere in the wild and impracticable projects of bad men, and thus accomplish the final destruction of your acquired liberty. A favourable opportunity presents itself to terminate her multiplied misfortunes, and you may confide in my sincerity when I assure you that no personal good fortune to myself could give me so much pleasure as to see this desirable event take place. A rational system of government in France can alone secure the repose of Europe; and, until this necessary measure is adopted and established, it would be extremely hazardous in the allied powers to sheathe the sword. I deliver myself to you without reserve, because I respect your understanding, and I have a confidence in the purity of your intentions.

I answered the letter of Madame de Montgeroult dated Baden, the 24th ultimo. It would give me great pleasure to know her sentiments on the subject of this communication.

## M. NOËL TO MR. MILES

Venice: September 27, 1793

I have just received, my dear Sir, the letter you did me the honour to write to me on the 10th instant, and I recognise with pleasure the confirmation of the friendly sentiments which you have kindly accorded to me. I much wish that I could receive this assurance from your lips; but, unhappily, there is every appearance of our separation being continued, for events do not seem of a nature to permit a speedy *rapprochement*. You remind me of all the efforts I have made to maintain peace; the result has shown you that they have been ineffectual, and my prudence has been charged with timidity and discouragement. I beg you to attribute the warmth with which I have written to the attachment I feel for my country and to my certain knowledge of facts. With regard to yourself, dear Sir, I shall always consider it a duty to express to you my gratitude, and I esteem myself happy in preserving the friendship of a virtuous and sensible philosopher, who pities the errors and the misfortunes of humanity. I have despatched your reply to Madame de Montgeroult. Monsieur de Montgeroult has just died in prison at Mantua.[1] Alas! my friends are almost all dead or in fetters. Brissot is in prison in the Abbaye, and they urge his trial. Condorcet has fled, and is in concealment. Pétion is arrested. Biron is in the Abbaye. I know not what has become of Dumouriez. One of his commissaries, whom he has abandoned, was amongst my best friends. I am cruelly tried. Le Brun is transferred to the Revolu-

---

[1] 'Dès la fin de Septembre, l'infortuné Montgeroult avait été trouvé mort dans sa cellule. Le *Moniteur* du 8 Octobre, 1793, semble indiquer qu'il avait mis fin à ses jours.'—Ernouf, p. 178.

tionary Tribunal, and I fear is in danger. It appears to me that it is for the assailants to make proposals of peace; but, depend upon it, we shall never receive the law from the foreigner, and the French will perish to the last man sooner than submit to such humiliation. This is my profession of faith, as it is also of all my compatriots, who, as you say, have yielded to you the *monkeys*. Le Brun has escaped from prison. I have lost sight of Sieyès for so long that I am unable to justify him from your imputations; all I can assure you is that for a long time he has taken little part in public affairs, and that he lives almost in retirement. I think you judge him very severely. *Salut!*

### MR. MILES TO MR. LONG
October 28, 1793

The following is an extract from a letter I received yesterday, dated the 12th instant. It is from a Minister Plenipotentiary of the French Republic at a Foreign Court:[1]

'Vous me demandez quel effet a produit sur mes concitoyens la proclamation de Lord Hood? C'est une haine immortelle pour la Maison de Bourbon et pour toute autre qui voudra nous donner un roi. C'est la ferme résolution de ne jamais recevoir la loi de l'étranger et de nous battre avec acharnement jusqu'au dernier homme, et jusqu'au dernier assignat. C'est en un mot de nous venger de la guerre de cannibales qu'on nous fait.'

I communicate the above to you, that Mr. Pitt may know the sentiments that prevail on the other side of the water. It is needless to tell you that you are the only person to whom this communication is made.

[1] The Abbé Noël at Venice. See Letter, September 17.

When I suggested to Mr. Pitt six weeks since the project of having a number of Lord Hood's proclamations distributed in France, it was in the persuasion that the Constitution, as it is called, of 1789 was the general wish of that country. I am afraid I am mistaken. Obstinate, however, as the French appear to be, I think that unanimity among ourselves will give force and ensure success to our military efforts and negotiations abroad. This is the object I have in view in the publication just gone to press;[1] and, if the bulk of the people are kept quiet, undisturbed by the arts of faction, if provisions, especially bread, are kept at low prices, I do not see that you have much occasion for alarm at home. I have proved by a string of facts and strong reasoning that it was not in the power of Ministers to avoid the war. You will perceive throughout the book a steady and determined zeal in favour of order and good government united to a proper degree of contempt for bad administration. I have written with some asperity against the emigrants, because I know that they intrigue and cabal. There is a vagabond adventurer amongst us; he parades Bond Street daily, he has contrived to get introduced into some good English houses, and he pretends to be esteemed by Lord Gower. I knew this man at Paris, where he arrived from the South of France in search of adventure on the Revolution breaking out. Lafayette gave him employment until his real character was discovered. He then applied to the Tuileries, and solicited charity. Afterwards he found his way to England, but not until he had apparently enriched himself in the affair of the 10th of August. He has spoken to me in the streets here, but I refuse to recognise him. You may rely upon it that he is not the

[1] *The Conduct of France towards Great Britain Examined.*

only man of that description in this country. I could say much against these gentry, but I will not trespass upon you further than to assure you I will not spare them.

### Mr. Miles to Mr. Pitt

November 28, 1793

An opinion has gone forth that you have wantonly plunged the country into war. It is to refute this opinion that I have given the statement of facts in the volume which accompanies this letter. In pronouncing on its execution you will have the goodness to recollect that it was written in the course of a very few weeks and at intervals of ease from pain. The letter quoted on page 29 was addressed to the Duke of Leeds, and the person alluded to is the Count de Romanzow. I had also much conversation to the same effect with the Prince Galitzin, in whose company I passed six weeks at Aschaffenburg, the country residence of the Elector of Mayence, in the autumn of 1789. I lament very much that this circumstance did not occur to me in 1791, when I published my pamphlet on 'The Expediency and Justice of Prescribing Bounds to the Russian Empire,' for, though my papers were at Paris, I could have had a copy of my letter from the Foreign Office.[1]

It is not in my power, Sir, to describe to you the extreme impatience I feel that this contest may be soon over, because I am apprehensive that, if prolonged, the consequences will be most detrimental to this country. It is for the interest of both France and England that

---

[1] The letter in question refers to an attempt to open negotiations with England for a *secret treaty* with Russia. Mr. Miles was sounded by the Russian Ambassador, Count Romanzow, at Frankfort, as to the practicability of *bribing* English members of Parliament in the interests of St. Petersburg. See the Introduction, p. 35.

we should be at peace and in alliance. The sincere personal regard I feel for yourself and for your talents leads me to believe that the nation has everything to hope from your patriotism and probity.

### THE DUKE OF LEEDS TO MR. MILES

North Mimms; December 5, 1793

I beg to return you my best thanks for the publication which you have had the goodness to send me. I did not quit it till I had read it through. I recollect perfectly the letter alluded to on page 29, and am not without my suspicions that what was at that time only hinted at was afterwards carried into effect. The book itself does great honour both to your abilities and political sentiments respecting this country and France. What can possess Government, unless the spirit of absurdity, to suffer such numbers of French still to remain here I know not, for some of the privileged orders now among us I take to be full as bad as any of the *sans-culottes* formerly attached to Chauvelin's mischievous mission.

### MR. MILES TO M. NOËL

December 6, 1793

I have written to you, my dear Noël, through the channel by which I have often requested you to direct your letters, and I shall be impatient until I hear of your having received *that* letter. It relates to what you and I have most at heart. If your ideas coincide with mine, or if you think that what I have suggested is practicable, you will make an effort to carry them into execution. The winter is the proper season for such an undertaking—the worst business of war suffers a suspension. Men have a respite from carnage, and can listen without risk to the dictates of humanity. But peace, I am aware, will never take place until France has recovered from her delirium and renounces the project of subverting all the old Governments in Europe. Let her leave other nations to themselves. In proportion as men discover and feel the pressure of grievances within their power to remedy, be assured they will correct them; they are not to be forced even into happiness against their inclinations. The battle of Jemmapes did your country an infinity of mischief. France became intoxicated with her successes, and bad men, profiting by her enthusiasm, led her further into error, lost her the affections of the Low Countries which had aided her, and deprived their inhabitants of the liberty which they had twice obtained. If you had left the Brabançons to their priests and to their superstitions, these would have taken care to keep the Austrians at a respectable distance. It is not only impolitic but iniquitous to force religious opinions. What would Sémonville have said of the justice of the Turkish Government, if, on his arrival at Constantinople, they had insisted on his being circumcised previous to their receiving his credentials?

I must entreat you to pardon the warmth with which I have declaimed in my recent publication against the depraved state of morals in France, the necessary and unavoidable consequence of a vicious Government. You will perceive to whom the last letter in the appendix is addressed,[1] and, though my censure is certainly general, your own discernment will inform you that exceptions are meant, and that you are among those exceptions. I cannot help entertaining a strong

---

[1] This letter, addressed to M. Noël, and dated October 26, 1793, is too long for reproduction here. See *Conduct of France*, &c., p. 186.

hope that the degeneracy of French morals will be succeeded by an entire change, now that a revolution so universal has ensued—indeed, it cannot be otherwise; and I should envy those who, a century hence, will have the felicity of seeing a new and respectable order of things arise in a country which has been the sink of profligacy and crime. I shall not live to see this desirable change; but it must happen, and I give you joy of an event which must in its consequences be beneficial to the whole human race.

### Mr. Long to Mr. Miles

December 7, 1793

I like many parts of your book much. I think, as I told you before, you are too severe upon the emigrants, although there are many whose conduct it is impossible to approve. It is very strong and pointedly written, and will certainly be of service.

### Mr. Miles to Mr. Long

December 7, 1793

I am much flattered by your letter of this date, as I take it for granted that with your own unaffected sentiments on my book you convey the approbation of Mr. Pitt.

It is to be regretted on moral grounds that Mr. Fox has so far lowered himself as to accept support from a voluntary subscription. The triumph of Mr. Pitt was never secure till that moment, and I will answer for it that Mr. Fox will risk his resurrection in this world, whatever he may experience in the next. If he had resisted the offer and braved poverty, he would have risen high in the esteem even of his enemies and been a thorn in the side of Ministers; but he wants fortitude, not courage, and in wanting fortitude he wants everything that is necessary to constitute the head of a party in times like these.

With respect to the emigrants, I cannot change my opinion, because it is founded on evidence. I tell you again that the fairest spoken of the crew would turn upon you to-morrow. I transmitted an account from Paris in 1790 of what was going on in England, Ireland, and Scotland. I communicated at that period what the views of France were, and, if every proper advantage has not been taken of my information, it is not my fault. Believe me when I tell you that we are not yet out of danger; our army in the Netherlands will not be allowed to sleep all the winter. I will not distress you by the mention of Toulon. Our Channel fleet is commanded by a man[1] so addicted to detail, so frivolous and yet so formal, that he would pick out a rope-yarn before he saw a cable, and stumble over it sooner. Such men are fit to measure tape behind counters. I would not say so much but that I know from whence his support arises, and it is from my regard for Mr. Pitt that I have said it. Nor am I less concerned that the army should be under the command of the Duke of York. You know my sentiments on this subject. I shall only add that, should he be taken, his ransom will be a peace at once ignominious and insecure. That Mr. Pitt should be so hampered frets me, for I am anxious for his success. He stands so high in public opinion that he may dictate in defiance of the Cabinet, which, by the way, he may throw off and whistle back as a huntsman does his hounds, for in the present situation of the country no party can injure him. I could say much on this subject. I have suggested to a very independent man in Parliament of my

[1] Lord Howe.

acquaintance the idea of a bill to prevent, under the pretence of personal regard, any of the royal family from commanding out of the kingdom, for this is not the moment for trifling with the interests of the nation, nor is its independence to be risked out of complaisance to any family whatsoever. My mind is so impregnated with this matter that I cannot lose sight of it, and, as I am no stranger to the Duke of York's conduct and character, I am the less disposed to confide in his prudence or capacity. I have no objection to your communicating this letter to Mr. Pitt or your telling him my intentions, as I should be sorry to do anything that would give him annoyance. It is my wish to fix him in power, if not from a full conviction, yet at least in the hope that he would not abuse it.

### MR. MILES TO MR. PITT

December 16, 1793

It is not for me to decide what degree of credit is due to the inclosed,[1] or whether it is of sufficient consequence to deserve your notice. The very warm interest I take in the success of your administration is at once my motive and excuse for transmitting this intelligence. Monsieur De La Colombe, from whom I have received it, is a native of Auvergne, and he is disposed to return to his country, where he will answer for a powerful diversion in favour of Louis XVII., provided the combined powers will consent that a *limited* monarchy shall be the future government in France.[2]

---

[1] The 'Declaration' on the part of the Cevennes, &c. See March 11 and July 10.

[2] '.... Et que le midi, qui était primitivement républicain ardent, n'ayant point d'inquiétude de la part des étrangers, est disposé à revenir à la monarchie limitée.'—*Lettres de M. de Talleyrand*, 8 Octobre, 1793. *Revue d'Histoire Diplomatique*, Paris, 1890, No. 1.

He has charged me to add that, if such a promise had been made previous to the siege of Lyons, that city would have been saved from destruction. By his account the inhabitants had been promised men and ammunition by the King of Sardinia, and on the faith of these assurances from the Court of Turin they engaged in the enterprise which, through the breach of promise on the part of his Sardinian Majesty, has terminated so fatally.[1] I am authorised to say that, if you should adopt the idea, he will at his own expense, instead of embarking for America as he proposed, proceed instantly to Auvergne and engage for an army of at least 24,000 men assembling and proclaiming the child, or, in case of the death of the young Prince, his uncle, Monsieur, as King of France. I must again solicit your pardon for this intrusion, and entreat you to place it to the account of my anxiety for the rapid termination of this sanguinary and destructive war.

*M. NOËL TO MR. MILES*

December 26, 1793

I have the honour to acknowledge your several letters, dated from October 26 to December 6. My position will not permit me to enter into any political discussion, but I regret sincerely that two nations, made to esteem each other, should mutually destroy themselves through the caprice of a Court and the vanity of two or three royal houses in Europe.

In order to support your views, I am impressed with the desire to make known in Paris your philanthropic

[1] 'Vos Piémontais sont de terribles gens; ils ne défendent point Lyon, et c'est là leur affaire. Ils ne reçoivent de l'Angleterre deux cent mille livres sterling que pour cela, et ils n'avancent point. Je crois que c'est pour toucher le subside plus longtemps.'—*Lettres de M. de Talleyrand*, 8 Octobre, 1793.

proposal, but it is at this very moment that I recognise with grief the impossibility of despatching an extraordinary courier on account of the most cowardly of plots. How could you expect, my dear friend, that I can believe in the pacific sentiments of your compatriots when cowardly and sanguinary assassinations are meditated against my fellow-citizens and myself? I must inform you of what passes here to the disgrace of the English name. All the hostile legations united with the scum of the emigrants conspire against us. Three couriers, to my certain knowledge, have been sent to post assassins on all points of the Valteline by which French couriers and travellers are wont to pass. The lives of all the French at this place are in danger. I am surrounded with spies. You have three ships of war in the Gulf whose sailors are at the disposal of your Resident.[1] It is not my intention to leave. If I should succumb, the Republic would not perish; but I have strong reason to count on the vigilance of the Venetian Government, and I hope that its wisdom will spare a fresh dishonour to the English name, already sullied by the assassinations at Genoa and Toulon. It was on the arrival of your Worsley that these infernal plots were first conceived; it is Worsley who is the soul of this project for an assassination which will be denounced throughout Europe; it is his criminal gold which hires the two vile counsellors who direct it—the one is a Frenchman named d'Hancarville, a scoundrel chased from almost every country in Europe, the other is d'Entraygues, a cowardly deserter from the popular cause, a titled scoundrel, selling himself for money to princes, and leading a life of immorality without shame. *Voilà le noble couple avec lequel Worsley s'est associé.* He

[1] Sir Richard Worsley, Bart.

thus inaugurates his political position here in a manner to forfeit all consideration.

Whatever may happen, my dear Sir, in the interests of a cause so excellent, I will brave—if only I receive the order from Paris—the poniards of assassins, the rigour of the season, and the dangers that would arise among the depths of snow, in order to co-operate in your philanthropic anxieties, only too happy if at the peril of my life I could contribute to pour a little balm on the wounds of suffering humanity. Your reflections on the battle of Jemmapes are judicious; but, believe me, the intoxication of which you speak has been in a great measure the work of emissaries from foreign powers, who made every effort to draw us beyond that success, and perhaps also of that base Dumouriez, whom I never regarded as a great man, and whose ambition, according to all appearance, is less visible in the courage of a French soldier than as the blind instrument of his own secret designs. One cause of the persecutions which I have experienced has been the boldness with which I pointed out certain individuals, who, exaggerating affairs, assumed, as I thought, the mask of patriotism and of philosophy only to render execrable both the one and the other, and to mislead the people with the view of thus prolonging our troubles at home. Events have proved that my *coup d'œil* was just. Before I left Paris I indicated these men to Danton and Barère. Since that day they have been unmasked by Danton and Robespierre. I have but a slight acquaintance with the latter, although we were almost companions in our studies, but I believe that his morals are pure and modest. As to the former, whom they picture in Europe under such hideous features, I will content myself with saying to you that he is a good son, a good husband, a good father, a good relative, a good friend; and I leave you, who lay so much stress on good morals, to infer the consequences. As to your attack on French morals, believe me, my dear Mr. Miles, that generalities can always retort with advantage. The English, who are so easily corrupted by their love of gold, would find themselves perhaps justly exposed to the same declamations. In general, European morals are bad—there is no question on this point.

*December* 27.—I have this moment received your letter of the 10th instant. I will take care to write to Geneva according to your request, and I would advise you to keep to the 'Moniteur.' I heartily wish I could further your views in respect to the pamphlets you desire, but my position is such that I can scarcely get anything from Paris, the sea being no longer free, and my packets cannot reach me by Switzerland, since they cross the Milanese territory, where they would be intercepted. I know nothing of the arrest of Chauvelin. Nor do I know anything of Descorches,[1] unless he is still at Constantinople. I am also ignorant of the fate of Le Brun, but I have too much reason to think that he has purchased an asylum among our enemies. I cannot agree with you in your animadversions on the French people. You confound the nation with the Court. The nation has always been frank in its character, naturally so; and its present distrust of others is due to the innumerable treacheries of which it has been the victim, and which were perpetrated by men of the former *régime*, who assumed the mask of patriotism only to serve their own passions, or else to bring about the failure of the Revolution.

[1] '*Ci-devant* Marquis de St. Croix, formerly the French Minister at Liège, and brother-in-law of M. Talon.'—W. A. M.

We must remember that generalities are always unjust; that, according to the remark of Rousseau, the inhabitants of large cities resemble one another in that they are equally corrupt, and that the people who have the least right to reproach others are the English, whose corrupt use of money, the worst of all vices, has become the principal resource of their Government. If you saw our papers you would judge very differently of the people whose traits of heroism and of disinterestedness draw from me tears of tenderness and of joy. I have just heard of the capture of Toulon. This event may smooth difficulties, for it would be impossible for us to listen to any negotiation with a power whose troops were still on our territory; it is a general resolution, common to every Frenchman, and from which none of them will ever depart.[1]

[1] 'During the night of the 16th of December, 1793, the English fort was attacked by a picked column and taken after a desperate resistance. The expectations of Bonaparte were immediately fulfilled. The allied council of war unanimously declared the place to be no longer tenable, and ordered the speedy embarkation of the troops. The consternation of the inhabitants, who were wholly taken by surprise, was boundless, and was but little calmed by the offer of the admirals to take every one on board the fleet who had reason to fear for his safety under Republican rule. Thousands thronged to the quays with their hastily collected goods, every one tried to get before the others, and in the crowd women were separated from their husbands and mothers from their children, and several of the overloaded boats turned over and buried the fugitives in the waves. Night came on and covered all this misery with darkness; the troops had already evacuated the forts on the hills, and the Republicans soon began to throw shells from thence on the confused mass of people, whose crowding now became so desperate that the ships were obliged on their part to fire upon the fugitives to prevent a fatal overloading of their vessels. At last, on the 19th, everything was at an end. More than 4,000 Toulonese, including all who had in any way taken part in the revolt, were crowded together in the ships. The English took with them a part of the French men-of-war, and set fire at the last moment to several others, as well as to a portion of the arsenal. When the columns of the Republicans marched into the city they found the streets deserted, the houses closed, and the whole place as quiet as the grave.'—Sybel, iii. 247.

### Mr. Miles to Mr. Aust

December 30, 1793

His sublime Excellency has arrived without his 550 wives, and, what is of greater moment to this country, without an intention to stay beyond six or eight weeks. I am much grieved to find that this son of Mahomet does not mean to establish here a longer residence, as I cannot but think it is practicable to have the Black Sea opened to us; and, as Spain and Turkey are as yet unexplored mines of wealth to this country, and well worthy the notice of Ministers, these latter will be highly criminal if they do not endeavour to enter into a commercial treaty with both without delay. If the French establish their Republic *malgré* the coalesced powers—and I am disposed to believe that this mischief to Europe cannot be prevented—the importation of all British manufactures will be prohibited, and, having everything within themselves, they will require nothing from us.

The printed letter dated Marseilles, the 11th instant, in the Bruxelles paper of the 17th cannot be authentic, though the fact may be true. The post is almost six days from Marseilles to Paris. How could a letter dated the 11th reach Bruxelles, which is seventy leagues farther than Paris, so as to be printed on the 17th? Reflect, and own that the printer of the circumstance deceives, or has been deceived.

### Mr. Miles to Sir Edward Newenham

December 30, 1793

You perpetually distress and vex me, dear Newenham, by misunderstanding my motive. *Je ne suis pas un écrivain aux gages; je ne le serais jamais.*

The productions of my pen are volunteer services, to which any Minister who deserves them shall be welcome without fee or reward; nor would the reversion of the Viceroyship of Ireland engage me to pledge myself as a writer to any Administration. I am much flattered by the reception you say my book has met with in your country. It is tolerably well liked here. Mr. Pitt has acknowledged that it will do much good, which is my object, not profit, and, thinking as I do that he has the interest of the nation at heart, and was forced into the war much against his inclinations, I will do everything to serve him under the conviction that in so doing I am serving my country. But do not mistake me, Newenham, do not suppose that I will make writing in support of this or any other Administration a trade, and do not suggest either to Mr. Pitt or to your Lord-Lieutenant the idea of my going to Ireland to support Government with my pen; for I have no wish to become an inhabitant of your country, nor should anything in the gift of the Crown induce me to pitch my tent even in Dublin. I dread the issue of the war. We shall be duped, plundered, and defeated, I am afraid. Adieu, and God bless you!

### Mr. Miles to Mr. Long

December 31, 1793

Do you recollect a passage in my letter of the 7th instant relative to Toulon? It has been wofully verified. I was told yesterday that the place had been evacuated, but, unwilling to furnish matter that might augment the general discontent, I heard it with sorrow and was silent. It is now no longer a secret, and the event must have a considerable effect on the public mind. A month has elapsed since I gave Mr. Pitt notice that 15,000 men were sent from Auvergne and the Cevennes, and from that neighbourhood, to the French army before Toulon. I also informed him that Carteaux was disposed to monarchy, and his being arrested favours the accuracy of my intelligence. At the commencement of hostilities I presented a proposal from several emigrants who are attached to a limited monarchy and were authorised by their countrymen to create a diversion in the South of France and raise an army of 30,000 men. They required no assistance from the coalesced powers, either in men, or money, or ammunition, and, from what I have since been informed, it is more than probable that Lyons would have been preserved, and of course Toulon, if this offer had been accepted.[1] The sole condition required was the release of Lafayette and his fellow-sufferers at Magdeburg; and, when it is considered that their detention could be of no advantage, it is without excuse that they were not restored to liberty. On the other hand, the benefit that might have resulted would have been important; every triumph of the French brings this Government into hazard, and it grieves me most sensibly to find crime triumphant. The failure at Corsica is a melancholy proof of the impolicy of allowing admirals commanding in chief to take relatives with them. The brother-in-law of Lord Hood was sent against Corsica. You know the lamentable issue of that expedition; it could scarcely be otherwise than unfortunate, for the man to whom it was entrusted is as dull and as heavy a lump of mortality, or rather of unkneaded dough, as ever Nature produced. Captain L—— is a good-natured

---

[1] 'At the beginning of the siege, and during the whole of October and November, the condition of the Republican army before Toulon was in the highest degree critical.'—Sybel, iii. 246.

man; I know him well; and so conscious is he of his own incapacity that I am sure he must have been astonished at the partiality of Lord Hood in sending him on that duty. No wonder that our military operations are unsuccessful! I know a variety of facts relating to the failure at Martinique as well as at Corsica, but I have most carefully preserved a strict silence on the occasion, and you are the only person to whom I have communicated my sentiments. I am sorry that my offer to put the Alps of France in motion was not received, as it must have influenced the war very considerably if these people had revolted. I have been extremely hurt by the silence of Lord Grenville. Good manners required an answer of some sort to the proposal transmitted to him from M. De La Colombe.

I am decidedly of opinion that no nation has a right to prescribe a form of government to another. A very considerable body of people in France are for a limited monarchy, and if the word republic is so offensive to our prejudices and our ears that we cannot bear the mention of it, and as we war in fact for discarded royalty, common prudence points out to us that the men the most capable of crushing Republicanism in France are the friends of limited monarchy. With those we should join; they are formidable and in credit; but as the red-hot Royalists detest the advocates for limited monarchy more than they do the Jacobins, and as our Government will see none, converse with none, and listen to the suggestions of none, except men of this description, the madness can only be corrected by experience, and sooner or later you will lament having allowed these people to influence our councils. They are more mischievous, and to the full as inimical to us as the Jacobins.

*Minute.*—No answer was ever given by Lord Grenville either to the declaration on the part of the Cevennes, Auvergne, &c., or to the letter from M. De La Colombe, dated March 11. This first offer was made through me. I took it to the office for Foreign Affairs, gave it to Mr. Aust, the Under-Secretary of State, and saw him take it in to the Cabinet, which was then sitting. The offer was repeated to Mr. Pitt on July 10. At the expiration of some months I received information that 15,000 of the Mountaineers, who were ready to declare in favour of limited monarchy, were, in consequence of the despondency in the French Alps, to be sent against Lyons, and that, if Lyons fell, Toulon would soon be evacuated by us, for the same force would march against this latter place. It was early in September when I transmitted this information to the Minister. Events have verified the intelligence. Lyons, which defended itself with a ferocity worthy of the animal whose name it resembles, was taken, and the catastrophe of Toulon can never be forgotten.—W. A. M.

### Mr. Miles to M. Noël

January 5, 1794

Your letter dated December 26th has just arrived and inspires me with the hope that our joint efforts will finally obtain the object for which I so ardently laboured last winter, and which I pledge myself to Heaven shall be yet accomplished if your friends in power at Paris will be temperate and sincere. Admonish Danton and Robespierre to be moderate; let them prove the justice of their dispute with Austria by the equity of their pretensions; and let them disavow and for ever renounce those sanguinary revolutionary doctrines which lead to the subversion of all government and of all order and subordination in society, and which, although sustaining their power to-day, may destroy it to-morrow.[1] The Low Countries, with the addition of Liège, may now become an independent state. I have some reason to believe that circumstances since I first proposed it have removed all that was offensive in the measure, and that it will not be strenuously insisted upon to restore them to their ancient tyrants. France does not want the Netherlands nor Savoy. Let your friends propose peace on such grounds as will prove their moderation and sincerity. I enclose you a variety of extracts from my book which may at first seem to bear hard on your countrymen, but if I have exaggerated the vices which, in my opinion, are the primary cause of the horrible excesses recently committed in France, I beg you to place it to an error in judgment, and not to a disposition to misrepresent. I have spoken with the same freedom of the Ministers in this country; and, accustomed to speak as I think, and to think for myself, my motives are just, however faulty may be my mode of expression. I am convinced that, if honourable men had come sooner into action, torrents of blood already shed would have been spared; but the spirit of intrigue and cabal which prevailed prevented the privileged orders from acting honestly, even as their ignorance prevented them from acting wisely, towards their country, and hence the crimes and follies that ensued. Let us hope that order and a pure and uncorrupt code of morals will ultimately succeed. I do not scruple to assert in all companies that France will rise a phœnix from her ashes. I stand alone in this opinion. All think that France will be crushed.

Be assured that the instant I receive a letter from yourself or from Danton, intimating a desire on the

[1] Danton and Robespierre were guillotined April 5 and July 28, 1794.

part of France to terminate the calamities of war in a manner suitable to the respective interests of both countries, I will see the Minister. This once done, I think Mr. Pitt will not hazard a further prosecution of the war. I am taking proper measures; but be moderate and just, return to order, rely on your efforts, and success must ensue if France will only be temperate and correct, and if vain punctilio and anger do not retard the business on your side. The further effusion of blood must be spared. Transmit my address without delay to Danton, and beg of him to indicate to me a town in Switzerland where I could converse with him on the subject of peace in the event of being sent by Mr. Pitt to confer confidentially with him on the best means of bringing about so desirable an event.

Robespierre I believe to be incorrupt, but he seems to be vindictive, and not very averse to the shedding of blood. That he is decidedly in favour of a republic, that he is from principle averse to any other form of government, and holds kings in abhorrence, cannot be denied; but in the prosecution of his favourite object, and to gratify his vengeance on the friends of monarchy, he has become sanguinary and ferocious. Lusignan laments the death of Mirabeau, and idly supposes that were he living he would tranquillise matters in France and *contenir les esprits*. I differ from the *ci-devant* marquis. Mirabeau had no character. I knew him well, and though his firmness at Versailles when he said to the officer of the guard sent to disperse the States-General, 'Va dire à ton maître que nous ne sortirons pas d'ici qu'aux buts de baïonnettes,' accomplished the Revolution, yet he wanted that integrity and credit which could alone have assured to him the direction of an event which he certainly accelerated. Mirabeau had survived his popularity, and, had he not died a natural death, would have been massacred or compelled like many others to be a fugitive. He avowed himself to me decidedly in favour of an alliance with England. In common with the Spanish Ambassador, he was a friend to the Family Compact, and the Court of Madrid thought it right to recompense his suffrage in its interests. Lafayette, although you dislike him, was more to be depended upon; but he is, *pour ainsi dire, nul dans le monde—l'autre n'existe plus*. If Sieyès, Robespierre, and Danton could be brought to act in concert, and adopt as a principle what many of their countrymen in high credit in 1790 and 1791 approved and sincerely wished, namely, an alliance with England, they would deserve well of their country, also of the world and of posterity. Adieu, my dear Noël!

### Mr. Miles to Sir Edward Newenham
January 6, 1794

As to my going to Ireland, as you propose, it is out of the question. I will not pledge myself to write for any Minister, for I will reserve the right which I derive from Heaven to think for myself, and perhaps occasions might arise where the surrender of my judgment would be required to favour wrong or folly. While the servants of the Crown act properly they shall have my support, and no longer. But this is not the kind of support that pleases them; they require it unqualified, and expect that men should prostitute or resign their judgments. I will do neither while I can live without ortolans or venison and quench my thirst with table beer instead of claret. My table is as simple as my manners, and, being equally an enemy to affectation and corruption, I will browse rather than purchase luxuries at the expense of either truth or my understanding. With a code so severe I am ill qualified for your meridian, as I will certainly never degrade myself to the condition of an automaton and move at second hand. It is the profligacy so openly practised and so impudently avowed, the scandalous barter of conscience for places and pensions, that have excited the clamour for reform, and to which I am yet a decided friend; but this is *not* the season; men's minds have been unhinged and too much agitated of late, and the rabble and rascals of society are too much elated with the prospect of plunder and bloodshed, too vigilant for an occasion to dissolve the bonds and break the links that keep them in order, for the sober part of the community to engage in any enterprise at present of the kind. But a reform must sooner or later take place, and it had better be done *in* Parliament than *out* of it. Such are my sentiments, and, if Ministers do not adopt similar ones, they will repent of their indolence or of their guilt, and wofully rue it hereafter.

Toulon has been evacuated, and under such circumstances as reflect no great credit on Lord Hood. The massacres that have depopulated Lyons [1] will again be

---

[1] 'When some one remarked in the Parisian municipality that the entire destruction of Lyons would deal a deadly blow at French commerce in general, Hébert replied that trade and the arts were the born enemies of freedom, and that it was, moreover, in the interest of Paris not to allow so considerable a city as Lyons to exist beside it on French soil. His partisans quite agreed with his reasoning, that if, according to Couthon's report, the whole population of Lyons was unpatriotic, it must be exterminated without distinction . . . The demolition of the houses went on at a great pace, and in a short time 14,000 workmen were engaged in it, and entire streets and squares were levelled with the dust. . . . On the 4th of December the executions were carried on *en masse* by volleys of musketry. In seven butcheries of this kind 484 persons were killed, and simultaneously, during the month of September, 101 persons were guillotined in the city of Lyons, and in the department 1,600 according to the lowest, and 6,000 according to the highest estimate.'—Sybel, iii. 241, &c. See Prudhomme, *Révolution Française*, vi. 40.

repeated; oceans of blood will flow, crimes will be multiplied in France, and discontents renewed in England. The British army in Flanders, from which, by the by, the French will soon expel it, is confided to a man without genius, capacity, or experience, and not very exemplary in other respects. The expedition against Corsica failed because it was entrusted to an officer who has no other merit than that of being brother to Lady Hood, and whose professional talents would never have raised him if his promotion had depended upon his merit. I know him well. When I reflect on these appointments, I am not astonished at the failure of our enterprises; but I am vexed, because, as I am yet disposed to think well of Mr. Pitt, I cannot bear that he should have millstones about his neck at this crisis. I wish him to display the same glorious and unsubdued spirit that animated his father, and, like him, be the Minister and the saviour of his country. I swear that, in his place, I would make all Windsor crouch to me if the Court obstinately persisted to thwart the interests of my country. Adieu!

*MR. PENROSE*[1] *TO MR. MILES*

Florence—(without date)

I take the opportunity of Mr. East's return to send you my thanks for your long and interesting letter. The complexion of affairs is such as to make the opinion of every one who has means of being well informed of infinite value; and, although I am tempted to wish that our political situation may not be quite so alarming as you describe, yet I am aware that the progress of an expensive, disastrous, and, what is more to be feared, an inefficacious war, may reduce things *de pire en pire*, and

[1] Secretary to Mr. Wyndham, Minister Plenipotentiary at Florence.

when once the scene of destruction commences, who can say where it will end? The campaign is opened in Italy. Our last accounts from Piedmont are that General Devins has ordered a camp to be formed at Acqui of 24,000 men, 14,000 of which are already on the ground, one part encamped, and another preparing to march towards Dego, Cairo, and Savona, with provisions and heavy artillery. An advanced post of the French was lately taken by the Piedmontese, who mean to make it an offensive campaign. It amuses me much to see in our last papers from England a conjecture that the Spanish men-of-war would join ours in the Mediterranean and effectually block up the French fleet at Toulon, or destroy it should it attempt to come out, so notorious is it that in no one instance have the Spaniards shown a desire to co-operate in the general cause. Indeed, when the division of the Brest fleet was sailing for Toulon, Langaro, although commanding nearly twenty sail of the line, made no attempt to intercept it, and, what is still more strange, a sham fight between a Spanish seventy-four and some of the French ships actually took place, and the Spaniard was permitted to escape! Nothing has been done on land, not a shot exchanged for these three weeks, all which are strong symptoms of a negotiation for peace, which I am told from good authority is only retarded by a dispute about some formality. We daily expect the arrival of the French Minister, Myotte, of whom report speaks favourably. His secretary, and a commissary, formerly a merchant at Courtrai, have been here some time; they conduct themselves with meekness, and have nothing of the Jacobin or Terrorist about them. If you are alarmed by a prospect of *disette* in England, we are not here in the utmost plenty, if one may judge from the riots that have happened at Arezzo and Cortona and the discontent shown in this place. If anything should occur worthy of communication, you shall receive it.

### MRS. WARE[1] TO MR. MILES

Ghent: January 6, 1794

If I had ever been blessed with a lively imagination, the intense cold we have in this place would freeze every sense, and make me stupid, although Nature had not intended I should be so. We have removed into a tolerable habitation, but there is no getting rid of the grievance of ill-shutting doors and antique casements.

You ask for opinions relative to the war. All the officers with whom I have conversed are most heartily sick of the business; but, as to the privates, I really believe they consider it as they would any other war, and though, like other individuals, liable every hour to danger, think all men mortal except themselves. The fatal rock upon which all success of the last campaign split was the expedition to Dunkirk. Who was the original planner I know not, but it is certain that Prince Cobourg was against it, and said in strong terms to the Duke of York, 'Sir, only stay with me six weeks, I will then accompany you, and I will almost venture to affirm that we shall succeed.' By the division of the army, Maubeuge could not be taken; it was a most important post, and our troops returned from Dunkirk, as I am well informed, minus 10,000 men, including the sick. One shameful mismanagement I cannot help mentioning. The bread during that time delivered out to our soldiers was so bad and mouldy that it was thrown away and lay in heaps round the camp. Our Royal Duke used to boast at his table when he had any visitor from England of his hardships during the campaign,

[1] Wife of Captain Henry Ware, Royal Horse Guards Blue.

and yet the officers in his own regiment have told me that six mules laden with provisions followed his baggage. Do you think any nation can prosper under such a commander? And yet I fear there is not a chance but for the trial of another campaign. My heart sinks at the idea.

I should be disappointed if I did not think you expected me to tell you how I liked campaigning, and how I bear the dirt and the very few comforts to be found in a Flemish hotel, whether dignified with the name of royal or imperial. I will be honest, and confess that the cold and inconveniences are abundant. How you would laugh if I should tell you all the feelings of my mind during one hour's progress through the chill galleries of the English Convent at Bruges! All that Héloïse thought and felt, I believe, possessed my mind for some minutes, and I declare I hardly ever took Ware's arm with so much joy as on repassing the precincts of this region of solitude, melancholy, and despair; for, however the good nuns might speak cheerfully and talk of peace, I could think only of the 'death-like silence and the dread repose in such a habitation.' To turn to a brighter scene. We dined by invitation with the Bishop of Bruges, and I was well pleased with the manners and hospitality of the first Flemish table to which I have been admitted. I do not dislike their cookery, but the comforts of a warm English home seem to be wanting everywhere in this country; at least I have not yet found them at Ghent, for at present we are in a miserable lodging, although it is in the Place d'Armes, but I have great hopes that to-morrow or on Wednesday we shall remove into a tolerably furnished house entirely to ourselves. I was carried through one scene at Bruges which I wished not to behold, for it brought home to my heart all the evils of war and the miseries of mankind : it was the damp cloister of a church converted into a hospital, where lay on straw covered with tattered blankets at least 200 miserable Hanoverian soldiers sick with various diseases. I felt the horrid scene in every nerve. Here it might be truly said, 'Despair tended the sick busiest from couch to couch.' Our apartment for a few days at Bruges, and the style we are in here, approaches very near to the comfort and neatness of strolling players dressing in a barn; but as it is not *solitude*, nor within the walls of a convent, I am satisfied and can take all the petty evils of life with good-humour, thankful that I am not a nun. I am very anxious for letters from England. At present we know of the evacuation of Toulon only from the French papers. We hear at Ghent that the French have beaten both Royalists and Prussians, and are everywhere triumphant. It is a common conversation that the British Parliament will not continue the war. I wish to Heaven it may have so much wisdom! I have heard many political opinions from well-informed persons here, but few that please me, and some relative to the conduct and character of certain chiefs that astonish me. Orders from my commanding officer are to present his compliments. Pray make mine to Miss Miles, and believe me, &c. &c.

### Sir Edward Newenham to Mr. Miles

Dublin : January 11, 1794

I am overwhelmed with all the bad news arrived here this day ! Toulon evacuated ; fifteen sail of the line and all the stores and arsenal left untouched ; no cannon taken away in lieu of those lost at Dunkirk ; part of our troops captured ; only three men-of-war carried off ; three English frigates said to be lost ; part of our commissariat left behind, also a number of the unfortunate Royalists; and, add to this, the defeat of the Royalists before even Jourdan's detachment arrived to assist the Republicans! Wurmser obliged to retreat across the Rhine, instead of being able to take Landau or Strasburg, by which retreat Luxemburg will fall. Mentz retaken, Trèves will be sacked, and so will Cologne and Mannheim, for I imagine they will pursue their victories before any new levies can be raised to enable Wurmser and Brunswick to make head against the armies of the Rhine and Moselle united. The vast army at Toulon will now reinforce all their other armies, especially those of the Alps and Pyrenees. Turin may fall. I also fear that, when they equip the ships left them at Toulon, they will burn Leghorn and Naples, for the English cannot always keep at sea. In short, my dear friend, I have great fears that France will rise victorious to all Europe, and dictate her mode of government to be adopted by every nation. Nothing but internal dissensions can injure her, unless Sweden, Denmark, and Russia enter into the confederacy. What is the Tigress of Russia doing? Her numerous armies might yet turn the scale by coming through Germany to Alsace: 100,000 of her troops would make a change if *speedily* sent. I am in despair, for I imagine I see the *sans-culottes* in full march to Hanover and Hesse, having burnt Frankfort, Darmstadt, Mannheim, and Hanau. I also fear for Lord Moira. I do not think he can make any impression on the coast of France unless Providence should raise a new powerful host of Royalists to receive him. The loss of Toulon will dispirit the Royalists throughout all France, and I am confident it was that news arriving at the French army on the 21st which induced them to make that desperate charge on the 22nd against Wurmser. Where are the 15,000 troops gone that were at Toulon? Where are the unfortunate Royalists gone—men, women and children? What will become of the unfortunate O'Hara? All this I long to know. Yet, under all these misfortunes, I have the best grounded hopes that the spirit and abilities of Pitt will plan and cause to be executed such measures as will restore our losses and annihilate the assassins; that York will be reinforced; that he and Cobourg will make a speedy and solid conquest towards Paris, by concentrating all our forces; that Lord Moira, if he does not find everything ready to his wish on the coast of France, will with his whole force join York. Surely Jourdan's army is much weakened by the detachments to Brittany and Normandy. What are the Mynheers doing? We relieved them, and Fame reports that they were the first to fly. Dutch gratitude! Not a ship of war to cruise in the Channel, nor off the coast of America, yet they find convoys for their own fleet, not one of which would have ever reached their European port but for the protection afforded them by the English fleet. I have such an opinion of your Minister, and of his ardent zeal for the welfare of Great Britain and Ireland, that I rely on him for restoring our foreign and domestic security, and forcing those who oppose the honour and glory of England to submit to terms of equity and justice.

I want to know whether my dear daughter, Mrs. Folsch, wife of Francis Folsch, Consul to the King of Sweden at Marseilles, is alive. We have not heard of her these twelve months. You have Lady Newenham's most ardent request to find out whether she is alive or guillotined. I rely upon your executing this commission for the mother of a darling child.

### Mr. Miles to Mr. Long

January 12, 1794

If the letters which I occasionally scribble to you are worth preserving, you will find on a reference to one you received on the 7th of last month the capture of Toulon announced as inevitable. I had previous to that period informed Mr. Pitt that 15,000 men had marched to reinforce the French army before that place, and, what will perhaps surprise you, those 15,000, with as many others, would have been attached to the cause of limited monarchy, and have preserved Lyons and Toulon, if a paper, the original of which I have in my possession and which was presented to the Cabinet in March 1793, had been attended to. An offer was made of a diversion from the Alps of France with from 24,000 to 30,000 men, and they neither required arms, money, nor ammunition. I could enlarge on this subject, for the torrents of blood that have flowed at Lyons excite my horror and indignation, and all the more as I know it could have been prevented by proper exertions even on the part of the King of Sardinia, who has shamefully violated his promise to the hapless victims who confided in his assurances. I do not know how Lord Hood will have merited at Toulon, but his sending an incapable man on the expedition against Corsica is a matter that deserves serious inquiry; and the question that naturally arises is, whether the interests of the nation at this momentous period are to be risked out of compliment to personal connections or from considerations of private friendship.

It vexes me to see crime triumphant in Provence and Alsace, but man cannot war against destiny. I said at the commencement of hostilities what I declared in

August 1790, that monarchy was destroyed in France, and the experience of the last year proves that it cannot at present be restored. An emigrant, one of the red-hot Royalists, a man much countenanced by Mr. Burke, read to me some evenings since a letter which he received from Brittany, stating that his countrymen would not receive Lord Moira. Whether it was true or false, it did not become the emigrant to publish it, and still less to comment on it as he did, but these gentry cannot be silent or prudent.

I have been endeavouring to obtain a knowledge of the extent to which the war has decreased that portion of the Duke of Grafton's income which he derives from the public revenue. Despairing of success, I apply to you to procure me that information. Several of my Norfolk friends have assured me that Lord Euston and Mr. Smith[1] have in vain attempted to divert his Grace from agitating a question in Parliament which, however assured Mr. Pitt may be of a majority in both Houses, is fraught with much mischief. This is not the moment to depend entirely upon majorities, for, the secret of obtaining them being revealed, their credit is diminished, and will be of little avail against public opinion. The people begin to be disgusted with the war, which they think has not been prosecuted with a vigour proportioned to the occasion, certainly not with success, and which cannot prevent the consolidation of the French Republic. To this last opinion I am strongly inclined, from a full conviction that it is no longer in the power of the Confederacy to prevent it, and those who hold contrary language are neither friends to their country nor to Administration, nor indeed—and which is of far greater import than either—are they the friends of truth and

[1] William Smith, Esq., M.P. for Norwich.

humanity. What personal sacrifice would I not make if Danton and Robespierre (the latter I knew in Paris, whose talents cannot be denied) would privately offer to Mr. Pitt such terms as he could entertain and, consistently with the trust reposed in him, recommend the King to receive. I was encouraged some short time since to hope that such an application would have been made. How far the expulsion of our troops from Toulon and the recent successes on the Rhine have produced a change I know not ; but this I know, that if France is wise she will offer fair terms, and if Great Britain is prudent she will accept them.

With respect to the intended motion of the Duke of Grafton, much as I wish for peace, I must condemn any public proposition of the kind at this moment as emanating from this country. It would be an acknowledgment that we are no longer in a condition to carry on the war; it would be a confession that the aggression had been on our part, and would give *beau jeu* to those gentlemen who wish to throw us into confusion. There are reasons why no such motion should be brought forward. Let the proposal come from Paris, and the face of the business will assume a different complexion. Accustomed as I am to penetrate into the motives of human actions, I cannot but inquire into the probable cause of the Duke of Grafton's proposed motion. When I recall to mind his political history—for the mischiefs resulting from his imbecile administration are not yet forgiven—and the sources from whence his income is derived, my suspicions are aroused. It is full time that the public interest should be administered for the advantage of the public, and not for the aggrandisement of individuals. When I reflect on the various factions that have contended for dominion in this country within my memory, and on the uses to which they have applied their power and patronage, I own to you that I have but little confidence in their capacity for government, and still less in their integrity.

Be so good as to send me an answer to my request respecting the Duke of Grafton.

### MR. LONG TO MR. MILES

January 13, 1794

I do not know to what degree the Duke of Grafton's income is affected by the war, but I suppose materially.

### MR. MILES TO M. NOËL

January 14, 1794

I have never ceased to revolve in my mind the subject on which I have engaged you to apply to Danton, nor am I insensible that, blinded by prosperity, mankind are apt to forget their own interests and to disregard those of others. It is more than probable that the wonderful resistance made to assaults from without and to a strong and powerful party within, may render France vain as well as fortunate; yet, although she may spurn the idea of making the first advances towards the tranquillity she so much requires, the cessation of hostilities may before long become to her an object of necessity when it will be no longer that of choice. I premise this to you from my apprehension that some difficulty may be felt by your friends at Paris to make the first advance towards peace; but, as France was the first to declare war, justice exacts that she should be the first to prepare its termination. We will not tear open a wound which ought to be healed by discussing matters antecedent to hostilities, and which could answer no other purpose than to irritate each party in the present contest, and thereby prevent the return of that harmony so necessary to the prosperity of both nations. The embargo on our shipping in your harbours,[1] and the declaration of war that followed on your part, were the direct acts of aggression which will justify the measure I propose of your making an overture for peace, and, when this is once done, I do not believe that Ministers would venture to reject it if made in the spirit of peace and of a nature to be accepted. The public mind in this country has been hurt by the violence of your councils, and yet it requires as a preliminary to friendly negotiations only such proposals as cannot possibly degrade you. While saying this, I am indefatigable in preparing the way to complete with full success our benevolent enterprise; and be assured we cannot fail if you are temperate, *prompt de bonne foi*, and reasonable. I did not recommend secrecy in my last letter relative to the diplomatic gentleman you mentioned to me. Your own good sense will suggest the propriety of great reserve, while your friendship for me will not suffer you to expose my name at the present moment. You will recollect that I write to you in confidence. The great object in view is peace. So many arguments may be urged in support of this view—it would so effectually terminate the horrible carnage which has deluged, and still threatens to deluge, your country with blood; it so unquestionably would restore that order and tranquillity among you which the coalesced powers pretend to have so very much at heart as well for their own security as for your comfort—that after debating the subject in my own mind I cannot discover one plausible pretext against it. Informed as I am of the general sentiments that prevail in England

[1] See Letter, Maret to Miles, February 7, 1793.

and of the advances expected on the part of France towards the return of peace, I do not hesitate to pronounce on the practicability, and to cherish hopes on the success of our combined efforts. I do not speak at random. If Danton and Robespierre come into our plan—and surely, if they have the interests of humanity at heart, and are actuated by a sincere desire to terminate the dreadful disorders that ravage all France, they will not refuse their aid—I feel assured that the blessing is attainable, and that the olive branch will again be displayed at Calais and Dover. I wish that you could convey to me a cypher. My letters will certainly travel in perfect security in this country; the cover under which they are enclosed is their safeguard, it is a passport that cannot be violated; but, unfortunately, this passport leaves my correspondence where it receives yours, and is no longer a guarantee for either your letters or mine on the other side of the Channel. If Danton should prefer sending a confidential person to the Minister, instead of intrusting me to make the overture to him, my house shall be at his service. I will receive him as my guest, and, in order to prevent all suspicion, let him be provided with a passport from one of the Thirteen Cantons, and travel as a Swiss merchant. It shall be my care to obtain for him an interview with the Minister, who alone shall be instantly apprised of the arrival of the welcome harbinger. Mr. Pitt is a perfect stranger to these well-meant and disinterested efforts to arrest bloodshed; but of this be assured, that I know on what ground I stand, and that, satisfied as to the equity of our proceedings, I shall not hesitate to exert all my zeal, and to come boldly forward should any opposition be made to proposals for peace from the quarter whose duty it is at all events to consider them, and to whom it is impossible that war can be a matter of pastime. Remember, my dear friend, it is not merely for the interests of our respective nations that we labour, but for those of humanity in general—it is for the peace of the world. Adieu!

### Mr. Miles to Mr. Pitt
*January 16, 1794*

By letters lately received I have reason to believe that it is in contemplation at Paris to make an overture of peace to you. A friend of mine who holds a confidential post under the present French Government, and who has both credit and influence in France, has suggested this measure to Danton and Robespierre, with whom he is in close political relations. He has assured me that his efforts shall not be wanting to put an end to the calamities of war. In his letter to me dated December 26 he expresses hopes of success from the circumstance of his country being again in possession of Toulon. I had an idea of imparting this information to the Duke of Grafton with a view to prevent his intended motion; but, as I do not think his Grace is likely to be influenced by any such communications, and as the information should of right be first transmitted to his Majesty's Ministers, the knowledge of my correspondence is restricted to yourself.

### The Duke of Leeds to Mr. Miles
*January 20, 1794*

Inclosed I return you Sir Edward Newenham's letter, with its enclosure, for the perusal of which I beg you to accept my best thanks. I am afraid any recommendation of mine to Government would not be attended with much success, but I think your old friend the

Marquis of Buckingham is extremely likely to be attended to, both by Mr. Pitt and Lord Grenville. Burgess[1] has not, I fancy, influence enough either with his principal[2] or anyone else to thwart your efforts, whatever his intentions may be. I shall be very glad to hear of your succeeding in the object of your wishes, that you should go to Basle for the purpose of endeavouring to obtain peace.

### M. NOËL TO MR. MILES
Venice: January 28, 1794

The English papers are deceived in respect to Venice. I know not whether it is Monsieur Worsley who has wished to anticipate his hopes of success; but at present this sagacious republic remains firm in its neutrality, and you will admit that circumstances are not exactly suitable to induce a departure from her resolution. Besides our triumphs abroad and at home, wisdom and reason regain their ascendency from day to day in Paris. All true friends of humanity regret that our Revolution should be sullied by crime. We have now reached the point when the political modifications of Europe are about to depend on the moderation of France. If I am able, since you think we may contribute in some measure to console bleeding and suffering humanity, you may be certain that I will not omit any effort to this end; but I must not dissimulate that men's hearts are sore, and that it is with England that France has a terrible account to reckon. Peace is a blessing so precious that, if it depended on any steps of my own, there is no sacrifice I would not make to obtain it, both for my own country and for the whole of Europe. But you must feel that in this matter my hands are tied unless

---

[1] Mr. Bland Burgess.   [2] Lord Grenville.

I have the formal authorisation of the French Government. I could not myself initiate interference in an affair so delicate unless I could brave every danger, rejoin you in London, and then together put our hands to the great philanthropic work which you have embraced with a zeal so laudable, so virtuous. Whatever depended on me I have done. I have written with the greatest precautions to my friends in Paris, and I am waiting for their reply; but I repeat my fellow-citizens are exasperated, and the unwarrantable measures taken by the Allies are in opposition to this great object. If they had been satisfied with making war against us and would cease to add insults, I think that peace would be more readily attained. They have not even considered us as worthy of the respect which they owe to nations; not only have they so thought, but they have published and re-echoed it in every Court, and, above all, they have had the *maladresse* to convert the French people into a nation of soldiers, and the whole of France into one gigantic camp. No less than fifteen armies are now in active service. Judge, then, if peace is easy of accomplishment! The French Republic is victorious, her cause is as just as we could wish. It appears to me that the Coalition should be the first to speak; and, besides, do you not think that the resolution never to treat with the enemy so long as he is upon our territory should be accepted with enthusiasm and spread abroad with ardour from the moment of its birth? This resolution is rigid, deliberate, and unchangeable. There can be no peace without this indispensable preliminary.

All your letters reach me in safety, under the cover which I indicated to you. Adieu, my dear friend! Preserve for me your friendship, and believe that I will refuse nothing that can contribute to the re-establishment of peace.

### MR. MILES TO M. NOËL
January 24, 1794

Our public prints, my dear friend, will have informed you that the minority in the House of Commons, notwithstanding all the efforts of the various factions in Opposition coalesced, amounted only to 59, and that the Minister had a majority in his favour of 218 on a question against him, the object of which was peace.[1] Do not, however, imagine that either the Parliament or the Ministry are obstinately resolved on war, or that they wish to prolong it wantonly or vindictively; on the contrary, it surely must be their wish to have it terminated; but the decree of the Convention which pronounces the penalty of death on whoever in France shall propose peace until the Republic is preliminarily acknowledged and the troops withdrawn from the frontier, seems to forbid every overture of the kind from your side of the water.[2] The universal dread entertained here of your attempting to subvert all the old Govern-

[1] Debate in the Commons on the 'Address of Thanks' on his Majesty's Speech.—*Parliamentary History*, xxx. 1088, 1287.

[2] 'There is one part of the argument of my noble friend to which I must particularly call your attention, and which, independently of every other consideration, precludes even the possibility of our treating with France in the present moment. A decree has been passed by the Convention, forbidding to treat with any enemy till they shall have evacuated the territories of the Republic; and on the 11th of April it was again decreed that those persons should be punished with death who should propose to treat with any power which should not have previously acknowledged the independence of the French nation and the unity and indivisibility of the Republic, founded upon liberty and equality. Thus, by any proposal to treat we should not only incur the disgrace of the most abject humiliation, but absolutely put ourselves at their mercy, and subject ourselves to the necessity of receiving any terms which they might be disposed to dictate.'—Extract from Pitt's speech on the opening of the session, January 21, 1794. *Parliamentary History*, xxx. 1285.

ments in Europe intensifies the situation. Could this nation be assured that no insidious means would be employed to disturb its internal tranquillity, I am convinced that offers of a pacific nature from Paris would be attended to by the Minister; and, if they were such as Great Britain could accept, I will take upon me to assert that the Minister would not venture to reject them against the decided sense of the country. It is not, however, through the medium of the Opposition that they can be presented.

I have great hopes that your suggestions to Danton and Robespierre will receive attention; but I foresee that our efforts will not be effectual unless the law pronouncing death on whoever shall propose peace in France be repealed. You cannot imagine how anxious I am to know what answer has been given to your suggestions at Paris. If the answer should be favourable, if your friends resolve to act with vigour and candour, more effectual service will be rendered to your country than by the most brilliant battles; you will obtain a victory of the noblest kind, and be the means of restoring peace, order, and comfort to millions who are now distracted and divided by animosities which the continuance of war must augment and aggravate.

Public report says that it is intended to try General O'Hara. I hope the report is void of foundation. The credit universally given to it does much injury, and will defeat all our hopes should the Convention really proceed to an extremity which cannot fail to destroy every immediate prospect of an accommodation. You cannot conceive the ferment a measure so atrocious would occasion throughout the whole country. Do not lose a moment, I beseech you, in obtaining for me a full refutation of a slander so injurious.

I conjure you, therefore, in the name of humanity, too long afflicted by the atrocious though frivolous disputes of mankind, to apply without delay to Danton and Robespierre, *if they have yet the confidence of the nation*, on the subject of my former letters. I am very zealous, very anxious to see a period put to the calamities of war; and where there is zeal there is sincerity. The wish nearest my heart is peace; and, if your countrymen would be satisfied with the extent of territory France possessed under the monarchy, and would engage not to disturb the repose of other nations, I have no doubt but a speedy stop would be put to the horrors that have desolated all Europe. Let me know in your next what I have to hope from your efforts in Paris.

Have the goodness to inquire without delay what has become of the Swedish Consul and his family at Marseilles. His wife, Madame Folsch, is the daughter of a near and dear friend of mine in Ireland, Sir Edward Newenham, and he and Lady Newenham are in the deepest affliction at not having heard from their child.

If the subject of politics should cease to be acceptable, let us change it for ethics. I once loved your country. I rejoiced at her emancipation in 1789, when on a visit at the Court of a German Bishop, and, if she becomes temperate and just, I will love her again. Adieu!

### Mrs. Ware to Mr. Miles

Ghent: January 31, 1794

Many thanks for the packet of letters you were so good as to send me, and for your own which accompanied them. I am infinitely obliged to you. What an

accumulation of public ills has a few weeks produced,
and how destructive of every hope of peace ! Austrians
and Prussians seem to be overpowered by numbers on
the Rhine, and, if these principals fail in their supplies,
what is to become of the little army of British? Our
chief will never contribute to its protection. I can only
give you the general voice, which speaks loudly as to
misconduct and precipitation of temper. The best
thing I have heard has been his declared resolution
that in the next campaign he will stick close to Prince
Cobourg. Never a day passes but I hear some officer
talking of his want of judgment. I am very anxious to
know the result of the meeting of Parliament, although
I fear it must be war, for how can peace be made? And
yet it is amazing what a general opinion prevails as to
the recall of the army to England. I am sorry to hear
of many desertions from our troops. The French stick
up papers near the picket-guard offering to any deserters the best reception and a retreat to the South
of France. If some of the very liberal subscriptions had
been applied for the better accommodation of the sick
soldiers, I believe it might have been of use, for what
they use as hospitals, I am told, are miserable scenes
of wretchedness, and there is great sickness amongst
the troops. I have great reason to like the society here ;
I have been introduced at the two great houses, the
Bishop's and General Murray's.

You affront me when you ask whether I am reconciled
to the abominations of this country. No, I am so truly
English that, if ever I live to awake again in what I call
a Christian-like apartment, and in a clean bed, I shall
think that, like Nell the cobbler's wife, I have died in
the night, and awaked in heaven! Imposition, dirt,
and incivility are natural to the inhabitants of this

country, but I cannot blame their prejudice against the forced occupation of their houses by the military. It is said here that the whole place is democratic. I have many very intelligent and pleasant acquaintances amongst Ware's friends. Captain Nicholson is a great favourite with me, as indeed he is with everybody; he dwells warmly upon the superiority of the English troops. He is upon the staff as aide-de-camp to Sir William Erskine. His account of the terror of Dumouriez at Ostend astonished me; the man who had braved danger in every shape, and made the Continent tremble during a whole campaign, actually shook with fear, and could not feel collected although Sir William Erskine assured him he was safe under the protection of the British. Captain Nicholson was aide-de-camp to the Duke de FitzJames, and served in the campaign under the Duke of Brunswick; all the mischief and misery of the retreat from Dunkirk I have repeatedly heard, but he thinks the Duke now listens with greater attention to the experience of Sir William Erskine, and it is pleasant to hear from all quarters how the latter is adored. Guards, cavalry, and infantry, all worship him. It is computed that the Allies will have 180,000 men ready to take the field early in the spring; but, if the Convention accounts are true that the French are to produce 90,000 cavalry, I fear they will still maintain their superiority. I dread the opening of the campaign: there is still a chance that Ware may get a troop before that time. It will be hard if they exclude the Blues from the benefit which the Dragoons are to have of an additional lieutenant-colonel and major. War, with all its advantages, is a dreadful evil, and converts men into savages. I am astonished at the majority in the House of Commons.

I think his Majesty talked too warmly of our brilliant successes.[1]

### Sir Edward Newenham to Mr. Miles

Dublin: February 1, 1794

Our victories in the East and West Indies are not of any consequence in my eyes; they appear to me, on the contrary, as rather injurious to our main defence, for we want both soldiers and sailors at home, and more troops on the Continent. The Brest fleet is thirty-two sail of the line. Hood has not sailors to half man his fleet, and I dread lest any detachment he may make from it will be captured. He cannot leave the Mediterranean, for, if he does, all the Italian states will be invaded; Rome, Florence, Leghorn, and Naples will be sacked, and all their wealth tumbled into the Treasury of the Convention. The French have soldiers sufficient to take Turin and the rest of Italy; the Spaniards will soon be forced back; the Toulon army will march to the Eastern, and the conquerors of La Vendée will march to the Western Pyrénées. The hope of plunder, want of bread in the interior parts of France, and the fear of the guillotine, will increase their Northern and their German army. Brunswick and Wurmser will never be able to make head against the adverse host, and a great part of Germany will be ruined. Where is this Northern Bear? Why does she not assist to save her own crown, which will be torn from her cursed head if Robespierre is successful? They have sent, I suppose, great reinforcements to their Northern army, and we have diminished ours in that quarter to increase the force of Lord Moira, who, I hope, will never attempt to land on the coast of France, for, if he does, he will be *burgoyned*. We have

---

[1] See *Annual Register*, 1794, xxxvi. 188: *State Papers*.

not heard of any plan fixed for Lord Moira. I fear his troops may be wanted in England, for it is not impossible but that the enthusiasm with which the Republicans are animated may induce them to make a desperate descent on the Kentish or Essex coasts, or, by their frigates crammed with soldiers, land a few thousands in Ireland.[1]

What are our cruisers doing? Why does not our fleet destroy Cherbourg? Our capture on the north of St. Domingo is of no value, nor any other *petite conquête* of that kind, for, if the French succeed in Europe, all such places taken by us must be instantly evacuated. Cape François would have been something. It is fortunate for England that Pitt is now Minister, for, on my soul, I believe that no other can save us from destruction. His speech delights me; it cheers our drooping spirits. He asserts that the career of the French is nearly over, and that they cannot show such a force much longer; he must know best, and his information ought to be well founded, yet the stocks have fallen from 77 to 68.[2] We talk of recovering all in the spring, but where are the men? Where is the money? May not Prussia make a separate peace? May not the German Princes de-

[1] 'Carnot hoped by the beginning of the summer to see the Army of the West before the gates of London, and he wished, in case of need, to be able to support it by a strong reinforcement; Pichegru, therefore, received instructions at all hazards to take up a position in Maritime Flanders with the greatest part of his division.'—Sybel, iii. 333.

[2] 'It has been urged that the French have distinguished themselves in the field. . . . They are compelled into the field by the terror of the guillotine; they are supported there only by those resources which their desperate situation affords; and, in these circumstances, what can be the dependence on the steadiness of their operations, or what rational prospect can there be of the permanence of their exertions? On this ground, the more monstrous and terrible the system has become, the greater is the probability that it will be speedily overthrown.'—Extract from Pitt's Speech, January 21, 1794. *Parl. Hist.* xxx. 1282.

clare a neutrality? Is Lord Howe strong enough for Brest?

This is the crisis for Great Britain; victory or defeat before the close of this month will decide the quarrel, for the French will make their grand effort at the East, the West, the North, and South, all at once. I know from the smugglers here that they have a vast force on the coasts from St. Malo to Boulogne. These smugglers left France the latter end of last month without any goods; they could not get as much brandy as would serve them for sea stores. All the Irish papers are filled with reports that York and Cobourg were completely defeated; not a word of that news in any of the London journals. They also say that Three per Cent. Consols have risen from 67 to 69; that is a trifle. We expect great debates to-morrow, as Sir L. Parsons has given notice that he will move for an account of the state of our defence. This is a dangerous measure, as it would betray our situation to the Carmagnoles; indeed, I am sorry to see, after all that has been taken from us and from the flower of our army, that more troops are ordered off. Our Militia is such a medley of men that we could not be sure of them. We have no forts, no place of arms or rendezvous, no magazines or stores of any kind except the few in the Castle of Dublin; internal foes and external enemies would soon lay waste this island. Lord Mulgrave is here, but I have not seen him; he is now with his regiment. Write often, and send me a good pamphlet now and then, and be sure to be the first at this crisis to communicate any important news to me, as I generally get my letters in the House of Commons.

I wrote to you long since to inquire about my darling daughter, Margaret Folsch, married to Mr. Francis Folsch, Consul for the King of Sweden, at Marseilles.

The Swedish Ambassador or Consul in London would inform you thereof, for, if she should be alive, any inquiry for her in France by an English correspondent would be the sure means of her being guillotined. Do, my dear friend, make those inquiries, though we have but little hopes of her life.

*MR. MILES TO SIR EDWARD NEWENHAM*

London: February -, 1794

Baron Nolcken, the late Minister from Sweden, informed me yesterday that Mr. and Mrs. Folsch were well at Marseilles, and that, as the wife of the Swedish Consul, she will be safe.

Your letter breathes the language of despondency, and the situation of the country justifies the gloomy perspective which you have given of public affairs I must repeat that, if my advice had been followed in 1790, England might now be still at peace, and the Austrian Netherlands would have been free. If Ministers had attended to the suggestions they received from me last March, Lyons and Toulon would have been preserved to the constitution as established in 1789, and humanity spared the horrors with which it has been afflicted. Lyons has been lost through our folly and the treachery of the King of Sardinia. The fall of Lyons necessarily produced that of Toulon. The King's partiality to his second son has occasioned defeat and disgrace in the Low Countries. The army is dissatisfied with the Duke of York, who, independent of his want of capacity, is without experience, and is violent and imprudent. Yet these nominations have been sanctioned by the Minister, and he relies on a majority in Parliament for support. Mr. Pitt, *after our worse than equivocal conduct towards France subsequent* to the 10th of August, 1792, most certainly could not have avoided hostilities. M. de Lusignan, a Frenchman of my acquaintance, acknowledged this to me last Sunday, and the ex-Minister of War, M. de Grave, has often said as much to me within the last six months. But the conduct of the war has not borne any proportion to the magnitude of the occasion; and, with France triumphant everywhere and the Republic established beyond the force of the combined powers to destroy it, we seem destined to play guineas against assignats, whilst some of the Coalition are as well disposed to this odds as if they had Mexico and Peru in their pockets, and did not know the value of money. Yet you appear to derive encouragement from Mr. Pitt's late speech in the Commons. It is only the uninitiated, or the sanguine, or the prejudiced, who are deluded by his statements on foreign affairs. He requires the aid of every gleam of hope to sustain the power he possesses. Time will prove the fallacy of his predictions, and show that in his forecast of the future he has not been gifted with prophecy, nor in the present entanglement of our Continental relations does he exhibit the qualities of a far-seeing statesman. Remember, I write to you in confidence.[1]

[1] 'England now made the first of her grand attempts to unite the powers of the Continent in a firm league against the gigantic and ever-growing Revolution. Pitt's Ministry, as we have seen, had entered into the war with the greatest reluctance, and had hitherto taken part in it with only half its strength. An army of scarcely 80,000 men maintained in Belgium, the blockade of a few French harbours, a war of privateers against the enemy's commerce, the capture of some West India islands —this was all that the English forces had hitherto effected. Nor had the Government of England shown any superabundance of sagacity or skill. *How deplorably had it neglected to support La Vendée and to make use of Toulon!* How short-sightedly had it helped to bring about the general disasters of the late campaign by the expedition against Dunkirk! With what narrow greediness had it now again sent off a consider-

Lately I met Mr. Charles Long near the German Chapel, St. James's, coming into the Park. He had been to call upon me. We walked towards the Treasury, and our conversation soon became animated. On remarking that I had preserved a correspondence with the Continent in the hope that much useful information tending towards peace might be obtained, especially since the Government were cut off by the rigour with which all direct intercourse with England was forbidden in France, Long smiled at the idea of peace as being entirely out of the question. He wished to assure me that the Cabinet was not without the very best intelligence. I replied that it did not appear so from their measures, but that, on the contrary, if Ministers acted on the intelligence they received, they were the worst informed men in the kingdom. I reminded him that early in this month I had forewarned the Government that the Allies in the Austrian Netherlands would not find the approaching campaign a summer excursion, that the French were resolved to expel them, and would bring at least 200,000 men into the field for that purpose. I told him, moreover, that, whilst I could depend on my information, I was no stranger to the characters, views, and capacities of some of the French, who were readily listened to, and that I deeply regretted to see that description of *émigrés* the best received who were the least entitled to credit or protection; that I was sure the Minister would find himself shamefully deceived in the end, and that I was sorry to observe how my information had been neglected. Mr. Long said that, although it was the wish of the Minister that I should not maintain

able force on a useless expedition against Guadeloupe or Martinique!'—Sybel, iii. 356.

my correspondence with the Continent, he understood from Mr. Pitt himself that I was well disposed towards his Administration. I replied that it was certainly so, but that my loyalty had its limits, that my first obligations were to the country, and that, passionately as I had been attached to Mr. Pitt, and highly as I thought of his talents, I would be the first to declare against him if I thought that his measures would be adverse to the restoration of peace or injurious to the cause of freedom. He entreated me not to quarrel with Pitt. I told him I had no such intention, but I must be left at liberty to decide on the utility or propriety of public measures. We now separated, after having walked for half an hour between the Treasury and the Canal.[1] Two days afterwards I had a long conference with Lord Buckingham. His Lordship told me that Mr. Pitt and Lord Grenville were outrageous at not being able to obtain any intelligence whatever from France, although they had tried a variety of means without success. I stated the conversation I had recently held with Mr. Long, who had so confidently asserted the contrary, and had conveyed the wish of the Minister that I should not keep open channels of communication.

You are not a stranger, dear Newenham, either to the natural warmth of my temper or to the zeal with which I have invariably supported the constitutional rights of your country and of my own. I have never been the hireling of Ministers nor of the Opposition; on

---

[1] 'In the inward park was made a formal canal 2,800 feet in length and 100 feet broad, running from the Parade to Buckingham House. On the south of this canal near its east end was the Decoy, a triangular nexus of smaller canals, where water-fowl were kept.'—Timbs's *Curiosities of London,* p. 652.

the contrary, I have reserved the right of thinking for myself. I see with my own eyes, hear with my own ears, and will not be the echo of any man or set of men. My politics are simple; they cannot be mistaken; they ought not to be misrepresented; and, what will equally offend Ministers and Opposition, they will triumph when the mischievous designs and the corrupt practices of *faction* on either side will be no longer suffered to insult the patience and honest plain sense of mankind.

Influential persons connected with the French Government have expressed a desire to see peace restored between the two nations. I communicated this information in confidence to Mr. Pitt. I am an enemy to war under every possible point of view, except that of self-defence; it multiplies crimes and calamities, it ought to be universally reprobated; and, if France will be temperate and just, and will abandon her wild and criminal projects, the British Cabinet, arrogant as it has become by mistaking the sense of Parliament for the voice of the nation, will be compelled to sacrifice its vindictive humour, and close a contest which must inevitably lead to the detriment, if not to the ruin of this country. God forbid that I should patronise guilt or become the advocate of plunderers and assassins; but, temperate in my resentments as well as in my loyalty, I should be sorry to see England become the associate of foreign princes in their wild and iniquitous project of restoring the ancient tyranny of France.

Lord Cornwallis has arrived from India in the 'Swallow.' The vessel was chased into Torbay by a French privateer. Adieu!

### M. Noël to Mr. Miles

Venice: February 9, 1794

I desire with all my heart to be able to hasten the success of your wishes. I wrote without delay to Danton and Barère—not to Robespierre, with whom I am only slightly acquainted, and I fully made known your ideas. No doubt they will determine as the interests of the Republic may appear to exact. All that is possible I have done, but distance and the difficulty of communication sufficiently explain why I have not yet received an answer. In the meantime blood continues to flow, but the *éclat* of our victories does not dazzle me, so as to prevent me from recognising that our military success has been purchased at the cost of the lives of innumerable Frenchmen. You say that everything depends on the uprightness and consistency with which Danton and Robespierre may act, and you appear by this phrase to portray them to your own vision as two Cromwells, in respect to whom faction has defeated all opponents. But this is a position that must be corrected. Danton and Robespierre, indeed, seem to possess influence, but they will lose it the moment that they abuse it. Power belongs no more to them than it belonged to the intriguing Brissot or to the feeble Condorcet. We cannot sufficiently convince the foreigner that it is not a faction, but the whole nation that desires liberty; and, although Danton and Robespierre should be crushed by the revolutionary movement, the impulse given to the people would not be enfeebled. It is this fact that the powers should know and believe, and not the crude notions and abominable falsehoods of the *émigrés*, whom, as I have already said, neither their nation nor their century recognise.

I think with you that France would not degrade herself by making the first overtures, but not, as you say, because she was the first to declare war. I would recall to your memory the crowd of hostile measures, the violent declamations, the manœuvres in every Court of Europe, well known to your Minister, the violation of treaties, and the repeated infractions of neutrality. France, however, could take the first step without degrading herself, because she has developed an energy without example in the annals of history, and she is victorious. But I must mention the difficulties which I foresee in considering the acrimony of the reproaches which are raised in every part of France against your Minister. I ask myself, not without disquietude, whether the idea by itself of treating with Mr. Pitt would not entirely fail.[1] I do not examine here whether these reproaches are well founded or not. The fact is, they are reiterated every day, the people are exasperated, and this difficulty is not a chimera. I fear, therefore, that you might be somewhat premature were you to mention to Mr. Pitt the possibility of an overture being made from Paris. Still, this is only my private opinion founded on the observation of facts; I know nothing of any official authority in respect to the above difficulty.

Is it a partial peace that is desired? Or is it a general peace? In the latter case I doubt whether France would consent to it. I am at too great a distance to know the dispositions of those who hold the helm of affairs, but as I reflect I say to myself, 'They have forced France to become a camp, and every Frenchman to be a soldier. Would it be prudent to

[1] 'Pitt, devenu, par un entraînement d'ambition, le plus belliqueux des ministres.'—Ernouf, p. 180.

recall suddenly to their homes this enormous mass divided into fifteen armies? Might it not be feared that this violent interference with the habits, tastes, and military licence would plunge us yet once again into fresh troubles? And would not policy counsel us to keep up a foreign element of disturbance and activity such as this war would necessarily develop? Will they not profit by this circumstance to assure the peace of Europe by retrenching some of the excrescences of that monstrous Colossus, the House of Austria, and thereby reduce it to its natural dimensions? It is perhaps what they would have done if passion had not been carried into politics. It might then have been believed that the Cabinet of St. James's had not committed the unpardonable and irreparable blunder of allowing Poland to be destroyed, and Russia to acquire so decided a preponderance in the affairs of the Levant and of the North, a preponderance which will involve the fall of the Ottoman throne in Europe, and which, perhaps, it will be no longer in the power of England to destroy. England might have played the noble *rôle* of mediatrix. But the time for that is past; she must now restrict herself to make peace for herself and for the other powers which have the most immediate relations with her.

The powers did not foresee the terrible development of force and energy of which this century is the witness, and, as I predicted to you in the Christmas of 1792, they judged the Revolution by the accounts they received from the nobles and priests, and they were obstinate in determining to see nothing but the poniard of faction in the manifestation of the general will.

You know that Le Brun has expiated his crime on the scaffold, but I cannot speak of him. I have too much cause to complain of his conduct towards me, and his country has judged him as a traitor.[1]

### MR. MILES TO SIR EDWARD NEWENHAM

February 12, 1794

I am so disgusted with the atrocious perfidy of the National Convention that I most sincerely wish it may be speedily and irretrievably crushed. I was among the first, and certainly among the most zealous, of those who admired the Revolution in 1789. I saw nothing in the events of that year until the 5th of October which could authorise the suspicion that more was intended than what was avowed; and even then I was rather inclined to attribute the violence offered to Louis XVI. and his family to a dread of falling again under the galling yoke of despotism than to any premeditated design to

[1] 'Ce n'est que le 2 Juin que l'Assemblée délibérant sous les piques rend ses décrets d'arrestation, et, conformément à la loi du 5 Avril, ordonne l'arrestation des ministres Le Brun et Clavière. Mais les ministres sont accusés, non destitués. Et c'est dans ces conditions que Le Brun prend encore des arrêtés, contre-signe des nominations—15 Juin, Grouvelle, envoyé à Copenhague ; Chauvelin à Florence ; Maret à Naples ; Noël à Venise. Ce n'est que le 21 Juin que son successeur, Desforgues, est nommé par la Convention. Quant à lui, en quittant le ministère, il s'est établi, toujours en état d'arrestation, rue d'Enfer. C'est là que le 5 Septembre vient l'atteindre le décret d'accusation rendu sur la proposition de Barère contre les Girondins.

'Lebrun, cependant, songe à échapper au décret qui le frappe. Ses amis, Ysabeau, entre autres, le poussent à s'enfuir. Il parvient à tromper le gendarme commis à sa garde et se réfugie rue de l'Egalité, maison d'Harcourt. Il se cache sous le nom de Lebrasseur, Liégeois. La nouvelle de son évasion est apportée à la Convention le 9 Septembre, et le comité de sûreté générale met immédiatement la police à la poursuite de l'ex-ministre. Il est arrêté dans la maison où il a cherché un refuge le 4 Nivose (24 Décembre) par Héron, chef de la police secrète du comité, incarcéré à la Conciergerie, mis immédiatement en jugement, condamné à mort, et exécuté le 7 Nivose (27 Décembre), An II., 1793. Son cadavre fut enterré au cimetière de la Madeleine.'—*Le Département des Affaires Etrangères pendant la Révolution*, 1787-1804, par Fred. Masson, Bibliothécaire du Ministère, pp. 281-283.

destroy either the monarch or the monarchy. I pass over the interesting and dreadful interval between his departure from Versailles and the period of his death, for, crowded as it is with events no less novel than extraordinary, it would require volumes to arrange the variety of facts and reflections which have occurred in that space of time. Nor is it necessary for those who are our contemporaries. The public prints record almost all that is needful to direct our judgment, and, being as it were spectators of the scene, we cannot want information. After almost four years of incessant and disgraceful labour, in which the most marked injustice and ferocious violence have repeatedly stained even the Legislature itself, it was reasonable to expect that, exhausted by the fatigue of such an accumulation of blunder and crime, France would have enjoyed a respite from those scenes of iniquity that dishonoured and debilitated her. It was natural to hope that the murder of the King would have been the term of her guilt, the last sacrifice to injustice and infamy; but I see no end to the crimes and blunders which disgrace and desolate that wretched country, where all is carnage, rapine, and horror. Six thousand victims have been again seized by the merciless tyrants that actually govern France, and these will most probably be sacrificed. I am dejected at the sad perversity of mankind, and feel a presentiment that this Revolution, so promising in appearance, will have a lamentable issue, and that, no less fatal to liberty than it is to individuals, it will eventually damn the sacred cause of freedom and in a manner legalise despotism. What shuttlecocks men are! How they are bandied about by fate or fortune, or, as is more probable in the present instance, by the incompetency and obstinacy of their rulers!

The Convention seem ferocious as cannibals; they thirst for human blood. On the other hand, the powers confederated against France appear, by their intrigues and cabals, to be inflaming this madness—mad enough already—in the hope that, when the vultures fall out among themselves, they may come in for a share of territory, or, perhaps, with the view of driving them as a *dernier ressort* from the evils of anarchy into the arms of tyranny once again. Adieu!

### MR. MILES TO M. NOËL

February 21, 1794

Your letter received on Tuesday last augments the apprehension I am under that the prospect of peace is less visible in 1794 than it was in 1793. I see such decided rancour, which increases from day to day, that I dare not hope for the termination of the war in which Europe is plunged. No doubt the shameful profusion and exorbitant power of your Court produced the Revolution; but the general depravity of all ranks and descriptions of people defeated in the first instance the object of that Revolution, and has occasioned all the misfortunes, anarchy, and crime, which have ensued from a measure just in itself beyond all question. This is the light in which I consider the present deplorable situation of France, and, since it was impossible that any event of moment could befall an Empire so vast in itself, and so powerful both in arms and science, without affecting, immediately and materially, the rest of Europe, no wonder that all the other States are involved in the consequences of your Revolution, and that their political existence and prosperity are brought into hazard. With respect to this country, I must maintain that France was assuredly the aggressor, for, so far from the British Minister having an idea of declaring war against her, he had not ships either to protect our commerce or to defend our coast from insult when the Convention declared hostilities against Holland and England. The more I reflect on the conduct of Dumouriez and on the series of extraordinary events since he proposed a declaration of war against the King of Hungary,[1] the more I am convinced it would have been a wise measure on the part of France to have secured her frontiers from invasion and to have left to her enemies the odium of commencing the conflict. If France had provided her fortified towns with sufficient garrisons and ammunition for a siege, and had taken the precaution of distributing an army so as to cover the numerous military positions from Strasburg to Dunkirk, neither Austria nor Prussia would have ventured to invade her territory. But the course she pursued has made her the aggressor. And, finally, your attempt to subvert every Government, and to cripple every State, by the introduction of principles which, taken in their ordinary sense, are incompatible with order and are destructive of security, has enraged all other nations against your country; and, so long as this alarm exists, they will be afraid to terminate the contest until either France is incapacitated for mischief or engages to leave other States in the tranquillity and independence which she claims for herself. Now, it is for these reasons I am anxious that France, as she has been notoriously the aggressor, and has undeniably aimed at the dissolution of monarchy throughout Europe, should renounce her unjustifiable projects, and give an example of moderation and equity by making overtures to the coalesced powers,

---

[1] 'Dumouriez, however insufficient might seem the grounds for doing so, resolved to propose to the National Assembly a declaration of war against the King of Hungary and Bohemia.'—Sybel, i. 448.

such as she may offer without self-degradation, and such as they may accept without danger. This is the only course that occurs to me as practicable for the opening of negotiations. I am sufficiently conversant with public opinion in this country to assert that such a step on the part of the Convention, whatever may be the secret views of our Court, would compel the Minister to pay a dignified regard to the proposal, and, if it should be rational and just, to adopt it. I have reasons for urging this point very strongly, through you, upon the earnest attention of Danton, of whose wonderful capacity I have ever spoken. I dare not, however, hope for so much good at present. The state of parties in Paris is too distracted. Barère seems all violence against this country, and inflames your people so as to indispose them to peace; he is hostile, it is said, to Danton and Robespierre, who are united, as I hear, only for the moment, and on account of their common danger. Collot d'Herbois wishes to be supreme in France, but Barère appears to have the most credit and the greatest aversion to peace. Let me know, if you can, the real state of parties in Paris.

Let me recall to your memory an incident of the past. You came to me one night about ten o'clock,[1] when Louis XVI. was arraigned, and informed me that, if our Minister felt any anxiety as to the fate of your unfortunate monarch, M. Talon, at that time residing in Sloane Street, Chelsea, could be of more use than any other man, and that, if the life of the King was to be saved, there was not a moment to be lost. You will remember that I refused to convey your information to Mr. Pitt on the ground that the Minister was not likely to meddle with the affairs of the French Government;

[1] See Minute, December 18, 1792.

and further, that, since your King had been put upon his trial, I did not believe that M. Talon or any other person would be able to rescue him. Had I gone to Mr. Pitt from motives of humanity, and if the Minister from the same motives had listened to the proposal, the Convention would have inferred that our Government did interfere with your domestic concerns, and would have made it one of the charges against us in excuse for the unprovoked rupture that ensued.

The 'Moniteur' arrives regularly at present, but can you contrive that I should receive it sooner? Adieu!

### M. Noël to Mr. Miles
Venice: March 14, 1794

As to your great object, the restoration of peace, I have not received any reply to my letters, and I infer from this silence that they do not wish me to interfere in the matter. I must henceforward restrict myself to my wish, and recognise with pain the necessity of renouncing the pleasure of writing to you. Despite the purity of my motives, it might be possible to give a criminal turn to our correspondence, and I must therefore be upon my guard against any such suspicions. Be content at present to communicate with M. Calandrini at Geneva; he will forward to you regularly the 'Moniteur.'

I have not concealed from you that I could do nothing towards negotiations for peace. What I promised I faithfully fulfilled—that is to say, I wrote to Danton and Barère, and conveyed to them your proposition, and, I repeat it, I have not received an answer to any of my letters upon this subject. Nor am I surprised, for how could they in Paris believe in the pacific dispositions of Courts which continue to employ in respect to us the same tone of insult and cowardly provocation? I avow that I see nothing objectionable in the eloquent report of Barère on the subject of peace; it is unanswerable; and, whatever you may maintain to the contrary, it is not France that desires to protract this terrible conflict. Our declaration of war has already cost England much. You say that, if our young Republic would limit itself to the territory of the monarchy, and not interfere with the internal affairs of the old Governments, you do not doubt but that peace would be easy. With respect to this second point, we have solemnly promised it, and why should the sanctity of our engagements be less believed than the assurances of regal courts? Have we, like those States who make war to-day against us, and notably Prussia, deceived successively in the space of two years all the powers of Europe?[1]

Then, again, you say that advances towards peace might be made by Danton and Robespierre. But no. Robespierre and Danton are certainly influential men so long as they remain the staunch friends of liberty; they will be overthrown to-morrow should they betray our cause. No, my dear friend. It must be with the

[1] 'At the fire-breathing impetuosity of the Jacobins, he [Danton] shrugged his shoulders, and considered it ridiculous to reject a useful alliance with a State merely because the ruler of it wore a crown. There was at first, indeed, much murmuring on the Mountain, when, on the 14th April, he laughed at the idea of a universal war with all kings, and put the question, who would be willing to waste the blood of a Frenchman to overthrow the Emperor of China? But he succeeded at last, and obtained from the Convention a distinct declaration that, as France would allow of no foreign interference in her domestic politics, so she, on her part, renounced all right to meddle with the constitutions of other countries. The object of this open renunciation of the revolutionary policy was declared by Barère on the 16th. "By this decree," he said, "you have laid the foundation of peace;" and that the majority were satisfied with this declaration was immediately proved by their granting a secret fund of six millions for the negotiations which had been commenced by the Committee of Public Safety.'—Sybel, iii. 42.

French nation, as represented by the Convention, that any negotiation can be opened. It is to this Convention that every proposition must be addressed, or, at least, to the Committee of Public Safety, which has its entire confidence. But instead of a pacific disposition I see in the hearts of kings and their adherents, only rage and knavery; and, although open rupture originated with us, it is true, hostilities underhand and secret on the part of the Coalition have been not less active and real. It is to this spirit that I attribute the report about General O'Hara. I have seen the French papers as late as the 2nd of February; there is not a word relative to him; it is a gross *ruse* on the part of your Ministry to render us odious.

It has been impossible for me to obtain the information you desire respecting the Swedish Consul at Marseilles, but I will still inquire. The little intercourse I hold with Paris and the prodigious difficulties of communication are the cause. Adieu!

### Mr. Miles to Mr. Long
March 30, 1794

I do most sincerely lament that Lord Grenville did not pay attention to the paper which I presented, and which I know was taken in to the Cabinet, in March 1793. If the offer then made on the part of the Royalists in the South of France had been accepted, the war would have worn an aspect more favourable for this country than it does at present, and Lyons and Toulon in all probability would not have been under the tyranny of the Convention. Should the contest have an unfortunate issue, and if Parliament should resolve to inquire into the causes of the failure of the war, his Lordship will find it very difficult to vindicate his conduct. Perhaps you have no knowledge of this incident, as the papers, the originals of which I possess, did not pass through your hands.

In the publication which accompanies this letter I have shown as little mercy to Mr. Burke as he has shown to M. de Lafayette; but the asperity with which I have treated the former is justified by facts known to all the world, whereas the virulence of Mr. Burke towards Lafayette is without foundation, and proceeds perhaps from a cause less excusable than prejudice.[1]

### Mr. Miles to M. Noël

April 11, 1794

The French papers dated the 6th instant have just arrived, and Danton, I find, is no more! His fall I long since predicted, as I did the triumph of Robespierre, from the personal knowledge I possessed of both

---

[1] The publication sent to Mr. Long was the *Letter to the Duke of Grafton, with Notes; to which is annexed a complete Exculpation of M. de Lafayette from the Charges indecently urged against him by Mr. Burke in the House of Commons on March* 17, 1794.

On March 17th General Fitzpatrick moved, "That an humble address be presented to his Majesty, to represent to his Majesty that it appears to this House that the detention of the General Lafayette, Messieurs Alexander Lameth, La Tour Maubourg, and Bureau de Pusy, in the prisons of his Majesty's ally the King of Prussia, is highly injurious to the cause of his Majesty and his allies; and most humbly beseech his Majesty to intercede with the Court of Berlin, in such manner as to his royal wisdom shall seem most proper, for the deliverance of those unfortunate persons." This motion was seconded by Colonel Tarleton, and supported by Fox, Grey, William Smith, Thornton, &c. It was opposed by Pitt and Burke. The latter, in the course of his speech, said: "The Abbé Foulon was now in London, and he often declared his anguish in these words: '*I will be revenged of Lafayette; it was he that had my father murdered; it was he who tore out and devoured his heart.*' I would not," continued Burke, "debauch my humanity by supporting an application like the present in behalf of such a horrid ruffian." The House divided, and the motion was lost by 107 votes.—*Parliamentary History*, xxxi. 28-54. On the death of Foulon, see vol. i. p. 259.

men. Danton, in February 1793, aspired to the Regency. I also knew from the same parties that he had facilitated the escape out of France of some Royalists. His character was not thought incorruptible. Robespierre was fully credited with being proof against money; how far he is able to resist the influence of ambition may be collected from the records of public events. Are we now to look upon it that a Government, consolidated and confirmed by public opinion, is established in France and will acquire stability and command respect?

I have received your different letters, and, while I acknowledge your personal kindness, lament that you should feel so inveterate a prejudice against the British Government, and attribute to the intrigues of the Cabinet the war in which you are engaged. It is incumbent on me to undeceive you on this very important matter. I must also declare to you that the English Ministers are totally ignorant of our correspondence. The suggestions communicated to you are certainly my own. It is not extraordinary that I should have expressed myself with so much horror and indignation at the execrable murders committed in France. I know that many of those who have fallen had rendered themselves obnoxious as well as dangerous, and that the crimes which have marked your country for these four years are easier accounted for than justified; but vice or crime, in any form, under any pretext, and from any quarter, vexes me, and I am apt to be warm when I feel that I am right. You will understand why I have written to you with so much solicitude to stop, if possible, the protraction of the war, and will perceive the motives for the language with which I spoke of Le Brun and others, whose irregular ambition or vengeance has deluged an immense tract of country with blood. Your letters, however, have not contributed to exalt my spirits, or to induce me to look forward with either hope or confidence to a speedy issue to this fierce and relentless war, and the Revolution that has lately happened in Paris inclines me to suspect that every such hope would now be visionary.[1] All correspondence, therefore, on a subject which I have had much at heart is at an end. The absolute impossibility of being ever able to accomplish my wishes is a discouraging reflection, and reduces me to silence and almost to despair. All I shall request of you is that, in case you should survive the tempest, you will do justice to my sentiments, and bear testimony to my unremitting but unsuccessful efforts to prevent, in the first instance, and afterwards to arrest, the war that has ensued between our respective countries.

I do not know whether you will think it prudent to communicate the contents of this letter to Robespierre, but you may at all events inform him of my disposition. Adieu!

### M. NOËL TO MR. MILES

Venice: April 30, 1794

You will have received my letter, in which I made known the silence observed in Paris with regard to your overtures, and from which I conjecture that they do not wish me to mix myself up in the matter. I learn that I am accused of being with Danton the author of this unfortunate war. You know, my friend, how little truth there is in this charge, but I do not ask you to bear witness to my innocence—your testimony would only aggravate the suspicion; we must wait, but, under

---

[1] See Sybel, iii. 291. Danton was guillotined on April 5, 1794, in company with Camille Desmoulins and thirteen others.

these circumstances, I think that our further correspondence would at least be useless, and, on that account, although your remembrance of me has been a great consolation, I proposed in my last letter that our communication should cease until better times. As to your suggestion with respect to Robespierre, I am not in a position to write to him. I have never had any private relations with him, and it is now with grief that I renounce the pleasurable thought of contributing my feeble help towards alleviating the sufferings of humanity. In truth I can do nothing.

A Frenchman who was at Marseilles not long ago has just arrived here; he gives me news of affairs at that place, and says that the Swedish Consul was quite safe at the date of his departure. Any irregularity in your receipt of the 'Moniteur' is due to the state of things in Paris. I will put you in communication with the lady who has kindly undertaken this commission. The 'Moniteur' can travel to you only by way of Geneva. At this distance I cannot do more for you. Adieu!

### M. NOËL TO MR. MILES

Venice: May 22, 1794

The very extraordinary position in which I am placed compels me to request you to send direct to Geneva your subscription for the 'Moniteur.' Please forward 156 francs in cash—not in assignats. The 'Moniteurs' of April will have informed you of what has passed in respect to myself. Certain people who do not know me accuse me of having been the author of this horrible war between our two nations.[1] You, my

---

[1] 'Saint-Just, rapporteur du comité de salut public, entre dans la salle et monte à la tribune.

'Le rapporteur obtient la parole. Un profond silence règne dans l'assemblée.

dear friend, know how false is the accusation, but you
would raise your voice in vain on my behalf—your
testimony would have no weight; and my case is an
additional proof that, in the time of revolution, purity
of intention and integrity of purpose are insufficient to
protect an honest man. At the moment that I write
to you, I am perhaps proscribed in a country I have
served only too well. I must wait with resignation the
arrival of terrible news, for I have no longer a single
friend in Paris—all have perished, all are either dead
or in irons. In this situation I have need to recall
to memory your kind and touching promises, and to
demand of you a great favour, which, however, I
request you to observe, is conditional. In the event
of an act of injustice being perpetrated against me, and
that I should have good reason to abandon my intention
to return to France, would you facilitate the means by
which I may find a temporary asylum in London, for I
meditate crossing as rapidly as possible to America?
Could you obtain for me a passport under the protection of which I could traverse Germany? And if I
send my baggage overland to your address in London,
do you think that it would safely arrive there—could

'Saint-Just, au nom des comités de salut public et de sûreté générale:
La révolution est dans le peuple, et non point dans la renommée de
quelques personnages. Cette idée vraie est. . . . Mais qu'as-tu fait
[Danton] depuis pour nous prouver que Fabre, ton complice, et toi aviez
voulu tromper la cour ? Votre conduite depuis a été celle des conjurés.
Quand tu étais ministre, il s'agit d'envoyer un ambassadeur à Londres
pour resserrer l'alliance des deux peuples. Noël, journaliste contre-révo-
lutionnaire, fut offert par Lebrun, tu ne t'y opposas point. On te le
reprocha comme une faiblesse; tu répondis: "Je sais que Noël ne vaut
rien, mais je le fais accompagner par un de mes parents." Quelle a été
a suite de cette ambassade criminelle ? la guerre, et ta liaison avec
Dumouriez et Brissot.'—*Gazette Nationale* ou *Moniteur Universel* du
12 Germinal, An II., Mardi, 1ᵉʳ Avril, 1794. See *Annual Register*, 1794;
*Hist. Europe*, xxxvi. 120, note.

you arrange for me that it should travel in security? I hope you will attribute any imprudence on my part to the singularity (*bizarrerie*) of my position, and I know enough of the goodness of your heart to be persuaded that you will reply promptly to this letter, the object of which is important as enabling me to escape from danger, and to seek some distant asylum where I may support myself by the labour of my hands.

Adieu, my dear friend! May you be more happy than I am, and may the misfortunes of France serve as a lesson to the different factions in England! God bless you!

*Minute.*—I instantly promised to do my best to procure for Noël a passport to travel through Germany, and I offered him, in the event of a counter-revolution, an asylum in my house. This good man, as I believe him to be, received a classical education at Paris, and was destined for the Church, but his inquisitive mind ill qualified him for a profession which had become degraded into a business, and the Revolution was an event too animating in itself, and too important in its consequences, for even a torpid mind to behold its progress with indifference. It acted like electricity on my friend, and his love of freedom induced him to espouse its interests with all the fervour that belonged to his ingenuous and ardent mind. In 1792, Le Brun sent him to London on a private mission, and soon afterwards he received directions to supersede Chauvelin, who had rendered himself obnoxious to our Court; but this gentleman, schooled by Talleyrand in all the craft of diplomacy, prevailed upon Noël to defer for reasons of state the notification of the proposed change, and his patriotism easily yielded to the request. The cunning of the ambassador was an overmatch for virtuous simplicity, and Noël sacrificed to public interest everything that was personal. He was sent to confer with Dumouriez at Liège; he then proceeded to Holland, whence he was recalled, and subsequently despatched to Venice as Minister Plenipotentiary. What has become of him during all the afflicting succession of revolutions in France since 1794 I know not, but I sincerely hope that he has survived the various tempests which have torn his country and Europe. He laboured in 1792, 1793, *de bonne foi*, with me, to avert the calamities of war, and if we had succeeded, what torrents of blood would have been spared to both nations![1]—W. A. M.

### MR. MILES TO MR. AUST
June 18, 1794

Every event tends to convince you that I did not augur ill or hastily of the catastrophe of the present contest. I told you from the first that the Republic was established; I asserted it in the year 1790, and my correspondence with Ministers will prove that I predicted the dissolution of the monarchy in the autumn of that year. France acts for herself; it is no longer the Court of Versailles, it is the nation; and Ministers are infamously imposed upon by those who tell them the contrary. If it was their wish to establish a rational government, they should have declared in favour of limited monarchy. Lord Grenville has more to answer

---

[1] The above 'Minute' is without date. Noël weathered the storm; and, like other Republicans who denounced crowned heads, accepted political office under the Empire. He was Prefect of the Haut-Rhin in 1800. He compiled several dictionaries and other works. Ernouf remarks: 'Voilà un début de carrière bien agité, pour finir par des dictionnaires!' Noël, whom Mr. Miles met in Paris in 1816, did not die until 1841. See Masson, p. 168.

for than he suspects by rejecting the offer which you took in to the Cabinet in March 1793; and should the contest have an unfortunate issue, and Parliament resolve to inquire into the causes of the failure, his Lordship will find it difficult to vindicate his conduct. If the proposal of M. De La Colombe had been accepted, the South of France, instead of being subjected to the tyranny of the Convention, would in all probability have been now in possession of moderate Royalists; but the great blunder was when Liège and the Low Countries in commotion were looking for a Protector against the duplicity of that royal swindler the King of Prussia, and against the despotism of the House of Austria. Adieu!

### Mr. Miles to Mr. Sheridan[1]

June 18, 1794

Do not attribute it to vanity when I tell you that I do not despair of making you a convert to the opinion I have uniformly supported, namely, that Mr. Pitt could not have avoided hostilities but on terms at once dangerous and dishonourable. With respect to the *conduct* and lately avowed *object* of the war, the difference in opinion between us, if any, cannot be great, and I do not hesitate to say that the Minister will act wisely by getting out of this terrible business as soon as he can, and as well as he can, whether or not he may have finally to treat with Robespierre. Thus far on public affairs, which, by the by, are at once so gloomy in perspective and so important in their consequences that they absorb in my mind all other considerations. Our accidental meeting the other day recalled past times; and, in recalling them, I felt the return of that

---

[1] Richard Brinsley Butler Sheridan, M.P. for Stafford, &c.

strong friendship which I once professed for you, and which would never have suffered the least diminution but for the idea I had conceived of your being accessory to all the excesses at Carlton House. Be assured that I shall always be happy to see you in Cleveland Row.

### Mr. Miles to Mr. Nicholls[1]

June 22, 1794

In my vindication of Robespierre I used the word *incorruptible* in a very limited sense; it goes no further than to say that he cannot be diverted from his present object by any pecuniary consideration; and I repeat that, if it were possible to present him with Mexico and Peru on condition that he would abandon his design or consent to restore royalty to France, I firmly believe he would spurn the offer. There are, however, other modes of corrupting the mind than by the temptation of money, and, when Sir Robert Walpole said that every man had his price, I am certain he did not confine himself between the extremes of a million and half a crown. Ambition, love, hatred, vengeance—in a word, all the variety of springs by which the machine is put in motion, may be considered as so many different instruments of corruption. I have known instances where a pretty woman has triumphed over gold at Wetzlar, and obtained a decree of the Empire which no bribe could at that moment procure. Those who suspect that Robespierre is to be bought by money know him not; but if his views in the very dawn or infancy of the Revolution had been attended to—that is, before

---

[1] Mr. John Nicholls, M.P. for Surrey. He sat in three Parliaments; and he is the author of a work entitled *Recollections connected with Public Affairs during the Reign of George III.*, &c.

circumstances authorised him to entertain any hopes of success to a project deemed extravagant in 1789, and which is as good as accomplished in 1794—his foible might have been discovered, and himself diverted from the vast design which even then he began to conceive. The misfortune is that, whenever a great popular commotion takes place in a nation, the men at the head of affairs generally *perdent la tête*, and are the least capable of allaying the ferment. The blockheads have recourse to rigour and violence. We lost America by attempting to dragoon only one town on that immense continent; the French Minister lost monarchy by surrounding Paris with troops, when his authority was in fact superseded. It is a perilous enterprise to war against opinion; the bayonet on such occasions may extirpate, but it can neither convince nor convert; and this is a truth which even the legislators of our own century have yet to learn. Believe me when I tell you that a general prejudice prevails throughout France against the *ancient* monarchy; nor do the fraudulent and swindling manœuvres of that unprincipled man the King of Prussia tend to make it respectable anywhere else on the Continent.

But what wealth could seduce Robespierre from his enterprise? This judgment of him is formed not only from the magnitude of his ambition as compared with the poverty of even the greatest pecuniary bribe, but from the knowledge I obtained of his character and habits of life when I was a member of the same club with him in Paris; and I tell you again, he is beyond the reach of gold. I do not think he could have been bought at any period of the Revolution, because his penetrating mind foresaw in 1790 that power would soon be wrested from the feeble grasp of the aristocracy, who, instead of taking precautionary measures against the tempest brewing in every direction through the indefatigable exertions of the Jacobins, were caballing and endeavouring to cut the grass from under each other's feet in order to get into authority. Robespierre foresaw the issue of all this imbecility as manifested in the National Assembly. Ardent in his pursuits, although cold in his manner—conscious of his power whilst looking for support, not to the nobility, but to the people to whom he belonged, knowing that the *people* would soon be everything and the *nobility* nothing— he waited patiently the course of events, and with a progress evidently and constantly in his favour he looked forward with certainty to the eminence he has now attained. What bribe of money could have diverted him from his object? *Ce n'est pas par l'argent qu'il faut espérer séduire un ambitieux, sûr de son fait, de ses projets.* I do not mean to insult Horne Tooke by comparing him with Robespierre, but on my soul I do not believe it is in the power of gold to purchase either of these men. I will even go further and assert that so convinced are his countrymen of the incorruptibility of Robespierre, that you will never hear —whatever convulsions may hereafter happen in France —of his being publicly arraigned and tried for a delinquency of this description, nor for leaguing with the enemies, or even with the pretended friends of his country for the restoration of monarchy. He may be assassinated or summarily condemned, but he will never be destroyed by a regular process as were his companions Brissot and others. I hope that this explanation will convince you that what I have elsewhere said on the subject of this extraordinary man, whom I personally knew, was more from my respect for truth than from any affection for the individual.

### MR. MILES TO SIR EDWARD NEWENHAM

June 25, 1794

I have just had a long conversation with your friend Mr. Jay,[1] who regrets very much that he cannot have the pleasure of seeing you before his return to America in about three weeks. Now, as the distance from Dublin can easily be measured, why not wing your flight to London at once, where my house will be your home, and greet the man who speaks of you and Lady Newenham with much rapture? His Excellency has promised to dine with me before his departure; we have fixed July 14, and I will invite Lord Rodney, Aust, David Hartley, and others to meet him. Come and join us. General Washington is in good health—never better. Mr. Jay is not aware that I exerted myself on behalf of the American prisoners at Forton, near Gosport. I assisted in raising subscriptions to relieve them on the spot, and engaged Lord Sandwich to order glass windows and a fire in their apartments, and the officers and men to be separated.

As for our mutual friend Lafayette, he has been transferred from one crowned head to another. He is at present in the clutches of the Emperor, confined in Moravia, where he is even worse treated than when under the dominion of the King of Prussia. He is denied the use of pen, ink, and paper; his friends are debarred all access to him; the rigour is increased in proportion to its continuance, and every day adds to his calamities. I have asked Mr. Jay if there are no means whereby Congress could apply to the Court of Vienna. America,

---

[1] Minister Plenipotentiary from the United States of America.

however, has acted very generously towards Lafayette, and, at the same time, very delicately towards France, by voting a sum of money to this victim of regal despotism, as *pay* due to him from Congress while in the American army, for, to his honour be it mentioned, he served without pay. They have in calculating this debt made it as considerable as possible in his favour, but how it will reach him I cannot conjecture. I am very sore on this subject; nor can I forgive Burke for his attack on Lafayette—an attack as false as it was cruel and as cowardly as malicious, for it was against a man in a dungeon, and unable to refute the charges brought against him. I am sorry that Mr. Pitt insists on considering him as his friend. I certainly shall not balance between my esteem for the Minister and what I owe to truth, for on the side of the latter I will wage war against all mankind.

P.S.—*Friday, June* 27.—Yesterday I received the following account from abroad:—The Prince of Orange, compelled to fall back to Nivelles, had demanded a reinforcement to sustain his position and cover Bruxelles. The Duke of York's baggage had left Tournay on the preceding Saturday *par la porte de Bruxelles*. On Monday Clairfait was attacked and defeated; the French were at that time within three miles of Oudenarde, Clairfait's baggage was coming into Ghent on Tuesday, and the people were flying to Flushing, Middelburg, and Antwerp, with their effects. I had an account three weeks since that the French were coming down in great force by Charleroi to take the Duke of York in flank, but I have discontinued my communications since Mr. Pitt has signified his wish not to receive any foreign intelligence. I told him in November last that the French would invade Italy, and that they would have 200,000 men in the Low Countries, but the Minister and the Cabinet were incredulous.[1]

*Midnight.*—I have just received further accounts by express. The French are at Ghent and at Bruges. Ostend was to be evacuated on Wednesday night; the troops were embarking, and the consternation was extreme. It was reported and believed that 70,000 French were galloping to Bruxelles. The Duke of York was at Tournay, not knowing where to go, and in danger of being surrounded. The French, expecting an insurrection at Amsterdam, resolved, whenever that event took place, to invade Holland. I will leave you to judge of the Duke of York when I tell you that his letter in the 'London Gazette' was dated on the field of battle, April 26, where he was not until long after the action—he was three miles off the whole time! I made many efforts last winter to have him recalled. I addressed myself to several members of the House of Commons, and particularly to Mr. Rolle, but they fought shy; all wished it, but not one of them had the spirit to move what they all confessed ought to be done. I meant to have gone farther, and had a bill brought into Parliament to prevent any of the royal family from commanding in chief either by sea or land; they cannot possibly obtain the necessary experience; but the excuses made were so frivolous and abject that I was hurt to see men in exalted political life so degraded.

If the offer I transmitted to Lord Grenville in the commencement of hostilities had been attended to, I have every reason to believe that the war would have

[1] See *Letter to the Prince of Wales*, 1808, p. 98.

been over, and a limited monarchy established in France.

Remember me affectionately to all your family.

### IMPRISONMENT OF LAFAYETTE

'Vous avez connu les circonstances de son départ et de son arrestation, jusqu'à Luxembourg, où des émigrés voulurent l'assassiner, et où il reçut une réponse de M. de Saxe-Teschen, qui, au lieu d'un passeport, lui insinua qu'on le réservait pour l'échafaud. On le conduisit à Wesel, avec ses deux amis, MM. de Maubourg et Pusy, et avec M. de Lameth, quatrième député constituant, qui eut le malheur de se trouver avec eux. C'est là qu'il a passé trois mois, ne voyant, outre son domestique (aux heures des repas), que l'officier de garde, à qui l'on faisait jurer tous les jours à la parade de ne lui rien répondre, même sur nous, et le bas-officier qui, enfermé avec lui, et relevé toutes les deux heures, était planté là pour le regarder fixement sans cesse jour et nuit, ce qu'il dit être un supplice insupportable. M. de Lafayette était d'ailleurs horriblement malade, tourmenté dans son grabat par tous les genres de vermine et une multitude de rats, ne sachant rien de ses compagnons; quoique M. de Maubourg, apprenant qu'il se mourait, eût demandé d'avance que, lorsque son ami se trouverait à l'agonie, il pût recevoir ses dernières volontés, ce qui fut expressément refusé.

'En arrivant à Olmütz, on dépouilla ces messieurs du peu que les Prussiens leur avaient laissé, ce qui se réduisait à leurs montres, leurs boucles de jarretières et de col, on leur confisqua quelques livres, où se trouvait le nom de liberté, et nommément *l'Esprit* et le *Sens commun*, sur quoi M. de Lafayette leur demanda "si le gouvernement les regardait comme objets de contrebande?" On déclara à chacun d'eux, en le renfermant dans sa cellule, "qu'il ne reverrait plus dorénavant que ses quatres murailles, qu'il ne saurait de nouvelles de rien, ni de personne, qu'on avait défendu de prononcer leur nom, même entre les geôliers et dans les dépêches à la cour, où ils ne sont désignés que par leurs numéros; qu'ils ne pourraient être rassurés ni sur l'existence de leurs familles, ni chacun d'eux sur l'existence des deux autres, et que, comme cette situation portait naturellement à se tuer, on leur avait interdit couteaux, fourchettes, et tous moyens de suicide;" à quoi M. de Lafayette répondit "qu'il n'était pas assez prévenant pour se tuer lui-même."[1]

### Mr. Miles to Mr. Pitt

June 28, 1794

When I reflect on the disastrous state of the campaign and the very little prospect at present of restoring the monarchical form of government in France, I cannot help calling to mind a paper which I transmitted to Lord Grenville soon after the commencement of the war, and which contained an assurance that from 25,000 to 30,000 men in Auvergne, supported by four other departments, were ready to declare in favour of a limited monarchy, and march to Paris, on conditions not only moderate, but as politic as they were equitable. The more I reflect on the importance of that paper, the more I am doubtful whether it ever came under your notice, for it must have engaged your attention, and, if the proposal had been adopted, it is more than probable that Lyons and Toulon would not have fallen, and that

---

[1] *Mémoires du Général Lafayette*, iv. 273, 275. Letter from Madame de Lafayette, Olmütz, May 10, 1796.

all the southern provinces, connecting themselves with
Brittany and Normandy, would have declared in favour
of limited monarchy. These hopes, so well founded at
the time on account of the numerous partisans of that
form of government, are, I am afraid, at an end for ever,
for the friends of the Constitution of 1789 and 1790 are
fled, or they have perished. If in the present state of
public affairs it should appear to you desirable to have
the intentions of those in authority at Paris sounded on
the subject of peace, I will avail myself of the resources
in my power for that purpose whenever I receive your
commands.

*Minute.*—The condition required was a declaration
from the coalesced powers that they would be satisfied
with a limited monarchy and the restoration of the
Bourbon family to the throne, and, as a proof of sincerity, Lafayette, Lameth, Pusy, and Maubourg, who were
known to be staunch supporters of that system of government, were to be released. All those who were attached
to royalty as above defined would have joined the
standard proposed to be raised in the Alps of France,
and, in a country so well fortified by nature, the force
would have been strong enough to have resisted any
army that the Convention could have sent against it.
Lyons was not far distant, and, from its known attachment to the royal cause, would have joined the five
departments and thereby have preserved Toulon. The
evacuation of Toulon was unavoidable after the reduction
of Lyons; and Lord Hood, who ought to have known
this circumstance, is the less excusable for not having
taken the necessary precautions in time instead of leaving
the destruction of the arsenal and the embarkation of the
troops to the last moment. The confusion that ensued,

and the number of victims most shamefully abandoned to the remorseless fury of their savage enemies, pressed as his Lordship was in this extremity, prove either incapacity in the Commander-in-Chief or scandalous neglect and a most atrocious want of humanity in some quarter.[1]

My servant took my letter to Mr. Pitt, who was at home. In the evening I went to Drury Lane Theatre, and, seeing Mr. Smith, the private secretary of the Minister, and with whom I have been on terms of familiar intercourse, I spoke to him as usual, but I soon inferred from his unwonted shyness that Mr. Pitt did not relish my letter. I am still convinced that if the combined powers, when England entered into the League, had declared for limited monarchy, the sword would have been sheathed, and an infinity of crimes would have been prevented. But these Governments are to the full as sanguinary as the merciless Jacobins whom they reproach with cruelty.—W. A. M.

### SIR EDWARD NEWENHAM TO MR. MILES

July 19, 1794

Our late retrograde movements and continued defeats, with the probable early capture of the garrisons of Nieuport, Condé, and Valenciennes, must weaken our

---

[1] 'A most curious circumstance in this affair [the engagement between the English and French fleets, March 14, 1795] is, that out of the fifteen ships of the line of which the French fleet consisted, six were actually ships said by Lord Hood to be burnt on the 18th of December, 1793, viz., "Le Tonnant," "Le Conquérant," "Le Mercure," "Le Heureux," "Le Timoléon" (then "Commerce de Bordeaux") and "Le Ça-ira" (then "La Couronne"), and a seventh, "L'Alcide," he reported to be unfit for service. If our readers will take the trouble to refer to the *Gazette Extraordinary* of the 17th of January, 1794, in the Appendix to the Chronicle of our *Annual Register* for 1794, he will find this to be the case.'—*Annual Register*, 1795, p. 64.

feeble army to such a degree as to render it unequal to the defence of Holland; for I suppose Cobourg must retire to Germany, and leave the Low Countries, and even Luxembourg, to Robespierre. I have but little hope that Cobourg can make a successful stand anywhere; Namur is not in condition for a siege, Maestricht may hold out for a time, but the open country will soon be in possession of the enemy, who may march to Hanover and Berlin for plunder; the petty Princes will all join the French, and no obstruction can be given to their advance, as the Hanoverians, Hessians, and Brunswickers are all with the remnant of our armies. These victories will consolidate the French, and Barère may send his hundred thousands from the interior part of the country to push into Holland and Germany. My fears extend to the French getting possession of Amsterdam, and renewing their fleet by the capture of the Dutch men-of-war which have been so long asleep. Can it be true that Spain has acknowledged Robespierre? What has become of the Spanish fleet and army? Not a soldier to assist in the taking of Corsica! But what is Corsica to us? The French may land 4,000, or even 2,000 men, and in a week they would retake the whole island. I do not believe the Corsican people would oppose them, for they did not assist us much in the reduction of it.[1] We have

---

[1] 'The local importance of Corsica, and the spirited efforts of its inhabitants to deliver themselves from the yoke of France, determined me not to withhold the protection which they sought for; and I have since accepted the crown and sovereignty of that country.'—His Majesty's Speech, December 30, 1794, *Annual Register*.

'The crown of Corsica, offered by Paoli and the aristocratical party to the King of England, was accepted, and efforts immediately made to confer upon the inhabitants a constitution similar to that of Great Britain—a project about as practicable as it would have been to have clothed the British plains with the fruits which ripen under its sunny cliffs.'—Alison, *History of Europe*, iv. 819.

not read of what is doing in Piedmont for three weeks. The Sardinian and the Neapolitan crowns are tottering, and the Gallery of Florence may soon ornament Paris under the direction of Citizen David. We have no prospect of a counter-revolution in Paris or in the provinces; all is quiet. What is Sir Sydney Smith about to do? We have read a great deal of gunboats and floating batteries. It is on Pitt alone that the salvation of these kingdoms depends. Has the King of Prussia really swindled us out of our money? Or is he re-slaving Poland with the assistance of British guineas? Surely it is agreeable to see some unanimity prevail at this awful moment, and therefore I rejoice that Windham, Fitzwilliam, and Portland have joined the Ministry. You must not drop your pen—I should detest you if you did —your country demands your continuance in support of it; your writings have to my certain knowledge done much good. Give the enclosed as soon as possible to the American Minister.

### Mr. Miles to Sir Edward Newenham

July 29, 1794

Your letter with its inclosure for Mr. Jay arrived last Friday, and in compliance with your request I delivered the packet to his Excellency myself.

The public prints will have informed you of the disasters without end which have befallen the allied powers; Flanders and the whole of the Austrian Netherands are again under the dominion of France. You will have heard of the retreat of the Prussians across the Rhine; of the arrival of the British troops on the territories of Holland; of the intention of the French to invade the Seven Provinces; and, indeed, I much fear that Liège is by this time added to the other conquests of a nation which aspires to the unexampled ambition of effecting an entire change in the systems of civil government throughout Europe.

Unhappily the misconduct of the powers on the Continent, without exception, bring royalty into general contempt and may accelerate its extinction. You may be sure that the scandalous and uniform perfidy of the Courts of Vienna[1] and Berlin will bring their own punishment. The safety of the British dominions, should we survive the wreck of other thrones, will be greatly due in the first instance to our ancestors in 1688, who took care that our Government should be safeguarded from despotic acts, and should be salutary, not mischievous, in the exercise of its limited power. It will be acknowledged by every thinking man that a revolution so wonderful in its extent as is now witnessed in France, a country rich in population, abundant in resources, and connected by a million of ramifications with the rest of the world, could not be accomplished without producing gigantic changes far and wide. This truth naturally escaped the common herd of mankind, who reason very little and not always correctly; but even our statesmen, whose duty it is to observe political events as they appear upon the horizon, and to act in conformity with these events, seem to have regulated their measures in the ordinary fashion, without either retrospect or forethought, and it is no wonder if they are now baffled by occurrences and contingencies as novel as they are extraordinary and

[1] 'I have often ventured, though with great diffidence, to communicate to your Lordship my own suspicions of the Court of Vienna. I cannot but consider them as entirely confirmed, as well by their conduct on this occasion as by the most extraordinary and unaccountable inactivity o General De Vins, who has now lain upon his arms a whole month with out attempting the most trifling attack upon the enemy.'—Mr. Wickham to Lord Grenville. *Correspondence of the Right Hon. William Wickham* August 1795, i. 152. See also p. 830.

alarming. Opinions, my dear friend, take root and vegetate with wonderful rapidity so soon as their force is discerned by the people. Hence the convulsions which at present annihilate the tranquillity of Europe. Adieu!

### Mr. Penrose to Mr. Miles

Florence: August 3, 1794

Owing to the progress of the French, the English mails have been considerably impeded. No less than seven were due yesterday; four, however, have now arrived, and I have received your letter dated June 29th. Your pamphlet against the Duke of Grafton I have received; your letter to Lord Stanhope [1] has not yet come; it will be heartily welcome, as indeed anything from your pen.

The very unpromising appearance of affairs and the great shock given to the tranquillity of Europe make me almost despair. We have had too long a childish trick of affecting to despise the French and their plans, and we are now, or at least ought to be, well assured that the exertions of a nation united in a common cause are not so contemptible. Do you see anything but ruin in the daily retreat of the Allies? And do you imagine that the extirpation of the Jacobins, as Mr. Jenkinson [2] absurdly proposes, can be so easily accomplished? Of our affairs here your Venetian correspondent will inform you. You have probably seen the constitution of Corsica, and know that Calvi still resists. The French fleet still remain blocked up, but I see no prospect of its being destroyed, for the intention of Lord Hood to burn the ships, which should have been kept profoundly secret, has been publicly

---

[1] A Letter to Earl Stanhope from Mr. Miles, London, 1794.
[2] Afterwards Lord Liverpool.

rumoured here. I am told he has twice failed. A French naval officer of distinction and courage whom I know wishes nothing better than to be employed in that affair; his plan is good, and, as he would risk his life, he must be zealous in the cause. Why they do not embody the French who are here in our pay (they amount to some thousands), and make a descent in Provence, I know not. The disaffection in the South would soon increase their army, and the diversion would diminish the French force on the frontiers. I have had applications from some of the finest men in the world merely to serve as privates, but I cannot find that any scheme is in agitation. Many thanks for your kind communications.

### MR. JOHN NICHOLLS TO MR. MILES

August 5, 1794

I see no reason for your separating from the Minister. But what is not likely soon to be the state of the Cabinet? It seems as if Holland would be overrun, and, if that should be the case, will not the indignation of this country against the Ministers show itself? I see no efforts on the part of Government to prevent the impending danger, and every man who tells them of the peril is called a Democrat and Jacobin. Why is there no attempt to reconcile the Stadtholder and his opponents? It is not to be done by such men as Auckland or Malmesbury, or, I believe, Lord St. Helens—though of this latter man I don't know much. Except the Government in Holland can be so modelled as that the mass of the people may wish to preserve it, the mass of the people will never exert themselves to preserve it: 'Id firmissimum Imperium, quo obedientes gaudent,' a maxim which should never be forgotten by a Minister. The

Dutch Government was neither a democracy nor a monarchy, but an aristocracy collected from the several towns, and to which a Stadtholder was unnecessarily and perhaps unnaturally tacked on. Yet the people, as they preferred this form of government, collected under its standard, and resisted the most powerful opponents. Spain, England, and France were all in their turn foiled by this little State. The inhabitants of the Austrian Low Countries asked for nothing but their privileges as declared at the 'Joyeuse Entrée,'[1] and these States, if their rights had been secured to them, would have repelled the French, for they could have armed 400,000 men, and they *would* have armed them if they had been attached to their Government. It will be the same with Holland. If the people cannot be brought to like their Government, and to rally under its standard, it will be conquered by France.

If you hear news not communicated by the public papers, send it to me. I am just going to dine with Thurlow,[2] who is much recovered by the air and bathing. I get all the knowledge I can from him, and he treats me in that respect with the same kindness as he used to do when I was a young man on the Western Circuit.

### MR. MILES TO SIR EDWARD NEWENHAM

August 9, 1794

There is no intelligence from the Continent. Two mails are due from Holland. The Stadtholder has applied for additional succour from this country, although we have already near 40,000 men in British pay on the Dutch frontiers, while the Dutch themselves have

---

[1] The Constitution granted to Brabant, as securing certain liberties or privileges to the people, was called 'Joyeuse Entrée.'

[2] Lord Chancellor Thurlow.

not even 10,000. The fact is, the Prince of Orange has a strong party against him, and we have to support him, not only against the French, but against those who have been hostile to his family and office since 1647, and quarrels of that date are not easily made up. The Danes and Swedes are disposed to be insolent, and to dispute our right to make captures in the Baltic. The neutrality of these seas will probably be insisted on by the three Northern Courts; and I should not be surprised if the Empress of Russia, whose perfidy equals her ambition and enterprising spirit, should in case of any disaster to our arms declare with Sweden and Denmark against us, or, if France should become very triumphant, unite with her to crush the power and commerce of this country. It is difficult, not to say impossible, to reason upon the fate of Europe. Our allies have proved the falsehood and futility of treaties, while France has clearly demonstrated the instability of alliances. England is arming with a view to curb sedition and resist invasion, from both which dangers she has cause to fear. I am sorry to see the necessity for our *militarising* ourselves. I love better to see men engaged in furthering civilisation. France will in all probability make a descent on Ireland under the idea of finding friends, but, since friends as well as others would have much danger to apprehend in times of anarchy, and since no security could anywhere be expected or protection given, I trust that all classes, including your peasantry, will be stimulated to unite in defence of their persons, and families, and fortunes. You will be surprised to hear that the Minister, whom I have so long and so warmly supported, should think that I have become hostile to him, and that the officials about the Treasury should dare to charge me with leanings towards democracy. My published writings are a sufficient proof of my personal respect and sincere attachment to Mr. Pitt; but I am afraid that the ill-advised conduct of ill-advised people about him may compel me to give explanations that will not be beneficial to Government.

### Mr. Miles to Mr. Woodfall[1]

September 8, 1794

I beg your acceptance of the different publications which zeal in the cause of our country and of humanity induced me to give to the world in the course of last winter. I believe that I may appeal to you for the purity at least of my intentions, if not for the correctness of my style, and you know that of all my fellow-labourers in the political vineyard no one has sought less or tasted less of the grape than myself. If men would be honest, disinterested, and decided, in proportion to the vigour of their intellects and the extent of their attainments, what an imposing check—what a powerful curb they would be on the conduct of those who govern their respective countries! How lamentable it is that men of letters, who ought to be the most united, should be the most divided!

There never was a period which threatened so much serious mischief to all Europe as the present. The war which desolates so considerable a part of it has none of the features in common with former wars except those of calamity and distress, and really its probable issue, judging from the conduct of those who are the most interested in averting its evils, has something that must alarm every sober and reflecting mind. *Je suis rien moins qu'assuré sur l'avenir*; and yet one of the

[1] Mr. William Woodfall, brother of the publisher of *Junius's Letters*, and himself a literary man of some celebrity.

despicable herd of that class of emigrants who would prolong the afflicting miseries of the times has just published a pamphlet under the title of 'Rassurez-vous.' That the Minister in this country could not well have avoided the war is a truth which cannot be controverted, and it is no less true that the French dare not at present terminate it. The miserable punctilios respecting Chauvelin, and which Chauvelin's mean and disreputable conduct perhaps provoked, did not decide the great event; and, what may surprise you, the two parties in France the most opposed to each other laboured to the same end, but from different motives and with different views. The Jacobins, or rather the Republicans, and the Royalists were both impatient for war, and Europe, at all events, would have been plunged in blood through the cabals of one or the other. It is not in an ordinary letter that I can go into this important detail, or give you the history of the intrigues of a class of men whom I hold to be more atrocious and dangerous than the most decided Jacobins; but, believe me, my dear friend, the red-hot Royalists, as I call them, are at least as much in fault as even Marat and Robespierre; and I can have little respect for people who sigh after the ancient despotism of France, rendered the Revolution necessary by their excesses, and sought to plunge Europe in blood through their intrigues. My writings will convince you that my principles have not changed since you first knew me, nor do I adapt my sentiments and language to the times, but to facts.

*Mr. Miles to Sir Edward Newenham*

September 25, 1794

I certainly thought that the nation was much safer in the hands of Mr. Pitt than in those of Mr. Fox, who had frequently blown hot and cold, and who had alternately supported and decried the most arbitrary measures. Mr. Pitt entered into political life with an unblemished reputation, and at a moment the most favourable to his views, for the nation, alike disgusted with the folly and tergiversation of Ministers and Opposition, was impatient and anxious to be rescued from the insolence and cabals of both. Time has taught me to be less credulous than in the past; and, allowing that my conjectures of Mr. Pitt were well founded in 1784, it does not follow that my opinion of him in 1794 is erroneous because it is less favourable than at the former period. I have nothing to object to his Administration down to the commencement of hostilities, which I will ever maintain could not have been avoided except on terms to which this country could not possibly have acceded; but I cannot approve of the conduct of the war—it has been faulty and ruinous in the extreme; and yet I have been silent on the subject, not only from much sincere personal respect for Mr. Pitt, but from a still better motive, that of not wishing to bring the measures of Government into discredit by exposing their absurdity. I have even prevented a very strong remonstrance from Lloyd's Coffee House being presented to the Admiralty on the little protection given to the commerce of the nation, and I will venture to assert that it was in my power to have exposed the First Lord at that Board to much censure, for the marine force has certainly not been distributed in the manner that it ought to have been; but I would not countenance what might embolden disaffection, and I maintained a reserve in the hope that Lord Chatham would better discharge the trust reposed in him, and that the Cabinet would make such an arrangement that the trade would be protected from the predatory war of the enemy. You will be astonished, perhaps, when I tell you that a million sterling will not pay the losses at Lloyd's Coffee House, and if more attention is not given to our commerce half of the underwriters will be ruined.[1] I communicate all this to you in confidence, and in proof that my disposition is far from being hostile. The only matter on which I have spoken without reserve is on the appointment of the Duke of York to the command of the British army—an appointment improper in every respect, as hazardous and impolitic; and events have fully demonstrated how incapable he was of holding so important a position. I confess that last winter, in conversation with several members of the House of Commons, I strongly insisted on the necessity of recalling his Royal Highness, and of following that measure up by a bill to prevent any of the royal family from commanding in chief, either by sea or land. I confined myself to mere conversation. I did not publish a line upon the subject. Mr. Pitt has had the game in his own hands and lost it once ; he may have it again if he will act with the spirit of his father, and I would then answer for his triumph. But it behoves us to act with a degree of vigour proportioned to the strength and resources of the enemy. This is not a war to be conducted by the common routine of office—an expedition here and another there, a few jobs and lucrative contracts, or improvident loans by way of stimulus. We seem to forget that we wage war with millions of men, not with an Administration which could be bribed to peace the instant that hostilities became irksome.

[1] 'In the last great war, 1793-1815, our Admiralty issued 10,000 letters of marque, yet, despite that vast addition to our naval strength, we lost close on 11,000 merchant vessels, and we captured but 1,000 of the enemy's privateers.'—See Norman's *Corsairs of France*, London, 1887.

The French are brave; they have infinite ingenuity, their perseverance is equal to their dexterity, and, without being the advocate of their guilt or an admirer of their follies, I will venture to assert that to such a mass of intellect, muscular strength, perseverance, and courage, an equal proportion of wisdom, fortitude, and activity must be opposed, or monarchy will be at an end in this country, as it almost is on the Continent. Ministers should well weigh the force with which they have to contend, and act accordingly; but the misfortune is, we have in the Cabinet men destitute of mental vigour. A legion of Jenkinsons are not equal in capacity to the men who take the lead in French councils, and we must not be surprised at the present deplorable situation of public affairs. Believe me, Newenham, this contest is more serious than is generally imagined, and, if it has not been properly conducted, it is probably owing to Mr. Pitt having been overruled in the Cabinet, whereby the welfare of the country and his own reputation are endangered.[1]

### Sir Edward Newenham to Mr. Miles

October 5, 1794

Do, my dear friend, be early in your communications. Can it be true that the Royalists have risen in force?

[1] 'We had made ourselves the principals and the paymasters of the world. We had thrust money down the throats of everybody; and we had forced nations to defend themselves whether they would or not. A war planned without wisdom had been conducted without energy; and we had contrived to monopolise the odium of France, though we had not gained the esteem of our allies. We had sent our brave men to be abandoned by those allies, and to perish in the defence of their territories.' —Marquis of Abercorn, House of Lords, December 30, 1794. *Parl. Hist.* xxxi. 991.

'The allied army meanwhile stood inactive on the Meuse; the Duke of York marched his troops up and down the country during the stormy autumn weather without any plan, and, immediately after the fall of

Nay, the papers say they have restored monarchy. The latter I think impossible. If Clairfait is defeated, there is an end of the Austrian army, and the Continent left to the mercy and rule of the Convention.[1]

### MR. MILES TO SIR EDWARD NEWENHAM

October 13, 1794

You forget, dear Newenham, that, as I have been absent from town and paying a course of visits in the country, you are almost as likely to hear of great events as soon as myself.

I really do not like the complexion of affairs either at home or abroad. The error of not being explicit at the commencement of the war by declaring to the whole world that the Cabinet had no other object in the contest than to resist aggression and restore order in France under a form of government most acceptable to the majority of the nation, is now acknowledged, but the acknowledgment comes too late. The friends of limited monarchy in that country are most of them banished or massacred; and the people, whose wonderful resistance and triumphs in every direction beggar all that history has recorded of the valour and heroism of the ancients, have shown to all Europe that they are not to be dragooned into despotism.

My letters from the Continent announce that the Dutch have solicited us to make peace and asked for money. Both these are out of the question by being out of our power. Lord Spencer has failed in his mission,[2] and that royal scoundrel the King of Prussia cannot

Crèvecœur determined to retreat again beyond the Waal.'—Sybel, iv. 264.

[1] The remainder of this letter is on the state of Ireland.

[2] 'On the same day (September 14), on which the diplomatic encounter between Thugut and Lord Spencer took place, Lord Grenville in London was drawing up entirely new instructions for his Ambassador in

spare us a man. The French have taken Bellegarde, and Spain is more than alarmed at the prosecution of the war. If the Convention would correct its own vices and become moderate, France would have it in her power to offer terms of peace; but its crimes, like its exertions, are in the extreme, and call for execration.

In a letter which I have just received from Madrid there occurs the following passage: 'Notre ministre à votre Cour sera chargé de vous proposer la paix; il n'y a pas d'autre moyen de sauver notre malheureux pays, et si votre Gouvernement s'obstine à continuer la guerre, nous serons forcé par des circonstances de faire la paix.'

### Mr. Miles to Mr. Rose
October 16, 1794

If you felt your mind relieved yesterday by an explicit declaration of your opinion on the French Revolution, it has not the less consoled me to find sentiments so congenial with my own prevail in a quarter where the measures of Government had led me to conclude that your ideas on an event so important were very different from those which you have now expressed.

The terrible excesses into which a Revolution—originally just and necessary—has degenerated must certainly convert the pleasure produced by the emancipation of millions into chagrin, horror, and disgust; but the evil the most to be deplored is that prescience itself cannot say where this savage enthusiasm will end,

---

Vienna. . . . . . Lord Spencer and Thomas Grenville, who had long been weary of these barren negotiations, and well assured that Thugut cared far less about the French war than the contest in Poland, declared that they were without instructions on this head, and left all further discussion of it to the regular embassy.'— Sybel, iv. 115-125.

or when it will stop. It sets distance of time and space at defiance. The poison is disseminated in every quarter of the globe; it is in no less activity on the banks of the Ohio than on those of the Vistula, and the resources of genius and courage to an extent unexampled in the annals of history are applied to render the desolation universal and complete. A people no less distinguished by their talents than by their crimes seem resolved on the destruction of all the old Governments in Europe, which, unhappily, by conduct at once criminal and childish, have contributed to accelerate their own destruction, and, however we may execrate the ruffians by whom they are assailed, there are some of them whose fall we shall behold without regret. With respect to this country, our insular situation is its best security;[1] but the Ministry seem to forget that, whereas all our former contests were with the Court of Versailles, whose exertions and resources, being inferior to those of England, gave us an advantage, and, in case of adversity, left a door open for successful negotiation, we combat the nation in mass, as it were, and are at issue with an entire people, who, at once intelligent and brave, have been driven by the folly and turpitude of the Allies to a knowledge of their own strength and resources, and whose triumphs in every direction show us the falsehood of treaties and the nonsense of alliances.[2] We must obtain peace by force, or descend to solicit it as a boon. The alternative is embarrassing, and it is difficult to say which is the greater evil, whether to yield or to contend. It can scarcely be doubted that an extremity so distressing might have been avoided if a candid and

---

[1] This insular security would be imperilled if the Channel Tunnel is permitted to be constructed.

[2] See Letter, November 15, 1792.

explicit declaration on the part of the Allies had been made at the commencement of hostilities. If it had been clearly announced that the restoration of order in France, as the only means of securing the tranquillity of Europe, was the sole object of the war, and that no objection would be made to the limited monarchy, which appeared to be the general wish of the nation, I feel assured in my own mind that the sanguinary Convention would have been dissolved, and a regal government established in its place. I do not know whether it ever came to your knowledge that Lord Grenville received through me an offer from five departments to rise in favour of the accepted constitution; the offer was repeated, and, although an answer was certainly due on the score of good manners and policy, no notice whatever was taken of the proposal. I certainly shall not be officious to mention this fact through any public channel, and I beg you to recollect that my communication is in confidence. My wish is to support Government, not to embarrass it, and, although it is my opinion that Lord Grenville has neglected his duty, yet, as the evil is without remedy, I shall be silent at least for the present.

### Mr. Miles to Mr. Sturt [1]

October 19, 1794

The situation of this country becomes every day more perilous, and I will candidly acknowledge that I foresee almost as much danger from peace as I do from the prosecution of the war. I have been since the year 1780 a strong advocate for an alliance with France; I counted upon the accomplishment of my favourite wish when the Bastille fell, and I really thought every obstacle

---

[1] Mr. Charles Sturt, of Crichel, Dorset, M.P. for Bridport, and grandfather of the first Lord Alington. Mr. Sturt was a supporter of Fox.

to so desirable a measure removed by the destruction
of the effete Government at Versailles. Confident of
success, I recommended the measure to those in London
and in Paris whom I thought the most capable to forward it; but cold water was instantly thrown on the
suggestion in England, and, unhappily, the conditions
insisted upon in France as preliminary to the union
would have defeated my views, even if the Cabinet and
Parliament of Great Britain had come into them. When
I proposed this union to some of those Frenchmen who,
by their extravagance and profligacy, had rendered a
revolution necessary in their own country, they scouted
the idea as being hostile to their views, which, in 1790,
were to plunge both nations into hostilities, under the
impression that a counter-revolution could be accomplished by no other means; and our dispute with Spain
on the subject of Nootka Sound furnished them with a
pretext. I speak from my own personal knowledge
when I tell you that the Royalists were indefatigable in
Paris, and employed every engine that low political
craft could devise in their effort to persuade the Jacobin
Club to force the National Assembly to declare war
against England. I combated their design in speech
and print. Nor was I altogether unsuccessful in coun-
teracting their criminal falsehoods. Several members
of the National Assembly listened to my arguments,
and I believe were convinced that this country did not
mean by arming to act hostilely against France. When
the friends of Louis XVI., as they had the effrontery
to call themselves, found they were baffled, they had no
other resource than to prejudice and indispose the minds
of their countrymen by persuading them that we had
postponed, not relinquished, the idea of crushing France
in revenge for her conduct towards us in the American

war. The virulence, therefore, which marks the language of the Republic is the result of this conduct on the part of the aristocracy; it is their poison which is now re-acting and operating with all its venom, and in every possible direction. The mischief which the dastardly fugitives left to chance to ripen and to hatch in 1790 is now in full activity, and God only knows when it will stop and where it will terminate. All this is history and merits attention. These men, driven out of their own country, have trailed their poison wherever they have been suffered to reside, and England more than any other nation will have cause to regret its hospitality and credulity. Would to Heaven that no credit had ever been given to their reports, which, founded in the spirit of revenge, have led us into errors which neither the efforts of wisdom nor of heroism can correct! I tell you again that the war could not have been avoided. France, intoxicated with the splendour of her successes in the winter of 1792, acted like a man who, quarrelsome in his cups, deals out blows on every side. Our interest no less than our honour is concerned in repelling the insult; and, as the aggressor is at once powerful, obstinate, and unjust, we have no alternative, I fear, except to fight it out. We are at war with the whole of the French nation; the odds are really tremendous, for, with a wonderful degree of intellectual knowledge which may be called genius, capacity, or invention, they command such abundant resources in courage as well as in the arts that the man who is not alarmed at their progress must be insane or torpid. Their talents and their atrocities are in the extreme; the one must extort admiration from even the veriest sycophant that crawls about the Court of a German despot, the most contemptible of all despots, for they are as arrogant and tyrannical as they are ignorant and unprincipled, while the crimes with which France is dishonoured must provoke horror in every feeling mind.

You may take it for granted that Cologne and Bonn are in the hands of the French; there is not even a redoubt to interrupt their march from Bonn to Coblentz. Germany is open to their advance, and, like the Caliphs of old, they are triumphant in every direction.

*Mr. Miles to Sir Edward Newenham*

October 27, 1794

We are certainly in a very deplorable situation. The French are everywhere victorious, and we have been everywhere defeated or *duped*. A very pretty negotiator is Lord Malmesbury to make such a bargain with the King of Prussia as to pay in advance a sum of money sufficient to maintain the whole herd of beggarly princes in Germany for seven years.[1] When I see all these improvident measures—this profusion and this thorough ignorance of foreign politics—I cannot support such conduct or think well of the capacity of those who have managed so ill. The conduct of the war has been faulty from first to last, and the fact is that it is equally ruinous to contend or to yield. The war must certainly be prosecuted—we have no alternative; we must obtain peace by force, or descend to solicit it as a boon from an enemy triumphant in every direction. We have to contend with an entire nation who are as

[1] 'This treaty obliged his Prussian Majesty to furnish an army of 62,000 men, under a Prussian commander-in-chief, to be subsidised by England and Holland, and to serve against their common enemies. This army to be in the field by the 24th of May. The maritime powers to pay his Prussian Majesty 50,000*l*. per month to the end of the year, and 300,000*l*. to put his army in motion, also 100,000*l*. on its return home. All conquests made to be at the disposal of the maritime powers.'—*Malmesbury Diaries*, iii. 91, *note*. See also Sybel, iii. 380; iv. 129.

rich in the resources of genius as they are ardent and enterprising in the field.

Burke, I hear, is attended by Dr. Willis.[1] *Sic transit gloria mundi!* May God keep this calamity from befalling Mr. Pitt, so that he may finish the quarrel in which we are engaged better than he began it!

Lord Malmesbury is coming back. Nothing more to be done with the King of Prussia. His head would fall beneath the axe in the metropolis of his own dominions far more justly than did that of Louis XVI. The mission has failed at Vienna. The Dutch will not trust either the Stadtholder or the Duke of York with the army. The Duke of Brunswick has been asked whether he will take it, and if he should refuse, or Holland refuse to accept him, I hope our Ministers will have the good sense to recall the troops. The Dutch have applied to us to make peace, but my letters from the Hague say that our Cabinet has given a refusal. The French are at Clèves and Coblentz.

The following *extracts* from the letters of my correspondents, persons in *confidential* situations on the Continent, may interest you:—

'*Coblentz, October* 15, 1794.—Vous serez surpris, mon cher Miles, de recevoir une lettre de moi, mais je ne puis laisser échapper une occasion si favorable qui se présente actuellement de vous écrire et sur laquelle je puis compter. Mon Dieu! que nous sommes malheureux de nous trouver après une dépense énorme, sans dire ruineuse, ou plutôt un épuisement général d' hommes et d'argent, réduits à la triste nécessité de mendier, pour ainsi dire, la paix d'une nation qu'on avait accablée d'injures et menacée d'exterminer. Tous les

---

[1] Edmund Burke died on July 8, 1797.

Electorats sur le Rhin tomberont. L'Empire même est menacé, et la Cour de Vienne désire très sincèrement pouvoir se tirer d'affaire. Le Roi de Prusse a fini, et tout scélérat qu'il est, il a mieux fait ses affaires que vous autres, car il n'a pas tiré de l'argent de ses amis mais de ses ennemis ; il s'est vendu à vous autres pour la guerre ; il a fait autant à la France pour la paix. Avouez, mon cher ami, qu'il sait très bien faire des marchés.

'*The Hague, October* 19.—Votre ministre à notre Cour a bien à faire ; il travaille jour et nuit contre le projet dont je vous ai fait part. Il a été proposé d'envoyer une députation à Londres. My Lord St. Helens s'y est opposé ; il a même prié en grâce qu'on ne le fît pas. Ce sera, à ce qu'on prétend, une démarche ruineuse ; cependant, c'est une chose certaine que quelqu'un ira toujours.'

'*October* 20.—My Lord Malmesbury doit se rendre en Angleterre ; il a aussi fini comme bien d'autres en n'ayant rien fait que perdre son temps et dépenser de l'argent inutilement, pour ne pas dire ridiculement.'[1]

## A FRENCH ÉMIGRÉ[2] TO MR. MILES

November 1, 1794

I do not believe that any treaty is signed with Prussia, but there is a communication between France

---

[1] 'For the correctness of the different statements in these letters I appeal to the official correspondence in the Foreign Department for the year 1794. If the whole of the foreign correspondence has been faithfully preserved for the years 1793 and 1794, there will be found matter that will justify something far more serious than impeachment ; it is really full time for Parliament to prove that the responsibility of Ministers is not a fiction. Ministers seem to claim, if not a legal, at least a kind of prescriptive right to impunity, and to brave public censure and resentment, while they are marching us with giant strides to revolution.'—Note by Mr. Miles. See *Letter to the Prince of Wales*, 1808, p. 196.

[2] A member of the Club, 1789.

and the Court of Berlin, and this intercourse has been preserved with more or less activity since our *intrigants* in 1789 contrived to send a copy of the secret instructions given to the Count de Ségur, our Ambassador at Berlin, to the King of Prussia. It was the policy of the popular party with us in those days to make an alliance with Prussia and break off all connection with the Court of Vienna, not merely on account of the Queen, but because the Emperor permitted the *émigrés* to assemble in arms and gave countenance to their projects. I agree with you that the war was inevitable, and that Le Brun, from vanity and personal pique on being refused the pension you solicited for him in 1787 from your Minister, may have inflamed matters, and, in conjunction with Chauvelin, forced us into a declaration of war; but, on the other hand, you cannnot dissemble that your Court was only too happy in the pretext which the folly and wickedness of our Executive Council gave for your entering into the confederacy; and this truth appears the more evident from the marked indifference of the Dutch to the free navigation of the Scheldt, for they would not even make it a matter of negotiation or of complaint. Then why should you? Your remarks on the conduct of the *émigrés* as being generally in favour of the old system are judicious. When we were in power in 1789 and 1790, we would not listen to their suggestions, which would have plunged our country into a war with England, because we knew that their drift was to serve themselves by accomplishing a counter-revolution. Your Minister has not been so prudent; he has believed their falsehoods and followed their advice.

*MR. MILES TO MR. JOHN NICHOLLS*

November 4, 1794

I certainly should have rambled towards Bedford Square, and have taken my chance of meeting you at home, if the Surrey election had not occupied your time and given me little hope of seeing you.

There is only one point on which you and I differ; it is on the war. I must again protest to you that Mr. Pitt could not avoid it at any period after 1791. I could convince you from papers in my possession that he was even eager to preserve peace in December 1792, and, although I condemn his dereliction from those Whig principles which first induced me to stand forth a volunteer in support of his Administration, I will never desert him where I know him to be right. To say that there is no power to treat with in France is absurd.

I am going to dine to-morrow and sleep at Sir J. Morshead's, but I shall be in town on Thursday, when I hope to see you.

*THE COUNT DE —— TO MR. MILES*

The Hague: November 18, 1794

The account that I sent you some time since is wofully confirmed, and to the loss of Nymegen you may add the affections of this country for ever. The intrigues of Vergennes, and the address of the French Court in the late war in fomenting the quarrel with the Stadtholder's party and detaching Holland from you, were not half so destructive to your interests as the haughty precipitancy of your Ministers, the infamous conduct of your troops, and the rapid advances of the French. Do not be surprised if we should unite with France and take part against you.

We never cordially loved you, but your Cabinet has contrived to make us most cordially hate you.

*November* 19.—On the 8th instant we were much alarmed, and our alarms are far from removed. Strong remonstrances have been made by your Ambassador on the interruption given to the emigrant corps in your pay. He says that they are to be considered and treated as English troops, that in proportion as the danger increases so must our exertions, and that every fresh difficulty should be an incitement to fresh efforts.

Lacombe is at Bois-le-Duc on the part of the Convention; he has made overtures of peace to us, one of the conditions being that we should recall our banished patriots. The Greffier has been instructed to state the particulars to your Minister, and he is also charged with a letter from the Stadtholder to the King. I do not hear that you are included in the propositions for peace. On the contrary, I believe it is the object of France to detach all your allies from you, and, in order to succeed in this policy of hers, she will yield much to her adversaries on the Continent, but nothing to you. If your Court is wise, it will consent to our making peace, provided France will make peace with you.

*November* 20.—What madness or imbecility governs your Cabinet, and what good can your Ministry possibly expect from the line of conduct they pursue, a line of conduct without stability, consistency, discretion, or vigour, and which has no one trait of plan, method, or uniformity, except that of blundering on at a venture, and trusting to accidents for a successful issue to their piecemeal, ill-conceived, and worse executed measures? If you have access to any one of your Ministers, ask if they were not informed of what passed on the 10th instant at a meeting with Lacombe, the French Commissioner at Bois-le-Duc. Ask Mr. Pitt or your Minister for Foreign Affairs if M. Lacombe did not declare to Mr. Van Breughel that he would undertake to effect a peace between France and our Republic upon the basis of those declarations, by which the former renounces all foreign conquests and disclaims all concern whatever with the internal government of other nations. Lacombe says he has no doubt of success; but he positively insists, as indispensable, that the ostensible overtures should proceed from the Hague, and be made without delay. You must remember this man: he was an officer at Douay, and a friend of your friend De Grave.[1] It was Van Breughel who undertook the commission, and he made his report to the Pensionary, who, anxious to know the sentiments of the Convention on the subject of a general peace, despatched Van B. to Lacombe. He was not absent more than a week, and the answer was as follows: 'That France would treat with all the combined powers on the general basis above stated, but that, with regard to Holland, its present situation was too critical to allow of sufficient leisure to consult so many distant Courts, and that a confidential person should be immediately sent to Bois-le-Duc.' Lacombe declared his readiness to undertake the business, and instanced in proof of his sincerity that he had arrested the celebrated General Daendels, a violent Dutch patriot, lest he should give intelligence of the negotiation and endeavour to defeat its success by engaging the Jacobins at Paris to declare against it.[2]

[1] Minister of War, Paris, for a short time, in 1792.
[2] 'During the Dutch troubles of 1787, a Burgomaster named Daendels had distinguished himself among the revolutionists, had fled from the country when the latter were put down, and after the outbreak of the French Revolution had joined the legion of Batavian patriots, with which

Your Court's aversion to a peace is inexplicable; all its remonstrances are couched in the strongest terms of inveterate hostility towards France, and all means are essayed to induce us to continue the contest; but we cannot; and so sensible is the Stadtholder of this, that he gives the country up for lost, for the party against him is too strong to admit of calling forth the full energy of the Seven Provinces. His power is crippled, and he is personally despised; this is well known in Paris, and, rely on it, Holland will either become attached to France by conquest or by treaty. Pray burn my letters after you have copied them.

P.S.—The answer is come back from Bois-le-Duc, and the Dutch Commissioners are gone to Paris to treat for peace.[1] As you are not to be included in the bargain, I think you will lament the extremity to which you have reduced us; but remember, whatever may be your fate, it is the fault of your Ministry, whose inconsistency equals their blindness and rashness. At the very instant when they are urging us to decline all treaty, to make every exertion in our power, and even to subsidize foreign troops, they assure the Courts of Berlin and Vienna that, if we should make a separate

Dumouriez intended to commence his attack upon Holland in 1793. Now again he was in the front rank of the combatants who were endeavouring to expel the Orange rulers so odious to him. . . . . The emigrant patriots, and among them the restless Daendels, distributed revolutionary pamphlets from the frontiers among the peasants, who were already filled with a thorough hatred of the Allies in consequence of the brutality of the English soldiers. The Government, threatened alike from within and without, appealed to their mighty allies with despairing prayers for help.'—Sybel, iv. 263, 266.

[1] 'The Prince of Orange resolved at last to present a humble petition for peace to the victorious enemy, and, on the ground of an expression of the Conventional Commissioner of the Northern army, Lacombe St. Michel—viz. that France aimed at no aggrandisement—to send MM. Repelaer and Brantsen to Paris to enter into a separate negotiation.'—Sybel, iv. 267.

peace, it will be better for them and for you, as your forces will then be at liberty to act on the sea coast and on shore in France. This is a curious fact, and you may rely on its truth; but if so, why take so much pains, and why offer men, money, and ammunition to us, if we will continue the war? *Avouez que vous êtes bien conséquent!*

### MR. PENROSE TO MR. MILES

Florence: November 22, 1794

The complexion of Italian politics has remained so uniform for some time past, that I cannot accuse myself of negligence in not sending you frequent letters. The escape of the French fleet from the Bay has spread some alarm on the coast, and perhaps with reason, for I have no great confidence in Admiral Hotham, nor in some of the ships' crews, who have lately shown a disposition to be mutinous, particularly on board the 'Windsor Castle,' where the men had secured the lower tier of guns, and threatened to fire on any ship that came alongside. I had been for some time prepared to hear without surprise the scandalous retreat of Prussia; nor shall I have much faith in treaties for the future, nor in English policy in paying *en avance*; but we are so lavish, and I suppose so rich, that the sum appears too inconsiderable for calculation, and is lost in the mass of public expenditure. We may attribute much of our loss to the misinformation of those dastardly *émigrés*, who deceived us by their plans, and found in our Ministry men as sanguine as themselves. I was ever of opinion that the united powers of Europe would be insufficient to obtain the end required, that a division of interest would diminish the powers of action, and that France, as it always had the capability of being the first nation in Europe, would not omit the opportunity of showing to the world how much could be effected by unanimity and energy. I cannot answer your query about Maret and Sémonville, not having heard of them for some time. If anything of importance occurs, I will write. The French remain quiet in Piedmont; but it is said they have intention to make a descent on Corsica or on the Gulf of Spezzia, but before they can do that they must beat our fleet, and then the game is up here. Corsica, I am afraid, will be a dear purchase. Meat that is sent from Leghorn costs eighteenpence a pound, and other things in proportion. The men are still sickly, and the natives not unanimous.

### COUNT DE —— TO MR. MILES

The Hague: November 26, 1794

The Greffier, I find, has entered at length into the object of his mission, and has informed your Cabinet of the offer of peace made to us by the French Commissioners. The substance of your answer is, that his Britannic Majesty is determined to carry on the war, and that, if we will act with vigour and exertion, he would supply us with everything in his power—money and men; but, if we judged it more advantageous to make peace, his Majesty could have no objections. He desired, however, that we should so concert it that the French should not dictate to us; that every proposition for recalling the patriots should be resisted; that we are to inform you minutely of all that passes, and that the Northern powers should not be permitted to interfere, as no mediation on their part ought to be admitted, Sweden being subsidised by France, and Denmark known to be unfriendly. France, moreover, should restore to us all our frontier towns—in short, all that she has taken from us; and the surrender is to be made at once, and not to be contingent on the end of the war with England; nor are we on any account to enter into an alliance with her. Would you not suppose from these conditions and this haughty language on the part of England that the issue of the war had been prosperous instead of disastrous? It is very possible that France may yield some of these points, but I much doubt it. I do not know what hidden resources you command so as to convert adversity into prosperity, but the course which, as it appears to all with whom I have conversed on the subject, you ought to have taken on receiving the Greffier's communication, was to have stipulated with us not to enter into any negotiation for peace without your being a party, and to have instructed us to offer to M. Lacombe our influence with your Court to terminate the war. If we had been desired to oppose every overture for peace unless you were included in it, we should have discovered the sentiments of the Convention towards England; and, if Lacombe had objected to it as inadmissible, it would have shown you what you have to expect from an enraged enemy. Surely, my dear friend, your Ministers are very unequal to the task they have undertaken. If it should be asked by Parliament whether France would not have included England with Holland, what answer can they make? They dare not reply in the negative, because they do not know—neither can they reply in the affirmative for the same reason—and yet they might have ascertained the fact if they would have condescended to ask the question. But, at all events, it behoved your Minister to know the intentions of France, and the terms on which peace might be obtained. He had it in his power to obtain this information, and he has ignorantly or rashly spurned it. The policy of France is to detach your allies from you, and your allies have all manifested a strong disposition to leave you. I have just seen Lacombe's letter, and he offers on the part of the Convention the *status quo ante bellum*.

My advices from Tuscany speak strongly in favour of peace. The Government favours the French strongly, and this disposition has been much strengthened by the violent and indecent conduct of the people you sent to Florence in the character of Ministers from your Court, so that the Tuscans, disgusted with the *hauteur* of your country, have the more readily listened to the suggestions of the French, and think the politics of the Jacobins more just and their manners more mild than those of the English Cabinet. Strong representations have been sent from Naples to Vienna on the conduct of the Tuscan Government, and, if the authority of the Imperial Court, or its influence over that of Florence, should be extinguished, it is probable from the tenor of Mr. Wyndham's conduct that your Minister will take hostile measures. The repose, however, of Italy this winter can only be secured by your fleet being victorious in the Mediterranean. The French will certainly be in great force in the spring, and, though they have withdrawn their troops in Piedmont, they still hold possession there of some strong fortresses and passes, from which there is not sufficient force to drive them. Their ships, so long blocked up, took advantage of a gale that drove your squadron away, and they made their escape; and so much the better for you, as I find by letters from Leghorn that your fleet had been crippled by the detaching so many ships, and that the crews were sickly by being kept so long at sea. This is a long letter, but its importance will excuse it. The Prince Galitzin is still at the Hague, and I believe is well disposed towards you.

I have not the least objection to your keeping copies of my letters, because the facts I send you at times may be interesting and valuable, but I rely on your honour and discretion to burn the letters themselves.

P.S.—*On vient de m'assurer qu'on croit pouvoir procurer la paix à l'Angleterre; on travaille même à ce but. Reste à savoir si votre ministre en sera content. Je vous embrasse.*[1]

### M. BARTHÉLEMY[2] TO MR. MILES

Bâle: December 17, 1794

I have just received two letters from London dated the 14th and 18th November. The writer, who does not give his name, begs that I will address myself to you and acknowledge their receipt. I have hesitated to take this step, not knowing if it would be approved by the Commitee of Public Safety, and because I am personally unknown to you. I do not remember having had the opportunity of meeting you during my long residence in your country; but the recollection of all that Count Maret said of you when he was here eighteen months ago decides me to address you.

You will believe, Sir, that I desire the end of the war, inasmuch as I am interested in the liberty and welfare of mankind. I yield to my wishes and feelings on this point with all the more readiness since the

---

[1] This letter, which is *abridged* here, was published, *in extenso*, by Mr. Miles in 1808. See *Letter to the Prince of Wales*, Appendix, p. 188.

[2] Minister Plenipotentiary from the French Republic at Bâle. This letter arrived in London on January 19, 1795. See Reply, January 20.

National Convention has just made its profession of faith on this matter, in consequence of a report presented by Merlin de Douai, the representative of the people, in the name of the Committee of Public Safety—namely, '*That all proposals in accordance with the interests, the safety, and the dignity of the French nation will certainly be welcomed by the Convention.*' But I think you will have heard of this resolution before my letter reaches you.[1]

It is very long since I have had any letters from the Citoyenne Montgeroult. I can, however, tell you positively that she is in Paris and is quite well. It grieves me to have to express my opinion on the atrocious violation of the Grison territory by the House of Austria, but, since you desire intelligence of the unfortunate Sémonville and Maret, I may tell you that I have been assured that they were transferred several months ago from Mantua to Küffstein, in the Tyrol. *Agréez toutes les assurances, monsieur, de la parfaite considération que je vous ai vouée.*

### Count de —— to Mr. Miles

The Hague: December 26, 1794

When Lacombe first communicated to us the pacific disposition of his country, our Government, imagining

---

[1] '. . . . qu'enfin, en traçant de sa main triomphante, mais généreuse, les limites dans lesquelles il lui conviendra de se renfermer, *il ne repoussera aucune des offres compatibles avec ses intérêts et sa dignité, avec son repos et sa sûreté.* Telle est sa politique ; elle marche à découvert, comme la gloire de ses armes. Il traitera avec ses ennemis, comme il les a combattus, à la face de l'univers, qu'il prend pour témoin de sa justice comme il l'a eu pour témoin de ses victoires.'—Extrait du Discours prononcé par Merlin (de Douai) à la Séance de la Convention Nationale du 14 Frimaire, An III., 6 X<sup>bre</sup>, 1794, Samedi.

*André Dumont.*—' Je demande l'impression du discours de Merlin de Douai, la traduction dans toutes les langues, et l'envoi à toutes les armées et à toutes les communes, afin que tous les français disent comme that peace would be very desirable to all the powers at war, inquired if France was disposed to a *general* peace, and, in our great eagerness to ensure such a blessing, we undertook to answer for you. France replied that she was so disposed. But your Ministry took fire at our officiousness, and, so far from consenting to the suspension of hostilities between the Austrians and the French on our frontiers, declared they would not consent to any such suspension. The idea of peace was reprobated in the strongest terms; we were implored to carry on the war with redoubled vigour, and were told that, if we would renounce peremptorily all negotiation with the French, we should be assisted with money and men to the very extent of your power. No argument was left unattempted to engage us to continue the war, and a positive assurance was given that your exertions should keep pace with the danger. Your Ambassador was directed, when it was first proposed to send the Greffier over to you, to oppose his coming with all his force—to declare that such a proceeding would not only be useless, but extremely offensive to the King. Our continuing in the war was held to be indispensably requisite to the prosecution of it with vigour and success; and we were solicited to allow some one to accompany Mr. Eliot [1] to Brunswick, and to join with him in a requisition from the two Courts of London and the Hague to his Serene Highness to take the command of the army destined to cover and secure the Seven Provinces. A part of Mr. Eliot's mission was to subsidise the two thousand Brunswickers on the same terms as those of Hesse. When the Greffier went over,

la Convention—La paix, mais une paix solide et glorieuse.'—Extrait du *Moniteur Universel*, 16 et 17 Frimaire, An III., 6 et 7 Décembre, 1794.

[1] The son of the late Lord Eliot, and brother-in-law to Mr. Pitt.

and communicated to your Court the offers of Lacombe and the inability of this country to carry on the war, it was answered that peace was absolutely inadmissible, and Lord St. Helens was again instructed to urge us to a vigorous prosecution of the war; but that, if we thought it more for our interest to make peace, his Britannic Majesty would not oppose it. Strong remonstrances, however, accompanied this notification; and we were enjoined not to allow Denmark and Sweden to interfere, nor to enter into an alliance with France, nor to allow of the recall of the patriots, and to insist on the *status quo ante bellum*. From the vehement and unremitting opposition of your Court to our making a separate peace, it would seem as if our adhering to the Confederacy was an object much to be desired. No such thing. Your Foreign Minister, in a despatch lately sent to Vienna, has declared in express terms that our making a separate peace will be for the advantage of Great Britain, as her troops will no longer be necessary to the defence of Holland, and that a considerable force will of course be left at liberty to be employed with effect in France and on the sea-coast, and that, thus relieved from what has hitherto been a burthen to you, the future exertions of Great Britain must have the desired success. Analyse this reasoning of Lord Grenville, compare the despatches of his Lordship previous to the 1st of December with those subsequent to the 19th of that month, and let any reasonable and well-informed man decide whether such a Minister, so at variance with himself, is fit to be intrusted with the foreign concerns of a great kingdom, or a proper person to have any share in the administration of her affairs.

Do ask Lord Grenville how much old Thugut

receives to be kept in good-humour and to continue the war. The Germans will do nothing without being paid for it, and they well know the value of English guineas. I tell you in confidence that you are obliged to subsidise foreign ministers as well as foreign princes; but you are rich, you feast, sleep, and live in gold, and may well spare some to *leurs altesses* and to *leurs ministres*. I do assure you that Baron Thugut will have his share, or if you will no longer pipe he will no longer dance.

If you knew the confusion and profusion that prevail among the *émigrés* in your pay, you would say that money grows as fast as weeds in England, and that no extravagance can exhaust your wealth and resources! The British army, it seems, is to act with the Royalists.[1]

*From —— to Mr. Miles*

Madrid: January 1, 1795

Our Government here was much alarmed on hearing that the Diet at Ratisbon had voted for peace; nor

---

[1] 'Thugut was always ready with the most satisfactory promises, but they remained entirely unfulfilled. In the first place, he said he had no money to send the troops into the field; and when England thereupon declared her readiness to pay subsidies, he bargained for months about the amount and the rate of interest. At last these points were settled, and the two powers concluded, on the 4th of May, a subsidy-treaty, which was followed on the 20th by a comprehensive treaty of alliance. But now the question was raised whether the principal efforts of the army should be directed against Franche-Comté or employed on the Lower Rhine for the relief of Luxemburg. And, unfortunately, it invariably happened that if Lord Grenville preferred the one course, Thugut maintained that the other alone was practicable, and consequently neither was adopted. Lord Grenville then declared that it was no matter which was the preferable plan, that he should be quite contented if the Austrians would but fight, wherever it might be; upon which Thugut expressed his deep regret that, in spite of the most energetic directions of the Emperor, General Clerfait for military reasons had declared that it was quite impossible for the present to assume the offensive. Meanwhile Luxemburg capitulated, and the

is the alarm confined to the Court, it is universal, and gone to such an extent that the Duke of Alcudia has not only declared to the Minister from your Court, but to those from others, that, considering the dangerous predicament in which Spain stood, it certainly was not advisable to go on with the war.[1] I have some reason to believe that this communication was not merely matter of opinion in common discourse, but made officially, as the Duke lately declared to a friend of mine that he received the most positive assurances from Lord Grenville, through Mr. Jackson,[2] that his Imperial Majesty paid no attention to what passed in the Diet; that he is determined to act in concert with Great Britain, and that he would increase his demand of contingent troops from 120,000 to 200,000 men from the Empire; that the King of Prussia was decidedly against a separate, though he wishes for a *general* pacification, and that he has sent his Minister, Mr. Goltz, to Bâle to explain his sentiments to that effect.[3] Your Minister urges our Court in the strongest manner to cooperate with you, but whether we shall think it prudent

---

prospect of a Royalist rising in Franche-Comté was entirely destroyed.'—Sybel, iv. 354.

[1] 'I have reason to suppose that no such communication was made to our Minister at Madrid—at least his despatches of that date, I believe, make no mention of it. I informed Mr. Pitt soon afterwards that passports were at Bâle in readiness for the Spanish envoy to proceed to Paris, but the intelligence was too unimportant to merit that Minister's attention, and, when Spain made her peace with France several months afterwards, he pretended to have been taken by surprise, and much hurt at conduct so little in union with her ancient character. If Mr. Pitt was really taken by surprise—if, as he said, our Minister assured him of th firmness of the Court of Madrid—what are we to think of the vigilance of our Envoy?'—W. A. M. *Letter to the Prince of Wales*, 1808, Appendix, p. 191.

[2] Minister from the Court of St. James at Madrid.

[3] See Sybel, iv. 161, 273.

for your security to hazard our safety is what I very much doubt.

*MR. MILES TO SIR EDWARD NEWENHAM*

January 15, 1795

I fully meant, my dear Newenham, to have written you a long letter, but I have been so much occupied and I am really so very unsettled that I do not possess the spirits necessary to exertion. The public prints will relate to you the very gloomy prospect before us; and yet there is as much cabal and intrigue for places, pensions, ribands, and peerages as if abuses in Government and the prostitution of political morality were never to close.

I wrote to you some time since that France would have Holland by treaty or by conquest. It is no longer a prediction. Spain wishes for a separate peace, Prussia proposes a general one. The French are very much enraged against this country, and seem resolved on a war of extermination. Your letter on Irish affairs which has just arrived does not contribute to elevate my spirits.

Just before Christmas I met the Rev. Dr. Jackson [1] in Aust's room at the Foreign Office, Downing Street. We were alone, and, after mutual civilities had passed, we conversed on the situation of public affairs, and on the evident incapacity of the present Administration to conduct the war to any happy conclusion. The Doctor informed me that the Duke of Leeds was decidedly for peace, that he thought we had no right to dictate to France what form of government she should adopt, and that his Grace was against the farther prosecution of

[1] Prebendary of St. Paul's, and Private Secretary to the Duke of Leeds when his Grace was Minister for Foreign Affairs.

the war. Pleased to find that the Duke entertained sentiments which corresponded so perfectly with my own, I inquired if his Grace wished to come into office again. He answered that the Duke was ready to accept any situation that the King would give him. I then asked how his Grace felt towards Mr. Fox. The Doctor replied that the Duke had no objections to act in concert with that gentleman, that his Grace had been too ill-treated by Mr. Pitt in the Russian business to act with him again, and that I should see the Duke come forward at the meeting of Parliament.[1] On mentioning that the Duke was not a man of business, the Doctor said such an idea was gone forth in the world, but that people were much deceived. I then observed that the manly conduct of his Grace in resigning the seals when he could no longer hold them with honour showed that he was a man of firmness and integrity; and, although I differed very much with his Grace respecting the Austrian Netherlands, and lament at this moment that the offers I brought him from the insurgents at Liège and Brabant were not attended to, yet his manner of resigning office and his advice on the Russian business made me think well of his talents. 'Yes,' said the Doctor, 'his conduct was noble on that

[1] 'The Duke of Leeds said that he felt himself about to enter on a most unpleasant duty. It was now said that it was disloyalty even to think of peace; yet peace, he would still confess, was never out of his thoughts. He did not mean to suggest disgraceful or submissive terms, but to recommend such a peace as could fairly and honourably be made. He saw no end of the war on the ground stated by Ministers; and, though he could not agree to the amendment, yet he could not support the Address, because it went to pledge the House never to be in amity with France whilst that nation continued a republic. In this case, a peace might never be made; yet, if France preferred a republican form of government, to dictate to her in this instance was neither just nor decent.' —Debate in the House of Lords on the Address of Thanks to his Majesty December 30, 1794. See *Parliamentary History*, xxxi. 991.

occasion, for, when Mr. Pitt handed to his Grace the despatch to sign which contradicted what had before been agreed to, he coolly answered, "You must excuse me, Sir, but Lord Grenville, I dare say, will have no objection."[1] It was arranged that I should meet the Doctor and Rolleston at the Duke's, and talk over the situation.

I send you a couple of papers, and my assurances of affection accompany them.

### MR. MILES TO M. BARTHÉLEMY

January 20, 1795

Your letter from Bâle of the 17th of December reached me only yesterday evening, and, since the French have taken possession of Holland, I know not when or by what route you will receive this acknowledgment. You have been informed by the unfortunate Maret, whose cruel and unmerited fate has often provoked my indignation, how much I desired to avert the terrible scourge of war, and what pains I have taken to preserve peace. Unhappily, all my efforts were rendered useless by the bad faith and obstinacy of Le Brun. But let us no longer consider the past. Your letter leads my thoughts to the future, and inspires the hope that a night which

---

[1] 'I told the meeting fairly that should the despatch in its present form be agreed to, Lord Grenville would perhaps have the goodness to sign it, for I could not. This direct disapprobation produced its effect; and Mr. Pitt altered it by stating the delay of a few days as desirable on account of various circumstances which had happened, and which in time would be communicated at Berlin. The delay being now proposed on general grounds, I acquiesced. The meeting broke up at near one in the morning, and the messenger set off by three. . . . . Thus ended this interesting, but not very agreeable day, I might say month.'—*The Political Memoranda of Francis, Fifth Duke of Leeds*, edited by Oscar Browning, printed for the Camden Society, 1884, pp. 56–58. See *Journal and Correspondence of William, Lord Auckland*, ii. 407.

has long been dark, dismal, and sanguinary may soon give place to the dawn of a bright day that will console and rejoice the world.

The letters dated on the 14th and 18th of November were written by me.[1] But the frankness with which you have explained yourself will not permit me to lead you into error, and I owe it to myself, as well as to the grandeur of our project, to advise you that I am in no way authorised by the Minister to enter upon our present correspondence, the object of which is not only to terminate a war which serves only to increase the implacable hatred by which the two nations are distracted, but to reunite them, if possible, by the bonds of common interest. This is the sole object in view. As to the form, it must for the time unfortunately be irregular, because, since official negotiations for peace are at a standstill, I have no other means of proving to our Government and to the nation that France is not indisposed to entertain pacific measures. It is asserted that there is no legitimate authority with whom we can treat. I wish to refute this unfounded pretension, for it appears to me that we may well recognise the power which by its numerous and brilliant victories has made itself felt throughout Europe; and it is important to destroy an opinion which, if erroneous, would blind and mislead the people. Unhappily, the crimes which have sullied France since the fall of despotism in 1789—and which the rapid and astonishing progress of events so great may have rendered inevitable—have given an advantage to the enemies of liberty; nor can it be concealed that the horrors perpetrated in your country have made the most zealous of her friends shudder; but in proportion as a free and enlightened nation advances

[1] Copies of these two letters are not among Mr. Miles's papers.

to dominion, so should each step be marked by justice and moderation. It then rests with you in this supreme moment to give a grand and sublime proof to the whole world that France is as magnanimous as she is victorious. Let the Republic boldly declare to the coalesced powers that, although her just grievances give her the right, and although the abundance of her resources and of her courage furnish the means of pursuing her victories, yet, far from breathing vengeance, she is ready to negotiate for peace on suitable and honourable terms. I know enough of the feeling of my country to assure you positively that such a proceeding on your side would cause the cessation of the war.

All the time that you were on a mission here, I was in America or on the Continent of Europe. When in January 1793 it was a question of sending you to London to replace M. de Chauvelin, I was written to, on the part of the Executive Power, to know if you would be well received in England. Maret no doubt made you acquainted with my reply. Circumstances that have occurred since the commencement of the war will teach kings and their ministers that there are events which direct men instead of men directing events; and believe me, Sir, we shall see those who know not either how to bend or to adapt themselves to circumstances compelled to bow to necessity. It is now for you to support my efforts towards the *rapprochement* of the two nations. *Agréez toutes les assurances de la parfaite considération*, &c. &c.

### MR. MILES TO MR. PITT

January 22, 1795

I have the full conviction that you will participate most cordially in the pleasure I feel in acquainting you that an assurance has reached me from a person authorised to make the communication that 'the Convention will readily receive any propositions for peace which you may think proper to offer, provided they are compatible with the interests, the security, and dignity of the French nation.' I leave to your discretion, Sir, the use to be made of the foregoing information, and have the honour to remain, &c. &c.[1]

### Mr. Miles to the Duke of Leeds

January 22, 1795

The sentiments of attachment and respect which I have uniformly expressed for your Grace, and which have been augmented by your recent declarations in Parliament in favour of an honourable and secure peace, will, I trust, apologize for my freedom in transmitting for your information at this momentous crisis the inclosed copy of a letter which I have this instant sent to Mr. Pitt. I have the honour, &c.

### Mr. Miles to Lord Buckingham

January 23, 1795

It is not from a wish to force myself into the confidence of Ministers, or into a negotiation which they may have destined for others, that I send to your Lordship a copy of the letter which I transmitted yesterday to Mr. Pitt, but merely to state that they have it in their

---

[1] 'Mr. Grey in one House of Parliament, and the late Duke of Bedford in the other, moved, on the 26th of January, 1795, that we should acknowledge the French Republic. Mr. Pitt then condescended to declare that *the form of government in France should be no bar to treating with her*. This, I have reason to believe, was the only effect the letter of M. Barthélemy produced upon the Minister—at all events, I never heard that any other notice was taken of it.'—W. A. M. See *Letter to the Prince of Wales*, 1808, pp. 90–101.

power to put a stop to the effusion of blood. I wish for peace, not only for the sake of afflicted humanity, but for the interests and security of this country. For myself personally I ask nothing; I will even pledge myself not to solicit anything; but, as I know my sources of intelligence to be valuable, I will, without any charge to Government except travelling expenses, undertake to go to the Continent—either to Bâle or Ratisbon—and obtain for its information a knowledge of the terms on which France is disposed to terminate the war. The great stake which your Lordship has in the nation, and the great concern you must naturally feel at the prolongation and certain increase of public calamity and private distress, convince me that you would have made no difficulty in communicating the above offer to Lord Grenville—with every renunciation on my part of pension, office, or emolument of any kind, in return for any service I could perform for my country—but to my astonishment I find that, instead of seeking to promote measures in the direction of peace, Mr. Wickham has been appointed Chargé d'Affaires at Berne in the absence of Lord R. Fitzgerald; the Duke of Portland and Lord Grenville having been persuaded to believe, erroneously as I think, that a successful *counter-revolution* would happen in France, and which the mission of Mr. Wickham is intended to support.[1]

[1] 'The great object of this gentleman's mission was to enlist volunteers for this notable enterprise, and, as it was no secret, the French Government, through M. Barthélemy, at Bâle, supplied him abundantly with recruits, who, after receiving bounty-money from Mr. Wickham, started for Paris, in many instances for purposes very different from the intentions of those by whose instructions they were enlisted. I had one of these recruits in my house in 1795. Whenever your Lordship examines the accounts at the Foreign Office and the expenditure for secret services from all the departments, you will be astonished at the facility with which Mr. Pitt permitted Mr. Windham and the Duke of Portland to squander

If the offer I delivered at the Foreign Office in March 1793 had met with the attention it deserved, the war in all probability would have been concluded. I hope from the circumstances of the times that the intimation which, as expressing the sentiments of the Convention, I have now forwarded to Mr. Pitt will meet a different fate.

Allow me to congratulate your Lordship on your return to Pall Mall, and to wish that you may long live to inhabit and enjoy the noble and elegant mansion you have constructed.

### The Duke of Leeds to Mr. Miles

Grosvenor Square: January 23, 1795

I beg leave to return you many thanks for communicating to me a copy of your letter to Mr. Pitt. The intelligence contained in that letter is, in my opinion, entitled to the utmost attention, and I cannot but flatter myself that the Minister to whom it is addressed will condescend so far at least as to think it worthy even of *his* notice. I return the copies of your letters to Mr. Pitt and the Marquis of Buckingham. Your offer is certainly a very handsome one, but I much doubt its being accepted.

---

the public money in pursuit of their favourite phantom.'—Mr. Miles to the Marquis of Buckingham.

'In my letter to the Prince of Wales, in 1808, I stated that Mr. Wickham had drawn for upwards of 700,000*l.*; but I would have been considerably under the mark if I had said a *million* had been paid by him in subsidies; in short, they throw away guineas as if they were playing ducks and drakes with them. Our Ministers are laughed at on the Continent, and England is plundered by the very French whom they thought they were corrupting and employing to their own purposes.'—W. A. M. See *Letter to the Prince of Wales*, by Mr. Miles, London, 1808, p. 59; also *The Correspondence of the Right Honourable William Wickham*, London 1870.

## Mr. Miles to the Duke of Leeds

January 24, 1795

My efforts to prevent the war in which we are engaged are but imperfectly known even to Mr. Pitt, whose repeated messages to me in November and December 1792 disposed me to believe that he was as anxious as myself to avoid what it was easy to foresee would inevitably destroy all his schemes of economy and finance. Before a Minister involves his country in a war, he should be well assured of its resources to support it, and of his own capacity to make a proper use of those resources; and, as I had communicated enough with Mr. Pitt, and with those immediately in his confidence, to convince me that he was very ill-informed in foreign politics, and very unequal to the task of conducting a war—novel in all its circumstances, as well as in its origin and objects, and which had nothing in common with former contests but the carnage, misery, and devastation inseparable from all wars —I considered the interest he had in preserving peace as an argument of his sincerity. My calculations were erroneous; and the wild counsels of madmen and bad men at Paris gave to men in this country who were not fit to be intrusted with the government of the smallest of the Scilly Islands the pretext they desired for plunging us into hostilities, the sad issue of which, in the event of another disastrous campaign, I dare not contemplate.

Hostilities, however, were no sooner commenced than an offer was transmitted to England from people residing in what is called the Alps of France to make a diversion in favour of the coalesced powers, without any expense whatever to this country, and with the assurance that they would be supported by five departments ready to declare for the Constitution of 1791, provided we would be satisfied with a limited monarchy. It was further told me that M. de Lafayette and his companions—if we would obtain their release in proof of our sincerity—would instantly repair to Auvergne, and march thence against the Convention at the head of 24,000 or 30,000 men. Major-General De La Colombe, who waited on me with this offer,[1] declared his readiness—in case of receiving a promise from the Minister that the influence of our Court should be exerted with that of Berlin in favour of the abovementioned proposals—to set off immediately at his own expense, hazardous as it was, and proceed direct to Auvergne, assuring me that they had cannon of their own casting, and did not require from us either men, money, or ammunition.

If the letters that I received soon after from Turin and Paris are worthy of credit, the King of Sardinia had pledged himself to succour Lyons, or at least to make a diversion in its favour, but he failed; and to our neglect of the above offer may be attributed the fall of Lyons and the loss of Toulon; 15,000 men from the French Alps were despatched to the latter place on the reduction of the former; and I have reason to believe that it was from me that the Minister had the first information of the march of this detachment. Your Grace will certainly be surprised when you are informed that Lord Grenville did not condescend even to acknowledge the receipt of this offer, and yet it was taken to him by Mr. Aust, who is well known to your Grace, and of whose fidelity no doubt can be entertained. If after so many fruitless efforts to pre-

[1] See March 11, 1798.

vent, and afterwards to terminate the war, I have incurred the displeasure of the Minister, I have at least the consolation to know that all good men lament that my exertions were not successful; and, with this conviction, I shall feel very little anxiety about the favour of men who ought to have acted with more forethought and wisdom.

It is incumbent on me to assure you that the intimation which I recently sent to Mr. Pitt comes from a person well known to your Grace, and who is in a situation to co-operate with anyone whom the Minister may appoint to open a negotiation for peace. If Ministers should think that I aspire to the Embassy—important and intricate as it is—they are much mistaken. I shall be perfectly satisfied with having been instrumental in paving the way for an accommodation so beneficial to mankind, and so indispensably requisite to preserve the internal quiet of this country.

### MR. MILES TO LORD LAUDERDALE
January 23, 1795

It has been suggested that the note at page 204 of the letters addressed by your Lordship to the Peers of Scotland alludes to a publication to which my name is affixed. It is incumbent on me to assure you that, so far from being 'employed by Government,' my interference with its measures towards the close of the year 1792, and my correspondence with the French Executive Council in January 1793, gave offence. My wish was to avert the calamities which have since ensued —for wars multiply and engender crimes—nor was I without hope of seeing accomplished at a future period an alliance between the two countries. It is what I have long had most seriously at heart. If the man then at the head of the Foreign Department in France, whose necessities I had relieved, and for whom I solicited, in 1786 and 1787, an allowance from the Secretary of State, had been either honest or discreet — if he had even kept his word with me — I would have defied the English Cabinet, however disposed it might have been to crush the infant liberties of a rising empire, to have gratified a wish so impolitic. In the last letter I wrote to Le Brun I traced so explicitly the route he had to follow, that, if his vanity and irregular ambition, mixed perhaps with some degree of personal resentment at the disappointment he received in 1787, had not blinded him to his true interests, as well as to all sense of duty to his country, the war would certainly have been avoided. I was well known in Paris, and in other parts of the Continent, where despotism, falling under the pressure of its own weight, had annihilated itself. It was understood that my mind, independent in all its operations, disdained the shackles of party, and that, influenced by a love of liberty and of justice, and uncontaminated by considerations of personal interest or ambition, I always judged for myself from facts and the best evidence I could obtain. It was with this stock of reputation in advance, and conscious of being right, that I conceived the project of preserving peace between the two nations, whose truest interests and best security, I aver, will ever be found in a close and intimate union. If my suggestions had been attended to by those who swayed the councils in both countries, the ruinous contest in which they are engaged, and the sad consequences of which I predicted at the time, would not have happened. It is, however, but justice to acknowledge that, if there were men in our Cabinet impatient to plunge us into a war, and which I am far from denying, there were others in France to the full as ready to furnish a pretext, and to irritate minds already too much inflamed into acts of hostility. Yet both these descriptions of people would have been disappointed if the Minister had accepted the advantageous offers I brought in January 1790 from the insurgents in Brabant and Liège. Having stated thus much of my conduct in vindication of the officious but well-meant part I took in public affairs, I trust that your Lordship, in the next edition of your book, will have the goodness to correct a mistake which admits of a wrong construction, and which, from your candour, I am satisfied was never intended.

## Mr. Sturt to Mr. Miles

January 24, 1795

I really understood when we parted that if I did not leave the House of Commons in half an hour you would not wait, and, as it was two hours after, I took the opportunity of Sir George Cornwall's carriage to go home, as I felt myself so extremely cold.

I still retain, dear Miles, the disposition to state my sentiments to the House next Monday on the subject of peace or war. What I think will be very strong is Lacombe's declaration at Bois-le-Duc. Fox told me at Mr. Bouverie's that he had heard of it, but did not credit it. I mentioned the offer of 30,000 men, and the revolt of five departments. This he doubts likewise, for, says he, it is such grounds for impeachment, that he would not hesitate a moment in bringing it forward could it be proved. If I can call on you I will, for I wish to know how far I may make use of your opinions and information. I mention no names. Fox is of opinion with yourself that France wishes for peace.

*MR. MILES TO MR. STURT*

January 27, 1795

Believe me, I was not hurt because you did not speak last night. I have no personal interest whatsoever in the communication I made to the Minister, whose duty, I aver, was to have declared explicitly in the House of Commons that the existence of the present Government in France should be no bar to negotiation for peace, whenever peace can be obtained consistently with the honour and safety of this country. With respect to the assurance I transmitted to Mr. Pitt, it came from a man authorised by the Convention to communicate it, and the reason for making choice of me for that purpose was, I conceive, that they knew at Paris of my having been in confidential relations with the Minister, and that it was through me, in the first place, that Maret had obtained a conference with Mr. Pitt. It is also known at Paris that I am influenced by a love of right, and that I do not come forward to get into office or power. I know the value of an honourable reputation too well to have made a communication to Mr. Pitt on the subject of peace if I had not been well assured of the quarter from whence it came; and I am convinced that, if the communication had come to the Opposition, your friends would have urged the Minister to investigate the fact and ascertain its source.

It is curious that, whilst I am represented by Opposition as being pensioned by the Treasury, I am held forth by the Ministers as disaffected to Government. It is certainly an unpleasant predicament; but it is what every man must expect in times so corrupt as these if he presumes to think for himself and to exercise that independence which is as much the pride of manhood

as is the intellectual faculty which distinguishes him
from the rest of animated nature. As I have never yet
been attached to any cabal, and as I shall ever reserve
to myself the right of declaring my opinion, I must
expect to be reprobated by the two parties, whose
wretched contentions, if continued, will finally beggar
and ruin the empire. Want of principle is, in my idea,
as complete a disqualification for government as want
of capacity, and, whether these two mischiefs act in
concert or separately, much ill must inevitably ensue.
If, however, Opposition are seriously disposed to peace,
and afterwards to Parliamentary reform—for this may
not be the moment for it—they shall have my decided
and full support, and that without exacting a mortgage
on the public estate as soon as they get possession of it.
I will see you on Thursday at noon. Adieu!

### MR. MILES TO SIR EDWARD NEWENHAM

February 14, 1795

The Marquis of Buckingham is in direct hostility
against Mr. Pitt, and, if there was any public virtue in
England, both Pitt and Grenville would be driven from
office. I shall take the resolution to retire from town
altogether and from politics. My mind cannot act
with men who have nothing in view but their own personal
interests. It is a scramble for plunder, and,
holding in abhorrence as I do the conduct of both parties,
finding by experience that they have little capacity and
less principle, and that no man is welcome to them, or
held in estimation by either, who will not go all lengths
with them, I feel it to be by far the most honest part to
renounce both, and honesty, after all, is wisdom. The
French have despatched 250,000 stand of arms to the
West Indies. They will arm our negroes as well as

their own in their cause. This summer will be an awful one for this country. I see matters tending fast to national ruin. The Prussians are negotiating for peace. I gave information of this to Mr. Pitt some time since, but those about him discredited my intelligence. He will, however, if he be wise, set about making peace himself, *avant qu'il soit trop tard*; but he is really incapable in foreign politics.[1]

### MR. MILES TO M. BARTHÉLEMY

London: February 14, 1795

My reply to your letter from Baden of the 17th December is still in England; the packet was obliged to return on account of the ice, and you may probably receive this communication before my letters of January arrive. I have already acquainted you with the steps I have taken to induce the Minister to open a negotiation for peace, but you are more likely to know his sentiments in Switzerland than I am in England. The country in which you now reside has become the centre of political intrigue, and it is rather in Bâle than in London that the pacific disposition of the English Cabinet may be gathered.[2]

Herewith you will find copies of all the letters I have written to you, also my reply to a letter which I

[1] '*January* 30, 1795.—O my country, into what a deplorable state art thou fallen ! And to what bungling politicians and statesmen are thine affairs confided ! This is the 30th of January—a memorable day in British annals, and for British freedom a proud one. I do pronounce it this very day that the Courts of Madrid and Vienna will desert us, and that we shall have foreign aid no longer than we can pay dearly for it. This war leads to the extinction of the old monarchies on the Continent, and, if unsuccessful, to a revolution in England.'—MS. note by Mr. Miles.

[2] 'My correspondence with the French Government, I have reason to believe, was known to Mr. Pitt and his colleagues.'—W. A. M.

received from a friend, a member of Parliament,[1] on the evening of the debate on the motion of Mr. Grey in the House of Commons. Mr. Pitt could not acknowledge my letter to him without compromising himself, but the extract from your letter which I sent to the Minister has apparently led him to renounce the unwise project of wishing to re-establish the *ancien régime* in France. You will learn from the debate that there will no longer be difficulty in recognising your Republic.[2] It is but a step, I confess; but a preliminary movement is always something gained, and the moment that the Convention declares itself ready to treat with England on bases suitable to both nations, you will see that the Minister, willing or unwilling, will advance steadily towards peace. He will have no choice. If your zeal equals mine, you will not cease to urge the Convention to take this step; it will enlighten the English people, and make it evident that it is not the intention of France to wage war to the death. This is all that is necessary to terminate hostilities. If you desire peace with England on conditions becoming her safety and her dignity, she is ready, I am convinced, to hold out her hand to you. I am not the organ either of the Ministerial party or of the Opposition. I only express the general wish of the people whose sentiments at a moment so critical you ought to know. In the name of God, do not allow yourselves to be

---

[1] Mr. Charles Sturt.

[2] Mr. Grey moved, 'That it is the opinion of this House that the existence of the present Government of France ought not to be considered as precluding, at this time, a negotiation for peace.' Mr. Pitt, in the course of his reply, said: 'The restoration of monarchy upon the old principles had never been stated by his Majesty, by Government, or by Parliament, as a *sine quâ non* preparatory to peace. Not only so, but it had never been stated that any one specific and particular form of government was deemed on our part necessary before we could negotiate for peace.'—*Parliamentary History*, xxxi. 1103, January 26.

dazzled by the fleeting splendour of your arms; there is for France an *éclat* infinitely more glorious than the most brilliant victories can procure. Let the Convention proclaim its readiness to accept honourable proposals for peace. It is the surest means of establishing the new order of things in your country; but to consolidate your power there must be justice and moderation in all your councils. Such wise conduct alone can put an end to the evils which afflict and desolate the world, and bring about the cessation of a war which, for its duration, has been more bloody and more fatal than any of which history makes mention. But I forget myself. I feel, Sir, that it is not my province to inform the French nation either of its interests or its duties; but my love of peace has encroached on prudence, and I must ask for your indulgence. I have exerted all my power in favour of peace. I can do no more.[1]

Captain Beaulieu kindly takes charge of this packet. Accept my assurances of the esteem with which I have the honour to be, &c. &c.

### Mr. Miles to Captain Beaulieu

February 27, 1795

I write yet another word, my dear friend, to tell you of the pleasure I have just experienced on reading the speech of Johannot, representative of the people, and also that of Rouzet, in the Convention on the 13th instant. Both speak in favour of peace, and the

[1] 'After two years of war, marked with a mixture of brilliant successes and melancholy disasters, both which had contributed to drain this country of its blood and of its treasure, we were not one point nearer to the object for which it was said to be undertaken. A melancholy reflection this—still more so, when the lives of perhaps 50,000 of our countrymen had been sacrificed, and when we had so enormously increased our debt.'—Mr. Grey, House of Commons, January 26, 1795.

former has repeated, almost word for word, what I had written by Captain Pévrieu to the Minister of the Republic in Switzerland. I do not know whether Citizen Johannot had any knowledge of my letter, but I am sure that we breathe the same sentiments, and I am overjoyed that they have been so favourably received by the Convention. I beg you to seek these worthy legislators, and acquaint them with all the steps I have taken to procure peace. Express to them also how much, as a citizen of the world, I feel indebted to their efforts, as philanthropic as they are patriotic, to promote the cessation of a war ruinous even to the conquerors.[1]

I repeat, my dear Beaulieu—and you know me enough to believe what I say—that, if the Convention would declare itself ready to treat on bases suitable to the two nations, peace will very soon be secured. I have already given you a faithful picture of the principles of the two political parties in this country. I beg you to enlighten your compatriots on this matter. You may assure them that the Opposition are not absolutely to be trusted, independent of party interest, as the advocates of peace. The present Ministry might be willing to make peace if it only knew how to set about it. That is the truth.

[1] 'Rouzet: Nous voulons tous une paix honorable et glorieuse, et telle qu'il nous convient de l'attendre lorsqu'elle nous est demandée par des ennemis voisins.'

'Johannot: Les annales de l'Europe ont montré souvent des rois qui, à la suite de guerres injustes, ne demandaient la paix qu'après des défaites, et ne posaient les armes que lorsqu'ils étaient contraints de les quitter. Il est temps que l'Europe donne un autre spectacle ; c'est celui d'un grand peuple qui, après avoir vaillamment défendu sa liberté contre la ligue des rois, ne se refuse point à la paix au milieu des triomphes les plus mémorables, et se modère dans ses succès lorsque tant de causes pourraient en faire excuser d'ivresse. . . . .'—Extrait de la Séance de la Convention Nationale du 24 Pluviose, An III., Lundi, 16 Février, 1795, *Moniteur*, No. 148.

Have the kindness on arriving at Havre, or in Paris, to procure for me the letters found among Robespierre's papers and which were printed by order of the Convention; this correspondence should be very interesting. You will do me a great favour if you will send me by the first neutral vessel leaving for London the complete works of M. Lesage; and if, on reaching Havre, you should meet with any *brochures* concerning the events of the day, I shall thank you very much if you will send them to me, together with copies of the latest 'Moniteurs.' I will either forward the amount or pay it to your order here. I still flatter myself that I may embrace you in France before the end of summer. Address your letters under cover to Messrs. Biddulph, Cocks, & Co., London. Adieu, my dear Beaulieu! *Je vous embrasse, et vous souhaite un bon voyage.*

### Captain Beaulieu to Mr. Miles.

Havre: March 11, 1795

It gave me great pleasure, my dear Mr. Miles, to receive your letter by Touzé.[1] He arrived on the 10th, the same day as myself. I had a wretched voyage of eight days. Here I am at last in my dear country; but rest assured, my dear good friend, that the joy I experience on being among my fellow-citizens can never in the least degree lessen the sentiments of esteem, friendship, and gratitude which I have vowed to you for life. Your kind and generous behaviour towards me will always insure my inviolable attachment. I will prove it on every possible occasion that presents itself.

I cannot yet tell you anything new, unless it is my agreeable surprise on setting foot on shore to find my

[1] Captain Beaulieu's servant, for whom Mr. Miles had obtained a passport.

dear fellow-citizens in the best frame of mind. They express sentiments which do honour to humanity, and are in conformity with the wishes we have both uttered. I hope to find the whole nation influenced by the same principles, which are very different to those attributed to it in your country. I trust that all will go well, and that I shall have the satisfaction of sending you good news.

I beg you to say a thousand kind things to Captain and Mrs. Hicks. Touzé begs me to express his lively gratitude for all your kindness to him, and to assure you of his humble respect; he leaves to-morrow to return direct to L'Orient. *Je vous embrasse de tout mon cœur, et suis pour la vie votre sincère ami.*[1]

## MR. MILES TO M. BARTHÉLEMY

April 27, 1795

I have just received, Sir, the letter addressed by you to Madame d'Osterwald, at Lausanne, acknowledging the receipt of the letter which she had the goodness to forward to you from me. You have certainly received all the communications which I wrote by Captain Pévrieu. I have nothing to add to those which M. Beaulieu undertook to convey. I can only regret that my power is so limited, and that my zeal for peace, or

---

[1] 'Captain Beaulieu commanded a ship in the service of the French East India Company, and, on his return to Europe during the American war, in 1779, unsuspicious of hostilities, he was made prisoner at St. Helena. He was captured a second time near the same spot by my friend Captain John Hicks, of his Majesty's ship 'Powerful,' and brought to England in 1793, he being then on his homeward voyage from Pondicherry to L'Orient. The French Government subsequently appointed him to the command of a fine frigate, 'La Force,' forty-four guns, and sent him to India. He encountered the 'Sybille,' commanded by Captain Cook, and, after a fierce and well-contested battle—in which both captains fell— the 'La Force' surrendered to the superior power of the British arms.' — W. A. M.

rather for the happiness of the human race, surpasses my means of contributing to it. Seeing how much rancour and personal interests enter into public affairs, and how difficult it is to reason with certain men, I have decided to take no further steps, but to wait on the course of events. I have ever had the opinion respecting the two countries to which we respectively belong, that it is the interest of both to be united. I preached this doctrine in 1780 to the Marquis de Bouillé and to Vicomte Damas; I urged it most vehemently in Paris and in London after the fall of the Bastille, and I am still firm in the same judgment. I believe that the best informed and the best intentioned men in France think as I do on this subject; and, if it was not the curse and misfortune of this country to be always wise too late, the English Cabinet would not delay a moment in making overtures to you for an accommodation between the two nations; especially since the very act of endeavouring to make peace would give that stability to your Government which it is pretended it has not, and which alone, it has been urged, is the obstacle to negotiation. My anxiety for peace and union with your country has given offence to the Minister; and, whenever his disposition becomes pacific, or necessity compels him to hold the language of conciliation, I am the last man he will select to convey the peace offering.

It is possible that in the course of the summer you may receive my personal acknowledgment of the kind attention given by you to my letters, as I have it in contemplation to visit Switzerland. This letter travels under cover to Madame d'Osterwald, at Lausanne, by Mr. C. W. Flint,[1] a friend of mine, who is going to

[1] Afterwards Sir Charles W. Flint, Under-Secretary of State for

reside at Berne, and with whom it is most probable you will have a personal communication whenever the season for negotiation happily arrives. In that case I hope you will pardon the freedom I take in recommending him to your acquaintance, for his goodness of heart and incorruptible fidelity entitle him to every attention he can possibly receive.

I obtained passports for three of your compatriots, prisoners of war, who returned some time since to France, and, if Captains Pévrieu, L'Héritier, and Beaulieu are still there, they will render justice to my efforts to ameliorate their misfortunes. Any further letters addressed to me may come under cover to George Aust, Esq., Downing Street, London. I pray you to accept the assurances of my very sincere esteem.

*MR. DUNCOMBE*[1] *TO MR. MILES*

Copgrove: August 2, 1795

My agent has sent me down the eleventh edition of your pamphlet, for which excellent performance you will accept my sincere acknowledgment. May your work do all the good for which it is calculated! I think it is so worded as not to endanger prosecution from those who love to revenge what they cannot answer, while it is written at the same time with much ability. I beg you would not trouble yourself to send me your publications on better paper, as it is the *matter* and not the *ornaments* of your composition I value.[2]

Ireland, and Resident at the Irish Office, Westminster. Lord Grenville had sent Mr. Flint from the Foreign Office to assist Mr. Wickham in his mission at Berne.— *Wickham Correspondence*, i. 89.

[1] Mr. Henry Duncombe, of Copgrove, M.P. for Yorkshire, and uncle to Mr. Charles Duncombe, created Lord Feversham in 1826.

[2] *A Letter to the Prince of Wales on a Second Application to Parliament to discharge Debts wantonly contracted since May* 1787 is the

The accounts you give of the disposition of people in town are alarming. The papers of to-day announce, what indeed I expected, the defeat of the emigrants, chiefly by treachery in the corps, which I no less expected. I entertain no sanguine hopes of success from the invasion of France, and I scarce see any advantages that could be derived from it not already attainable from peace and a recognition of the Republic in France. It does not seem that there are many in France disposed to unite with those willing to introduce the *old* Government, and it is something like infatuation in us to continue this unavailing struggle at an expense as ruinous as it is fruitless. I cannot but believe Pitt overruled in the Cabinet, and that, not having his father's spirit, he submits to pursue the measures he cannot approve.[1] The public accounts tell us that the army of the Prince of Condé is to be augmented to any possible number, for which the King of Great Britain will be answerable. This is rather too much!

I enjoy myself much in the country, released at length from the hot town, and the venal chapel at St. Stephen's. I congratulate you, too, on your quitting London in order to enjoy the calmer pleasures of the country. The scarcity of corn is yet grievous, but the farmers begin now to bring out their stores more freely from the approach of harvest, which we hope will be abundant. We are obliged to the volunteer corps for having preserved peace and tranquillity.

publication mentioned by Mr. Duncombe. It appeared in 1795 under the signature of 'Neptune,' and passed rapidly through thirteen editions.

[1] 'It appears from the Harris Papers that Lord Grenville was ever for prosecuting the war against France, and opposed to all the negotiations for peace which Pitt proposed at different periods subsequent to these events.'—*Malmesbury Diaries*, iii. 96. Note by Editor.

*MR. MILES TO MR. LONG*

August 6, 1795

I was much surprised to find that the very first article in the 'Times' of yesterday was a positive denial of the Minister having any knowledge of the negotiation for peace between France and Spain.[1] That the Court of Madrid has given assurances to our Court to the contrary, I know; but Ministers were informed that, notwithstanding these assurances, Spain would make peace with France. This information was transmitted to Mr. Pitt by me very soon after I received a letter from M. Barthélemy, an extract of which was sent to the Chancellor of the Exchequer on the 22nd of last January. My intelligence relative to Spain came from a friend connected with an Italian Court, and also from Switzerland. My authority was unquestionable. I told Sir Ralph Woodford last February that Spain was in treaty with France, and, I added, would also join France against us; and in April I told a diplomatist of rank attached to Government that passports had been made out for the Spanish Minister, who was to pass through Switzerland.[2] Indeed, Mr. Pitt might have collected,

---

[1] 'Whatever resentment the Court of Spain might yet feel against Great Britain on account of what passed at Toulon while the Allies were in possession of that place, or with respect to the issue of the St. Jago prize-cause, we were the less inclined to expect so speedy a conclusion of a separate peace, as all our diplomatic advices from that Court, particularly since the arrival of Earl Bute at Madrid, seemed to discountenance the probability of such an event. If we consider the manner in which the operations of the coalesced powers have been directed during the present war, we cannot feel any strong disposition to admire or praise their political morals. .... We see the younger branch of the House of Bourbon hasten to fraternise with the murderers of the chief of it, and to persecute all the other branches of the same house; a proceeding unworthy that proud and generous character which once distinguished the Spanish nation.'—*The Times*, August 5, 1795.

[2] See Note by Mr. Miles appended to Letter from Madrid, January 1, 1795.

without the information he received from me, sufficient proofs of the intention of Spain from the equivocal and frivolous excuses of Don Langaro [1] for not cooperating with Admiral Hotham.

It is my intention to return to town in about ten days, unless it is your wish to see me sooner, in which case I shall, on receiving a line, proceed instantly to London.

### MR. MILES TO LORD FORTESCUE

August 10, 1795

The only nail which your Lordship thought would drive, and which I called *notre unique espoir*, has failed. My hope is vanished, and your nail has been bent by the hammer! To add to the sum of public misfortune, Spain has followed the example of Prussia, and, by way of palliating the evil to the world, it is asserted that this defection was alike unknown and unsuspected by the Administration. I was grieved to see advanced an excuse which, in the opinion of the present Minister's father, would be an argument of criminal negligence, and I cannot admit any apology for the Cabinet having remained ignorant of an event of such magnitude, and which is likely to be productive of the most serious consequences to the commerce, dominion, and liberties of this country. Nor is the excuse founded in truth, but, on the contrary, it is the fact, as Ministers knew at the time from me, that a negotiation for peace was absolutely going on between France and Spain in the latter part of the winter, and that passports had been made out for the Spanish Minister, who was named to proceed on the important mission to Bâle. I am at a loss to conceive what apology they will offer to Parlia-

---

[1] Admiral in command of the Spanish fleet in the Mediterranean.

ment and the nation for their strange and inexplicable conduct.[1]

I received a letter last January, previous to the motion of Mr. Grey for peace, from M. Barthélemy, assuring me that the Convention was ready to receive propositions from us for peace, provided they were compatible with the interests, security, and dignity of the French Republic. I transmitted an extract from this letter to Mr. Pitt, and I followed up this information by making known to him a disposition on the part of the Court of Madrid to come to terms with France. It then became a question with every well-informed man to whom I communicated the above intelligence on finding that our Cabinet remained obstinate in folly, whether it was not for the interest of Great Britain to close with France—a Republic—rather than see France throw herself into the arms of Spain, or Spain into those of France, and revive that 'family compact' which Mr. Pitt, to my positive knowledge, was so desirous to have dissolved in the summer of 1790. That object, indeed, was part of my mission to Paris; and, if my correspondence with Ministers from that

---

[1] 'Count Cabarrus, Tallien's father-in-law, was able to continue the negotiation in secret, to which the intelligence received in February of the conquest of Holland and the departure of Count Goltz for Basle gave a fresh impulse. Alcudia once more recurred to his old jealousy of England; he had a reconciliation with Valdes; and, in a great Cabinet Council held on the 22nd of March, in presence of the King and Queen, the question was formally mooted of concluding a peace with France on the sole condition of the liberation of the two royal children. . . . . Don Domingo Yriarte, an able but frivolous man of business, who had been formerly banished from Madrid on account of his Jacobin sympathies, and sent as Ambassador to Poland, was selected to go to Basle, and open negotiations of peace with Barthélemy.'—Sybel, iv. 360. The peace was signed by Barthélemy and Yriarte on the 2nd of July.

See official copy of the treaty between the King of Spain and the Republic of France in the *Annual Register*, xxxvi. 297: *State Papers*.

city has been thought worth preserving, it will be found that, in my repeated conferences with Lafayette and Mirabeau, I supported this anxious wish of Mr. Pitt with every argument the subject would admit, or rather that my recollection at the time afforded. In my mind, the question of making peace with the Republic does not admit of a doubt, and Ministers would possibly think as I do if it had ever occurred to them at any one period of the contest that we were at war with the whole of France.

There is a strange fatality attending men in power, or, what is infinitely worse and less pardonable, a supercilious arrogance and contempt for all opinions that militate against their own, as if infallibility was attached to office. I had conversed often enough with Mr. Pitt, and seen enough of his measures in 1787, to suspect that he was extremely uninformed on Continental affairs. What was merely suspicion in 1787 became a certainty in 1790; and I told Lord Buckingham early in February 1793 that the Minister did not understand foreign politics. It was from this conviction that I interested myself so warmly, and rather officiously, in the winter of 1792, with the French Executive Council —with whom I had some credit—to avert the calamity which those intrusted with the conduct of public affairs in both countries seemed equally anxious to invite; and, however servilely obsequious some of the Ministers might have been to gratify his Majesty in the desperate attempt to avenge fallen monarchy in France, I would have defied them to have indulged the King in this his dominant wish, if Chauvelin, instead of being an intriguing mischievous blockhead, had been as circumspect as he ought to have been, and if Le Brun had followed the counsel which he received from

Maret, Noël, Reinhard, and myself. If the war had been conducted on the obvious and rational plan, which was expected from the character for capacity which Mr. Pitt possessed, it would in all probability have been over with the campaign of 1793. The inhabitants of the Auvergne would at that early date have risen in their thousands in favour of limited monarchy; but the deputation who were commissioned to bring the offer to England received no countenance from our Cabinet, and, being afraid to return to their own country, M. De La Colombe and his companions sought shelter in America. Circumstances, moreover, were unfavourable to the prolongation of hostilities. The Convention had excited universal disgust by the sanguinary disposition it manifested, as also from its want of vigour to repress that brutal ferocity which sent several of its members to the scaffold; and, as the disaffection was directed towards individual usurpers of the Government, and not against the Revolution, the course of events might by skilful management have been turned to good account in the interests of royalty itself—an object, as it appears, much at heart in this country; but, unfortunately, the very means which the British Cabinet adopted to crush the power which deluged France in blood, and spread alarm throughout Europe, has consolidated that power. I will do Mr. Pitt the justice to say that I believe he was disposed to peace until he found himself pressed on one side by the King, and on the other by his own conviction that the Executive Council was trifling with him, that it was impossible to maintain any measures with Chauvelin, whose object was to throw the country into commotion, and that the succession of impostors and adventurers, pretending to have come over on a secret mission of importance, made it dangerous for him to confer with any.

Your Lordship knows from our acquaintance of many years that I am averse to faction of every description. I consider it as the bane and mischief of our country. I have hitherto endeavoured to support Administration from the conviction I felt that the public interest was safer in their hands than in those of the Opposition; but I am as averse to censure Mr. Fox when he is in the right as I would be to uphold Mr. Pitt when he is in the wrong. It is the misfortune of both these gentlemen, and it will be the ruin of the latter, as it has been that of the former, to discredit and undervalue all friendships which will not go all lengths with them. Anything short of this will not answer their purpose; and the man who respects his own character, and will not make dishonourable surrender of his judgment, is decried alike as a person hostile and obnoxious to both parties.

Lord Bute, who made himself ridiculous in his diplomatic character at Turin some years since, and received an admirable reproof for the ignorance and pertness of a question which he had the folly to propose to that Court, unauthorised by his own, has, according to the uniform pernicious practice of all Ministers seeking places for men in preference to a proper selection of men for places, been sent to Spain, invested with the highest diplomatic rank, merely to be told that the Court of Madrid has no longer any occasion for our friendship.

*Mr. Sturt to Mr. Miles*

August 22, 1795

I am not enthusiastically mad for Mr. Fox, I assure you. In the course of his political life he has committed errors, but they are trifling, and his country has received benefit and sterling advantages which will more than compensate for any errors he may have committed. The Coalition was against his own private opinion; it was the generosity and benevolence of his disposition that induced him to accede to the pressing request of men whom he loved and respected. All that he predicted has happened; and I have little doubt but he will be right respecting the long duration of the war. I think the report about the French Navy, and the decree passed in consequence, more alarming to Great Britain than any one act done in the time of Robespierre. I perfectly agree with the reporters that large ships are only an idle and expensive parade; light privateers will more effectually distress us than line-of-battle ships.[1]

The sad fate of the *émigrés* may probably draw from you a tear. I consider it the most infamous expedition ever planned. May those who advised it suffer the death they deserve! I was at Southampton a few days ago. The *émigrés* are stationed up the river by themselves, and neither our soldiers nor officers mix with them, which occasions some unpleasant remarks from the French.

Doyle does not know where he is destined to. I think Gibraltar, where we have a very weak garrison.[2]

---

[1] See note Letter, September 25, 1794; or, the *Corsairs of France*, by C. B. Norman, London, 1887.

[2] 'Count Puisaye was actively employed for eight months in England, in trying to induce the British Government to lend a powerful support to the Royalists. At first he had no small difficulty to overcome, for the *émigrés*, by their ostentatious boasting and the ignominious failure of all their promises, had forfeited all credit in Europe, and had alienated the English Government more than any other by their fanatical abhorrence of all liberal and constitutional principles. Puisaye . . . completely succeeded in gaining over Pitt and Windham, the Minister of War, to his

## Mr. Duncombe to Mr. Miles

September 3, 1795

I have been some time at a cottage I have on the moors for the sake of shooting. The place is wild, sequestered, and delightful; but, as for shooting, it no longer affords me the same diversion from aches and pains which age has brought upon me, but I still find exquisite satisfaction in the quiet of this retirement.

The reflections which the situation of public affairs inspires are certainly not of the most consolatory kind;

views. . . . . Pitt granted all that he asked. Colossal supplies of uniforms, muskets, and ammunition were collected, and Puisaye's summons was sent to the *émigrés* through the whole of Europe to assemble in the English harbours for the intended expedition. . . . It was an unfortunate idea of the English Ministers to strengthen these troops by recruiting from among the French prisoners of war in England. D'Hervilly, an old soldier and a strict Royalist, warned them against burdening the expedition with such untrustworthy elements; but Pitt thought there was no need to be so particular in battle.'—Sybel, iv. 374, 375.

On June 25th, Sir John Borlase Warren, in command of the naval force, anchored between the Gulf of Morbihan and the peninsula of Quiberon. The *émigrés* were landed on the 27th, the Republican General Hoche advanced against the Royalists with superior numbers, the French prisoners deserted to the Republicans, and the capture of Fort Penthièvre soon followed. 'The *émigrés* retreated hopeless and in disorder to the extreme point of the peninsula, with no other prospect than that the English might perhaps be aware of their position and send off boats to their succour. . . . . Women and children pushed their way between the ranks of the soldiers to the boats, wounded officers were dragged along by faithful servants, and the crowding of the terrified mass was so great that the English sailors were often obliged to use their cutlasses to prevent the boats from being overcrowded. All order was abandoned. Puisaye, thinking that he could serve the cause more effectually in England than on the scaffold, had already escaped to the Admiral's ship.' . . . . Sombreuil 'was resolved to be the last to quit the shore, and, if possible, to save his wretched comrades by his own death. He was the son of the last Governor of the Hôtel des Invalides, a venerable old man, whom a devoted daughter had rescued from the blood-dripping hands of the September murderers, but only to see him die a year afterwards under the axe of Robespierre.'—*Ibid.* iv. 387; *Histoire de la Révolution*, par Deux Amis de la Liberté, xiv. 114, &c.; *Mémoires sur l'Expédition de Quiberon; Wickham Correspondence*, i. 82, 125, 134.

and, did not this latter teem with consequences of uncommon importance, I should be desirous of banishing them altogether from my thoughts. The perseverance in this mad war is deserving of the severest censure, and, with all my former partiality for Pitt, I confess my good opinion of him to be tottering. I cannot but think that, since his last coalition, he is little better than a cypher in the Cabinet, where the King's friends, I fear, outnumber and outvote him. I now find Lord Moira's expedition at an end, and it has served only as another means of shameless expenditure of the public money.[1]

*MR. PENROSE TO MR. MILES*

Florence: September 10, 1795

I send you our two latest newspapers, that you may judge yourself of the state of politics on this side the Alps. The advantages gained by the Austrians in the Rivièra de Gênes at the opening of the campaign have served only to increase the vigilance of the French, and to occasion great reinforcements to their armies, which have become in their turn victorious, and are forcing the Austrians to retreat. The inactivity of the Imperial Army for some months has been an object of universal surprise, but accords well with the politics of the Court of Vienna, which, if it be not too strong a term, I

[1] 'Yet notwithstanding this very promising appearance of affairs on that side' [Britanny and La Vendée], 'it is much to be feared that the disciplined troops which the Convention is marching against the Royalists from all parts may arrive in time to avail themselves of their natural superiority over the less regular force of the Royalists, though assembled in greater numbers; and, consequently, that the beginning of this great plan may be crushed before the succours of British troops, which the King is about to send there, under the command of Earl Moira, can reach the place of their destination.'—Lord Grenville to Mr. Wickham. *Correspondence of the Right Hon. William Wickham,* i. 125, July 24, 1795.

should accuse of fraud and duplicity.[1] You will see that a squadron of six sail of the line has left Toulon to join the Spanish fleet, it is said, which is a sufficient reason for Hotham to stay at St. Fiorenza, where he now is, but he has sent an equal force after them under Admiral Mann.

A friend of mine informs me that he found the emigrants on their march to join the Prince of Condé's army a compound of deserters and blackguards, many of whom enlisted when there was nothing to do merely to receive the English pay, and now, when they are likely to be made useful, run off by dozens with their clothes and accoutrements. It is a pity M. de Puisaye cannot meet with them, as he might make another expedition with the probability of as much success as his last. I should have imagined that the indignation of the people would have demanded some punishment for such a scoundrel; but the fact is, we are ill served, and it is no paradox to assert that

> The age of virtuous politics is past,
> And we are lost in that of cold pretence.

This is brought by a servant of Mr. Wyndham, who will return when the office has anything to send, and will bring any letter you may have for me.

P.S.—I must add that by a letter from Leghorn, dated the 5th, to the astonishment of all the world the squadron under Admiral Mann had not then sailed in quest of the French. In a former letter I mentioned that Noël had left Venice some time ago for Paris.

---

[1] 'It affords matter of the utmost concern and uneasiness here to see that the inactivity of the Austrian army on the Rhine has left the enemy at liberty to detach so very considerable a part of the force which is opposed to Marshal Clerfaye.'—Lord Grenville to Mr. Wickham. *Wickham Correspondence*, i. 126, July 24, 1795.

*MR. MILES TO MR. LONG*

November 10, 1795

Men are apt to be sanguine in proportion to their own conviction of the correctness of their views and of the practicability of what they advise, and this is the excuse I have to offer for the warmth, or, if you will, the intemperance, with which I opposed a rupture with France in 1792, and for the vehemence with which I urged in all my letters from Paris in 1790–1791 the importance of keeping on good terms with a nation broken loose from all restraint and with whose force and resources we were unacquainted. On my return to London I told Mr. Pitt that he could not stop the Revolution, but that, with a little address, he might guide it. I thought it my duty to write truths and nothing else when on the mission which he had confided to me; and, as I had mixed with all parties, as I dined almost every day either with my old Bruxelles friend the Duc d'Aremberg or M. de Lafayette, as I met the red-hot Royalists with the former and men of all shades of opinion with the latter, as I was a member both of the Salon, which the Corps Diplomatique and *noblesse* alone frequented, and also of the popular clubs, as I narrowly watched every public commotion and was at once communicative, sociable, and inquisitive, I thought I saw the French Revolution in a more correct point of view than Mr. Pitt; and, certainly, I had as good an opportunity of informing myself of the true state of affairs as any of the gentlemen whom the Minister had sent to Paris. I was so convinced of the dangerous tendency of public opinion, and of the hapless destiny of the Queen, that I proposed to the Princesse de Tarente, whom I frequently met at the Duc d'Aremberg's, to arrange measures for her escape to England. The Princess delivered my message. The answer of the Queen marked her generosity and heroism. She acknowledged her obligation to me, and said that, although aware of danger, she would not separate herself from her husband. I recur to these details merely to show that, commanding every facility to form an accurate judgment, I did not consider my mission as a jaunt of pleasure.

When I discovered that our Cabinet was resolved to break with France so soon as Spain and Russia could be prevailed upon to join the league, and that it was meant to act upon the resolutions adopted at Pilnitz, I ventured again to interfere; and, be assured, real regard for Mr. Pitt had nearly as great a share in my interference as affection for the honour and welfare of England. You know with what zeal I interested myself to prevent hostilities, and that my final warning to the Minister at the Foreign Office on the 7th of January, 1793, when he came out from the Cabinet to return M. Maret's despatch, was, 'Remember, Sir, if you war with France you will ruin your country.' I foresaw even at that period what hostilities would lead to, and your groom can now decide, as well as either of us, as to the correctness of the vision. Mr. Burke was that day at Council. Would to God that he had been anywhere else, for he has caused by his unfortunate influence with Mr. Pitt irreparable mischief! I have never ceased to maintain the same doctrine, from the conviction that those who would conduct the war were in total darkness with respect to the resources of France, that they were misinformed of the genius and character of the French people, and that they seemed not aware that, in the event of a rupture, they would be at war for the first time with the entire French nation. I took the liberty to state to Mr. Pitt that all our wars hitherto had been only with the Court of Versailles, from which Court we could always obtain peace by the judicious distribution of 100,000*l.* in the event of matters being adverse, but that, under the circumstances in which we were going to plunge into war, no such refuge would remain—it would be a national war.

Every effort on my part to prevent or arrest the shedding of blood has been ineffectual. Nor is this all. The offer made from the southern departments of France in March 1793 to raise an efficient army, free of all expense to England, against the Convention, and which was sent through me to Lord Grenville, was not even acknowledged. The intimation I gave to Mr. Pitt, on the authority of a letter I received from a member of the Executive Council in January 1794, that the French were determined to drive us out of the Low Countries in the following campaign, *coûte que coûte*, was discredited. M. Barthélemy, by order of the Convention, wrote to me in December last from Bâle that France was disposed to treat with England for peace. I sent a copy of this letter to Mr. Pitt, notwithstanding his avowed disinclination to receive intelligence on the subject of peace from France, and I offered to proceed to Bâle merely to sound the Convention without any recompense from Government; but the Cabinet remained immovable in their resolve to continue the war. At that time Spain was still with us, Holland might have been saved, and Italy preserved from being revolutionised. You are too well informed not to know that occasions occurred in the first contest favourable to peace, and you are too candid not to allow that we committed an oversight in not availing ourselves of the opportunity to terminate the fierce conflict. Prescience itself could not have predicted the result such as we behold it at this moment, but every man who had attended to the progress of the Revolution in its commencement and had marked the character and genius of the French people must have foreseen that a war between the two nations would be a struggle for existence, and that this country could not expect to escape from great disasters. Experience has taught us that we had nothing to hope from the fidelity or exertions of the Continental powers; I intimated as much to the Foreign Office in the very dawn of our approaching difficulties;[1] and Ministers, when they sin against experience, have little claim to compassion.

I could bring a crowd of facts to your recollection in justification of the forecasts and opinions which, although they alienated Mr. Pitt from me, subsequent events have proved to have been well founded. There is still reason to believe that peace is practicable if an open and manly course is adopted; but I also think that the longer it is deferred the more difficult it will be for attainment, and especially if the enemy should succeed, as they hope, in throwing some twenty or thirty thousand men into Ireland.

### Mr. Miles to Mr. Hugh Elliot [2]

November 29, 1795

With respect to public affairs, the general talk is in favour of peace, but I believe on no other ground than that it is the general wish. I dare not hope that so great a good is near at hand; it might be practicable if the desire for it was made clear on the part of our Government, but I know not any man at present in this country capable of conducting so complicated

---

[1] See Letter, November 15, 1792; also Letter, October 16, 1794.
[2] H.M. Minister at Dresden.

and delicate a negotiation. *Tout est bouleversé*, and precedents can no longer serve as guides. The Court of Vienna is governed by Thugut; he declares that he is resolved to carry on the war, and, as he is said never to break his word, the prospect of peace from that quarter is at all events deferred. The letter I received from M. Barthélemy, at Bâle, last January, and which I communicated without delay to Mr. Pitt, might have led, if it had been properly noticed, to a cessation of hostilities; but all the good it apparently produced was to draw forth the declaration in the course of the debate on Mr. Grey's motion, that the *form* of Government should be no impediment to negotiation with France. The terrible scenes enacted make me deplore the mistakes that have been committed, and I am still convinced that, if the Principality of Liège and the Austrian Netherlands had been united as a republic under the guarantee of Prussia, Holland, and England, the war would not have happened; but the Duke of Leeds, of whose amiable and excellent qualities no man can think more highly than I do, was Secretary of State, and you know as well as myself that his Grace is a much better poet than statesman—that he has not vigour or comprehension enough to keep pace with political and social changes so wonderful and extensive as are those involved in a revolution which has already shaken the foundations of all the Governments in Europe, and which bids fair ultimately to overwhelm and destroy them. *L'histoire des révolutions n'est pas encore fini.* Men whose mental vision is not strong cannot look steadily at these great events, and, habituated to one track of thought, they find it difficult to contemplate without disquietude any other. They think that the Low Countries cannot be detached from the House of Austria. If they would tread back only to the American war, they would find that nations must adapt their politics to circumstances, and, if they had ever travelled out of a turnpike road, they would have known that men must have learned how to drive if they do not wish to overset or break the carriage. The French have demanded 12,000,000 of livres from the Genoese, and Sardinia is said to be in serious insurrection.

There are speculations in our funds to the amount of many millions, but, as these manœuvres are beyond my science, I do not pretend to explain them. The great commercial prosperity of this country has debauched its morals and manners. The spirit of avarice and a rage for dissipation, which excites a thirst to acquire wealth by any means, tend equally to increase our distress and to debase our minds. As to the Minister, I have no longer any direct intercourse with him. Mr. Burke, who was once his bitter enemy, has contrived to obtain his confidence; but my best wishes will continue to accompany Mr. Pitt even after I have yielded to many powerful calls to withdraw from the turmoil of political parties. I long for a retreat amidst that simplicity of rural life which has resisted the contagion of the times. It is not absolute solitude that I want. I know that my mind is capable of great exertions, but its pursuits must have *utility* for its object and *rectitude* as its guide. Among all my diplomatic acquaintances I have met few men whose character and talents I so much appreciate as your own; your dignified conduct at Berlin showed that you were incapable of stooping to anything that is unjustifiable, a trait which I heard mentioned at Lord Torrington's table ten years ago; and I know not how to express the intense pleasure I derived when Mr. Huskisson brought you to my house in Paris in the autumn of 1790. Your relations with Government, and my knowledge of your good qualities in mind and heart, induced me to throw off all reserve, and I spoke freely of the propriety of the measure then adopted, but weakly pursued, and soon afterwards ignorantly and unfortunately relinquished.[1]

My present idea is that, unless peace is obtained very soon, Spain will take part against us. I said so several months ago; it was then, however, mere conjecture, and as such only I offered it; but now I have very good grounds for saying that Spain will soon join France.[2] If anything worthy of your attention should occur, I will certainly write to you. In the meantime it will give me pleasure to hear that this letter has reached you. I send it at a venture to the Foreign Office. Your last letter now lies upon my table.

*MR. MILES TO MR. STURT*

December 8, 1795

Do not write to me again, dear Sturt, until you hear from me. I am weary and disgusted with the conduct of all parties; but so far from expecting men to be angels, as you say, I desire nothing more of mankind than the exhibition of that candour and frankness which I profess, and which is certainly within the reach of all

[1] The allusion is to the Family Compact and the mission to Paris.

[2] 'The Spaniards, on the 10th of August, 1796, concluded a treaty of alliance, offensive and defensive, with France, on the footing of the Family Compact. By this treaty, the powers mutually guaranteed to each other their dominions both in the Old and the New World, and engaged to assist each other, in case of attack, with 24,000 land troops, thirty ships of the line, and six frigates. This was followed in the beginning of October by a formal declaration of war on the part of Spain against Great Britain. Thus England, which had commenced the war with so many confederates, saw herself not only deprived of all her maritime allies, but the whole coasts of Europe, from the Texel to Gibraltar, arrayed in fierce hostility against her.'—Alison, v. 806.

people. I never belonged to any party or political club in this country, and, if I went to the latter at Paris, it was to amuse myself, and to study, as a philosopher and politician, the wonderful change which the Revolution in France had produced on the minds of men. My great objection is, that political parties are composed of men who have their own personal interests or ambition more in view than the good of their country.

My opinion of Mr. Pitt will never change. I will adhere to it to the last moment of my existence. Until the commencement of the war, I consider him to have been the ablest and best-intentioned Minister that this country has witnessed since his father was in office, and, if he had possessed the fire and dignity of his father, he would have been as great a War Minister; but he wants the authority and firmness of his intrepid and magnanimous sire. If, indeed, he inherits the noble qualities of Lord Chatham, it is evident that the corruption of the times will not allow him to exert or display them, and the necessity of temporising with the vain and arrogant will finally disgrace and destroy him. In a word, the country owes the most serious obligations to Mr. Pitt for his having destroyed the Coalition, for his having prevented the India Bill of Mr. Fox, or rather of Mr. Burke, for his Commercial Treaty, and for his general measures of finance; and, thinking thus well of him, I must allow all these great and superlative merits to weigh much in his favour against the opposite scale, which by-the-by, would never have been attached to the balance but for this unfortunate war—the sad consequences of which I deprecate as much as any man, but which, pressed as he was by the King, it was not in his power, as I have repeatedly told you, to avoid. I am not a man of compliments, but my love of truth will not allow me to withhold that justice which is due to another because I differ with him in opinion. My recent publications prove that I differ much on many of the late public measures of the Minister; but Mr. Pitt is, nevertheless, in my opinion, the only man to make peace, because he is the only man in whom the nation can confide with the least risk. The party, Sturt, with whom you act have no share in the public confidence. The nation cannot trust them, and your own confessions to me of the selfish and interested views of many of them are so many proofs of this truth.

I wish I had sufficient influence with Sieyès and Rewbell,[1] who are both known to me, to engage them to make overtures of peace. The return of the Stadtholder and the independence of the Netherlands might perhaps facilitate a negotiation; but France is not yet wise enough, or impoverished enough, I am afraid, to come into such reasonable terms. Once more, Sturt, I swear to you that I am weary of the duplicity and malevolence of the political world, and, though reasons which must occur to you forbid me to accept your offer, I shall certainly get out of town somewhere, and rest quiet, as soon as I can meet with a place to my liking. Adieu!

### MR. MILES TO SIR EDWARD NEWENHAM

Froyle, near Alton: December 20, 1795

Your letter, my dear Newenham, was an acceptable treat, for friendship with me is a sentiment, and I look back with pleasure through some twenty years of life to the date when our acquaintance first commenced. I have fled from the metropolis, the scene of noise and guilt

---

[1] One of the five members of the Directory. Sieyès had been also elected a member, but, declining for the present, his place was filled up by M. Carnot. The Directory superseded the Convention, October 27, 1795.

and the arena of political dishonesty and incapacity, in the hope of finding repose; but my too busy mind, the assassin of its own tranquillity, brings to my recollection past and happier times, and, no longer blessed with that constant and impetuous flow of animal spirits which marked the earlier period of my manhood, I may linger out my days in solitude, and, unless circumstances shall recall me to a sphere of mental activity, I may moulder away amid the luxuries of a country life. Say, Newenham, if you think that my present resolution to retire from conflict with this busy world is in harmony with my natural character or disposition!

With respect to politics, I am not competent to speak on the present lamentable state of Irish affairs from want of information; but this I predict, that in declaring any part of Ireland out of the King's peace, the Government virtually pronounces that part to be independent, and independence to a part will ultimately give independence to the whole. Our prospects are not bright in any direction. I have no wish to see the Opposition return to office, because I believe that Fox has even less political rectitude than Pitt, and that he would have recourse to the same corrupt means to keep himself in office that Mr. Pitt now has to keep the Opposition out. The country would not be benefited by the change of men, and, as a change of *measures* does not suit the views or the capacities of either party, the machine—ponderous and deranged as it is—must go on till it breaks down. I do not know from what part of Lord Malmesbury's conduct you augur so favourably of his abilities; *il n'est ni plus ni moins qu'intrigant*. The horizon everywhere is hazy, and, when I tell you that we are not yet at the term of our calamities and humiliations, I shall only repeat a truth that is felt and acknowledged by every man of candour and common sense. Pitt has had a tremendous fall; and it is not in the nature of things that he should ever recover his former position. He courted and obtained the assistance of Burke, and then thought that he would be invincible with such a champion at his side. But he will not strengthen his position by the unnatural alliance; nor do I envy him the acquisition of such a man, but, on the contrary, I lament the influence the latter has obtained and the counsel he has given. I have had one steady, uniform line in politics, founded upon a thorough investigation of the principles and purposes for which governments were instituted, and from which I cannot swerve to humour avarice, vanity, or ambition. I bitterly lament that Pitt should have fallen from the glorious, the stupendous height on which he stood at one period of his life—noble and erect—the arbiter of other nations and almost a divinity in his own![1]

It was this appreciation of his talents, sagacity, and rectitude that drew me forth into public notice as a warm supporter of his Administration, after I had sought seclusion on the banks of the Meuse; and,

[1] 'From the day on which Pitt was placed at the head of affairs there was an end of secret influence. His haughty and aspiring spirit was not to be satisfied with the mere show of power. Any attempt to undermine him at Court, any mutinous movement among his followers in the House of Commons, was certain to be at once put down. He had only to tender his resignation, and he could dictate his own terms. For he, and he alone, stood between the King and the Coalition. He was therefore little less than mayor of the palace. The nation loudly applauded the King for having the wisdom to repose entire confidence in so excellent a Minister .... To such a height of power and glory had this extraordinary man risen at twenty-nine years of age. And now the tide was on the turn. Only ten days after the triumphant procession to St. Paul's, the States-General of France, after an interval of a hundred and seventy-four years, met at Versailles,' &c.—*Macaulay on Pitt.*

while he pursued the line of right, I followed him with
an ardour that mocked alike the smiles and frowns of
fortune. It is not possible here to enumerate the
points on which I have materially differed from him.
They are not unfamiliar to you. In all matters that
relate to our foreign interests he wants information—
he is without knowledge and without system. In the
conduct of the war he has failed in judgment, and,
what is no less to be regretted, he wants that bold,
vigorous, and decisive character—quick in conception
and prompt in execution—which ensured glory to his
father and prosperity to his country. His want of
vigour of mind was never more evident than in not
seizing upon the Spanish fleet then in his power when
Spain violated the faith of treaties by a separate peace
with the common enemy. He knew from me last
February that the Court of Madrid was negotiating
with France, and I informed him at the same time that
passports were waiting for the Spanish Ambassador to
proceed to Bâle. In January he received, through me,
assurances from the Convention of the readiness of
France to entertain propositions for peace. In January
1794 I forewarned him that the French army in the
Low Countries would, if necessary, be augmented to
200,000 men, and that France was resolved, *coûte que
coûte*, to expel us from the Netherlands. In March
1793 five departments in the very Alps of France
offered to march from 25,000 to 30,000 men against the
Convention in favour of the constitution which Louis
XVI. had accepted, provided Great Britain would
declare herself satisfied with a limited monarchy. In
1792 every effort was employed by me to prevent the
war; and in 1790 an alliance, to my certain knowledge, might have been formed with France. I was sent

to Paris in that year, as you know, for the particular purpose of detaching France from Spain; and, if those who employed me had been consistent and allowed me to accomplish what they desired me to undertake, the present war would have been avoided, and France, detached from Spain, would have been the friend, not the enemy, of England. What is now the situation of our country? It is as deplorable as mismanagement amounting almost to imbecility can make it, and Mr. Pitt, whether he strives for peace or prefers the continuation of war—if he has not already rendered a revolution inevitable—has, at least, by his profusion and want of system and energy, brought us into a position of incalculable embarrassment and danger both at home and abroad.

I have thus rapidly glanced back to the year 1790 to convince you how inadequately Pitt has comprehended the great revolution that has happened in France and its very obvious consequences. This is a long letter. It is my manifesto. My sincere regards to Lady Newenham. God bless you.[1]

### MR. MILES TO LORD BUCKINGHAM
Froyle, near Alton: December 25, 1795

It is not to harass your mind in a moment of multiplied difficulties and dangers that I entreat your Lord-

[1] 'So convinced was Pitt that the enterprise before him would be short and easy, that this great financier entirely abstained at the opening of the war from imposing any considerable war taxation, and at once added enormously in its very earliest stage to that national debt which he believed it to be his great mission to liquidate. A speedy peace, the rich colonies that were certain to be wrested from France, and the magical virtues of the sinking fund, would soon, he believed, restore the finances of England to their former prosperity. It was only very slowly and painfully that the conviction was forced upon him that England had entered on a mortal struggle, the most dangerous, the most doubtful, and the most costly she had ever waged.'—Lecky, vi. 134.

ship's deliberate perusal of the manuscript which accompanies this letter, and which is addressed to the King on the lamentable state of his affairs.[1]

Unconnected as I have ever been through life with every description of party—in love with peace, and desirous of that obscurity in which I have sought refuge in vain from the distractions of the times—I can be influenced only by a high sense of public duty to emerge from my retreat, in hope that the strong facts produced may induce his Majesty to come forward and perform his part in the great struggle. The improvident counsels which have involved us abroad tend to multiply the imminent dangers which threaten us at home. I have forborne to expatiate on the imbecility which has reduced the country to its present deplorable condition, not from motives of tenderness towards those who have so fatally misled their sovereign and the nation, but from the conviction I feel that retrospect can answer no good purpose, and that a detailed account of blunders and omissions, with an exposure of pernicious and ill-advised measures, would serve only to stimulate the people to acts of outrage at a moment when their entire force and energy are necessary to repel the gigantic efforts of a powerful enemy, resolved, as it would appear—unless, indeed, successful negotiations for peace intervene—either to destroy us or perish in the attempt. It is from this consideration that I forbear to enumerate the fatal errors which mark the whole of Mr. Pitt's Administration, so far as it is connected with foreign transactions.[2] It is from this same

[1] This manuscript is still intact among Mr. Miles's papers. It was never published as intended. The necessity for *Parliamentary reform* is warmly urged in the address.

[2] 'His first Administration lasted seventeen years. That long period is divided by a strongly marked line into two almost exactly equal parts.

consideration that I am silent on the fatal abandonment of his well-conceived project to dissolve the Family Compact at the very moment when I had disposed the public mind in Paris to such a measure, and had transmitted the fullest assurances from M. de Lafayette and from the elder Mirabeau that the dissolution of that Compact should have their most cordial and strenuous recommendation, provided they could be assured of the pacific disposition of Great Britain, and, above all, if they could hope that it would lead to an alliance between the two nations, whose mutual interest it was that they should love and respect each other. It is not for me to inquire into the motives that decided Mr. Pitt to change his plan. I shall only beg leave to remark to your Lordship that, if he had persevered, he would have accomplished the object which he seemed to have very much at heart in 1790, and it would have ensured peace and prosperity to both countries. If peace with France was a desirable object under her ancient form of government, it was infinitely more so when she became emancipated, and restored, as it were, to the full exercise of her own powers and to a perfect knowledge of her strength and abundant resource. If it was the interest of Great Britain to preserve a good understanding with the French Court, it was no less so to keep well with the French nation, bursting, as it had unexpectedly done, into full-grown political existence, fearful of losing its new-born liberty

The first part ended and the second began in the autumn of 1792. Throughout both parts Pitt displayed in the highest degree the talents of a Parliamentary leader. During the first he was a fortunate and in many respects a skilful administrator. With the difficulties which he had to encounter during the second part he was altogether incapable of contending; but his eloquence and his perfect mastery of the tactics of the House of Commons concealed his incapacity from the multitude.'— 'Macaulay on Pitt,' *Encyclopædia Britannica*, ninth edition.

and jealous of the hostile powers by whom it was surrounded.

In 1786 I transmitted to Mr. Pitt the rough sketch of an alliance between the two kingdoms projected by the late Duc d'Aiguillon when Minister, and in which it was proposed that France, in order to avoid causing any jealousy to England, should have no more than fifty sail of the line. The Marquis de Joviac, from whom I received the project, was to have come over to make the proposal, but a change in the councils of Louis XV. put an end to the business. In the year 1790 the popular party in the National Assembly were well inclined to revive and realise this project; they even looked wistfully towards England; and those with whom I conversed in the infancy of the Revolution were ready to give the British Minister every assurance of good faith. So far as my fallible judgment and the means of information I possessed enabled me to decide, it appeared evidently to be the interest of England to secure an alliance with France, after she had become free, rather than allow her to throw herself into the arms of Spain. Mr. Pitt seemed to have entertained the same idea when he sent me to Paris for the purpose of dissolving the Family Compact; and what pleaded most strongly in its favour was the impossibility of France and England living, under actual circumstances, on any other terms with each other than those of allies or of inveterate enemies. In the event of the latter alternative it behoved the King's servants to have been fully assured of the capacity of this country to engage in war with a nation that would act against us in a mass and not by platoons.

I would not have recurred to the ruinous contest in which we are engaged were it not to justify my predictions to Mr. Pitt and to Lord Fortescue—predictions often reiterated to yourself and to Mr. Long, Mr. Aust, and many others, from 1790 to 1795. I wish also to make your Lordship sensible of the gross error on the part of the Minister in not espousing the cause of the Constitutionalists when they offered in March 1793 to secure Lyons, and to proceed with an army against the Convention, under conditions that required absolutely nothing from Great Britain except the assurance of being satisfied with limited monarchy. By the rejection of this proposal, which emanated spontaneously from men in possession of the most inaccessible parts of France, and who still retained credit and power, we consigned some of them to beggary or exile, others to the guillotine, whilst the rest were forced, as a measure of self-defence, to become Republicans, as your Lordship or myself would have done, perhaps, under similar circumstances.

On the subject of Parliamentary reform, it is most probable that my opinions are in direct opposition to your own, but it is not to give pain and still less to oppose you that I assert them. I am no stranger to the many excellent virtues that adorn your character in private life, and, if the influence of which the nation complains was everywhere exercised with the same regard to dignity and discretion as it is in the county in which your Lordship resides, the abuses which have excited the clamour against the interference of peers would never have had an existence. This is an acknowledgment due to your candour and integrity. I have considered the influence at elections as a violation of the principles of the Constitution, and my chief inducement for coming forward in support of Mr. Pitt's Administration was his solemn pledge to the country to restore to Parliament the independence it had lost. My several letters to you, and a long essay, under the signature of 'Neptune,' in the 'Morning Post,' in January 1785, as also many of my pamphlets, are proofs that I have consistently and strenuously insisted on the policy and justice of such a measure; and, if I have ventured to come forward again in a letter addressed to the King upon this important subject, it is under the fullest conviction —and I appeal to God as an evidence of my sincerity— that on the measure of reform depends the preservation of monarchy in these realms. Among the numerous pamphlets which I brought from Paris in 1791 for your Lordship there is one entitled, 'Que deviendra de nous?' I did not expect that a similar question would in my time become fully as applicable to this kingdom as it was to France. The question startles me; but, however much I may have the misfortune to differ from you on the several topics contained in my letter to his Majesty, I do entreat you to give me credit for purity of intention, and to consider it, as it really is, the production of an ardent and ingenuous mind labouring under the conviction that, unless the measure of Parliamentary reform be adopted by the House of Commons, serious calamities may befall this kingdom, and the reform will be undertaken by men the least qualified for a business so delicate and important.[1]

[1] 'In office Pitt had redeemed the pledges which he had, at his entrance into public life, given to the supporters of Parliamentary reform. He had, in 1785, brought forward a judicious plan for the improvement of the representative system, and had prevailed on the King, not only to refrain from talking against that plan, but to recommend it to the Houses in a speech from the throne. This attempt failed; but there can be little doubt that, if the French Revolution had not produced a violent reaction of public feeling, Pitt would have performed, with little difficulty and no danger, that great work which, at a later period, Lord Grey could accomplish only by means which for a time loosened the very foundations of the commonwealth.'—*Macaulay on Pitt.*

## M. MARET TO MR. MILES

Bâle : December 26, 1795

Votre lettre et votre amitié, mon cher Miles, m'ont comblé de joie. Je suis libre depuis une heure, et c'est en recevant la liberté que j'ai eu le précieux témoignage de votre souvenir. Je rentre à l'instant en France, et vous écris à la hâte ces deux mots de peur que les communications soient plus lentes ou moins faciles. Vous aurez une lettre de moi incessamment. Mes hommages à Mademoiselle votre fille. Mourgue, qui est à Paris, vient de m'écrire. Il apprendra de vos nouvelles avec grand plaisir. J'écris à Viotta. Recevez, mon cher Miles, les assurances de mon inviolable attachement.[1]

---

[1] 'Le projet du cartel d'échange dans lequel étaient compris Maret et Sémonville avait été présenté par Treilhard dans la séance de la Convention du 30 Juin 1795, et approuvé à l'unanimité. Néanmoins, plus de six mois s'écoulèrent encore avant leur rentrée en France. Dans cet intervalle le régime conventionnel avait fait place à la constitution de l'An III., et ce fut seulement le 11 Janvier 1796 que les deux ambassadeurs, enfin libres, furent présentés au Conseil des Cinq-Cents. Par une coïncidence évidemment préméditée, c'était alors Treilhard qui présidait.'—Ernouf, p. 189.

M. Maret was sent by the Directory to Lille in 1797 as one of the plenipotentiaries charged to treat, in conjunction with Lord Malmesbury, on the subject of peace with England. He afterwards attached himself to the fortunes of Napoleon—'fut nommé comte en 1807, et duc de Bassano deux ans après,' and became Minister of Foreign Affairs under the Empire. Reinhard, writing to Mr. Miles, August 6, 1814, says : 'Quant à M. le Duc de Bassano, il est à la campagne et son règne est fini.' However, he returned to power during the Hundred Days, witnessed the disaster at Waterloo, and, for a short period, resumed office as Minister of the Interior under the restored monarchy. 'Maret ne vécut pas assez pour assister au retour triomphal des restes de Napoléon. Il était mort l'année précédente, le 13 Mai, 1839, âgé de soixante-quinze ans, à la suite d'une courte maladie. Ses derniers moments, comme toute sa vie, dit le *Moniteur*, furent l'objet des plus honorables sympathies.'—Ernouf, p. 678.

### Mr. Miles to the Duke of Leeds

Froyle, Alton: December 30, 1795.

If I refrain from giving a public contradiction to the report propagated in certain circles that I am disaffected to Government because I cannot approve its measures when badly conceived and ill conducted, it is because I am fearful of inflaming the public mind, already too justly irritated against the King's servants for a series of blunders which, as your Grace observed to me last Sunday, 'could not have been exceeded by any twelve hackney coachmen taken from the first stand.' How far the present Cabinet is entitled to our forbearance is a question that would admit of no debate if the nation was not unhappily embarrassed with an Opposition which it cannot trust; and, under these circumstances, we have only the choice of two evils—we must either submit to the incapacity of those now in power, or recur to means which may involve the innocent in consequences that ought to fall exclusively on those whose criminal imbecility has brought our lives and fortunes into hazard. Enclosed for your perusal is a copy of the letter which I have just written to Mr. Pitt. I have preferred a private to a public condemnation of certain parts of his administration.

If my correspondence with your Grace is still preserved at the Foreign Office, it will be found that, in the summer of 1787, I forewarned you, as Secretary of State, that the Belgic provinces and the Liège country would inevitably fall under the dominion of France unless the British Cabinet adopted one of the two measures which I took the liberty to suggest at the time. In the year 1789 the necessity for this interference became more evident, and, consequently, I published, whilst on the

Continent, my 'Reflections on Public Men and Public Measures;' and in 1790 I was authorised by the insurgents to make propositions to your Grace which it would have been wisdom in this country, as you have since acknowledged to me, to have accepted. I do not know whether Mr. Pitt ever communicated to you the object of my mission to Paris—it was a confidential mission—but, if you are acquainted with the circumstances, you will, I am sure, agree with me that, if he had been consistent on that occasion, the ruinous and direful contest in which we are unhappily involved could not possibly have happened. In 1794 he discredited the information so fatally verified that our troops would be driven out of the Low Countries during the ensuing campaign; and your Grace is already aware that overtures for peace were transmitted to him through me from the French Minister at Bâle in January of the present year. A sad detail of failures swells the charge against the administration of Mr. Pitt during recent years, but, as the summing up of the account for the purpose of overthrowing his Cabinet cannot be accomplished in the present state of parties without risking a commotion of serious dimensions, the Minister must be allowed to remain in the security he is ill entitled to, but which he may find, as our difficulties increase, to be as delusive as it is unmerited.[1]

[1] 'The impulse which drove the two nations to a collision was not to be arrested by the abilities or by the authority of any single man. As Pitt was in front of his fellows, and towered high above them, he seemed to lead them. But in fact he was violently pushed on by them, and, had he held back but a little more than he did, would have been thrust out of their way or trampled under their feet. He yielded to the current, and from that day his misfortunes began. . . . . It was impossible that a man who so completely mistook the nature of a contest could carry on that contest successfully. Great as Pitt's abilities were, his military administration was that of a driveller. He was at the head of a nation engaged in a struggle for life and death, of a nation eminently distinguished by all

## Mr. Miles to Mr. Pitt

Froyle, near Alton: December 30, 1795

It could not have been difficult for an enlightened statesman to foresee some stupendous result in the direction of national freedom on the assembling of the States-General at Versailles. The temper manifested throughout the Third Order announced as much when the nobility and clergy, who brought little else than their prejudices and intolerance to the First Legislature, obeyed with reluctance the order of their sovereign to unite with the Tiers État. The resistance which the higher orders had the indiscretion to make was ill calculated to conciliate the minds of the people, awakened, as they were, to a sense of their rights, and indignant at the usurpations under which they had groaned for centuries. It is to the criminal indiscretion of these unfortunate men that we are indebted for that spirit of

---

the physical and all the moral qualities which make excellent soldiers. The resources at his command were unlimited. The Parliament was even more ready to grant him men and money than he was to ask for them. In such an emergency, and with such means, such a statesman as Richelieu, as Louvois, as Chatham, as Wellesley, would have created in a few months one of the finest armies in the world, and would soon have discovered and brought forward generals worthy to command such an army. Germany might have been saved by another Blenheim; Flanders recovered by another Ramillies; another Poitiers might have delivered the Royalist and Catholic provinces of France from a yoke which they abhorred, and might have spread terror even to the barriers of Paris. But the fact is that, after eight years of war, after a vast destruction of life, after an expenditure of wealth far exceeding the expenditure of the American War, of the Seven Years' War, of the War of the Austrian Succession, and of the War of the Spanish Succession united, the English army under Pitt was the laughing-stock of all Europe. It could not boast of one single brilliant exploit. It had never shown itself on the Continent but to be beaten, chased, forced to re-embark, or forced to capitulate. To take some sugar island in the West Indies, to scatter some mob of half-naked Irish peasants—such were the most splendid victories won by the British troops under Pitt's auspices.'—*Macaulay on Pitt.*

revolt, a spirit as contagious as it is irresistible, which has been displayed from one extremity of France to the other, and which, even on its first appearance, was a sad but certain presage of the gigantic stature which that kingdom seems destined to attain. It is not impertinent to state how very much the guilt and imbecility of her neighbours have contributed to the astonishing force and rapidity of her growth, nor will I refrain from mentioning the deplorable consequences that have resulted from the ill-conceived and worse executed contest with which Europe is at this instant embarrassed, and which presents no other figure to our dejected minds than that of a dark and dismal night, with no prospect of returning dawn to enliven or console us, in which murder and rapine, let loose to desolate the world, seem alone to be awake, scrambling with barbarous and impious speed over the bleeding, mangled corpses of butchered thousands intent on massacre and pillage.

On topics so fearful I have neither the courage nor the capacity to dwell; but it is not irrelevant to this disastrous state of affairs to recall to your memory the idea which you entertained of detaching France in the very infancy of her Revolution from her alliance with the only maritime power that could effectually co-operate with her at sea. When my stay at Liège was no longer of any utility to Government, I quitted the principality, and in the summer of 1790 you sent me on a mission of considerable importance to Paris, and which to a certainty would have succeeded if it had been pursued with the same wisdom that dictated it. The sagacity of the project, however, is its only eulogium.

The mission in itself had for its object the dissolution of a compact which, although little more than mischievous under the ancient monarchy, threatened the most serious consequences to the power and commerce of this country whenever France acquired the energy, and knowledge, and industry, which are the infallible characteristics of a free Government. When this mission was offered to me, and I was asked if I had any objection to go to Paris on so delicate a business, the mode suggested did not seem adequate to the end proposed; but, as I was in a manner abandoned to my own resources, and left at liberty to act as circumstances might require, the latitude allowed was sufficient to leave full play to my judgment, and, considering the dissolution of the Family Compact only as a preliminary to a far more important event, my sole anxiety was to obtain the object of my mission with as much promptitude as possible.

An account of the insult offered to the British flag at Nootka had just reached Europe, and satisfaction had been peremptorily demanded of Spain. The outrage, although committed at the extremity of the globe, was considered by many persons in Paris as having been previously concerted in Europe, *préparé de longue main*, between the two Courts of Madrid and Versailles, in which the latter might take part as an ally and avoid the odium attached to aggression. It was said that the Court of Versailles, aware of the discontent that prevailed, saw no refuge from tumult and insurrection but in war; that war alone could divert the public mind from the contemplation of domestic calamity; that the measure, desperate as it seemed, had its recommendation as well as its necessity, and would at least be palatable, if not popular, from the circumstance of its putting an end to the Commercial Treaty, against which all France had in a manner exclaimed and revolted. Such were the arguments I heard on my arrival at Paris, and such the chain of reasoning by which the officious and unauthorised violence of a Spanish officer towards our traders was traced to the Courts of Versailles and Madrid.

These opinions derived no inconsiderable support from the impatience for a war with England as manifested at the same moment by the emigrants, whose cabals have unhappily contributed to deluge Europe with blood. They avowed that war alone would restore them to their privileges and the monarch to his power, a power which he had neither the capacity to exercise nor the courage to defend; and, while this language was held among themselves, every artifice was employed to impress the people with the idea that England intended her armaments to act, not against Spain, but against France; that it was not likely a nation so circumspect and wise would go to war for the mere purpose of recovering a few wild cats' skins; and that, anxious to gratify her vengeance against France for having assisted the Americans in their revolt, England expected to find in the distractions and weakness inseparable from a revolution the sure and easy means of vengeance and of triumph.

The Spanish Minister at Paris did not neglect to give currency to these opinions, and asserted the evident necessity of adhering most strictly to the conditions of the Family Compact, adding that, if France should supinely allow Spain to be attacked and vanquished, both nations would be ultimately sacrificed to the insatiable avarice and ambition of their inveterate and common enemy. It did not form any part of my mission to transmit to you the different conversations that I heard in private or in public, but I felt it my duty to apprise you of the general disposition of a people in a state of fermentation. No doubt also Lord Gower, perfectly well instructed in the transactions of the period, informed you of the manœuvres of the Spanish Minister to engage France to enable his Court to resist the demand it had received from that of London.

No efforts were left unattempted by me to convince those with whom I conversed that it was neither the interest nor the intention of England to add to the calamities with which France was afflicted; and, but for the mysterious silence you observed, and the imprudent declarations of the emigrant Royalists that they would be supported by Great Britain, the pacific disposition of this country would never have been questioned. The Family Compact had fallen into disrepute; it was called the League of Despots; and, as Spain was naturally suspected of taking a personal interest in the fate of the French King, a dissolution of the alliance with her was recommended from the press soon after I reached Paris, and was urged with vehemence when she became suspected of conniving with the Royalists to plunge France into war for the purpose of re-establishing her sovereign on the throne. Those whose credit and influence enabled them to follow your views were not averse to the dissolution of the Compact. I had cautiously sounded them and found them in general well-disposed. Even Mirabeau, who received a thousand louis d'or from the Spanish Ambassador for the vote of forty-five ships of the line, whose blaze of eloquence in spite of public odium influenced the National Assembly, and who was regarded as the only pilot that could navigate the vessel through the tempest, had no insurmountable objection to the annulling of the treaty. He would have preferred a union with the Court of London. The Republican party then beginning to reveal themselves were to a man for the measure; and those who were for a limited monarchy, and wished for an alliance with this country from their partiality to its form of government, would cheerfully have broken with the other branch of the House of Bourbon if they could have been assured at the time of the friendship, or even of the neutrality of England. All these facts were fully and repeatedly stated to you in my letters from Paris, accompanied by suggestions which would probably have ensured success to the enterprise. Every obstacle to your wish seemed as if it were removed, and a very little more—a very small advance on the part of this country—would have detached France from Spain, and perhaps have preserved a hapless monarch and his throne from destruction. Little more was required from you than to have been explicit as to the conduct that this country meant to observe towards France in her then perilous and distracted state. It has ever been matter of surprise to me, and no less so of serious regret, that this little was not accomplished, and that a measure so wise in itself, so beneficial in its consequences, and so admirably well timed, with a train of circumstances so decisively in its favour, should have been unaccountably abandoned almost as soon as it was adopted—the fatal renunciation, I must repeat, of your project for detaching France from Spain at the very moment when its completion was within your grasp. An open and manly avowal of neutrality at that time would have secured to you the friendship of the former country; and it will be confessed that it was more for the interest of England to unite with France, even under a republican form of government, than that she should have been allowed to contract a stronger and more efficacious alliance with Spain than she ever derived from the Family Compact. The policy of such conduct on the part of this country appeared to me in the very infancy of the Revolution. Would to Heaven, Sir, that your perseverance, or attention to the obvious means of accomplishing so desirable an event, had corresponded with the wisdom of the measure!

If that unfortunate description of men, whom the barbarous licentiousness of the day had branded with the odious appellation of aristocrats, did not succeed in forcing the Constituent Assembly into a declaration of hostilities, they at least inspired a universal distrust of your pacific intentions which your fatal reserve, while the troubles in France were augmenting, and the still more fatal Convention of Pilnitz, unhappily confirmed. Do not be offended if I say that it would have been wise on the part of this country, if it had meant to dissolve the Family Compact, to have removed this distrust—the ruthless cause of the relentless war that has ensued. As no measures were taken by Government to contradict these injurious, and I trust ill-founded reports, they propagated and established themselves throughout France, and probably suggested the terrible expedient of incapacitating England for mischief by involving us in all the horrors of anarchy.

It was not likely that France, weakened by internal commotion, would hazard a separation from Spain without an equivalent for the sacrifice, and least of all was it likely that she would consent to such a separation at the very instant she was taught to believe that this country was only waiting for a favourable occasion to attack her. I am far from insinuating that it would have been policy to have proposed at that date a treaty offensive and defensive with France; but it was certainly incumbent on us, in honour as well as in policy, to have assured her of our pacific intentions at the very moment when we were endeavouring to detach her from the only power to which she could resort for assistance in the hour of danger.

The above observations reflect the views I entertain as to the irreparable mischief occasioned by the absence of an intelligent and decisive grasp of the political situation in 1790. My letters to Mr. Long elucidate the part I took towards the close of 1792, when I strained every effort to avert the war, and when I felt assured that, if my language might displease by its warmth, the sentiments I expressed could never offend, unless indeed you had totally relinquished the principles which you professed in earlier life and on which you had grounded your claim to public confidence. Opinions founded on principle, such as you once publicly avowed, cannot change; they are as immutable as are their foundations in the minds of men who prefer rectitude and consistency to favour, or fortune, or power. To explode those principles, or even to bring them into disrepute, may lead to consequences never intended even by writers whose pens have been so unworthily employed. Yet such were the purposes which Mr. Burke, and other authors of that description, appear to have had in view when they misrepresented the transactions of the last century in this country, and took advantage of the wild excesses of our neighbours, not only to vilify the Revolution, but to deny the utility or necessity, and even the right of recurring to such expedients, when despotism leaves to free-born man no alternative but submission or revolt. I feel myself perfectly secure from

the reproach of disaffection so long as liberty holds its
full value in your estimation. I do not mean the wild
licentiousness into which a thoughtless multitude released
from the fetters of slavery are apt to precipitate themselves in the frantic extravagance of their joy, but sober,
rational, well-organised liberty, as the result of profound
reflection, and which time and experience have corrected,
the liberty which you, Sir, once professed to love, and
which stands proud and erect, like a colossus, with one
foot upon anarchy and the other upon despotism.

I am no friend to tumult and insurrection. It is
not anarchy or chaos that I love, but order. Revolutions are very serious things; they are sometimes very
terrible things; but they are always the result of
a series of vexations and oppressions long endured
and hopelessly resisted. Nor can their progressive
course be arrested. The multiplied abuses and ex-
actions of Rome under the most splendid of her
pontiffs led to the emancipation of a considerable part
of Europe from the fetters of ecclesiastical tyranny. A
horde of fishermen, provoked by the inexorable cruelties
of Philip II. and after a contest of seventy years with
their proud oppressor, freed themselves from the Spanish
yoke and established in the swamps of Batavia a
republic which soon after disputed the dominion of the
sea with Great Britain. Our ancestors punished one
sovereign with death and another with banishment.
The criminal infatuation of Parliament even in our
days authorised the revolt which gave independence to
America. And we have seen an imbecility still more
criminal and more extensive in the Court of Versailles
give rise to an insurrection in France which seems to
have been a prelude to a series of revolutions which
may eventually lead to the extinction of monarchy in
Europe. If princes and ministers were susceptible of

admonition, if it was not inseparable from their general character to consider advice as reproof and to spurn the good counsel that is offered by the unquestionable authority of history, the examples I have cited would serve as lessons of instruction. Each calamitous event would be a beacon to forewarn governments of their danger. The folly, Sir, which misfortune cannot cure nor experience reach is incorrigible, yet, if none were involved in the consequences of that folly except those who are guilty of it, the mischiefs that result would deserve neither consideration nor regret. But, unhappily for the quiet of the world, the happiness of millions, as we see at this moment, is involved in the errors committed by the few; and perhaps it is due to the impunity which apparent security offers that princes have sometimes been seduced into acts of injustice, and their ministers entangled with enterprises not always honourable in design and far beyond their ability to conduct. In such a state of things all remonstrance is vain and nugatory. It is at once the error and the crime of most governments to think concession meanness, and to persevere in the very course which endangers their existence. The evil in this case must work its own remedy, and the machine go on until it breaks down with the weight of its own accumulating pressure.

### MR. MILES TO M. MARET

Froyle, near Alton: January 28, 1796

Your letter from Bâle, dated December 26, my dear Maret, arrived this morning, and I was overwhelmed with joy on hearing that you are at last set at liberty and in France. It would give me infinitely more pleasure if circumstances permitted me to proceed to Paris and receive the charming news from your own lips. A score of my letters are at present travelling over Europe in despair of finding you, or have become buried somewhere. It does not signify if they should fall into the hands of the despots who seized and banished you; they will find only proofs of my friendship and of my indignation at injustice. I wrote to you about a month since by M. Jacques Guyot, of L'Orient, who had come to England under a flag of truce, and whose liberation I had the happiness to obtain a year ago by procuring from Government permission for him to return to France. He has promised to forward my letter to you. I have just written to M. Rewbell, also to Mourgue, asking them to obtain for me permission to pass through France on my way to Switzerland, and, if successful, I may have the pleasure of assuring you in person of my undiminished friendship. Tell Mourgue that his letter dated on the 5th of this month, without signature, has found me. Adieu, my dear Maret! Recommence, I pray you, the work of peace, which the folly and crime of Le Brun unhappily interrupted. Once more, adieu!

### MR. MILES TO MR. ERSKINE [1]

Froyle: December 10, 1796

I find that Mr. Fox intends to make a motion to obtain the liberation of M. de Lafayette from the dungeon into which he has been iniquitously and cruelly precipitated. It is an effort in favour of afflicted humanity in which every well-constructed mind and honest heart will cordially join, and, as I cannot be indifferent to the fate of a man for whom I have the sincerest friendship, and with whom I have lived in past and happier times in habits of intimacy, I shall feel it as a personal kindness if you will have the goodness to inform Mr. Fox

[1] The Honourable Thomas Erskine, Lord Chancellor in the 'All Talents' Ministry of 1806.

that a refutation of the calumny advanced by Mr. Burke in the House of Commons, when General Fitzpatrick made a similar motion, is in my possession and at his service. I will forbear all asperity on the unpardonable rancour and falsehood of a charge which was meant to check the operations of national benevolence in favour of a desolated family by branding my friend with having connived at the imprudent, not to say treacherous flight of Louis XVI., for the foul purpose of acquiring popularity and confidence by bringing him back to the slaughter-house. The assertion was made, although one of their own party attached to the King vindicated M. de Lafayette from the calumny at the time, and whose claim to veracity derives additional strength from the circumstance of his being in declared hostility to the person whom he defended from slander. I have also the history of those times written by M. Montjoye, and dedicated to the late King, in which M. de Lafayette is represented to have exerted his utmost efforts to save the life of M. Foulon, at whose massacre Mr. Burke asserted that my friend had connived.[1]

I am aware that the part I have taken in politics cannot have been very pleasing to Mr. Fox, yet, offensive as it may have been to him, it has been much more so to Mr. Pitt. But I have done little more than represent objects as they appeared to my view, and, inflexibly attached to the principles of justice and humanity, I have gone straight forward, without respect to persons and certainly unbiassed by party attachments—imprudently, perhaps, as connected with my fortune, but at all events with great sincerity. On such a question I am sure Mr. Fox will feel interested, and, as it is not the only one of late years in which it has been my happiness to

[1] See Note, p. 107.

agree with him, I trust he will not reject the information I wish you to communicate, or decline to use it in the event of the slander being repeated when the motion comes before the House. Dare I ask you to quit your briefs and numerous suitors for substantial justice, and give your vote on that occasion, that it may stand recorded among the other innumerable proofs you have given of a correct and excellent heart? Would to God that the assembly calling itself the House of Commons, degraded to the condition of *commis* or clerks to the Chancellor of the Exchequer, could feel as well as hear the groans of despair uttered by an affectionate wife and her children from the cavern of sorrow, and, feeling as men ought to feel, call upon the Minister to disavow the infamy of his imperial associate, and exert his credit for the release of a gallant and honourable man! This is an effort on my part, due to the esteem I bear towards Lafayette. I say an effort, for I am retired, disgusted with the bustle and perfidy of politics, and live by choice here in solitude, self-banished and self-devoted to poverty and obscurity. If pleasure or business should bring you into Hampshire, I have a bed, a mutton chop, and a glass of wine or ale, with an affectionate welcome, at your service. Adieu!

### Mr. Erskine to Mr. Miles

London: February 18, 1797

I am very much obliged by both your kind letters, which I could not acknowledge before to-day, as I am not my own master for a minute till after dinner on Saturday. It is a great satisfaction to me that you approve of my pamphlet, by which I mean of my intentions in writing it, which were the purest that can be. I am no candidate for literary fame, nor indeed for any other. I see the vanity of it more and more every day I live, and I long to be able to leave the labours and pursuits of the world, to live amongst my friends; but I feel that I have probably much to act and to suffer before I am much older.

You may depend upon my reading your work whenever you bring it out. That I shall admire its composition and spirit I have no doubt, and that I shall agree with you in the greatest part of it I have no doubt either; and, however differently as a public man you may think of public men whom I esteem, that will make no difference. There is, besides, no inconsistency in changing opinions concerning men, because men themselves change. I look to principles, and shall only support men as they are faithful to them.

I am afraid that nothing will save the country; its destruction appears to me to be nigh. I have had a great deal of prosperity in life, and am now prepared for my share in the reverse, conscious that, with all my faults, my country has no charge to bring against me.

### MR. ERSKINE TO MR. MILES

London: March 12, 1797

I should have much sooner answered your very obliging and liberal letter, had I not been in the country, and since my return I have been detained past post-hour every day. I think the decision you have come to does you honour, and it will leave your talents for writing on many most important subjects which will crowd upon us every day. Undoubtedly, the coalition between Mr. Fox and Lord North was an unfortunate event; it was before the beginning of my political life. It was doubly unfortunate because it gave many honest and intelligent men an opinion of Fox which has enabled bad men to do mischief. I am quite sure that Fox will be found to be a man of the clearest integrity. His views at this moment, I am quite sure, are such as you would heartily subscribe. You will see that he never will compromise the people of England on the one hand or endanger the constitution on the other, if, indeed, Mr. Pitt leaves a constitution capable of being preserved. Much as I regard and venerate Fox, you may depend upon it I shall never follow him or any other human creature a single step out of the direct line of conduct for which I must be hereafter answerable to God for filling up the little space in which He has willed me to move. Whatever serves best to promote the universal happiness and improvement of the world is our duty, which we are bound solemnly and at all hazards to fulfil.

Mr. Robert Adair is the nephew of my old friend Keppel, and from that relation I wish him well; but I seldom have agreed with him wholly in political matters, and have never interfered or concerned myself directly or indirectly in any of his publications, nor ever read them with attention—his late one, which you mention, never at all. As to newspaper calumnies, I advise you never to regard them. I am abused from one year's end to the other, but without the smallest effect. I consider my character as safe as my feelings are certainly untouched. Whenever I feel that I am doing right I never care for anything else.

With regard to the country, I despair of it. No Minister will ever be trusted by the King whom the people ought to trust; the consequence will be factions and heart-burnings, oppression of the people in the first instance, and, afterwards, greater danger to the monarchy than I wish to think of or would choose to express.

*From* ——[1] *to Mr. Miles*

Paris: le 5 Juin, 1797

L'objet qui vous intéresse, mon cher Miles, la paix, est à present sur le tapis. Mon information est tirée de la meilleure source. Je n'oublierai pas ma promesse ; les délices de Froyle ne me sont pas indifférentes. Avant que ce mois soit fini, vous m'y verrez.

Votre ami Barthélemy est élu. Je le regarde comme un des hommes les plus capables de remplir les devoirs de l'important poste qu'il va occuper, et je regarde son élection comme une chose heureuse pour les intérêts de ce pays-ci.

Adieu ! Votre affectionné.

*Mr. Miles to the Marquis de Lafayette*

Froyle, near Alton : September 27, 1797

Retired, my dear General, and living recluse from politics, it is only by accident that I hear of what is transacting on the great theatre of public affairs. The papers of this date announce the release of my much valued friend from a rigorous and iniquitous captivity. May you enjoy in security those laurels which, in the first instance, the ferocity of anarchy, and at a later period the no less barbarous ferocity of regal despotism, would have torn from your brow ! The warm friendship I professed for you would not allow me to be an indifferent spectator either of the unprovoked calumnies of your enemies in this country, or of the foul treatment you experienced under the merciless gripe of imperial tyranny ; but my voice was too feeble to be heard, and my means too circumscribed to render you the service

---

[1] 'From a friend in office announcing a prospect of peace. God grant it may be realised and pave the way for an alliance with France!'—W. A. M.

which my heart desired, and which was due to your virtues and sufferings. I could only contradict the atrocious slanders levelled at you by men whose rank and education should have taught them to better respect truth and misfortune. One of these men, Mr. Burke, is no more.

If this random shot should happily reach you at Hamburg, I beg you to recall me to the memory of Madame de Lafayette, and assure her of my sincere concern that I could only sympathise with her, and that, strong as was her interest in your restoration to freedom, the interest is no less felt by the friends of liberty dispersed over the surface of the globe. It will give me great pleasure to hear from you; but the pleasure would be infinitely greater if I could personally greet you on your resurrection from the tomb at Olmütz, and repeat to you the assurances of my sincere and affectionate regard.

### *Mr. Miles to Mr. Nicholls*

Froyle : April 10, 1798

It may perhaps have appeared to you upon reflection, as it has since done to me, that every effort towards accommodation with France would at present be ineffectual, bent as she is on the wild scheme of subjugating all Europe to her merciless gripe; and, as we are an obstacle of no inconsiderable force to the achievement of such an enterprise, there is little prospect of her consenting to sheath the sword until she is convinced that her project against this country is as impracticable to execute as it is extravagant in design. Her recent invasion of Switzerland must convince the warmest partisans of France *que la République française* deserves the reproach so often and so justly made *à la monarchie française d'avoir ni foi ni loi*; and, considering the danger with which the northern powers are menaced, their conduct appears to me at once criminal and inexplicable. France leaves us no alternative between ruinous dishonourable concession and eternal warfare. Reduced to such a dilemma, and abandoned as we are to our fate by the rest of the world, our only resources are unanimity, vigilance, and courage.

Now for Ireland. The inclosed will convince you that an alliance between France and Ireland is not a very novel idea. At the period when I wrote to Sir Edward Newenham I saw letters from M. de Vergennes to an Irishman, from which it plainly appeared that the Court of Versailles was then endeavouring by her intrigues to accomplish the separation of the two countries. I will not enter into the questions of grievances and aggressions; the sword is unhappily drawn, and all discussion is at an end on those fruitful causes of the present ruthless contest; but, while we lament the sad issue to which this unfortunate misunderstanding is come, do not let us be insensible to the atrocity of inviting France to become a party in the quarrel, nor to the folly—if conduct can be so called from which so much calamity and distress must ensue—of becoming the blind and ferocious instruments of unprincipled ambition. The infatuation must be extreme that supposes the French espouse the cause of the discontented in Ireland from personal affection for the people of that country, or from a wish to render them free and happy. The Directory consider them as a lever by whose astonishing force they hope to prize Great Britain out of her political position, and their calculation proves equal wisdom, malignity, and accuracy. Hence the promised succour to the deluded insurgents, who do not perceive that they are the dupes of a nation whose sole object in aiding their revolt is to cripple and destroy us. From the extravagant pretensions of the 'United Irishman,' I am doubtful whether any reform in their representation would have satisfied them. I am afraid that their views point to independence, and if so, tell me, I conjure you, how the attainment of such a design is to be prevented but by force. All reasoning with men so determined would be nugatory, and at the same time that I say this I almost despair of recovering Ireland by coercion, because all history, with a very few exceptions, informs us that a revolution commenced is virtually accomplished, and that it has no retrograde motion.

On the subject of Parliamentary reform I have but one opinion, which is that, if it is not done within doors, it will be done without, and then God help us all! Force can at any time take a gate off its hinges, but it requires address as well as strength to put it on again. I dread the great body of the people undertaking this business, and yet the incurable obstinacy of Parliament in not doing it will expose us to that danger. The business of reform belongs to a deliberative assembly, not to a mob, which I cannot assimilate to anything but wildfire; and, if the locality involved is considerable, the mischiefs resulting from the explosion will be terrible and incalculable. Let me know if we agree on this topic as well as we do on most others.

### THE MARQUIS DE LAFAYETTE TO MR. MILES

Widmold, near Plön, Holstein: August 2, 1798

My answer to your last most kind favour has been long delayed, my dear Sir, for which I could not forgive myself if I had not understood that a private opportunity for the transmission of my grateful acknowledgments was a safer mode of conveyance than by the post. I have now applied to a friend in Hamburg who will either deliver this to a trusty passenger or send it to London under a secure cover. In the meanwhile I hope that your kind consideration of me has anticipated an apology which I should be happy to make in person either at your house or mine. I wish I could properly express the high sense I entertain of my obligations to you in the time of adversity, when friendship is put to the test. That you should have aroused political enemies by your generous interference on my behalf is a matter of deep regret, whilst it is a consolation to know that you have been supported by every lover of liberty as the worthy advocate of the sacred cause. I heartily thank you for your spirited correspondence on my behalf in your Ministerial papers. On the testimony of your affection and esteem I shall ever put a great value. Mr. Burke, on arriving at the conclusion that France would become a blank in the politics of Europe, thought proper in his fits of passion to make me one of his principal objects of attack, but I forgive him out of respect for those friends among whom he had the honour to rank. Indeed, I ought to be thankful for the opportunity he afforded for a refutation of the calumnies repeated against me. You know how highly I value your own efforts on my behalf, how much I feel indebted to the labours of your able pen. Let us hope that with the cessation of despotic monarchies the governments of the future may be founded on the basis of liberty and justice, so that the dignity and happiness of mankind may be assured.

Adieu! With affectionate and grateful attachment.

*MR. MILES TO MR. FLINT*

Froyle : May 19, 1799

The papers which you sent to me I have read under an agitation of mind not experienced since the massacres of the 2nd of September, 1792. Such events make my heart weep tears of blood, and, when I consider that these atrocities are committed by the same class of beings as those to which I belong, I recoil from the reflection that no animal is so remorseless, so ferocious, as man. The papers in the pay of Government seem to soften the guilt of the Austrian assassins.[1] It is for the credit of the British Government that the public prints in this country should reprobate an outrage that has been offered, not only to France, but to the whole civilised world. Suppose that Lord Malmesbury had been waylaid on his return from Paris or Lisle, suppose that Sir Gilbert Elliot or my friend Liston had been seized on neutral ground on their way to Corsica and Constantinople, as Maret and Sémonville were when charged with missions to Naples and Constantinople, would not every Englishman have been stimulated to resent the

---

[1] 'The French envoys, Roberjot and Bonnier, were ordered to quit Rastadt at twenty-four hours' notice, April 28, 1799, and soon afterwards they were cut down by Austrian hussars during their return to France by night. Suspicion fell upon the Austrian Court. The officer in command of the outpost, Colonel Barbaczy, explained the deed in a letter as follows : —" I feel myself deeply oppressed with anxiety caused by the account of a horrible act perpetrated on the persons of the Ministers of the French nation by some common plunderers, who had availed themselves of the protection of the night for that purpose. . . . With respect to the safe escort of the embassy in question, the situation of the country did not permit me to restrain my troops from overrunning this neighbourhood; and I am convinced that no danger would have arisen, nor would this cruel act have been committed by any criminals blinded by a thirst for plunder, if the French Embassy, who had twenty-four hours to arrange their affairs, had set out on their journey in the daytime." '—Extract from the Paris papers, Strasburg, April 29, 1799.

outrage offered to their country in the persons of her ambassadors? This is a matter that concerns all nations, and all nations should make common cause with France, through whom their rights have been attacked and violated. I hope that our Court will not be tardy in expressing its abhorrence of the crime.

It is painful to contemplate the horrors that sometimes seem to carry the sanction of men in high power. May rectitude and humanity be the compass by which you steer your course through life! Thrown upon the world to explore my way through its dark, intricate, and dangerous mazes, my own master before I had attained the age of eleven,[1] I have escaped the contagion of the bad example with which I was surrounded; and with passions as violent, and with a mind as ardent and volatile as ever swayed the human breast, I have not allowed myself in my intercourse with men to be seduced or intimidated from the love and practice of right. It is this inflexible attachment to right that consigns me to my voluntary exile.

### M. BARTHÉLEMY TO MR. MILES

Londres: 30 Juillet, 1799

Monsieur,—La lettre que vous m'avez fait l'honneur de m'écrire le 28 de ce mois me parvient dans ce moment. Je m'empresse de vous transmettre toutes les assurances de la sincère reconnaissance que je dois à la manière pleine d'amitié avec laquelle vous voulez bien m'engager à vous aller voir à la campagne. J'accepterais avec grand plaisir, je vous assure, monsieur, une invitation aussi obligeante, si ma situation présente me

---

[1] Mr. Miles had lost both his parents at this early age, and, being the sole heir of a small private fortune, he had never been subjected to any material control.

le permettait. Je n'avais pas besoin de tous les malheurs que je viens d'éprouver pour désirer avec passion de revenir dans un pays où j'ai reçu autrefois tant de bontés ; mais, si les circonstances font que je n'y reste pas, et que je pars sur-le-champ pour le Continent, vous croirez sans doute, monsieur, que ce n'est pas de ma part une affaire de choix, et vous aurez raison. Quelque part que je sois, soyez bien persuadé de la vérité de tous les sentimens de reconnaissance et de dévouement avec lesquels j'ai l'honneur d'être, &c. &c.[1]

### Mr. Miles to M. Barthélemy

Froyle, near Alton : August 2, 1799

I do most sincerely regret, dear Sir, that circumstances are likely to deprive me of an opportunity to convince you that my esteem for your character and my concern at your unmerited sufferings are the unaffected effusions of a heart sensibly touched by your misfortunes. For reasons obvious to you I am silent on a subject which folly and crime have rendered no less painful than interesting.

The part that I have taken in the unhappy contest which separates two nations that ought certainly to be united is no secret to you, and it is in solitude, sorrowful and dejected, that I deplore the fatal excesses which efface from my afflicted mind the hope of an early restoration of peace beween our respective countries. I will not renounce the hope of seeing you at my hermitage, where I arrived this day and was greeted by your welcome letter, but, should your departure for the Con-

---

[1] 'The above was transmitted to me from the Chief of the Alien Department a day or two after the arrival of M. Barthélemy in the 'Vengeance,' Captain Russell, from the West Indies. Barthélemy and General Willott came home together (both had been banished by the Directory to Cayenne), September 1797.'—W. A. M.

tinent deprive me of the felicity of congratulating you in person on your happy escape from exile, my best wishes will accompany you, and, if you meet with my old friend M. de Lafayette, I entreat the favour of you to assure him that the same affection and regard he experienced in the midst of his afflictions shall continue to influence my conduct towards him while I live. It is with sincere pleasure I inform you that he was well very lately. I desire also to say that, if I had been permitted to continue my correspondence with you in 1795, I had the commands of the late Duke of Leeds to assure you of his ' sincere regard for his friend Barthélemy.'

### MR. MILES TO CAPTAIN BALL [1]

Froyle, near Alton : September 20, 1799

Your letter dated off Malta on the 3rd ultimo came to me this day, and I judged part of it so important, not only on account of the immediate fact that it stated, but with regard to the probable effect which the jealousy you mention may have on the future operations of our Government, that, without naming you, or even furnishing a clue to the discovery of my correspondent, I sent an extract to the Minister, which, with a copy of what I wrote to Mr. Pitt, you will receive enclosed. Our diplomacy is so shamefully bad, owing to its being formed entirely by Parliamentary corruption and cabal, that it is very possible our Court will receive through your means the first intelligence of the sentiments of the Emperor of Germany respecting Malta. You appear to me to have pushed your delicacy too far in hesitating to comply with the general wish of the Maltese to have you for their Governor. In your place I would have

---

[1] Afterwards Admiral Sir Alexander Ball, First Commissioner of Malta.

allowed their supplications to travel to England, and have apprised the Minister in whose department you serve of the measure, stating all the circumstances in detail, so that your frankness would destroy all suspicion of cabal or intrigue. To be set up by a party, whether as Governor or Grand Master, has nothing very flattering in it, but when called by the unanimous or general voice of the community to be their chief, from confidence in your talents and rectitude, it is a matter for your discretion whether you accept the important charge or not. You could only comply with the approbation of your Government. It may be your duty to acquiesce in the prayer in consideration that it represents the desire of almost an entire people. With respect to Sicily and its monster of a King—for he is everything but a man—the less you have to do with his Court and Government the better. I do not suppose that Malta will be in any way under the control of his Neapolitan Majesty. You will have a difficult card to play with the Congress, of which you are President,[1] if France, now that Bonaparte is no longer formidable to the Turk, should make her peace with the Porte. Should any private agreement with the Court of Petersburg hereafter appear by which it has been stipulated by our Cabinet to cede Malta to the Emperor Paul, I feel no difficulty in saying that, if the public virtue of this country bears any proportion to the delinquency of such an arrangement, the Minister will be impeached.

Do not be surprised, my dear Ball, if you should hear of the defection of the Emperor, and of a confederacy in the North against the Court of Petersburg, unless the Court of Petersburg, as in the war of 1760, hitches the business and goes to the other side. The

[1] See Letter from Sir Alexander Ball to Mr. Miles, August 2, 1807.

jealousy which Russia has excited at Vienna, and her conduct towards Hamburg, Denmark, and Sweden are ill calculated to ensure her respect or affection. I do not know who are the counsellors of Paul, but they are certainly men of address, for they have gained most completely the weather-gauge of our Ministers, and are taking such strides that it will be a work of difficulty to restrain them within those limits which are necessary to the commerce and independence of Great Britain. Perhaps they mean to play us foul. The Turk and the Austrian have an interest in confining the Great Bear to his place in the zodiac; and so have we; but it is not always that John Bull can distinguish his interests from the phantoms and bugbears that court his good offices. The same maxims by which I thought Europe ought to be governed in 1790-1791 hold yet their influence on my mind. I am fully persuaded that Russia ought to be kept in the background. Mr. Pitt was once of this opinion, and, as the same reasons exist now for her exclusion as existed then, I cannot accompany the Minister in the curve he has thought proper to make, but, on the contrary, I remain firm in the conviction that not so much as a row-boat ought ever to be allowed to pass the Dardanelles, lest it should eventually lead to their getting possession of Constantinople. Unfortunately for the country, as for himself, Mr. Pitt entered too young into the highest offices, and as he had to struggle with a powerful party in order to hold what he had obtained, and to consume portions of his valuable time in buying majorities in Parliament,[1] he had not the leisure to study the history of modern Europe, or acquire a proper knowledge of foreign politics, without which it is morally

---

[1] See *Correspondence between the Right Hon. William Pitt and Charles, Duke of Rutland*, London, 1890.

impossible that any Minister can be a statesman, or be competent to decide the question as to which of its various peoples it is the interest of this country to unite itself with. He had to contend with an Opposition more formidable from its talents than from its virtues, and which was headed, not only by aristocratical families of the kingdom, but by the heir-apparent to the throne. Thus the early manhood of Mr. Pitt was lost, both to himself and the country, until the war broke out and for ever opposed a barrier to his acquisition of those attainments, the want of which we shall most wofully feel before the present contest is over.[1]

I happened to be in town when the news of Mantua being taken arrived, and it instantly occurred to me that, as the great object of the Court of Vienna was gained in Italy, it would relax its ardour, and perhaps withdraw itself from the confederacy. I mentioned my apprehensions at the Foreign Office, and was advised to be more confident. I have watched the conduct of Austria since that period, and almost every occurrence confirmed me in my suspicions. Your letter decides the matter. It is very probable that, as the army of Bonaparte appears to be destroyed in Egypt, the Grand Seigneur will perceive an enemy in one of his present friends. The Turk has much more to fear from the Emperor Paul than from the French Directory. Many years have

[1] 'Pitt may, indeed, well have felt conscious that to preside over the war was not his natural vocation. His conduct in it betrayed no extent of views, no commanding notions of policy. Anything more commonplace can hardly be imagined. To form one coalition after another in Germany, and subsidize the Allies with millions of free gift, or aid them with profuse loans, until all the powers in our pay were defeated in succession, and most of them either destroyed or converted into tools of the enemy—such were all the resources of his diplomatic skill.'—*Historical Sketches of Statesmen*, &c., by Lord Brougham, London and Glasgow, 1855, i. 281.

elapsed since I hazarded my opinion on the necessity of prescribing bounds to the Russian empire. It is no longer a secret that Mr. Pitt has been most shamefully duped, and the country pillaged by every power with whom we have been in alliance, and this delusion has not been corrected by experience.[1] Even the Directory have had the address to filch some thousands from the Minister by availing themselves of the correspondence of a Frenchman employed as an agent by us, who, being detected at Paris, purchased his safety by betraying his trust. The *émigrés*, believe me, have had their full share of our money and confidence, and you are as capable of judging as myself of the *good* we have derived from their services.

Your situation since the victory at Aboukir must have made you acquainted with the tricks and intrigues of courts, and have shown you how very little rectitude is estimated in their transactions with each other. In the little commerce I have had with them, I attempted to walk in a direct line and was only the dupe of my purity; but when I sought to enforce upon those with whom I was in political relation to direct their steps by the same line of right, I fell a victim to my zeal and was taunted with the charge of expecting honesty from knaves. Profit, dear Ball, by my experience and adopt the wholesome advice which I offer, but which I do not follow—never to count men for more than they are worth, or to give to the coin of Birmingham the value and currency of sterling. I do very sincerely respect

---

[1] 'Let Parliament call for an account of the subsidies paid by Mr. Wickham to Bavaria, Würtemberg, and the Elector of Mayence, the nation will then judge of our wisdom in selection and economy in expenditure.'—*Letter to the Prince of Wales*, by W. A. Miles, London, 1808, p. 87.

Mr. Pitt, but my respect for truth is still greater than it is for the Minister.

Thus matters stand at present. I vegetate among the clodpoles and hop-poles at Froyle. My books are a vast resource, and the fidelity of my memory makes my own history amusing in this solitude. I preserve a correspondence with several friends, who are not displeased at receiving letters from the *dead*, and who sometimes visit me in my *sepulchre*, from which they occasionally seduce me to make an *apparition* either at Portsmouth or in London. Macnamara Russell has just left me. He brought home one of my Gallic correspondents, Barthélemy, whom Sieyès sent to Cayenne, and has been despatched to the Continent or somewhere on a mission of some sort, but from which I augur no good if I may form a conjecture from the depression of mind under which he left me. I was lately on a visit to Pickmore, and before I left Portsmouth I dined with Sir Peter Parker. My rambling for the present is over. Captain Irwin, of the 'Queen Charlotte,' conveys to you a letter in which I mention having accidentally met your brother George. I carried him off to Froyle for the purpose of recruiting his health. Adieu!

### Mr. Miles to Mr. Butler [1]

January 17, 1801

Your letter containing an inclosure from the Rev. Herbert Marsh did not reach me until yesterday, or its receipt should have been sooner acknowledged. I have to lament that the disordered state of my papers and books puts it out of my power at this moment to give your friend the information he desires. If, however, he

---

[1] Charles Butler, barrister of Lincoln's Inn, and a controversial writer, theological and political.

should deem it prudent under present circumstances to say anything more respecting the origin of the hapless contest in which we are involved, you may inform him that, when the perfidy and arrogance of the Court of Vienna—combined with its unjustifiable interference in the internal government of France—provoked the latter country to hostilities, not only as a measure of self-defence, but as absolutely necessary to consolidate her Revolution, it was no longer possible for England to avoid being drawn into the terrible vortex of war. I am not acquainted with the work of Mr. Belsham to which Mr. Marsh alludes;[1] but it will perhaps be doing the Minister, whom the latter gentleman wishes to serve, a very essential injury to pursue this literary controversy any farther, or to call on me for M. Le Brun's last letter to the British Court, the publication of which would prove that, on that occasion at least, the French Minister argued like a well-informed statesman.[2] Foreseeing the sad consequences which would inevitably result to this country from a rupture with France, broken loose from all forms as well as from the fetters of despotism, and that, in the event of a quarrel, it would not be an ordinary conflict but a war between nation and nation, I left no means unattempted to prevent it, and took the liberty from the intercourse I had with Mr. Pitt at the time to suggest to him in the very infancy of the Revolution the wiser and safer line of an alliance with France

---

[1] William Belsham, a political pamphleteer and historian, published, in 1801, 'Remarks on a late Publication styled *The History of the Politics of Great Britain and France*,' which latter work was written by Herbert Marsh, Private Secretary to Mr. Pitt. Belsham also published, among other things, *Remarks on the Peace of Amiens*.

[2] See Letter from M. Maret to Mr. Miles, January 7, 1793, which is an official document written by direction of the Executive Council, and which must be the letter referred to above as sent by Le Brun to the English Government.

rather than to excite her jealousy or provoke her resentment. My voice was too feeble to be heard. Disgusted with the conduct of all parties, and, finding as little capacity on one side as there was want of principle on the other, I quitted the tumult of public affairs, and retired to the country, as soon as I had vindicated the Minister from the unmerited but interested aspersions of his opponents, and cleared him of the guilt of aggression which was most industriously attempted to be fixed on him, and of which he was rather the dupe than the author. A very sincere personal regard for Mr. Pitt, combined with a strict love of truth and justice, was my sole motive for refuting the reiterated calumnies of Mr. Fox and his adherents respecting the mission of my friend Maret in January 1793. He has at this instant my best wishes, and it is this feeling towards him that renders me the more sensible of the delusion under which he has acted since 1789, and leads me to deplore with a very heavy and aching heart, as a great and irretrievable misfortune to himself and the nation, that he should have been so fatally misled by a man[1] whom he should have guided by his better understanding.

*The Marquis of Buckingham to Mr. Miles*

Stowe: January 26, 1801

I am grateful to you for the obliging offer contained in your letter of the 23rd, which, owing to my absence from home, I did not receive till last night. As I always see the French papers from my brother's office,[2] I need not trouble you on that chapter. I have considered the very able and active politics of France to have been of late so systematically levelled in all their various bear-

---

[1] Edmund Burke.  [2] Lord Grenville, at the Foreign Office.

ings at the very existence of this country as a *bellum internecinum*, that I am not sanguine in my expectations that any consideration would induce France to suffer the Brabant corn to be shipped for England. You will, however, have the greatest satisfaction, for you will have had the greatest merit, if you can assist your commercial friend to effect this object.

*MR. MILES TO THE MARQUIS OF BUCKINGHAM*

January 28, 1801

I wish to unfold to your Lordship, with all that frankness which belongs to me, my sentiments on that part of your letter which attributes to France a systematic design to destroy the existence of this country as a nation. I am ready to admit that her conduct justifies such an opinion, and I feel in some sort warranted to assert that the project was conceived early in 1795, when Pichegru accomplished, by the conquest of Holland, a resolve of the French Government in January 1794, namely, ' de nous chasser des Pays-Bas cette année, coûte que coûte,' were they even forced to devote 200,000 men to that purpose. This resolve was instantly transmitted to me by a man high in credit in France—a leading man in the Revolution, and who was soon afterwards consigned by Robespierre to the guillotine. It was as instantly transmitted to Mr. Pitt, who forbade me to send him any more French intelligence—an injunction faithfully obeyed until I received an overture for peace from M. Barthélemy, in a letter dated Bâle, the 17th December, 1794, and which I thought it my duty to forward to the Minister, in whose welfare I feel as warm an interest at this moment as I did at the time of the Regency in 1788, for it is his character as a Minister and not emolument for myself that I have at heart;

and it is matter of deep and sincere anguish to me
to behold a man whose abilities I almost idolised, and
in whose triumphs I partook, so fatally misled, not only
in his objects, but in his mode of attaining them. You
will surely remember that I told your Lordship, in
February 1793, in Bolton Street, that Mr. Pitt was an
infant in foreign politics, and a succession of events
have unhappily proved that the assertion was not ill-
founded. The facility with which the Duke of York
was driven out of the Netherlands, where, by the by,
he ought never to have been sent combined with the
consequences resulting from that expulsion, convinced
Sieyès and those who acted with him that his idea of
the possibility of destroying the power of this country
was very practicable; and from that period the very
able and active politics of France have, as your Lord
ship has very justly observed, been levelled at our existence. With such an object in view by a power so near
to us and with such resources, very different conduct
should have been observed by this country, and while
we lament the sad extremity to which the contest is
reduced, and take measures to resist the catastrophe
with which we are threatened, we cannot deny that the
difficulty has been drawn on us by ourselves, or that
this spirit of revenge has been provoked by our wild
and imperious attempts to restore the old government
and by our folly in subsidising almost the whole of
Europe for that more than criminal purpose. It was
scarcely possible for any man conversant with the
internal affairs of France previous to the 14th of July
1789 not to be well aware that her Government would
acquire a considerable degree of accession of mental and
physical strength by the Revolution, and that France
restored to freedom would no longer resemble France

under the wretched management of the Court of Versailles.¹

If I may be permitted to hazard another opinion, it is that I do not think the present Councils in France are disposed to consider the quarrel as a *bellum internecinum* any farther than as it may be a measure of self-defence. In other words, if we are resolved to go on with the war in order to subvert the present state of things in France, France, on her part, will aim at our destruction as the only means by which she can hope to find security and repose. I really do not believe that she is resolved at all events to attempt our extermination; and I tell your Lordship in confidence that a person high in credit at this moment in France is decidedly against any such measure, and is fully convinced that this country should continue to exist as a great power. I have some reason to believe that this opinion may be rendered the common opinion of France, and that it will be our own fault if the door to all amicable accommodation should be finally shut against us. I have opened my heart to you without reserve. As the passports are not arrived from Paris, and I shall not cross the Channel without them, my departure is postponed for a week. I am fully aware of the difficulties I shall encounter in negotiating the great and sole object of my mission, and, in order to carry my point, I mean to submit to the Lords of his Majesty's Council the propriety of my offering a supply of

[1] 'Il me semble que deux ans de guerre avaient assez démontré que contre les étrangers, tout le monde est soldat en France, et les honnêtes gens qui détestent la Convention et les scélérats qui sont dévoués à son service, parce que les étrangers se sont toujours présentés ou comme voulant conquérir le territoire, ou comme voulant détruire la liberté.'—Lettre de M. de Talleyrand à Madame de Staël, Londres, 8 Octobre, 1793. See *Revue d'Histoire Diplomatique*, quatrième année, No. 1, Janvier, 1890.

colonial produce, for which France is, I am told, very much distressed.

P.S.—If the late Duke of Leeds communicated to Mr. Pitt my correspondence from Frankfort in the year 1789, the Minister must have known from that period what he had to expect from Paul[1] whenever he succeeded to the throne. Mr. Pitt knew from me in 1786 and 1787 the indisposition of the late King of Prussia towards this country, and the little dependence to be placed on his friendship. Knowing all this, and retracing in my afflicted mind the little credit given to my efforts, with the train of melancholy events which have since occurred, I feel the more sensibly the injury done to our country and its Government by the information and counsels which have misled its Minister. Allow me once more to repeat to your Lordship that I do not believe it is impracticable to disarm France of her anger and detach her from her northern connections.

*Mr. Miles to the Marquis of Buckingham*

January 28, 1801

I submit the enclosed paper to your perusal as a proposed preface to my pamphlet entitled 'An Inquiry into the Necessity and Expediency of Prescribing Bounds to the Russian Empire,' and which was published in 1791 at Mr. Pitt's and your Lordship's request. It was my conviction that all the powers of Europe were interested in keeping Russia in the background. Mr. Pitt in those days was of the same opinion. He has had reasons perhaps for changing it. I have not. It is still my conviction, and I have reason to believe that France will not allow Paul or a Regency to add an

---

[1] Emperor of Russia.

inch of territory to the Russian empire. I know to a
certainty that France has resisted some attempts of the
kind on the part of Prussia which I am not at present
at liberty to reveal, but, if Lord Grenville has been
well served at the Court of Berlin by those whom he
has sent there, his Lordship can confirm this fact.

On the subject of the present contest I have only to
observe that, from what has occasionally come to my
knowledge of the disposition of people in Paris, Mr.
Pitt has it in his power to treat for peace on terms far
from being disadvantageous, all circumstances considered. My wish certainly is that Mr. Pitt should
make the peace, not only from the strong personal regard I once had for him, but from the full conviction—
and I think that this conviction must be general—that
no man in England is more capable than himself to
make a better use of peace after he has obtained it; no
man could possibly turn it to a better account. His *forte*
is finance, and the wonderful height to which he raised
the public credit of this country after a very disastrous
war is my voucher. Thus thinking of his talents, as
far as they relate to political economy, and believing,
as I firmly do, that he has through the whole of this
unfortunate quarrel been *seduced* or *compelled* to act in
opposition to his better judgment and disposition, I
cannot but most cordially wish that the styptic may be
applied to the bleeding wounds of my country under
his auspices. If he is *allowed* to act, I feel assured that
the splendour and the power of the nation will be
restored and preserved. I know that there is no objection on the other side of the Channel to treat with
him, and that, whatever opposition may be made from
a certain quarter to all accommodation with France, he
would be supported in this country by a majority

decidedly strong enough to strait-waistcoat insanity should it refuse its assent, or to punish the criminality that would dare to oppose it.

### The Marquis of Buckingham to Mr. Miles

*Stowe: January 30, 1801*

I return to you the paper which you transmitted to me on the subject of the Russian quarrel. Part of the reasoning applies to the present moment, but the contest stands on far different grounds. As to the *bellum internecinum*, I use the word as the shortest to express an opinion on which I shall be glad by the result to find that I have been mistaken. But I certainly impute the origin, the continuance, and the present state of the war to a systematic plan on the part of France—however her rulers or Ministers may have changed—to strike at the greatness of Great Britain, and I conceive that this system will impede your commercial negotiation for corn.

### Mr. Miles to the Marquis of Buckingham

*February 8, 1801*

Your Lordship is certainly justified in asserting that France under her various rulers since the Revolution has uniformly levelled her blows at the greatness of this country. I know it was the opinion of the Abbé Sieyès in 1790, from several conversations with him in the club of 1789, that France had nothing to fear in the event of a war with Great Britain. I know that he was anxious for the contest, which he did not deign to consider at that time as a trial of strength, but as a measure of policy. As he endeavoured to inflame the public mind with the apprehension that we were re-

solved to replunge the people in despotism, restore the
fetters from which they had broken loose, and dis-
member France, we, on our part, should have carefully
abstained from whatever seemed to corroborate that
mischievous error and to give a complexion to the
opinions that were circulated. When you told me that
you would not be at the head of affairs in England at
this crisis, I drew the inference that you have marked
as injudicious the entire conduct of the King's servants
since his Majesty gave the mandate for war and the
aristocracy of France beheld the extinction of their
titles in the acknowledgment of the Republic. The
sad issue of the war I predicted to Mr. Pitt and Mr.
Long before its commencement.

### MR. MILES TO THE MARQUIS OF LANSDOWNE

*February 4, 1801*

It gave me infinite satisfaction to find—for it announced a pacific disposition—that, on applying to the
Duke of Portland for leave, no opposition was any
longer made to my going to Paris. Since, however,
the idea prevailed with our Government that the war,
on the part of France, was a *bellum internecinum*, I
was induced to recur to such channels of information
on the Continent as I could depend upon, because, if
this idea is correct, it is not likely that France would
lend her aid in a moment of calamity to succour the
country she was resolved to crush, and, in that case,
my journey to the Continent to negotiate for corn could
not possibly answer any good purpose. I have, therefore, a very sensible pleasure in informing your Lordship, and from an authority that I know to be unquestionable, that it will be entirely the fault of this
country if the sad contest in which it is involved

becomes a *bellum internecinum*. On the contrary, France is at this moment disposed to treat for peace; but, whilst I impart this information in confidence, I am bound to reveal that the Government, which had the criminal imbecility to reject the overtures of the First Consul in a tone of arrogance which its situation neither at home nor abroad justified, must submit to the well-merited humiliation of making an overture in its turn, and so atone for the insult it offered to those towards whom policy as well as justice dictated a different line of conduct. With this disposition on the part of France I cannot suppose that Ministers will be mad enough to stand upon a punctilio to which they have so little claim. All good men should pause before they allow Ministers to prosecute a quarrel beyond the possibility of honourable reconciliation.[1]

With respect to the object of my proposed journey, I am by no means sanguine; not that the hostility of the two nations will be a bar to my success, but the fact is—and my information is full and correct on this occasion—that the Government in France, afraid of the rise in the price of bread, has prohibited the exportation of grain from the Low Countries, and, on the Brabanters

---

[1] The letter of Bonaparte, 'First Consul of the Republic, to his Majesty the King of Great Britain and Ireland,' is dated, 'Paris, 5th Nivôse, 8th year of the Republic.' In this letter the question is asked, 'The war which for eight years has ravaged the four quarters of the world, must it be eternal? Are there no means of coming to an understanding? How can the two most enlightened nations of Europe, powerful and strong beyond what their safety and independence require, sacrifice to ideas of vain greatness the benefits of commerce, internal prosperity, and the happiness of families? How is it that they do not feel that peace is of the first necessity as well as of the first glory?' The reply of Lord Grenville, dated Downing Street, January 4, 1800, was sent, *not to Bonaparte*, but to the Minister of Foreign Affairs at Paris. See *Letter to his Royal Highness the Prince of Wales*, by W. A. Miles, London, 1808, Appendix, p. 204, &c.

remonstrating that agriculture languished in consequence, they were threatened with a cordon of troops, and a merchant of great credit at Paris was forced to unload at Antwerp a cargo shipped for Holland. I beg your Lordship to attribute this detail to the strong desire I feel to give you every information in my power at this momentous crisis.

## MR. MILES TO MR. ERSKINE

March 1, 1801

I hope that you will follow the example of your friend, so that your joint efforts, supported by the good sense of the people at large, will give to this distracted country that peace which has become necessary, not only to her comfort, but to her very existence as a nation. I wrote to you from Froyle, the place of my voluntary banishment, in 1797, that Mr. Fox, whose errors had made me take so decided a part against him, should exert the talents he possesses and which appear so well adapted to the exigencies of our times. If Mr. Pitt had remained steady to the genuine Whig principles he avowed in early life, and if his Administration could have been so formed as to have admitted Mr. Fox to a share in it, the former confining himself entirely to the fiscal department for which he is so admirably fitted, and the latter to the direction of foreign affairs, such a combination of talents, aided by the strength which each would have brought into the field, would have rendered the French Revolution, disastrous although it has been through improvident counsels, a blessing to mankind and not a curse. I did not fail to suggest to Mr. Pitt that, as the Revolution was an event which would spring a mine of intellect in France and give a world of mental and physical force to her new Government, he would do well to avoid even the possibility of a rupture with her. Who knows what will be the issue of this sad contest! My latest information from Paris is that France will make peace with England if England will ask for it.

### Mr. Miles to the Marquis of Buckingham

*March 29, 1801*

The enclosed letter has this instant been brought to me from Mr. Addington, and seems meant to throw me into a difficulty, or to engage me to pledge myself to an unconditional support of his measures.[1] I will enter into no such engagement, as he calls it, with the new Government, nor indeed with any Government, new or old, with whose character and objects I am totally unacquainted. If Mr. Addington means to oppose the Catholic question, I shall most decidedly be against him, for the reasons which I have already stated to your Lordship and Mr. Long. I will not answer the letter without consulting you; but this I premise before I have the honour of seeing you to-morrow, that no consideration shall induce me to abandon the Catholic question whenever it is brought forward, and in support of which I am actually preparing my opinions for the public press.

### Lord Wycombe to Mr. Miles

*Dublin: October 9, 1801*

I have a thousand apologies to make for not having sooner thanked you for your very obliging and friendly letter, but I have been so taken up with a variety of

---

[1] 'I offered to mention you to Mr. Addington as a person who might be of service to him, provided your opinions enabled you to exert your abilities in his support.'—Mr. Long to Mr. Miles, March 29.

little arrangements that I have hardly had leisure to attend even to that little correspondence which I am in the habit of carrying on. On my way from Cork hither I learned, to my great and very agreeable surprise, that the grand object of peace was at length attained. A glorious peace for France, it must be owned! I hope it does not necessarily follow that it is a disadvantageous one to England. It might have been desirable to limit the accession of contiguous territory to the Low Countries and the Ecclesiastical Electorates within the Rhine, instead of letting them into Piedmont also, or, in other words, into the dominion of Italy, for which they have not even the pretext of natural limits. All circumstances, however, considered, I am heartily glad to receive the peace as it is given to us, and rejoice from the bottom of my heart in the termination of a war which has at the expense of 250 millions[1] aggrandised France beyond what the imagination of the most sanguine Frenchman could expect, founded a military Republic, and, instead of restoring a dynasty, confirmed a usurpation. A consul who can govern arbitrarily at home and appoint kings abroad may well be considered on a footing with an emperor. The pageant Bonaparte has set up in Etruria is feebly supported. Mrs. Wyndham writes from Padua that by the arrival of Madame M—— from Pisa on her way to Vienna they have accounts of the new King's dissatisfaction. He is so poor that he arrived with the Grand Duke's old carriage and liveries, has plated forks and has borrowed 100,000 crowns on the Queen's jewels. It is said that he has made great remonstrances, and has even gone the length of signifying that, if the French troops do not withdraw, he must. I hope the

---

[1] Alison states the expenditure to have been 200 millions (viii. 68).

money to be contributed by Hanover will not be taken out of the pockets of the English people, though it would be as well bestowed as that which you say is to be given to the Duke of Portland. I beg you will make my compliments to Mr. Garland, and tell him that I shall be very happy to renew his acquaintance either in England or Ireland. It would give me great pleasure to be of service to his son if it lay in my power, but the fact is I have never asked the slightest favour of my friends in office. With Markham, notwithstanding our old and constant friendship, I have literally not exchanged a letter these many years, and I have had no communication whatever with Lord St. Vincent for nearly as many.

When you see Charles Sturt tell him with my best compliments that I have taken the place in Ireland which most resembles Crichel, and that I hope he will come and see me in his schooner—a little above the Cove of Cork, where I intend going to reside very early in the spring. In a few weeks I shall probably go to London for a couple of months, and will not fail of asking you how you do, though I cannot think of quartering myself upon you. I had great pleasure in seeing Mr. Donovan here; he is gone again into the County Waterford.

### Mr. Miles to the Marquis de Lafayette

London: October 22, 1801

It is no longer high treason, my dear General, for an Englishman to correspond with a Frenchman, and I seize the first opportunity after my return to town to felicitate you most sincerely and warmly on the great event that has happily taken place. The interests of the whole civilised world imperiously demand that friendship between the two nations should be formed and consolidated. I have uniformly maintained that the Revolution, notwithstanding the misfortunes and crimes it engendered, was a justifiable measure, that nothing short of such a measure could reform the abuses of the French Government, and that good to humanity will ultimately result from it, however deep the crimson may be that has marked its chequered fortunes. Such was my belief in the commencement of the Revolution when freedom dawned upon France, and such it has continued to be through all the process of the furious contest. Accept the expression of my sincerest regard, and allow me to offer my best compliments to Madame de Lafayette.

*LORD WYCOMBE TO MR. MILES*

Dublin: November 3, 1801

The state of parties in England, if it be anything like what you describe, must be extremely curious. Yet it will lead, I think, to little else than an unworthy scramble on the score of booty or of station. If, uninformed as I am, I were to hazard a conjecture, it would be that we shall find Pitt come forward, approve the peace, reprobate the doctrines of Burke's disciples on the one hand and those of the Reformers on the other. Mr. Addington may then receive an honourable *quietus* in a peerage, and the immaculate ex-Minister may return to his old quarters. This, however, supposes that the King has not in good earnest quarrelled with the author of the income tax. The difference which peace will make in our situation here is almost incalculable. I would willingly persuade myself that the narrow policy of fomenting divisions in this unhappy island, and the concomitant practice of sacrificing Irish to English interests, were likely to be discontinued, and certainly this much at least is wanting to atone for the injustice of the Union. Yet I confess I am not sanguine enough to believe that these comparative blessings are in store, and for this reason amongst others, I consider the treaty concluded with the French Republic as having afforded us a respite rather than security. The American contest has been compared to the first Punic war. We have survived the second, let us beware of the third. Now that peace is concluded it will be unpardonable if measures are not taken to extricate the civil list from its embarrassments. I cannot guess what aspect the revenue may assume in England. Government is about to sacrifice the morals of the people to it here, for the evils of whisky are about to be once more let loose upon us. In the South, whither I am going on Thursday, I am sorry to say we stand more in need of civilisation than you can well imagine.

### THE NEWFOUNDLAND FISHERY.

In 1791 a committee of the National Assembly at Paris, on a representation of the merchants concerned in the Newfoundland fishery, proposed that considerable bounties should be given to the adventurers in that trade, with the view, as their report stated, to encourage a nursery which, on an emergency, could furnish seamen enough to man forty sail of the line. Aware of the importance of this trade to the maritime strength of Great Britain, I attended very closely to the proceedings of the French Legislature, and was fortunate enough to obtain copies of the memorial of the merchants, of the report of the committee to which the memorial was referred, and also of the *projet d'un décret* of the National Assembly in consequence of this report.

These papers I gave to Mr. Pitt towards the close of the year 1791, reserving copies of them for myself, and, as soon as the preliminaries of peace were signed in October 1801, I transmitted these copies to Lord Hawkesbury for his guidance in arranging the definitive treaty, accompanied by some additional information respecting the great importance which France attached to a participation with us in that valuable branch of commerce. I have since the commencement of the present rupture been apprised that France keeps an eye steadfastly fixed upon Newfoundland, and, as she will most probably avail herself whenever the season for negotiation arrives, not only of the law which supposes the island to be evacuated every fall, but of her gigantic attitude, to demand a part of it to be ceded to her for the purpose of curing and salting fish, it becomes a question whether such a claim should not be prevented by instantly colonising Newfoundland and giving it the same rank and consistency as our other colonial possessions. The French merchants concerned in the fishery are for very obvious reasons decidedly against the island being made a colony by law, although it has long been one in fact. The number of people who constantly reside in Newfoundland with their families is considerable. The population was very great when I was there in 1779, as appears from documents which I obtained on the spot, and which I still possess. Its wonderful increase since that period may be accurately ascertained by referring to the annual returns delivered to the Secretary of State's office, and these will best demonstrate the policy of establishing a regular fixed government, of investing the inhabitants with municipal rights, and giving them a tribunal which will preserve them, and especially the laborious classes, from those innumerable vexations and depredations which must perpetually occur in a population so vast and left to its own guidance nine months in the year.

W. A. MILES.

### MR. MILES TO LORD HAWKESBURY

December 4, 1801

I take the liberty to transmit to your Lordship the inclosed communication received this day from my friend Mr. Garland, the member for Poole, who, whatever personal interest he may have in the Newfoundland trade, is no less anxious on national grounds for the preservation of this branch of industry, from the full conviction derived from long experience and local knowledge of its vast importance to this country. I did myself the honour to forward to the Foreign Office lately a copy of the 'Petition of the Merchants of St. Malo and Inhabitants of Saint Pierre and Miquelon for the Dry Cod Fishery,' presented to the National Assembly at Paris in 1791, and which illustrates the high value annexed to the fishery by the Legislature of France. I should have felt it my duty under the circumstances of the present moment to send this document at all events to the Secretary of State. Your Lordship will also receive herewith a copy of the *projet d'un décret* as submitted by the memorialists to the National Assembly, and which procured, on the report of the committees of Trade and Finance, the passing of decrees favourable to the appeal for increased bounties in the interests of the French fishery.

### EXTRACT FROM THE PETITION.

'If the existence of our maritime power did not essentially depend on the cod fisheries, if France could procure without it a sufficient number of men to equip her naval forces, we would not hesitate to say that the sum they absorb must be put to a better use. But this trade is the best school for seamen; without it we could have vessels, but not men to equip them, whereas at the moment when war is declared it furnishes crews for forty sail of the line.

'It is evident that this branch will become extinct if the nation does not quickly assist it by sufficient encouragement, for it is not possible to sustain the competition of the English and American fishermen in foreign markets. Let the bounty in our favour be exactly the difference of price between their fish and ours: we have fixed it at eight livres per quintal for Europe, and can assure that this computation is reasonable. Since France has been deprived of Canada and adjacent islands, the coasts of Gaspé and Labrador, in short, of all ownership in the island of Newfoundland, what have we now left? The arid rocks of Saint Pierre and Miquelon, with the liberty of fishing on the most barren part for fish off the island of Newfoundland, from which we are obliged every year to transport men and craft used for the fishery, which is attended with very great expense; whilst our rivals have over us the advantage of settled fishing, carried on with less expense and risks, and, moreover, the profits that result from the spring and fall fishery, of which we are deprived.'[1]

### THE DEPUTIES FROM MALTA, 1802.

On the arrival of the deputies from Malta and Gozo, Sir Alexander Ball came to me, much agitated, and complained of the injustice of Ministers in imputing this occurrence to him, stating that the Government were perplexed by their presence and embarrassed as to what to do with them; that they were resolved not to give

[1] See *Archives Parlementaires*, xxiii. 712.

them an official reception, as their object was to avoid causing umbrage to France and not to excite her jealousy; that they wished to conceal the arrival of the Maltese in England and get them sent back as fast as possible. I observed that, whilst it would be impracticable to keep the affair secret from a nation which had a spy for almost every chimney, it would be policy, if Malta is worth keeping, to treat these gentlemen with the greatest liberality and show them every attention, so that they might return home impressed with a high opinion of British hospitality, urbanity, and generosity. Ball agreed with me, and said that he was hurt that Ministers should show such a dread of offending Bonaparte; adding that the possession of Malta and Egypt was absolutely essential to the security of our territory in India. I remarked that, if these deputies had been sent to Paris instead of to London, an elegant hotel would have been instantly allotted to them at the public expense, and every art employed to impress them with the munificence and power of France. My friend admitted that, as the possession of Malta is an object to us, it was desirable to conciliate the natives and win their affections, especially as there was a formidable party in the French interests residing on the island and in actual correspondence with the Government in Paris. The most effectual way to obtain a preference, I observed, is to deserve it by acts of courtesy and kindness.

Ball reported our conference to Lord Hobart,[1] and, returning to me the next day, said that the deputies were to leave England immediately; that, in compliance with my suggestion, their travelling expenses to Portsmouth would be defrayed, for which purpose 50*l.* would be allowed; and that, as I declined the honour under the

[1] Minister of War.

circumstances of the case, they would be escorted to Portsmouth by a captain in the Navy as a mark of respect. But this sum, I replied, would be quite insufficient in the event of their being detained on shore by contrary winds. 'No, my dear Miles,' answered Ball, 'they will drive direct to the Sallyport on their arrival, a boat will be ready to receive them, and they must embark immediately.' I commented on the indecency of driving the Deputies post-haste to the water-side, and remarked that the Government would have done well to recognise the propriety of dismissing them in a manner due to the Islands they represent. Ball thought as I thought. He said that Mr. Penn, the Under-Secretary, had invited them to dinner.

It will appear from the memorial which, at the request of Sir Alexander Ball, I wrote for the deputies, that the object of their mission was to obtain a recognition of the *independence* of Malta, which should be sanctioned by Great Britain and France; but, in the event of this being evaded or refused, 'they prayed that they might be placed under British protection and become an integral part of her empire, or that, if this latter boon could not be granted, they might be assured by his Majesty, in the presence of France and Russia, that the Order should never return to Malta to trouble their hearths and expose them again to the misfortunes from which they had just escaped.'[1] I inquired whether the

---

[1] 'The islands of Malta, Gozo, and Comino, shall be restored to the Order of St. John of Jerusalem, to be held on the same conditions on which it possessed them before the war. . . . The Government of the French Republic and of Great Britain, desiring to place the Order and island of Malta in a state of entire independence with respect to themselves, agree that there shall not be in future either a French or an English *Langue*, and that no individual belonging to either the one or the other of these powers shall be admitted into the Order. . . . The forces of his Britannic Majesty shall evacuate the island and its dependencies

two islands, Malta and Gozo, produced corn enough to feed the inhabitants, and, if not, for how many months their supply would hold out. They answered, for only three months; and that their resources for the rest of the year were Tripoli and Sicily. These gentlemen dined with me. I invited Ball and Liston to meet them. At a subsequent private interview the deputies repeated that, notwithstanding the utmost exertions and industry of the natives, they could not reckon on less than nine months for the supply of food from external sources. In that case, I replied, the *independence* of your islands is *impracticable*; and I advised them to submit themselves without hesitation to the dominion of Great Britain.[1]—
*April*, 1802.—W. A. M.

within three months from the exchange of the ratifications, or sooner if possible,' &c.—Extracts from the Treaty of Amiens, Article X. See Cobbett's *Political Register*, i. 823.

[1] '*February* 5, 1802.—A deputation from the principal inhabitants of Malta has arrived in London. The object of their mission is to put their country under the protection and government of his Majesty. No doubt can exist but that this overture will be accepted by his Majesty's Ministers as some small equipoise to the sovereignty of Italy, which the First Consul has acquired since peace was signed. *April* 11.—As his Majesty was coming out of church he was met by several gentlemen from Malta who had been waiting for some time to see the King. His Majesty was accompanied by Earl Morton. The King conversed a long time with the Maltese gentlemen. It must create some surprise that those gentlemen, who attended as ambassadors from their State, should not be admitted officially to a regular audience. Surely this did not proceed from any servile fear of the displeasure of Bonaparte to our Ministers.'—*Annual Register*.

The memorial drawn up by Mr. Miles, written in French, is a document of some length, and reviews the position of the Maltese when under the government of the Order; it touches on the appearance of the French squadron off Valetta in June 1798, mentions the artifice of Bonaparte to effect a landing of his troops, and how, contrary to treaty, he succeeded through the treachery of the Order; and shows that, in 1800, the Maltese Militia, although undisciplined as soldiers, compelled the French to capitulate and retire, whereupon the English entered the harbour, and took possession of the island at the special desire of the inhabitants. Internal evidence plainly indicates that portions of this document were dictated by

### MR. MILES TO SIR ALEXANDER BALL

April 24, 1802

If I offered, my dear Ball, to escort the Malta deputies to Portsmouth and to do the honours of my country to these people, it is from the perfect knowledge I have of the vast impression made on all foreigners by even the most trifling attentions. If it be a national object with this country to preserve an interest in Malta sufficiently strong to counteract any efforts which France may make to regain her former preponderance, permit me to say—and I speak from experience on subjects of this nature—that the most effectual way of doing it is by emulating our rivals in those civilities for which they are distinguished, and which have enabled them to acquire more in the cabinet than they have done in the

the deputies themselves. There is extant in Malta the original memorial, in Italian, brought over and signed by the deputies—Il Marchese Mario Testaferrata, Dr. Emmanuele Ricaud, Filippo Castagna, Michele Cachia, Sacerdote Dr. Pietro Mallia, and Antonio Mallia. The deputation was accompanied by Antonio Casolani, as the confidential agent of the Government, and Eugenio Formosa as his clerk. Why Sir Alexander Ball should have requested Mr. Miles to draw up *another* memorial after the deputies had arrived in London does not appear; but the fact is so. In Cobbett's *Political Register* the affair is thus announced: 'Six deputies have arrived from Malta, bringing a memorial, the object of which is to solicit his Majesty to keep possession of that island' (i. 120).

By the Treaty of Paris, May 30, 1814, it was provided that Malta—the ostensible cause of the renewal of the war after the Treaty of Amiens—should be ceded, with its dependencies, to Great Britain in perpetuity. Opposite to the Palace of the Grand Masters, which is now the residence of the British Governor, is the Piazza, where, facing the Palace, stands the principal 'guard,' a building which has the following inscription under the royal arms of England:—

> Magnæ et Invictæ Britanniæ
> Melitensium Amor
> Et Europæ Vox
> Has Insulas Confirmat
> An. MDCCCXIV.

field. Our manners are not the best calculated to win the affections of mankind. There is nothing seductive in them, and we have a coldness and *hauteur* which not only offend, but disgust other nations. It is a mistaken notion that we can purchase opinion, friendship, and even zeal with gold. Any schoolboy can go to market with his guinea, or exchange his one pound one for its full value, which he knew by calculation before he went, but no skill in arithmetic can estimate the profit on civilities of even the most trifling nature, and, believe me, more is to be obtained by urbanity and address, if well timed, than by subsidies. Prepossess foreigners in your favour, win them by flattering that *amour propre* which all of us possess in a greater or lesser degree, and of which all of us are jealous, and by doing this all that diplomacy can acquire will be achieved. If I had been allowed to do the honours of my country in a manner worthy of my country, it would have been my care to send these men away strongly impressed with ideas, not only of our power and opulence, but of our urbanity, munificence, and hospitality.

Deputies from Malta do not arrive daily. It is one of those occurrences that may only happen in a century, and the money expended for their accommodation would have been well laid out. A hundred pounds, more or less, can be no object to a nation whose annual expenditure is thirty-six millions. I feel on this occasion no less for the honour of my country than for its interests, and I could not think of travelling with these gentlemen to Portsmouth as if I were conducting eight convicts to be shipped to Botany Bay. Whatever their individual characters may be, they are here as the representatives of an entire people, whose entire confidence it behoves us to acquire, and, as the representatives of Malta, they are entitled to respect. It is their public and not their own individual personal characters or capacities that I look to. Adieu!

### SIR ALEXANDER BALL TO MR. MILES

Clifford Street, London : May 29, 1802

I saw Mr. and Mrs. Liston yesterday, and talked with them much about you, dear Miles, for he is very anxious to have you with him, that he may have such a very able second to enable him to surmount the many difficulties he will have to encounter. With respect to myself, I am so sick of attending public offices that I am surprised that men of independent fortunes will submit to it, and I have been so out of humour at times that I have wished the people in office would be out of humour with me, that I might have a pretext for retiring; but the wish to secure a good provision for my son sometimes intrudes itself, and makes me bear with little rubs and inconveniences for his sake. This stimulus is wisely ordered to prevent men of independent minds retiring from the chicanery and rubs of public stations. I shall endeavour to see Lord Hawkesbury or Mr. Hammond to-day, but the chances are against it. But I shall hope to see Mr. Rolleston, and I will ask him about you.

All my family desire to be kindly remembered. We are very busy preparing for a voyage at least as far as Gibraltar; but I shall not go beyond that unless I have ample powers. My task will be an arduous one. I have extricated the Maltese from the greatest difficulties and dangers, which made them call me *Saint* Ball, but I am aware that a saint circumstanced as I shall be at Malta cannot work miracles without a little money.

All the powers are arming again—another storm is
brewing, which I think will burst over the Turks, and
I am apprehensive that we shall soon have a most difficult part to act. Pray give me your full opinion of the
state of politics; it is so completely jumbled that I am
quite lost in conjecture. Adieu, my dear Miles!

### Sir Alexander Ball to Mr. Miles

Malta: December 10, 1802

Your letter, my dear Miles, of the 24th of last August
is the only one I have received from you since my arrival
here. I rejoice to find that your body can keep pace
with the activity of your mind to enable you to explore
the country and visit your friends, as it will lead me to
hope that you will not think Malta too long a voyage
when this Government is a little more settled. At present the minds of the inhabitants are in a most unpleasant state between hope and fear, and my situation
very arduous as well as perilous. I have had warning
from priests, who have received the intelligence by confession, that it has been agitated by some conspirators
to take away my life. All the Maltese Republicans who
are attached to the French and went with them to France
when they capitulated are now returned, and they are
so desperate at observing the influence I have over the
greatest part of the inhabitants, that I should not be
surprised if they attempted to poison or attack me at
night; however, as I have reason to consider myself born
under a fortunate planet, I shall continue to hope it will
protect me from the hand of the assassin. I am now
carrying on a paper war with the French Minister, who
has been working hard to undermine me; but I do not
think him very skilful in diplomatic science. I suppose
you have heard of the insolent conduct of Bonaparte in

Italy. He ordered the King of Naples to send some of his statues to Paris. The poor King of Sardinia was not allowed to live quietly at Rome; he was ordered to reside at a small town about twenty miles from thence. The late Duke of Parma died suddenly, and under very suspicious circumstances; he had scarcely closed his eyes before the French Minister ordered the Duchess to quit the country. The French Minister at Florence does not allow a carriage to leave the opera before him. Their insolence and plunder exceed what you can imagine of Frenchmen. If I had your abilities and leisure, I would make the nation rouse from their apathy and feel that the French Government is conquering them in peace! However, my dear Miles, we may differ in opinion on political subjects, be assured it will never in the smallest degree break in upon our ancient friendship. I am sure we shall agree in moral points; as to others, I am a friend to every person thinking and even speaking to the utmost extent when it does not infringe on the happiness of society.

We have not any dates here but what come from Barbary. I will send you a few oranges next month with some wine. You will not receive any by the 'Alexander;' she sailed from hence before I arrived. My wife keeps her health tolerably well, but complains of the intense heat; my son is well, and improves very much. Mr. Laing, his tutor, is one of the best young men I know; we live as brothers; he is much respected here. My time is so much occupied that I can seldom ride out or use any exercise. All the families here live sociably together, and I shall have to regret their departure when our troops evacuate this. My situation here will not then be very enviable. Delightful weather—sitting with my windows open. I think this the finest climate in the world during eight months of the year; the remaining four are certainly too hot, and require management. All my family unite in every friendly wish to you, my dear Miles. Adieu! Yours affectionately.

### Mr. Miles to Mr. Rolleston[1]

June 10, 1803

I take no credit for having pointed out to Mr. Pitt in 1786 the importance of having an establishment in Egypt and maintaining the free navigation of the Black Sea. I received these ideas from a man whom I accidentally met on the Continent, and from a perusal of the memoirs of Baron de Tot and the travels of Savary and Volney. My project went no further than to acquire by negotiation what has since been obtained by the sword; nor would I have broached the subject had it not then been evident to my senses that France kept the same objects in view, and that, as informed at the time, wheat grew most abundantly without much culture on the shores of the Euxine—a statement which Sir Sidney Smith has since assured me is a fact. The Revolution opened vast sources of important political information to the principal actors in that great event.

Not having the treaty of Amiens to refer to—and I very much regret not having it—I am not qualified to appreciate the arguments in favour of our retaining Malta, to which the 'summary account' is merely an *avant-propos pour mettre le lecteur au fait* as to the importance of that fortress to this country, possessing, as we do, a vast empire in Asia, and apprehensive, as we may be, of the great danger that would result from an enemy planting himself on its confines. I think, however, that the veil between the ratification of peace,

---

[1] Mr. Stephen Rolleston, of the Foreign Office.

which Mr. Canning more properly defines as 'a feverish
repose,' and the recent rupture, is not sufficiently thick
to conceal from even ordinary penetration an impatience
to catch at anything like a fair pretext for retaining Malta.
It seems to me as if Ministers, ashamed of the cession,
were unwilling to let it slip through their fingers, and
were anxious to withhold it, if they could without committing the honour of the nation by a violent breach of
its plighted faith.[1] If Harlequin could put his magical
wand of truth to the breasts of Mr. Addington and Lord
Hawkesbury, I have no doubt but that their confessions
would tally with my surmise; and, thinking as I do, it
is probable that I should have snapped, as they have
done, at the first opportunity of keeping so important a
position. Had I been Minister, no consideration would
have induced me to surrender it—fortified, as we were, in
the possession by the expulsion of the French and by the
acclamation of the Maltese—the inhabitants, approaching to 80,000, being desirous to be under the British
Government, since it is impossible from the sterility of
their soil to maintain their independence. You do not
know, perhaps, that the memorial presented by the
deputies to Lord Hobart was drawn up by me. These
deputies were left to shift for themselves, and when
desired to quit the kingdom they were hurried off to
Portsmouth without any consideration. Had they gone
to Paris instead of coming to London, they would have
been well lodged, a table would have been kept for them

[1] 'The clause regarding Malta, which became of so much importance
in the sequel, from being the ostensible ground of the rupture of the
treaty, was in these terms: " The island of Malta, with its dependencies,
shall be evacuated by the English troops, and restored to the Order of St.
John of Jerusalem. To secure the absolute independence of that isle
from both the contracting parties, it shall be placed under the guarantee
of a third power to be named in the definitive treaty." '—Alison, viii. 55;
Dumas, vii. 319; *Parl. Hist.* xxxv. 18, 19.

at the public expense, every attention would have been shown, and they would have found the fable of Calypso realised, not in Gozo, but in France.[1]

### Sir Alexander Ball to Mr. Miles

Malta: November 2, 1803

If you have received all my letters, you will be convinced that neither distance nor time can make me forget an old friend. I am continually regretting that you are not induced to employ the abilities you are blessed with in the active support of the Government at this critical period. I have read with much satisfaction the many spirited and patriotic publications which have lately come out, and which no doubt have had the desired effect upon the public mind; but we are not made sufficiently sensible that we must all submit to privations, or risk losing our property by a convulsion which has been long threatening us, and giving sufficient warning of our danger, unless we act with unanimity, firmness, and patriotism. You must give the people a philippic upon this subject. I have established a Malta 'Gazette' in Italian, which circulates all over the Mediterranean—it even reaches Cairo—to counteract the effect of the poison disseminated in the 'Moniteur' and other French papers. I endeavour to awaken my readers to a sense of the danger in which they are placed by the ambition of Bonaparte, who, in one of his late official communications, says: 'Avec trois

[1] 'Malta (*Melita*), with its sister Gozo, has from time immemorial been a place of importance to whatever race wished to hold the highway of the Mediterranean, whether Phœnician, Punic, Roman, or Arab. Thus even the stories of Homer have a semblance of truth, for the Ogygian isle where Ulysses took refuge has been supposed to be Malta or Gozo, in both of which tradition, born of the poem, yet points out the grottoes of Calypso.'—*Encyclopædia Britannica*, ninth edition, xv. 341.

jours de brume et cinq jours de provision je serai maître de Londres, du Parlement, et de la Banque.' This is in the true spirit of French gasconade coming from a fellow who the other day declared that the chance of his success was one hundred to one against him. In my next I shall give you an account of what I have been doing. All classes here are getting rich and happy, and we should be inundated with people from all parts of Italy if we did not prevent it. We have great intercourse with Sicily; many Sicilians visit us from curiosity, and many for commercial purposes, the whole of whom give so favourable a report of our government that all the inhabitants are anxious to annex their beautiful island to Great Britain. Two thousand men and a good proclamation would do the business. The people of property say they would favour us privately, but not publicly, for fear we should desert them at the peace. The lower and industrious class to a man would fight in our cause. General Veal declared at Naples that he had not in the least succeeded in his endeavour at Malta. His party, and those of the Order, have reported the most infamous lies in the foreign 'Gazettes' against me, which I understand were in part translated in the 'Morning Chronicle.'

P.S.—Lord Nelson having in the last peace, or rather suspension of hostilities, declared that Malta is of no importance to a fleet blockading Toulon, he takes every opportunity to support that opinion, and he is always pointing out the superior advantages of Sardinia and Minorca. It may be observed that the Toulon Fleet have twice escaped his vigilance. The first time they sailed he was in a bay on the north side of Sardinia, the last time he was in a bay on the south side of Sardinia. I shall soon send you a paper tending to prove that Malta is to be preferred to any of the islands, and that it will be regarded as the watch tower of the Mediterranean, the great military and naval depôt as well as the commercial storehouse of Great Britain.

### Mr. Liston[1] to Mr. Miles

Pall Mall: May 10, 1805

I perceive with regret that it will really be impossible for us to pay you a visit at Brownsea during our present excursion. I have been persuaded by my friends, and indeed induced by a national curiosity, to protract our stay in town till we should see the issue of the late shock of parties; and, this appearing to be now nearly at an end, we must think of making immediate preparations for our journey to the North, where every operation connected with the *utile* or the *dulce* is neglected during our absence.

The conduct of the contending parties has struck me nearly as it has done you—a coincidence, you know, not very frequent. That our great men should, at such a crisis, be exclusively occupied in measures of personal attack and defence appears to be really criminal. Never had I such difficulty to examine political contests in the calm lights of mild philosophy. Were we to meet, I could talk a little misanthropy with you with pleasure.

The mention of the word suggests to me to say that, from the strain of your last letters, you do not appear to me to be by any means cured; I would say, I allude to those of the 25th of April and the 3rd of this month, but that I do not suppose you either keep copies or notes

---

[1] Afterwards Sir Robert Liston, Ambassador from the Court of St. James at the Porte.

of the contents and the dates of your epistles; I must therefore give my opinion, both as your friend and your physician—and in this last capacity I pretend to some skill and great experience—that you must not upon any account be allowed to *escape* from your present confinement, or to seek refuge in the larger Bedlam you allude to. You must endeavour 'pensive to show a countenance serene,' and quietly resign yourself to the custody of your amiable and excellent keeper, Mrs. Miles, of whom my wife and I think and feel, and very frequently express, all that you say, and more.

You have not answered my question with respect to your manner of spending your time—for I did not allude merely to amusement—in your present retreat in the manner I wished and expected. You tell me what you cannot do because you are sick, but I wanted to know what you do when you are not sick. If you had a cottage of your own, with an acre of ground, I should expect you would employ yourself in digging in your garden; but as the property of the soil is not yours, I take it for granted your chief occupations are in the house, reading and writing; and it has struck both me and my better half that you might make a most excellent and interesting book if you would sit down and write the history of your life, in the same easy, animated, and candid way as you told us some anecdotes of it one day in town. You might not be able to publish names, but you might either have blanks or delay the publication till a later period. We have been reading the 'Memoirs of Marmontel,' written by himself, and published after his death, which are highly interesting. Think of this. I beg you will assure Mrs. Miles of our respect and love. Ever most truly and affectionately yours.

### MR. MILES TO MR. JEKYLL[1]

Brownsea: January 9, 1806.

I thank you for your very flattering reception of my rhapsody. If anything contained in my letter should have induced you to think more seriously on the perilous state of the empire, I shall most sincerely rejoice. With respect to the terrible prospect before us, my too irritable feelings disqualify me, as much as imbecility could do, for discussing or judging of public affairs; yet I cannot refrain from hazarding my opinions at a moment like the present, and the more so, as I cannot suppose the possibility of any man being silent or indifferent on the very critical situation into which the country has been brought. It is full time that the age of imposture should cease, and that the worst description of charlatans should be incapacitated from doing us any more mischief. While the nation is lost, as it were, in a delirium of joy at the brilliant achievement of Nelson, it seems insensible to the giant strides of Napoleon, whose fortunes appear to be in a ratio with his genius. The splendour of his marches seems to us to be totally eclipsed by the valour of our tars. But we must not forget that while we take ships he takes cities and subdues empires. I told Mr. Pitt in 1793, and I repeated it to Lord Buckingham, that *foreign politics* were not his forte. Turn to the map of Europe, as at the commencement of the war, and compare it with the map of Europe for 1806, and say whether I calumniated the Minister. Allow me to describe it to you as it stands at present, and I may trust your memory for what it was at the former period:

---

[1] Mr. Joseph Jekyll, a barrister on the Western Circuit, appointed a Master in Chancery in 1815, a favourite with the Prince Regent. See *Life of Romilly*, iii. 186.

Austria—all but blotted out, and her authority in Brabant, Flanders, and Italy annihilated.

Genoa, Tuscany, Lucca, &c. }
Switzerland, the Electorates on the Rhine . . . . } Extinguished.
The Bishopric of Liège, and the seven United Provinces . . }

Naples, Spain, and Portugal—almost eclipsed.

Prussia and Bavaria—trembling for their existence as independent states.

Russia—palsied, and France, perhaps, at this moment offering to restore her to vigour by a treaty of alliance.

Sweden—its thoughtless King saved from being dethroned by his neighbours.

Denmark—irritated by our vexatious aggressions and become French at heart.

Saxony and the whole herd of German Princes—*Rien!*

This was the state of Europe when Mr. Pitt, in 1804, impatient of place, drove Mr. Addington out of office.[1] On what ground, then, could he expect any effective co-operation on the Continent, debilitated, broken down, and disjointed as it was? I feel convinced that the mischievous counsels by which the nation has been governed during the last fifteen years have brought the possibility

---

[1] Pitt was 'uneasy being out of harne s, a d in his heart of hearts longed to return to Downing Street.' 'Mr. Pitt is, I hear, more and more bitter against the Ministers, and feels strongly what he deems the embarrassment of his situation.' 'On the 10th May Mr. Pitt was enabled to announce to the King, and to obtain his Majesty's approval of, the new Administration.' 'On Mr. Pitt resuming office in May 1804, he saw the camp of Napoleon still on the heights of Boulogne, and the flotilla of boats not yet dispersed.' See Walford's *Life of Pitt*, and Jesse's *Memoirs of the Life of George III.*

of her being conquered by France very much within the area of the chances. Look at the evidences in favour of my fears, and judge for yourself. I merely give you the opinion of a private individual who, sitting as it were on an eminence in his voluntary retirement, whence he fancies he has a commanding view of affairs, cannot avoid weeping over the sad destiny of his native land!

If you see Lord and Lady Lansdowne in London, do me the kindness to recall me to their remembrance and to make my affectionate respects acceptable. I wrote last Sunday to his Lordship at Southampton a letter nearly similar to this.

### Mr. Miles to the Marquis of Buckingham

Brownsea: January 21, 1806

If it should be the idea of your Lordship that our safety lies in peace—and in a peace which points ultimately to an alliance with France—and if it is your intention to act upon that idea, the talents which you have done me the honour so frequently to mention are at your absolute disposal to marshal and to regulate their march as you please. Content with the income I possess, I disclaim all thoughts of emolument in offering my exertions through the public press to forward these views. My idea of an alliance with France is now twenty-five years old. It originated in a conversation which I had with the late Marquis de Bouillé in 1781. It was afterwards much insisted upon when Mr. Burke in his splendid nonsense declared France was 'blotted out from the map of Europe,' and to counteract such mischief I asserted in a paper which I showed your Lordship in 1791, and which you entreated me not to publish, that she would rise a 'phœnix from her ashes.' The present state of Europe decides very fully between Mr. Burke and me.

The 'indemnity for the past and security for the future' of Mr. Pitt [1] may now be entombed with the 'unconditional submission of Lord North,' and to the historian the melancholy task will be consigned to ascertain which of these men accelerated with the greater rapidity the ruin of the British Empire. The present generation will have enough to do to fence itself against the mischiefs they have done to our hapless country.

### MR. FLINT TO MR. MILES

London: January 23, 1806

I write a line to say that Mr. Pitt died this morning at half-past four o'clock. Poor man! His star has set in clouds indeed! A thousand thanks for your interesting letter. I cannot answer it as it deserves at present. As you will be anxious to hear the probable turn things will take, I will put you in possession of my view of them. I think it likely the King will send for Lord Sidmouth, and desire him to form an Administration. The Lord have mercy upon him if he does not insist on a union of parties, without which we shall have no internal peace, not that I think that a union will accomplish much good. We are in a wretched situation, and nothing can avert our ruin, I think, but a miracle. Adieu! [2]

[1] *Parliamentary History*, xxxi. 633.

[2] The circumstances which accelerated the death of the Minister are full of mournful interest. The defeat of the Austrian army by Napoleon at Ulm gave him a shock from which he never recovered. News of the victory of Nelson at Trafalgar brought a gleam of hope. This was but a momentary rally. 'Austerlitz soon completed what Ulm had begun. Early in December Pitt had retired to Bath, in the hope that he might there gather strength for the approaching session. While he was languishing there on his sofa arrived the news that a decisive battle had been fought and lost in Moravia, that the Coalition was dissolved, that the Continent was at the feet of France. He sank down under the blow. Ten days later he was so emaciated that his most intimate friends hardly

*MR. MILES TO MR. FLINT*

Brownsea: January 26, 1806

*Il est donc parti après nous avoir fait infiniment de mal!* But the errors of Mr. Pitt may be entombed—*de mortuis nil nisi bonum*. Would to God that we could as easily dispose of the consequences of those errors! In his situation, with his eloquence and popularity, he had it in his power to 'ride in the whirlwind and direct the storm;' he might have turned the French Revolution into a blessing for the whole civilised world. When Mr. Burke asserted that France was 'blotted out from the map of Europe,' I wrote instantly to the Minister to counteract the danger of such an opinion. The present state of Europe decides very fully between Mr. Burke and myself. I admonished and conjured Mr. Pitt to cultivate the confidence of the French by an open declaration that Great Britain would not suffer any interruption to be given by foreign powers to the course of the Revolution. Such conduct on the part of England —hitherto regarded as a rival and an enemy—would have been hailed as magnanimous; it would have deserved and secured the admiration and gratitude of the French people; and the world would have escaped the catastrophe of being torn to pieces by warfare during the last fifteen years. If he had been a statesman he would have recognised the impossibility of this country

---

knew him. He came up from Bath by slow journeys, and on the 11th of January, 1806, reached his villa at Putney.'

'He ceased to breathe on the morning of the 23rd of January, the twenty-fifth anniversary of the day on which he first took his seat in Parliament. He was in his forty-seventh year, and had been during near nineteen years First Lord of the Treasury and undisputed chief of the Administration.'— Macaulay, *Encyclopædia Britannica*, ninth edition. See *The Diaries and Correspondence of the Right Hon. George Rose*, vol. ii.

being allowed to remain neutral, menaced as France then was by the powers which she has since annihilated or left eclipsed in total darkness. My great anxiety in the first years of the Revolution was to preserve Mr. Pitt from error. Unhappily, he yielded to the influences of Mr. Burke and the *émigrés*. I had no share in misleading him. As soon as I contended with that warmth which is natural to me, as to every man in love with right, that the wisest line of conduct for this country to pursue would be an alliance with France—which I had first discussed in person with the Marquis de Bouillé in 1781, and which Mr. Pitt, as I thought, favoured when he sent me to Paris in 1790—I became marked as *un patriote enragé*, as a man who had mounted *à la hauteur de la Révolution*. I was very far from being in sympathy with the early revolutionists; on the contrary, I recoiled from the horrors of their excesses; but I foresaw that they would exhaust themselves, and, when recovered from their delirium, would leave impressed on the French nation an entirely new character.

Nor has Mr. Pitt been without the opportunity for terminating hostilities. If he had accepted the invitation to treat for peace transmitted through me by order of the Convention in January 1795—or even if he had attended to the wise admonition of the late Lord Lansdowne, after the affair of Aboukir, to make proposals to France for peace, for the hour of victory was the time to propose it—do you think Napoleon would have been Emperor of France and King of Italy? Certainly not! If it should be said that he was controlled by the King, who desired war, I say that Mr. Pitt should have controlled the King by telling his Majesty that the nation desired peace.

I agree almost with you that nothing but a miracle

can save us.  The salvation of the country, however, is not so much to be looked for in the union of parties as in the concentration of sterling talents combined with great political integrity and firmness.  The union of parties means little else than a conspiracy more extended —a more ample distribution of the loaves and fishes to the numerous followers of each faction.  Mr. Fox, who certainly has the comprehensive mind of a statesman and clearly understood the character of the French Revolution in its commencement, is at the head of one party, and the old adherents of Mr. Pitt, until they file off to the right or left, form another; but the country, which is the most interested on this occasion, unfortunately has no party to espouse her cause.  It can scarcely be said that Lord Sidmouth is known to the country.  If the King, instead of referring to him, would send for Mr. Fox, it would be the best method his Majesty could adopt to form under existing circumstances an unexceptionable Administration.  Not that Mr. Fox is free from the reproach of having contributed his share to the calamities which have befallen us; his coalition with Lord North brought the Opposition into contempt by the strong and general discredit it threw upon the profession of public men.  Had it not been for this coalition, Mr. Pitt would probably not have been in office at the epoch of the French Revolution, and we might indeed have heard of Napoleon as a general but never as an emperor.  We are still robust, and must repel the blow aimed at us by the giant arm of Bonaparte.  Let me know who the new men will be, and stop the 'Sun,' if you can, from blazing forth its abominable impudence.[1]

[1] 'The *Sun*, a newspaper set up by Mr. Pitt and others in 1793. Its owners were George Rose, Secretary of the Treasury, and Francis Freeling, Secretary at the General Post Office.'—Note by Mr. Miles.

*Mr. Donovan to Mr. Miles*

St. James's: January 23, 1806

For ten days past I have danced more attendance and experienced more trick and shuffling at a certain great office not far from the Horse Guards than I can possibly describe. The death of Mr. Pitt, which is now stated to have taken place at four o'clock this morning, places me perhaps in a worse situation than hitherto, for my claims and services were known to him. The reports of the day are various and contradictory: some people talk of a Regency, others of a coalition of the three parties; some again that the King, who is not easily put from his opinion, will form an Administration to the exclusion of the old Opposition, which, should it take place, it is thought, cannot keep its ground; and I was present where a foreign nobleman declared that he had heard on good authority that Lord Hardwicke is to be a member of the new Cabinet. Why do you not come to town at this moment—more critical, perhaps, than at any former period? Every man of talent should be ready either to support the measures of men who may deserve it, or to crush them if they should be found unworthy of their position. Recollect that the talents which it has pleased God to bestow upon you ought to be exerted in time of public emergency like the present. Pray exert yourself on this occasion; run up to town and show yourself to your old friends, who would rejoice to have you again amongst them. According to your advice I called at Lansdowne House on Monday last. His Lordship was not at home, and I left my card.

### Captain Pickmore to Mr. Miles

Ramillies, St. Helens: January 26, 1806

I have been so plagued with executors and attorneys since returning to this anchorage that I could not write with comfort to Brownsea, and now the wind is become fair, and the signal is made for sailing. I will not, however, go off without a few lines to my valued old friend Miles. Of our destination I can no otherwise judge than a belief we are to go in search of one of the squadrons escaped from Brest, and in that cruise I am assured of your best wishes. What a change is the death of Mr. Pitt likely to make! I have my fears it will be a change without a benefit, for I think there is much more appearance of party than of patriotism. Clamour and disloyalty may ensue, and in the squabble poor old England suffers the most serious injury and injustice. I do not conceive much evil would arise from a change at the Admiralty, unless an imprudent attempt should be made to put Lord St. Vincent there. What will become of us in that fatal event is most difficult to say; but it ought to be considered that the Navy should serve with confidence and encouragement; and I hesitate not a moment to say that no man who can avoid it will serve while that character presides. The loss of Mr. Pitt's talents must be seriously lamented, for, whether Minister or not, I believe him a great and an honest man. I hope on our return to learn that your valuable friend the Marquis of Lansdowne has taken a distinguished share in the Government. It is from such abilities and independence that we should look for the independence of old England, and, should it be the case, he will no doubt, for public benefit, take my friend Miles by the hand, who is too much a lover of his country to refuse his aid, so useful and so much wanted. Your verses on poor Lord Nelson are much admired for their strength and beauty. It would be well for us if our Government thought the Navy of as much consequence as you do; but the present people are only warm in outward show, while their hearts are like a dead man's hand. Let no such men be trusted. Their conduct to the heroes of the glorious battle of Trafalgar has been full of suspicious jealousy. The men have been separated and drafted when there did not appear a want of men, and while the ships are refitting they have lent the officers to other ships, instead of indulging them with leave for recreation. The anchor is just tripping, and I must close my letter, assuring you, my dear Miles, that I am with truth and faithful regard, &c.

### Mr. Miles to Lord Moira[1]

December 1, 1806

It appears as if the winds only blew to waft us disastrous intelligence, and that the day only dawns to give a stronger glow to the vast ruin that seems ultimately to await us. In whatever direction your Lordship looks, an afflicting perspective stares you in the face, and confirms with additional and bitter evidence the fidelity of my unavailing predictions to Mr. Pitt from 1790 to 1793, that, if he warred with France broken loose from all restraint, and under the wild dominion of an enthusiasm which no human force could extinguish or control, he would ruin his country. Neither he nor any of his colleagues knew, or would know, the character of the

---

[1] Francis Rawdon, Earl of Moira, County Down, first Marquis of Hastings, as Governor-General of India, entered the Cabinet on the death of Pitt, 1806, as Master-General of Ordnance.

French nation or its Revolution, but what they wanted in science they amply made up in rashness and presumption. The errand on which Mr. Pitt despatched me to Paris in 1790 was rendered nugatory by him at the very moment when its object might have been accomplished, and I believe that Mr. Hugh Elliot and myself were the only persons who gave him a faithful account of the progress and objects of the Revolution.

The French, as I had the honour to predict to you a fortnight since, are actually at Hamburg. I knew and communicated the fact at the time to the Minister that they had their eye upon that emporium as far back as 1795.[1] It was an event to which Government might have looked forward from the instant that the enemy took possession of Hanover, and I have no doubt from what was transmitted to me from Paris in those days, and what has come to my knowledge since, that the peace which Russia has perhaps made, or will be compelled to make with France, will be a prelude to an alliance with her and to our consequent exclusion from the Baltic, the effect of which on our navy needs no comment. As to Sweden, if our missionaries at Stockholm have well served their Court, your Lordship must know that its sovereign holds his diadem and his life by a thread much finer than that from which the sword was suspended over the head of Damocles, and that his own subjects have an account to settle with him to the full as serious as any which the malicious ingenuity of Bonaparte can possibly fabricate against him. Thus circumstanced as the country is, forgive me if I conjure you to use the whole force of your talents and influence to produce an entire change in that system

---

[1] 'A cartel came to Poole, Christmas, 1795, and by that opportunity I received a letter from Paris saying I must not think of peace, and that our expulsion from Hamburg must be accomplished.'—W. A. M.

which has brought us to this awful precipice, for nothing short of an entire change can possibly rescue us from being drawn into the terrible vortex of the Revolution. If I obtrude myself thus almost daily on your Lordship's notice, and with a warmth that certainly argues sincerity, it is not that I have more sensibility or that I pretend to be more alive to the interests of my country than other men, but that I have had the means of obtaining better information than falls to the lot in general of persons so far removed from power as myself, and that I have perhaps reflected more deeply on the causes, the conduct, and the consequences of this unfortunate contest, than even those to whom the King has confided the management of his affairs. I told Mr. Pitt in 1791 that the curse had never fallen upon our nation till now, and from that period to the present calamitous moment I have never lost sight of the proceedings and probable views of the belligerent powers. To any other man than yourself an apology would perhaps be necessary for obtruding these observations, but you, who will judge of their importance by their intrinsic worth, will require no excuse. You are aware that in a vessel during a hurricane the aid of the meanest individual is acceptable and may be useful, and that in a storm, where the lives of all are in equal danger, it may be permitted for a man to fly aft from the forecastle to the quarter-deck with his best efforts to prevent shipwreck without being guilty of a breach either of discipline or of decorum.

*MR. MILES TO BARON DE NOLCKEN*[1]

February 18, 1807

It was fully my intention to have personally solicited you this morning to favour me with your company on

[1] Swedish Ambassador at the Court of St. James.

Saturday next to dinner, but from various causes I was unable to go out. Our good friend Liston would have joined the party, but he is, unfortunately for me, prevented by a prior engagement. I have no right to complain, for, shooting him as it were flying last Sunday, I had him the whole day to myself, and, since he is a man universally beloved and sought for, this is to the full as much as I am entitled to expect. I love him because I know his moral worth to be equal to his talents and attainments, *et c'est beaucoup dire*. That such a man should have been recalled in times like the present from a Court where he was idolised has something in it so marked by imbecility that I know of no terms strong enough to express my indignation at Lord Hawkesbury's conduct on that occasion. Sweden and Denmark, no longer secondary powers, seem to be alone capable of prescribing limits to that tide of conquest which is not yet at its highest flood, and which has already inundated almost the whole of Continental Europe. To have recalled at such a moment Mr. Liston from Copenhagen, and allow his talents and great acquirements to wither in the shade, has more of political crime than of folly in it, and when we see public trust so abused, it is absolutely impossible to remain silent. *Lui et son père nous ont fait beaucoup de mal*, and from the terrible prospect before us it is not improbable but, old as the latter is, *qu'il s'en repentira*. I have asked Lord Folkestone and Sir John Gifford to dine with me, and need I say that I shall feel flattered and honoured by your company at a quarter-past five on Saturday next? I beg the favour of your presenting my best respects to Madame la Baronne de Nolcken.

*Mr. Miles to Lord Moira*

Foley Place: July 17, 1807

As your Lordship has done me the honour to communicate to me freely your unreserved opinion on the lamentable state of the country, and as your opinion coincides with my own, I take the liberty to state to you that I am still firmly convinced that the far wiser line for this country to pursue is an earnest endeavour to obtain peace—not a mere patchwork truce, *seulement pour respirer*, but a peace that would conduct us to an alliance with France. It was an alliance, not war, that I preached to Mr. Pitt in 1791 and 1792, and in urging it I assured him that, if he adopted the latter, he would ruin the kingdom. I took the liberty to urge this incessantly until he interdicted me, January 7, 1793, from corresponding with the French Government on the subject of peace or war. In 1801 I recommended Mr. Addington to look forward to the achievement of a cordial understanding with France; assuring him that a peace which had not that event for its ultimate object would be fallacious, precarious, and mischievous. My predictions have in part been verified. It is reserved, I hope, for your Lordship to prevent their entire accomplishment. Our position is certainly less favourable for such a project in 1807 than it was in 1792; but I think it practicable, and, if attempted in time, may prevent a treacherous combination dictated by fear or selfishness, as well as by resentments and jealousies. Russia has surely little claim on us for much delicacy toward her, and the Russian councils are too fluctuating and Austria too weak in men for us in the present state of affairs to stand upon punctilio, and especially as such a punctilio may eventually prove our death-warrant. I dare not trust my pen with the subject of Sweden and her worse than indiscreet sovereign; and, as to Denmark, all that it behoves me to say is that she is no longer a secondary power, and that we should have done well to follow her example. We must not, however, forget that she has injuries to resent, and that even her neutrality may become an object worth obtaining.

A favourable opportunity offers for my going to the Baltic, if the Prince would have the goodness to authorise Colonel McMahon to see Mr. Canning upon the subject of the secret mission, which your Lordship desired might be suggested to him by Mr. Sheridan. An old friend of mine, Admiral Essington, hoists his flag on board the 'Minotaur' at Yarmouth, and will most readily give me a passage. Admiral Gambier goes Commander-in-Chief, and Sir Home Popham Captain of the Fleet. Baron Nolcken assures me that matters are not so bad as they have been represented, and that Bonaparte was no less ready to agree to the armistice than Russia was to propose it. I have some reason to believe that the cession of Malta and the Cape, and even of Hanover, will be no obstacles, and, as I have been assured that France is disposed to a general peace, such a disposition on her part, if true, would give the greater facility to my communications with my old friend M. Maret. I am to see Colonel McMahon by appointment to-morrow at Carlton House, and I will repeat to him what I have taken the liberty to point out to your Lordship; but I am too well aware of the force which suggestions of this kind must have when they come from you not to wish that you would give them your powerful aid. I would propose going to Memel, where I might communicate confidentially with Lord Hutchinson, but the place of my destination can be discussed with greater ease and propriety when it is resolved to send me.

### SIR ALEXANDER BALL TO MR. MILES

Malta: August 2, 1807

I am concerned, dear Miles, that the late changes in the Cabinet have prevented Lord Moira from providing you a situation that would have employed your talents, but I hope that the zealous and generous disposition which he has evinced to serve you cannot fail to procure some appointment for you under any Administration.

Mr. Eton and Mr. Dillon have lately published two books on Malta, tending to prejudice me in the public mind, and to get me removed from this situation, that they and their friends may come here and direct the Administration under the Duke of Sussex. I have answered Mr. Eton's charges, and his Majesty's Ministers have been pleased to express in handsome terms their confidence in me. Mr. Eton complains of the discontent of the Maltese because they are deprived of their popular assembly; and he says that, the moment they revolted against the French, their first act was to convene this Consiglio Popolare, at which I was made President on my landing. This is the most impudent falsehood that ever was asserted. The fact is, Lord Nelson gave me the command of a squadron to blockade the French in La Valetta, and to assist the Maltese in the country who were in arms. On my arrival I found the inhabitants split into parties—the farmers refusing to pay rent; the lower class going in bodies at night to commit every kind of devastation and plunder. In this state the chiefs were continually applying to me for advice and assistance; and after five months of experience they found themselves under the necessity of requesting me to land and direct the civil and military departments. At this period the Maltese had never thought of convening an Assembly. I perceived the advantages to be derived from having a Congress, and I drew up a plan of one, which was immediately formed, and at which I was President; and I can positively declare this, it was entirely a suggestion of my own, and done with the view of making the Assembly bear the odium of the necessary regulations for restoring order.

I did not write to you on the late mutiny and the two explosions we had within the short space of eight months, because it was a subject upon which I could not speak fully without casting a reflection to the prejudice of some persons. The Ministers are fully informed of all the circumstances. The mutiny of Froberg's regiment put beyond all doubt the attachment of the Maltese to the British Government. We had at that period only two British regiments in garrison, and we had Froberg's regiment (about 800 men), 1,000 French prisoners, two Maltese regiments, and Dillon's regiment, many of whom were Greeks and French; and, if the inhabitants had been disaffected, they might have had 4,000 armed soldiers to have joined, but, instead of showing discontent, they evinced the utmost zeal, ardour, and courage in our cause.[1]

---

[1] The concluding part of this letter got astray in Malta, when lent for perusal by the Editor of these volumes to the late Mr. Harper, the much respected magistrate in Valetta, about the year 1863, and has not yet been recovered. Sir Alexander died at Malta in 1809. Before the close of the same year the Maltese opened a subscription for a monument to be erected on the island to his memory. 'We should feel ourselves guilty of ingrati-

*LORD MOIRA TO MR. MILES*

Donington: August 23, 1807

From circumstances which I cannot explain, it would be altogether inexpedient for me to write to Mr. Canning at this moment on the subject to which you refer. At the same time I see in the most important light the advantage of learning what may be the disposition of the French Government towards peace. The delay of our operations at Copenhagen is not a promising symptom, nor has it an appearance favourable to the moral quality of the measure. It removes the colour of necessity—a plea which would have required instantaneous effort. Surely, Ministers have placed the King in an odd situation. They make him say to the Prince Royal that which, construed into honest English, would be just this: 'You are my nephew, resting on the security of that relation, as well as on the ordinary good faith of nations. But you might, if you would commit a scandalous act, take a step injurious to me by attacking me unawares; therefore I will do a scandalous act by attacking you unawares. And, as you have the claims of consanguinity upon me, in addition to those of the established law of nations, I will give you a pleasing option: you shall surrender your fleet to me, and have your Continental possessions taken from you by Bonaparte for the supposed collusion; or you shall have your capital burnt and its unoffending inhabitants buried with you in the ruins.' And we talk of Bonaparte's treatment of independent states!

tude,' the deputation observed to his Excellency the Royal pro-Commissioner, 'were we to fail to give to the world, now that Sir Alexander Ball is dead, some token of the gratitude we have ever felt and expressed for him during his lifetime.—Valetta, December 22, 1809.'

### LORD MOIRA TO MR. MILES

Loudoun Castle : September 19, 1807

Since our troops made good their landing, I have thought the surrender of Copenhagen certain. I speak on the supposition that our cruisers command the Belt so entirely as to prevent any succour from crossing. My opinion against a favourable issue was founded on the probability that the Danes would be upon their guard, and that their army would be brought back from Holstein before our fleet reached the Baltic. That this was not the case will afford a strong presumption against there having been any hostile dispositions towards us; because the army could be kept in Holstein for no other purpose than to watch the French. From us it is evident they apprehended no danger; whence it may fairly be argued they had no consciousness of offering provocation. Once the city was invested, the business was done. A town of that sort cannot stand a bombardment. So much the worse for the plea of those who make a gratuitous attack, which is to be attended with such horrors to a mass of peaceable inhabitants.

### LORD MOIRA TO MR. MILES

Newcastle : October 24, 1807

All the further particulars which I have learnt convince me more and more that our procedure against the Danes was adopted on the loosest of possible surmises. Everything seems to prove that there was no rational ground of presumption that they meditated hostility towards us. A scandalous cupidity may advance their well-provided arsenal as a cause of suspicion, but common sense will not. A subscription would be of no real benefit to the unfortunate sufferers, and it would be liable to much misrepresentation. I am on my way, though by very easy stages, to Leicestershire. I shall stay there but a few days and then repair to London.

### Lord Moira to Mr. Miles

Donington: November 15, 1807

I should have acknowledged your obliging letters earlier, had I not expected to have been in town before this time. A slight indisposition has made Lady Loudoun delay her journey, and I am thence detained. I have many thanks to return for the intelligence from abroad. If our procedure against Denmark did not excite real indignation in other powers—and it is unnatural to think it should not—it was at least sure to afford a pretext for the abandonment of all previously implied arguments with us, and for the adoption of any system hostile to our interests. We have nothing now, as you truly observe, to wish for but peace. A wretched one it will be; and its consequences will be as mortifying to our feelings as they will be seriously destructive of our pre-eminence. But these consequences will not be the effect of a cessation of hostilities; they are the result of our past miserably improvident conduct. A continuation of war would afford no chance, I fear, of diminishing them, and would give scope for very additional mischiefs.

The bustle of the time has made it impossible to obtain the opportunity of discussing your immediate object. There shall not be any avoidable delay on my part. I have always been earnest about your being employed abroad, and I do not place that wish on the footing of an attention to you, but as thinking your talents would in the line proposed be exerted very beneficially for the public.

### MR. MILES TO MR. LONG

November 19, 1807

The entire front of Europe from the Bosphorus to the North Cape is in hostile array against us, and our Court must have been very badly informed of the temper and feelings of the Continent towards us if it has yet to learn that we are everywhere detested. I agree with you that the present measures of Bonaparte strike at once at our maritime code; but, as we have by repeated indiscretions, and in some instances by wanton aggressions, brought on this state of things, it behoves us to devise the means by which the present gigantic league against us may be rendered as little mischievous as possible, and the means to avert the final ruin with which we are threatened are to be found in peace. You acknowledge that whoever can procure us peace, or be instrumental in procuring peace upon fair and honourable terms, will render us a most essential service. But *fair* and *honourable* are vague terms; at all times they are relative terms; and we must not expect to have them so advantageous in 1808 as we might have had in 1795. As soon as this country had acknowledged Bonaparte as the legitimate chief of the French nation, its policy ought to have been directed to conciliate his confidence, and to withdraw the reproaches that had been personal against him. In 1802 we were at liberty to change our system and form other connections, and an alliance with France, considering her strength and position, her views, and the means she possessed for accomplishing these views, was preferable to an alliance with Austria, Russia, and even Prussia, by way of forming a tether to the ambition of Bonaparte, or to the milder project of accomplishing a counter-revolution. I took the liberty to state this to Mr. Addington, not from any confidence I had in his talents, but in compliment to his official station. If France was not warmly cordial to us in the late peace, it was because she doubted our sincerity in making peace. She as little confided in our sincerity on the former occasions, and under Mr. Addington's weak, I had almost said his contemptible administration, France considered us as desiring peace for no other purpose than to organise new coalitions against her. Conduct more frank and manly on our part would have consolidated the peace.[1]

I have already told you that it was contemplated by a member of the late Administration, before the change took place, to have sent me *pour tâter le pouls de Monsieur Maret au sujet de la paix*, and, as I aspired to nothing more than to open the door of the vestibule, I made my arrangements accordingly, and with hopes of a successful issue to my secret mission. I have been assured by different people in credit with the present Government in France that, if I had been sent at any period of the war to the Continent for such a purpose, my mission would have been considered as a proof that the British Court was sincerely disposed to peace by having selected a person known to have been hostile to the war from its commencement—and not an *intrigant*. Should the present Cabinet be as well inclined to put an end to the ruinous contest as my noble friend to whom I have alluded, I can almost take upon me to assert that I should not be a week in Gothenburg before I had permission to pass through Copenhagen into Holstein,

---

[1] 'Is there to be no compunction for the effusion of human blood on the Continent? Were we sincere in our treaty for peace?'—Letter to the King, by Hampden, in the *Independent Whig*, April 26, 1807.

and reside at the house of a person[1] of consideration, within a short day's journey of Hamburg, even at this season, until I was permitted to proceed to Paris. I am not sanguine enough to expect any offer of service would be accepted from me by the present Cabinet, but if your colleagues are disposed to employ me as a confidential *avant-coureur* they may have reason to be pleased at having made the experiment. I hope that our country may once more be restored to the blessing of peace, and that you may have a share in procuring that inestimable blessing.[2]

### LORD MOIRA TO MR. MILES

February 5, 1808

Many days ago—indeed, so long ago as that I expected to have been able to say something upon it when you were to call on Wednesday—I had requested a friend to speak in my name to Mr. Canning, and I authorised him to say to Mr. Canning that I was sure his employing you would be gratifying to the Prince. The person undertook it cheerfully. He called on Wednesday and Friday, but I unluckily missed seeing him. I am

---

[1] M. Erneste de Hennings, gentilhomme de la chambre de S.M. le Roi de Danemark, à Rantzau, près Elmshorn, Holstein, and cousin of M. Reinhard, French Ambassador at Hamburg.

[2] The Cabinet as formed in March, 1807 :—

| | |
|---|---|
| Earl Camden | President of the Council. |
| Lord Eldon | Lord Chancellor. |
| Earl of Westmorland | Lord Privy Seal. |
| Duke of Portland | First Lord of the Treasury. |
| Lord Mulgrave | First Lord of the Admiralty. |
| Earl of Chatham | Master-General of the Ordnance. |
| Earl Bathurst | President of the Board of Trade. |
| Lord Hawkesbury | Home Secretary. |
| Mr. Canning | Foreign Secretary. |
| Lord Castlereagh | War and Colonial Secretary. |
| Mr. Perceval | Chancellor of the Exchequer. |

confident he did not omit what I desired. I wish you were on the Continent. There is a fermentation there at present, of which we gather the intimation so tardily that we cannot improve the opening; and it would be of infinite consequence to have you in a situation such as would enable you to get at the intelligence for which you possess so many keys.

Your news about the King of Sweden is too likely to be true. He had long been doing everything to ruin himself. I thank you for the very obliging activity in forwarding the intelligence so immediately. Much might be done for the interest of England by new moulding the states of Sweden and Denmark. The greatest obstacle is the inveteracy with which any individual under the latter crown regards the English since the mad and mischievous enterprise against Copenhagen. Still, a trial could entail no inconvenience.

### LORD MOIRA TO MR. MILES

Donington : September 20, 1808

I am truly sensible to the obliging motive which induced you to send the turtle, though I grieve at having thence deprived you of partaking of it. The more regret attends it, because the Prince, who was to have been here as yesterday, has been prevented from coming hither by an attack of illness which seized the Duke of Sussex, and which was so violent that the Prince could not think of quitting him. Accept, I beg, my best acknowledgments for your politeness.

The mortification to which we are subjected by the convention in Portugal is directly chargeable to the Ministers, for they left it open to Sir Hew Dalrymple to assume a command, if they did not absolutely instruct him to join the army, which it was clear he would with such latitude unavoidably undertake. He is a gentlemanly and amiable man; but his unacquaintance with service gave every reason to apprehend that he might be bewildered and overpowered by the novelty of his situation. The same ignorance of human nature exposed our interests to a hazard which ought not to have been left on the cards. It was sure that Sir Arthur Wellesley, unless restrained by positive orders, would endeavour to gather laurels before a superior could arrive—that is, before the force calculated as necessary for the enterprise could assemble. Fortunately, the issue has been in our favour; therefore, the risk will be overlooked. The game is by no means over in Spain. Napoleon has made a profession which binds him to great exertions there. No! I fear the successes of the patriots have been egregiously magnified, except as to the surrender of Dupont, and that they have smothered the notoriety of many severe blows. The French ought ultimately to fail in an attempt which has been no less absurd than iniquitous; but there must still be a rough contest, and skill might outweigh probabilities.

### Lord Moira to Mr. Miles

Bridlington: September 27, 1808

I hope you will not have taken amiss a liberty of mine in directing that a tureen of your turtle should be sent to you, as you were not near enough for me to ask you to partake of it with me, and, as it was dressed in London, I thought I might repose myself on your obliging confidence, and trust you would not misconstrue my sending back to you a portion of the luxury.

You will see that all our vast and most expensive preparation will ultimately have produced no other result than the facilitating the retreat of Junot from

Portugal, which he was deeply anxious to effect and which he was hopeless of achieving. It is a lamentable consideration that the resources, and, still more, the noble energy of this magnanimous country should be so inefficaciously applied. Remember what I said of the necessity there was to gain a decisive influence in Spain —an object easy to have been secured—and my opinion of the inanity of any operations which did not proceed on the principle of our wielding the Spanish force. Bonaparte will fail in his enterprise. But we shall not overthrow him. The parties will remain nearly as they were; and the strength of France will blight us if we cannot blast it.

### LORD MOIRA TO MR. MILES

Donington: April 3, 1811

My absence from town has only thus much of political in it, that it was awkward to be on the spot and to be supposed to be influencing measures when the natural impatience of our friends inclined them to be dissatisfied with the delay of steps which the Prince really could not take with either propriety or effect. I admit that the present state of Government is injurious to the country. The Prince, however, can pursue no other line, unless he turn out the Ministers at once and dissolve Parliament; and, reflect what the extraordinary inconvenience of the latter measure would be were the King, unlikely as it is, to regain his tone of mind sufficiently to be brought forward immediately into power! Unquestionably it is disadvantageous for the Prince that his friends should be left unrewarded, while the Ministers are bestowing on their adherents the offices which become vacant; yet this cannot be otherwise unless the Prince should ask as courtesy from the Ministers these appointments—a degree of connection which I trust he will never have with them.

The interesting letter of Admiral Pickmore has reached me safely. It shall be returned when I have the opportunity, for it is too heavy for one cover, and my number of franks is exhausted for to-day. I will write to Admiral Pickmore.[1]

*MR. MILES TO LORD MOIRA*

July 12, 1811

I am not competent to decide on the propriety of Lord King's circular letter to his tenants, nor whether it was meant by indirect means to bring the question of public credit to an immediate issue, or whether it originated in that mercenary disposition which is attributed with very little reserve to his Lordship by all his tenantry in that part of Surrey where I possess a small copyhold under him; but, from whatever cause it proceeded, it has most clearly shown the deplorable state of the country; while the speech of Lord Eldon, marked as it is by indecision, and by that timid caution which is the characteristic of his mind, prepares us in advance for the desperate remedy of making bank notes a legal tender; *ainsi la Grande-Bretagne se trouve précisément dans la même position où était la France en* 1790. At that period I lived in confidential intimacy with the late M. Mirabeau, and I believe I was the only Englishman whom he consulted when he brought forward his favourite measure of finance, for my friend, his old schoolfellow, Governor Elliot, had not then been sent to

[1] The letter from Admiral Pickmore to Mr. Miles was designed to show the desirableness of retaining the island of Minorca. 'The importance of Minorca was even acknowledged to me repeatedly by the late Sir Alexander Ball, notwithstanding his infatuation for Malta.'—Mr. Miles to Lord Moira.

Paris by Mr. Pitt. The first issue proposed of assignats was four hundred millions of French livres, and I have a perfect recollection of Mirabeau's acknowledging the justice of my remark when he condescended to ask my opinion, on my telling him that his object was not so much to sustain public credit and provide funds for a war with Austria as to place the new order of things beyond the reach of counter-revolutionary measures, which were then plotting at the Tuileries, Coblentz, Turin, and Vienna, by ranging under the standard of the Revolution a vast part of the population of France, which would come forward and purchase what he called 'national domains,' which assignats, by the by, fell 15 per cent. as soon as they were issued, and very soon afterwards to 30 per cent. The streets leading to the Palais Royal were crowded with men exchanging them for money, nor did Peregaux or any of the bankers ever take them at par. With respect to America, I am happy to find that your Lordship views the ill-advised measures of our Government towards our former colonies in the same light that I do, because it is to me a confirmation of the correctness of my own opinion. Ministers do not seem to be aware that a war with America involves in it the loss of Canada and Nova Scotia, with probable ruin to our sugar colonies, besides ensuring to France a navy capable at least of facilitating the transport of troops to Ireland. I am not, however, less astonished at this infatuation of the King's servants than at the forbearance of the Prince and of the country, whose ruin will be ensured unless his Royal Highness comes forward and takes those bold and decisive measures which can alone save him and his family from destruction.

### Lord Moira to Mr. Miles

London: August 13, 1811

Mr. Liston is too accurate in his view of things. Affairs appear to me to be now on such a declivity that it is almost impossible they should not suffer a rapid descent. In addition to former evils, a ferment, and a subversion of confidence which will hardly be re-established, must be reckoned upon in Ireland from the strange measure of the recent proclamation. The Prince has been misled into it by a colouring which totally disguised to him the nature of the question. But, as that cannot be explained, a most mischievous attaint will be given to those expectations from him which more than anything kept within moderation the discontent of the multitude in Ireland.

With regard to your own situation, nothing can be done during the existence of the present Ministry. Painful as it may be to repress your anxiety to be of use, I can give you but one counsel—which is, to remain quiet. The condition of the King appears to settle again into comparative tranquillity, in which state things may go on for months. I shall, of course, in a day or two return to the country.

### Mr. Miles to his Wife

London: February 17, 1812

I believe there will only be a partial change in the Ministry. Lord Grenville and Lord Grey have acted a very injudicious part, and thrown themselves out; but I have yet the hope that all will go well, and that the Prince will act in a manner to ensure him the confidence and respect of the country.¹ I am not at liberty to repeat all that has been told to me, but I think that certain persons who, dexterous as they may be, without abilities, delicacy, or honour, are endeavouring to mislead the Regent, will be disappointed. I met Lord Moira as I was returning from the House of Commons, just as I parted with Lester, and his Lordship made me walk with him to the Horse Guards. He was extremely friendly and communicative. I only wish that the Prince would confide entirely in him. His Royal Highness does not see anybody, and I do not press for an audience, but I have desired Colonel McMahon to say that I am in town and will await his Royal Highness's commands. This day week I hope to transmit you a letter more acceptable, inasmuch as it will inform you of our destiny. If the new order of things should be realised, I am to be employed. Mrs. Liston, who sends her love, fags incessantly at Italian. You must do as much at French.

### COLONEL MCMAHON TO MR. MILES

Pall Mall: February 20, 1812

Illness and business have made me delay returning my sincere thanks for your most kind letters from Southampton, and for your obliging note on your arrival in town. I entreat your pardon for this omission, and beg you to accept my warmest acknowledgment of your repeated proofs of friendship. As I had not the pleasure of seeing you when you called, I did not lose a day in

¹ 'Sunday, February 3, 1812.—The friends of Lord Grenville are going about the whole of this day, expressing in unqualified terms their strong disapprobation of the conduct of the Regent; complaining bitterly of not having had earlier information of his change of sentiments, the inconvenience of which they must have felt to a considerable extent, from many of their party having discovered that they were to have been left out of the intended arrangement.'—*Diaries of the Right Hon. George Rose*, ii. 478.

writing down your name at Carlton House, and in acquainting his Royal Highness particularly that you had done so.

### Mr. Miles to his Wife

London: February 20, 1812

I wrote to you yesterday under Charles Flint's cover, giving an account of the strange and injudicious conduct of the Prince. It has been a disappointment to me, and has again put off my expectations; but my spirits are not at all diminished, for I shall find in your affections a mine of inexhaustible happiness, far beyond anything that public employment could convey, and more than a counterpoise for all the vexations to which political men are exposed. Nor am I so much grieved on my own account as on that of the Prince, in whose elevation I really feel much interested. I wished to see his Royal Highness rise in the opinion of mankind, and redeem a character which duty should have urged him to recover from the state to which his imprudences had reduced it. He has lost the finest opportunity to become the idol of his country and thereby fortify the throne. As it is, he has rendered it more rickety, and he may possibly find the sad effects of his want of firmness. Lord Moira has acted a manly and a noble part. He has declared that he will not, cannot, support the present Ministers, but that, from his attachment to the Prince, he will abstain from leaguing himself with any Opposition. This is the real state of things, and in this state it would be worse than dreaming were I to entertain any hope of being employed; and certainly I shall not become a suppliant to the present Minister. We shall soon see whether the Prince was sincere in the promises he made to me at Carlton House. I protest to you that I am more hurt at the crooked and unexpected turn that public affairs

have taken on the Prince's account than on my own.
Time, our great instructor and best preceptor, will tell
us more. I am afflicted at the perversity which has preferred a restricted and intricate path to the broad and
open turnpike road which was before him, and which it
was his interest as well as his duty to have taken, for
he had long since *solemnly pledged* himself that Lord
Moira should be his Minister. His Royal Highness has
broken faith both to his Lordship and to the hopes of
the country. The present people stay in, with the exception of Lord Wellesley. Lord Powis goes Lord-Lieutenant to Ireland;[1] and Lord Moira, who has remained inflexibly attached to the Prince from his infancy,
and has vindicated him when aspersed, has been disregarded at the very moment when he alone should have
had the whole arrangement of a new Administration and
the entire confidence of the Prince. All this derangement is owing to the intrigues of unprincipled persons
who exercise an unhappy influence at Carlton House.
I write to you in confidence. Men of honour have already sent Lord —— to Coventry. Yet, after all, the
little integrity and public virtue in the Opposition is
the cause of this shameful triumph. Had their conduct
been correct, the country would have been with them,
but, as it is, the country does not care a straw for them,
knowing them to be place-hunters.[2] I will see Lord

---

[1] '*February 2.*—Mr. Coutts Trotter called on me this morning, having just left Lord Moira, who told him he was going Lord-Lieutenant to Ireland, which seems to render the removal of Ministers certain. Notwithstanding which, Mr. Brougham told Mr. Arbuthnot last night that the Ministers certainly would not be changed immediately.'—*Diaries of the Right Hon. George Rose*, ii. 478.

[2] 'I have heard from one channel that his Royal Highness, in forbearing to change the Administration, acted upon the advice of Lady Hertford and Mrs. Fitzherbert; and, through another channel, that Mrs. Fitzherbert was sent for to London, and that the Prince was some hours with

Moira on Saturday, and, as I shall then have a better view of the land, I will write to you after my interview.

I breakfasted with the Listons. Their hopes of going to Constantinople are very faint; that Embassy, I am afraid, is at an end, and they may have to return to Scotland.[1] I have seen Mrs. Elliot, who, with all her family, inquired very kindly after you. Lady Ball has asked me to dinner, but, being engaged, I could not accept her invitation. Willoughby and the Flints desire to be remembered to you.

### Mr. Miles to Lord Moira

February 21, 1812

I am well aware of the vexations, the difficulties, and the insurmountable obstacles you have had to encounter. To me it seems that his Royal Highness, in disappointing the hopes so generally entertained by the country, has greatly injured himself. No man ever had a more glorious opportunity of redeeming his character. No man could have acted more perversely injudicious. I protest that I should have felt more gratification in beholding the ascent of his Royal Highness in public estimation and his becoming deservedly the object of national applause, than in receiving from him the most lucrative employment in the gift of the Crown; but I will forbear all comment on the fatal step he has

---

her. After which she told a person who talks freely with her that she was not at liberty to state any particular, but that some people would meet with a disappointment they were not in the least aware of—alluding to the Opposition.'—*Ibid.*, p. 483.

[1] '*February* 7.—Lord Wellesley came to tell me he had proposed my son to his Royal Highness as Ambassador Extraordinary and Minister Plenipotentiary to Constantinople, which he had acquiesced in very graciously. This communication I received gratefully, expressing, however, great doubts whether my son could accept; for reasons not necessary to detail here.'—*Ibid.*, p. 482.

taken until I have the honour of seeing your Lordship to-morrow. I am also far more concerned at the wound your sensibility has received than by the failure of any hopes I ever entertained of public employment through your influence or authority. At no period of my life have I been much swayed by considerations of personal interest, still less so since you have honoured me with your confidence.

### MR. MILES TO HIS WIFE

London: February 27, 1812

I have this moment left Lord Moira, who is much perplexed by the importunities of the Prince to join the present people, but no consideration will ever induce his Lordship to unite with any Administration that refuses to accede to Catholic emancipation. I have had a long conversation with him on the uncertain state of affairs. It is his Lordship's opinion that matters cannot go on as at present. The Prince sent for him: an expostulation ensued which cannot be communicated in a letter; suffice it to say that his Royal Highness has since flinched on the Catholic question. I know it to be a fact that he wishes to get rid of Perceval. Lord Moira continues to see the Prince. I do not believe the world possesses a better man, a man with a nobler and more virtuous mind than Lord Moira, and I am vexed that the Prince, whose fortunes are at stake, should not show a greater appreciation of his counsels. I told everybody that his Royal Highness would act a manly part when the *restrictions* were at an end; all his friends did the same everywhere, and *everywhere* disappointment has been felt. The Opposition are united, firm as a rock, indignant, and they will give no quarter. Public indignation against the Prince rises every day. Perceval will find that chicanery and trick are not always to escape with impunity. All the world reprobate the conduct pursued by his Royal Highness towards Lord Moira.[1]

It is now my wish to return home. I am afraid that Ministers, unless there should be a change in the Cabinet, will not employ me; they are impressed with the idea that I am as mad for peace as they are for war. I have been assured that, although on the request of Lord Moira they would readily place me at one of the boards, they would not on any consideration send me to the Continent in a position enabling me to become the channel of communication on the subject of peace or war. When, however, I proposed returning to the country and to await there the course of events, entreating his Lordship not to allow my pretensions to embarrass him for a moment, nor my presence to importune him,

[1] 'The details of the Regency Bill were afterwards brought forward, and discussed with great spirit and minuteness in committees of both houses of Parliament. Most of the clauses were adopted with no other than verbal alterations; but a protracted debate took place on the clause which proposed to lay the Regent for twelve months under certain restrictions, especially in the royal prerogative of creating peers, or calling the eldest sons of peers to the Upper House by writ. These restrictions, however, for that period, were inserted in the Bill by a majority in the Lower House of twenty-four, the numbers being two hundred and twenty-four to two hundred—a majority which fell, on the matter of the limitation as to creating peers, to sixteen in the Commons, and in the Lords to six. This rapid diminution of the Ministerial majority clearly indicated what an insecure tenure Ministers now had of their places, and how strongly the now confirmed malady of the sovereign, and the known partiality of the Prince of Wales for the Whig party, had come to influence that numerous party in Parliament—the waverers—in the line of policy they thought it expedient to adopt. . . . It was generally expected, however, that the Prince would still revert to his earlier friends when the year during which the restrictions were imposed by Parliament came to an end; and the opinion was confidently promulgated by those supposed to be most in the Regent's confidence, that February 1812 would see the Whig party entirely and permanently in office. The event, however, again disappointed the hopes entertained by the Opposition.'—Alison's *History of Europe*, xiv. 23, 27. See *Diaries &c., of the Right Hon. George Rose*, ii. 447, &c.

he took me most kindly by the hand, and said, 'No, you must not leave town yet; wait some days longer; there may yet be the means of sending you to Sweden or Denmark.' Hence I infer that matters are not finally settled, and that arrangements are in contemplation which may enable him to have me sent to the Continent. The rejection of Lord Grenville, he observed, would not affect me. I stand well at Carlton House. Lord Castlereagh is Secretary for Foreign Affairs. I do not know that he would oppose my going to Sweden should it be mentioned to him. Liston says that, as there is no opening at present in Sweden, he would like to see me appointed Consul-General at Philadelphia in the room of Mr. Bond, who desires to remain in England. I am now going to look for lodgings for Sir Home, who has gone to Portsmouth to bring Lady Popham to town. He inquired after you. I dined last week with Mr. Whitbread. I met my old friend Nicholls, and he has engaged me for Saturday. I dine with Cooper on Sunday. Your packet I found at the Foreign Office, where I generally come to write my letters. The Prince met with a rebuff in the vote of the House of Commons, on Monday evening, against the appointment of Colonel McMahon. The House was in riotous applause on the occasion. I took Lester[1] to an evening party at Lady Ball's, and, having introduced him, I withdrew.

*LORD MOIRA TO SIR HOME POPHAM*

April 23, 1812

While matters in the Northern States of Europe are so capable of receiving useful direction with a little management, could you not suggest to Lord Melville the expediency of employing Miles in Denmark on some

---

[1] Benjamin Lester Lester, member for Poole.

negotiations for an exchange of prisoners—his *real object* being to acquire information how far it be practicable to heal the soreness about Copenhagen, and to detach Denmark from Bonaparte's interests. There is not a man within my knowledge anything near so well calculated for a mission of this sort as Miles : his quickness, and even the eagerness of his manner, would enable him to throw out propositions which would ascertain what might be done without committing Ministers.

### MR. MILES TO SIR HOME POPHAM

April 30, 1812

I take it for granted that Lord Moira, who was prevented by the death of Mr. Fox from having me sent as envoy to the Corcyra of the ancients, has pointed out to you his perfect conviction that I could be usefully employed at this moment in the public service at Copenhagen, and that, under the ostensible character of Agent for Prisoners, I might possibly be instrumental in removing the excessive acrimony of the King of Denmark towards this country. The prospect is so brilliant in the Peninsula that, if the Northern powers could be engaged to unite with us heart and hand in the contest, I have no doubt but that France would be ultimately driven within her former frontier, and the way be prepared for the return of peace. You are aware that I passed the whole summer of 1789 at the Court of the Elector of Mayence in readiness to succeed Mr. Heathcote, the accredited Minister to the Elector of Cologne, as soon as the expected vacancy occurred, and that I was sent to Paris in 1790 on a secret mission, as was also my friend Hugh Elliot, and precisely for the same object.

*LORD MELVILLE TO COLONEL MCMAHON*

Park Lane: May 2, 1812

May I request you to take the trouble of desiring Mr. Miles to call at the Admiralty to-morrow at two o'clock, or on any subsequent day about noon?

*MR. MILES TO LORD MELVILLE*

Hythe, Southampton: May 3, 1812

The post of this date has brought a letter from Colonel McMahon intimating that it was your Lordship's wish to see me this day. I hasten to express my regret at having been unexpectedly called home on domestic business, but I hold myself in readiness to proceed to the metropolis the instant I am honoured with your commands. I avail myself of this opportunity to inform your Lordship that my correspondent, whose letter dated Vienna, October 25, 1811, Colonel McMahon gave you to peruse, has returned to Copenhagen, and, in the event of my being sent to the Baltic, I would count much on the good offices of my friend, who is in the confidence of the Court of Denmark and is most anxious to accomplish a reconciliation between the two nations.

*MR. MILES TO SIR HOME POPHAM*

Hythe: May 13, 1812

You will be no less concerned and surprised than myself when I inform you that the tragical fate of Mr. Perceval[1] was hailed by the labouring classes in this neighbourhood as an auspicious event. They inquired

---

[1] Mr. Perceval, the Prime Minister, was shot through the heart in the lobby of the House of Commons by a man named Bellingham on the afternoon of May 11, 1812. See Introduction, pp. 109, 110.

of each other whether they had heard the *good news*. I know this is only loose chit-chat; but the feverish state of the country, the high price of provisions, and the little horror expressed or felt at an act which in better times would have been execrated, prove that these symptoms are more the result of public sentiment than of the malignant and brutal triumph of the few. If the assassination of the Prime Minister should be everywhere received as it has been here, the unhappy manifestation will have nothing equivocal in it, and the destiny of Mr. Perceval will be a lesson to which the ill-advisers of the Prince would do well to attend. Peltier, as other vagabonds, has in his publications justified and recommended assassination.[1] We are now able to appreciate the practical effects of such abominable doctrines when we find that the private virtues of an individual are no fence against the assassin. Whatever may have been the political errors of Mr. Perceval, he was an honourable man in private life, and his exemplary conduct as a husband and father gives him a claim to be lamented. I do most sincerely feel for his family. When lately pointing out to you his political difficulties, how little I thought that all these difficulties would be so soon removed! The Prince will do well to dismiss Lord Liverpool from his councils for ever. His talents are below mediocrity. I enclose a letter for Lord Moira, whose value may now be felt. I hope the Prince will send for his Lordship and ask him to form an

---

[1] Jean Peltier, a French Royalist, had been convicted in a trial before Lord Ellenborough, February 1803, for instigating the assassination of Napoleon. As hostilities were soon afterwards resumed between France and England, he escaped punishment. Peltier was defended in a celebrated speech by Sir James Mackintosh. He had sought refuge in London, where he employed himself as a political writer in a paper called *L'Ambigu*.

Administration. It is full time his Royal Highness should look about him, discriminate persons, and fence himself with men of honour and talents.

*Lord Melville to Colonel McMahon*

May 14, 1812

As the arrangement suggested in Mr. Miles's letter to you was one which could only be carried into effect in conjunction with the Secretary of State, I am sure you will not be surprised that any further discussion upon it has been during the last week suspended, and that nothing can be done in it at present. No doubt the same explanation will occur to Mr. Miles himself. There will be no occasion for his coming to town until his business is arranged, if his plan is to be carried into effect.

*Colonel McMahon to Mr. Miles*

Carlton House: May 14, 1812

Many thanks for your favour of yesterday. The enclosed is from Lord Melville in answer to another application I had made on the subject of your proposed mission. The reasons his Lordship assigns for your not yet being sent for are unquestionable, and certainly nothing can be expected to be done until an Administration shall be formed.

*Sir Home Popham to Mr. Miles*

May 14, 1812

It was my intention to have written to you yesterday from the House of Commons, but I was so jammed in that I could not get out. Really there was not anything to convey. To-day there is the same blank. The Prince has not yet decided upon the person to be his Minister. He looked fat and well when he received the address from the House of Parliament. It was said that the Prince sent for Castlereagh to try and unite him to Canning, and, if he could, he meant to put the seals in Lord Wellesley's keeping. If so, I apprehend that Lord Wellesley may apply to Lord Moira. I want an audience with the Prince about my signals,[1] but I have not yet ventured to write to McMahon. I saw Lord Moira yesterday, and expressed my great anxiety that you should be employed. Your letters shall be forwarded. The death of poor Perceval may give me some anxiety on private matters. I am sure that Lord Castlereagh would employ you if they would make a point of it. If I should be sent to the coast of Spain, and you like to take a view of the country, a cot and as honest a welcome to my table as any man ever had shall be at your service, and I will send you back when you are tired. Adieu!

### Mr. Rice[2] to Mr. Miles

May 16, 1812

I have been anxious to communicate some intelligence which could repay the very great interest I derived from your letters. Each day I expected would furnish the materials I had anticipated. I have been as constantly disappointed. The result of the Cabinet Council of to-day will decide everything, and, if I can hear what this is before the hour of post, you shall receive it at the conclusion of my letter. Lord Wellesley has, I know, been sent for, but what his Lordship's answer is likely to be is only guessed at. I think him too ambitious a man to refuse power, and too needy

---

[1] A code of signals prepared by Sir Home Popham for the use of the Royal Navy.

[2] Mr. Spring Rice, Chancellor of the Exchequer in 1836, and raised to the peerage in 1839 as Lord Monteagle of Brandon.

a one to be indifferent to emolument. Canning has declared his willingness to act with Castlereagh; the pride of the latter has, I believe, succumbed. What is likely to be the result? If Wellesley acts up to his gigantic schemes of Continental warfare, our best resources are risked. If Huskisson comes in at the head of the Exchequer, will he venture to interfere with the issues of the Bank? The great question, however, is, whether an Administration will be so constituted as to possess the confidence of the people. Time alone will answer it. Lords Camden and Westmorland may perhaps give way to more popular characters, but will the probity of Government appear less doubtful under the direction of Canning, or its economy under the ruler of India? A rumour was circulated, and believed, that Lords Holland and Moira had been invited to a coalition with the parties I have described. I presume not to conjecture whether the report is true or not. It is impossible to deny that the intemperance of Opposition has in a great degree destroyed all chance of their return to office; and this state of things has been still further aggravated by their unfortunate entanglement with the Grenvilles—a family whose abilities none can doubt, whose popularity none can maintain. Without this connection, would not Lord Grey at this moment be our Minister, and would he not be more strongly supported than almost any other man in the political world? I consider that the Whig party ought to come in with any Administration that would propose popular measures.

*P.S.—Tuesday.*—I missed the post yesterday from the wish to give you more certain and intelligent news, but I am still unable to do so. The seals were at a late hour last night in Lord Ellenborough's possession.

I have heard that Wellesley and Canning have declined, though Castlereagh was willing to make an entire sacrifice of his pride, so as to give efficiency to the Administration. Things are to go on with the present men as long as they can keep the ball moving. The Prince has promised to carry them through by the weight of his own authority, rather than surrender at discretion. My informant added that in the House of Commons the Ministers could not maintain themselves. This I do not admit. However weak may be their talents, the strength of possession is great, the aid of influence is powerful.

Have you any thought of republishing your letter to the Prince? There are so many endeavours to procure it, and it is now almost impossible to be met with. I am glad your son William is at Winchester. During my Cambridge life, the four best men I met were from that school, and three of them are among my most valued friends. The execution of Bellingham took place without any disturbance. The mob exclaimed, 'God bless you! You'll go to heaven at least!' But no attempt was made to riot. All was over in three minutes. He was not allowed to speak.[1] Adieu!

### Mr. Miles to Lord Moira

Hythe: May 20, 1812

Lord Melville has had the goodness to explain to Colonel McMahon the reason why I have not heard from his Lordship, and which indeed I had anticipated. In the event of your suggestion being adopted by Lord Melville, it will be necessary to arrange with the Secretary of State. Of course his concurrence must be obtained; but in the present dislocated state of Govern-

---

[1] Bellingham, the assassin of Mr. Perceval, died on the scaffold at Newgate, May 18, seven days after the commission of the crime.

ment I see no immediate prospect of a settled Administration. The Regent is little aware of the low ebb of his credit at this moment in the country, and, shut up like the Grand Seigneur, the first information that would cure his delusion may be the forcing of his palace gates. To your Lordship I open my heart without reserve. I do not communicate to others my thoughts so freely. Were you at the head of the Government, unshackled, and without Lords Grenville and Grey, the calm would be instantly restored to a distracted country and the Prince find a tower of strength in your very name.

### Sir Charles Flint to Mr. Miles

May 26, 1812

I have much to say, dear Miles, but my time is very limited. No arrangement is yet made. Lord Wellesley has collected the sentiments of Opposition and Administration on two points :—

1. A consideration of Catholic concession.
2. Carrying on the war with vigour in the Peninsula.

The Cabinet, with the exception of Lord Melville, have adhered to their opinions respecting Catholic affairs. Lord Melville says he is not averse to the principle of taking them into consideration. But Lord Liverpool and he have both declared in writing that they never can sit in the same Cabinet with Lord Wellesley! They are offended at the publication of Lord Wellesley's correspondence with them and at his last reply to Lord Liverpool. Lords Grenville, Grey, &c., have given in their ultimatum, and so have Canning and his friends. The only difference between the latter and the former and Lord Wellesley is the war in the Peninsula. They postpone their ultimate decision in this respect until they can peruse the official documents, in which alone a sound opinion can be formed. Lord Wellesley laid all the different opinions before the Prince yesterday, and to-day he was to see him again. What has been settled within the last hour I know not, but I cannot help hoping it will end in a union between Lords Grenville, Wellesley, and Canning, as I think *that* chance offers the best hope of a strong and permanent Government. Your friend Lord Moira will of course go to Ireland, and I shall be truly happy if he can carve out for you there some comfortable appointment.

I have been offered to be proxy to Sir Henry Wellesley at the installation of the Knights of the Bath, and the offer was made in such a gratifying manner, originating with Mr. Pole, that I have accepted it, and I hope you will agree with me that I should have done wrong in not accepting an honour intended to mark approbation of my conduct. I shall be knighted on Friday next. Adieu! *Consider this letter as confidential.*

### Lord Moira to Mr. Miles

November 3, 1812

I really feel myself a sad delinquent towards you in correspondence. But the letters which I get from all quarters, from individuals utterly unknown to me, are so numerous that it would be ludicrous were not the accumulation attended with serious inconvenience. The persuasion of my influence with the Prince Regent is so general that every one who has an application to urge endeavours to make me the channel, and so many of these solicitations come from persons in the higher walk of life that the acknowledgment of their letters is an oppressive labour. To most also I cannot explain that, literally, I have not interest enough to make an exciseman, and I must thence seek evasions which double the toil of writing. To me, all seems going on as ill as possible. The Ministers, on the contrary, are buoyant with the expectation of the fall of Napoleon, whom they state to be at this moment surrounded, and by the troops over whom he has gained a succession of victories, which must at least have dissipated their field resources. This self-duping is perhaps the worst symptom of our situation.

My appointment to India affords me no scope for employing you in that part of the world. The restrictions of the Act of Parliament, and the natural jealousy with which the Directors enforce them, leave to the Governor-General no power of taking out persons beyond the defined and very narrow personal household allowed him. The object of this regulation is to preserve advantages for the Company's servants alone, and the principle is certainly just. The intercourse, however, which this appointment must give me with Ministers will probably enable me to manage something gratifying to the activity of your spirit before I embark. I shall not sail till the end of January. Hitherto I have kept so much at arm's length from Ministers as not to have asked the minutest favour from any one.

### MR. MILES TO LORD MOIRA

Hythe: November 3, 1812

The post of this day has brought me letters of congratulation on the certainty of my being employed in consequence of your Lordship having been appointed Governor-General of India. If I have importuned you to realise the hopes held out to me, it was more with a view to benefit my country than myself, and to justify the favourable opinion entertained of my zeal and abilities, not only by your Lordship, but by the Prince Regent, whose spontaneous expression, uttered in your presence at Carlton House in 1807, 'that the instant he had it in his power to call me into the service of our country I might depend on being employed,' led me to expect an appointment on the Continent. It is now due to your Lordship and to the affectionate attachment I feel for you to relinquish all thoughts of a foreign mission under the present Administration, whose objection to employ me, I am told, is due in a great measure to my declared sentiments in favour of Parliamentary reform and peace—the apprehension that I would aim at *forcing* peace upon Ministers; but, if so, it is precisely the very reason for which they ought to employ me, provided it is their wish to preserve the Prince Regent from the danger of intestine commotion and to arrest the further effusion of blood. I give up all thoughts of being sent abroad. I am now arranging my MSS. for the press. They will prove that, if I have mistaken my own interests through life, I have been perfectly correct as to those of my country. It will be for my children to pardon the sacrifice I have made of their fortune by pursuing a course which I conceived to be for the public welfare.

### Mrs. Liston[1] to Mr. Miles

Pera: July 15, 1812

A Frankfort paper shocked us very much soon after our arrival here with the account of Mr. Perceval's untimely end, and a subsequent one has given us a partial change of Ministry, by which I find Lord Moira goes to Ireland. Is all this true? We long very much

---

[1] Wife of the British Ambassador at the Porte, afterwards Lady Liston.

for a mail from England. This place has the same fault that I found with America—the distance is so great that one is always sighing after *news* from England, for whatever intelligence is received here comes through France, and one knows not whether to believe or doubt. I ought to ask whether, if these changes have actually taken place, *you* have experienced any change, or whether, like a sensible man, you are following the plan that Mr. Liston suggested to you, and which he was so very anxious you should pursue, for *literary work* would be more permanent than any occupation that depends upon the fluctuation of Ministers. I anticipate the pleasure you and Mrs. Miles will feel on hearing that we arrived on the 28th of June in perfect health after a voyage which, considering how many stops we made, must be reckoned short. The weather was quite delightful throughout. Pera, where all foreign Ministers live, is called the suburbs of Constantinople. The house appropriated to the mission is situated in a high and airy position, large and handsome, but very much out of repair, and may be perhaps very cold in winter. The climate here is by no means so charming as has sometimes been described. There appear to me already two seasons—the north wind bringing cold in summer, and, as I am told, the south wind bringing a certain degree of heat in winter. I cannot speak of Constantinople, because as yet I have seen only the *coup d'œil* at our entrance, which is certainly the finest in the world. Mr. Liston has been very busy, and, as Mr. Canning returns in the 'Argo,' I have written myself almost *blind* from anxiety to avail myself of the opportunity, as the intercourse with England is neither regular nor frequent. There is an ugly report of plague which has alarmed us much. From various causes we have not yet been abroad—at least I have not—and Mr. Liston only on business. When you write, give us a great deal of news—I do not mean the philosophical or political reasonings, with which we were very well pleased when we had time to read them at the distance of a hundred miles; but here, where we are in another world, and I fear not a better one, at the distance of some thousand miles, we want the knowledge, not of what ought to be done, but of what is actually doing—not what philosophers think, but what men actually say, and particularly what are likely to be the consequences of Mr. Perceval's death. Should your letter disappoint me, my next shall be to Mrs. Miles, who is always both indulgent and considerate. Mr. Liston joins me in kind wishes to you both, and to the children. Affectionately yours, &c., &c.

### *Mrs. Liston to Mrs. Miles*

Pera: January 11, 1813

Mr. Liston received Mr. Miles's letter, and has often talked of replying to it, but I can with truth assure you that the situation he holds in this country is not a sinecure; it is indeed perpetual occupation. It must at all times be so, but at this moment the business of writing is considerably increased by the state of the war betwixt France and Russia. Soon after our arrival Mr. Liston sent Sir Robert Wilson to Petersburg on business; he has since been permitted by Lord Cathcart to join the army, and his couriers to Mr. Liston are still more frequent than those received by the Russian Minister here. This keeps us in a bustle of news, and, as all the Ministers and governors in the Mediterranean depend upon Mr. Liston for this news, which reaches them much sooner than it can from

England, it is perpetual writing. You and Mr. Miles will be surprised to hear that public news is obliged to be as regularly sent to Bagdad, and to the Governor-General in India, as to Malta or Sicily, for the messengers make it out by land much sooner than it can reach India from England, so that if Mr. Miles—as I think not impossible—goes or is sent to India by my Lord Moira, whose appointment there in place of Lord Minto we have seen in the 'Frankfort Gazette,' he may hear from us more frequently. Pray write and tell us the particulars, whether Lord Moira really goes or not, whether his family accompanies him, and, what is infinitely more interesting to us, whether this matter makes any alteration to Mr. Miles; and particularly tell me how you all are, and what doing, not forgetting our godson Robert Henry.

The plague has, since a week after our arrival, raged with inconceivable violence, and for four months we were prisoners, though not idle ones, within our garden walls—not even a servant permitted to go out, the one who bought our provisions living on the outside of the gate. Upwards of a thousand died daily, and the scene was truly dreadful. At last we went to a small house in the village of Belgrade, where Mr. Liston, after great fatigue in writing, caught a cold, and was some weeks confined with a smart fever, but is now quite well again, and as busy as ever. We returned to town about Christmas, and the weather has been so cold since the 8th of last month as greatly to have diminished this most dreadful malady, and, as the frost continues, we hope to be entirely freed from it in a short time.

If Mr. Miles takes the trouble of carrying or sending your or his letter to the Foreign Office, Rolleston will take care to forward it, and our letters come by the Malta packet, which quits England once a month at least. If you are within reach of our friend Mrs. Gamble, remember us kindly to her. I presume her husband is again in the Baltic. Mr. Liston joins me in every affectionate wish to you, to Mr. Miles, and to the children. Believe me, with perfect regard and attachment, yours, &c.

### MR. MILES TO THE MARQUIS DE LAFAYETTE

Hythe, Southampton: December 28, 1813

I have long had it in contemplation to transmit to posterity what I know on the subject of the Revolution in 1789, with the view, I confess, of vindicating from aspersion those who embarked in that enterprise with motives as pure as your own. Unconnected as I have ever been with the two great parties in this country who claim the right alternately of governing it, I shall at least have the merit of being impartial, and it is from an impartial pen only that posterity can be enabled to form a just opinion of an event which, after having produced a series of revolutions, does not yet appear to have exploded the whole matter with which it has been freighted by the vices and misconceptions of mankind. I find few of my countrymen who think as I do on this important subject, and it is, perhaps, the circumstance of finding myself alone that emboldens me to feel qualified for the task I am desirous of undertaking. I have preserved a voluminous correspondence with a variety of persons, many of them in official situations; and my MSS., whenever they are given to the world, will prove that I have been through life the steady friend of rational well-defined liberty, the determined foe of despotism and anarchy under whatever form of government they dared to present themselves. If you can give any assistance by furnishing me with authentic materials for the history I propose to write, I shall be obliged to you, but, great as my obligations will be, my dear General, the obligations of posterity and of the future historians of these lamentable times will be much greater. This letter travels under cover to my friend Ernest de Hennings, who is at Vienna, and whose father you remember at Plitz. I trust to the friendship of his son to forward this letter to you, because I know that he holds you in the highest esteem. He is in my confidence. I have a high opinion of his talents and rectitude. If the Continent was restored to that repose to which it has been a stranger for more than twenty years, it is to Switzerland that I would transport myself and my papers, and there accomplish the great object which, next to peace, I have most at heart.

### MR. MILES TO THE MARQUIS DE LAFAYETTE

Hythe, Southampton: June 12, 1814

Your friendly and affectionate letter dated from Paris on the 26th ultimo conveys to me the first information of the irreparable loss you have sustained in the death of the best of wives and mothers, leaving you to perform the worst part of this journey of life alone. My deep sympathy with you is the tribute I pay to departed excellence. A tempestuous night of twenty-five years' duration, uninterrupted except by a momentary glimpse of dawn which served only to make the darkness more terrific, has been a severe drawback on the few comforts attached to our existence and to its sad remnant blighted by the storm. My love of liberty in the very infancy of my manhood induced me to draw my pen, as it did you at the same period to draw your sword, when oppression traversed the Atlantic to reduce three millions of freemen to 'unconditional submission,' and happily and irretrievably failed. The same principles separated me from the Prince Bishop of Liège in 1787, at whose Court I resided and with whom I lived in habits of intimacy, when, led and misled by evil counsellors, he ventured to play the despot and was banished for his temerity. Soon after that period, Mr. Pitt sent me to Paris, and, as he was no stranger to my political opinions, as he well knew that my attachment to him originated solely in his having avowed himself the champion of Parliamentary reform, I felt persuaded that he beheld the French Revolution under the same impression as I did, *et que la pierre fondamentale* of an alliance was laid—an alliance which I had recommended ever since 1780, and that France and England, united in one happy bond, would ensure peace and prosperity to the world for ever.

I long to see you, and it shall go hard with me but I will shake you by the hand most affectionately before winter arrives and congratulate you on the return of peace. I have preserved many of my letters, and my memory has much in store. I have it much at heart to write the memoirs of the French Revolution, in which I would justify your conduct, your disinterestedness and heroism. Mr. Elliot, who has been in the Corps Diplomatique since 1773, was at Paris when I was there in 1790–1791, and we were the only two who did not humour the erroneous wishes of our Court by assuring Ministers that a counter-revolution was on the point of being declared. On the contrary, we respectively wrote, not in concert—for we were ignorant of each other's letters at the time—that the Revolution could not be interrupted in its march, and that any attempt to stop it would only enrage an immense population broken loose from all restraint, and that, ignorant of the force and resources of a nation which had sprung a mine of intellect, we should await patiently the course of events and seize the first favourable calm moment to propose an alliance, offensive and defensive, with so powerful a neighbour. In this sense I wrote to Mr. Pitt, so did Mr. Elliot, and, holding this language to the Minister on my return, I implored him not to quarrel with France. But he listened to a legion of emissaries, priests and laymen, unworthy of credit, the oracles whom Edmund Burke consulted and believed.

I have now given you, my dear Marquis, a short detail of some events, the rest you shall receive *de vive voix*; but your recent history will be far more interesting to me than my narrative will be to you. I must remain in England until my eldest son, for whom Lord Moira has obtained an appointment in the Civil Service of India, and who, on leaving Haileybury College, will join his Lordship at Calcutta, has embarked for his destination. I shall count the days until I again see and embrace you.

*Mrs. Liston to Mr. Miles*

Constantinople: October 25, 1814

The delirium of joy described in your letter of April last, my good friend, has, I trust, in the month of October subsided to tranquil satisfaction. No! 'I cry thee mercy,' we have not yet heard the result of the congress, who is to get and who is to give; and a letter from a politician the other day says Bonaparte is not quiet, he turns his eye to Turkey. A native of this country, a Frank, not a Turk, advanced a very strange opinion in this house very lately. If Bonaparte, said he, chooses to come to Constantinople, the Grand Seigneur will make him Grand Vizier. But *religion*, I observed. Has he not already been a Mahometan, and may he not be so again? *Language*, added I. There are enough of dragomans, replied he, to translate French and Italian into Turkish. Well then, I observed, if the Sultan makes Bonaparte Grand Vizier, I'll answer for it he will very soon make himself Grand Seigneur. I leave you to comment upon this.

The Regent, I presume, has a mind more at rest since a certain great personage has visited the Continent. I wish she had done it sooner; perhaps then a certain marriage, which I regard as a circumstance important to the happiness of the country, might have taken place; but you, on the spot, ought to know more about it, and whether things are likely to come round.

Mr. Liston joins me in affectionate wishes to you and Mrs. Miles, not forgetting Robert Henry. *A propos* of the name, you will very soon, I hope, see Robert Elliot in London. Mr. Liston sent him home some weeks ago by way of Vienna, but, as he had quarantine to perform on the frontiers, he may not arrive so soon as this letter. I mean to recommend him to our friend Rolleston, or Mr. Liston will, at his first leisure. I took what I thought the prudent method. I began with the lady, and gave him a letter to Mrs. Rolleston. I am anxious to hear that he is safely restored to his father and mother. He has had the finest weather in the world. I am rather pleased that Mr. Liston has not time to write by this occasion. I don't think we ought to write at the same time. We are in perfect health. This country has a thousand faults, but it is certainly the best and healthiest climate possible.

*THE MARQUIS DE LAFAYETTE TO MR. MILES*

Paris: August 28, 1815

The events which have taken place in France and the actual situation of the country have nothing inviting for you to come over. How long this state of painful uncertainty will last I cannot pretend to judge. The declarations of the Allies have hitherto been a very erroneous ground to build upon for the anticipation of their conduct, nor can the sense of this nation be found in the debates of the two Houses which are likely to act as representatives of the French people; so that we must rest in the dark, under a cloud of ignorance and uneasiness, big with unforeseen events, the ultimate result of which must prove to be favourable to the cause of reason and general freedom.[1]

Your opinion of Bonaparte seems to me very accurate. His talents were prodigious, his intentions illiberal, his temper incorrigible. While I wonder at the enthusiasm of some friends of liberty for the greatest enemy, considering his circumstances, that liberty ever had, I despise the ungenerous, and, in many cases, the ungrateful hatred which now turns his former flatterers or submissive instruments into vile abusers or merciless enemies. He has done more harm, and missed more opportunities of doing good, than any man I know of.[2]

---

[1] 'It is said that Fouché and Talleyrand received money for betraying their master in 1814, and that Marchmont, Clarke, and Fouché were concerned in the second treachery in 1815, with some others whose names I have forgotten. In this latter year, I am told, sawdust was mixed with the powder sent to Montmartre from Paris, and ball of calibre not adapted to the artillery, and that, if the garrison had been permitted to act by the ruling powers in Paris, the Allies would have been destroyed.'—MS. note by Mr. Miles.

[2] 'Entre 1804 et 1815, Napoléon fait tuer plus de 1,700,000 Français

When the aristocracy of France, the European Continent and its sovereigns, were in his service, I refused to be his friend or even his visitor, nor would I consent to wait upon him at the very time that I supported a national defence of which he necessarily was the military chief. It has been my lot, in the hour when he meant to dissolve the House of Representatives, to promote his fall, but I ever reprobated the idea of his being given up to you. I would have assisted his escaping, as he might have done, to the United States. I do not see what Government in Europe would have a right to hurt him.

I have deeply lamented the loss of the excellent Mr. Whitbread. My personal obligations to him during my captivity had endeared to me the duties of fraternity which more than ever ought to unite the friends of liberty in every part of the world. He was a good judge of the influence of French affairs with respect to general civilisation. I thank you for your very valuable verses on the melancholy and most affecting occasion.[1]

When you determine to visit France you will find me either at Paris or at Lagrange, where I shall resume my life of retirement. Had you persisted in your intention to come over shortly after the date of your letter, you should have been over by this time. I conclude you have postponed the journey. At any time I shall be very happy to see you. Present my respects to Mrs. Miles, and believe me very affectionately yours, &c.

nés dans les limites de l'ancienne France, auxquels il faut ajouter probablement deux millions d'hommes nés hors de ces limites et tués pour lui, à titre d'alliés, ou tués par lui, à titre d'ennemis.'—*Revue des Deux Mondes* 1 Mars, 1887; *Napoléon Bonaparte*, dernière partie, par M. Taine.

[1] Mr. Whitbread had committed suicide.

*THE MARQUIS DE LAFAYETTE TO MR. MILES*

Lagrange: January 5, 1816

I wish it were in my power to answer your queries as fully as it may suit your patriotic purposes. The several pieces here annexed, and numbered, will in a measure enable you to take useful notes. Permit me to make a few observations.

1. I believe it indispensable to begin your collection of notes agreeably to the chronology of the times; the want of order in the succession of the facts inquired into has sometimes puzzled my memory, and would, in my opinion, be an obstacle to the good arrangement of your materials.

2. The enclosed documents having been partly dictated by me, partly drawn up by friends, American or French, as you will see by their partiality to me, I put them under your care, so that none in the world but Mrs. Miles and you may be admitted to see them.

3. You are welcome to take notes, extracts, translations, as freely as you please, requesting that the source of the information be unknown, and that the books and manuscripts may be returned to me when I come to town at the end of the month.

4. Permit me to ask you not to write either upon the books or the manuscripts, as a part of them I may be obliged to restore, and I wish the totality to remain free from annotations, which, if you are pleased to make some, I beg you to write on a separate paper.

5. In the said documents you will find answers to the greater part of your queries. I am going to peruse them again, and answer what is not touched upon in this mass of information. Should you think proper to

ask new questions, I beg leave to suggest the propriety to put them in a half margin, chronological order, large paper, as you go on in the notes and extracts you are going to take, to be given to me at the end of the month when I receive back the voluminous *envoile* here annexed. Some of these papers are not mine, although under the same hand as the others. It is an additional motive to wish their not being communicated, and their being returned as soon as possible. In the two printed books, which it is somewhat improper for me to submit to you for perusal, and extracts, as they are full of partiality to me, I think you will find answers to a part of your queries.[1]

Now, my dear Sir, it remains for me to wish you and Mrs. Miles a happy New Year for yourselves and family. Most truly and affectionately yours, &c.

### Mr. Miles to Sir Matthew Wood

Paris: February 20, 1817

Do not be too sanguine of your security, nor fancy that concessions extorted by fear will interrupt the march of those who are resolved in their demand for a reform which Government cannot refuse without risking its existence. I am certainly an enemy to mobs, riots, and insurrections. I am also hostile to annual parliaments and universal suffrage, because I do not see my way through them, and conceive they would lead to more

---

[1] A few of these original MSS. are still extant among Mr. Miles's papers—'Mémoire manuscrit sur les anciens tems;' 'Mémoire sur les Noirs et les Protestants;' 'Notes d'un Citoyen américain sur les Cents Jours;' 'Bulletin d'un Citoyen français sur la Situation Politique de la France, au 1er Octobre, 1815'—which piece is written by Lafayette in the form of an elaborate letter addressed to Mr. Miles; also an exhaustive article on the Coalition of the Continental Powers, and Memoirs of the Duc d'Orléans—Egalité, and Monsieur—Louis XVIII.

disastrous events than have resulted from a corrupt and perjured House of Commons; but, firmly as I object to so dangerous an innovation, and averse as I am to all popular tumults under the guidance of men ill qualified for legislators, I am immovably fixed in favour of reform and retrenchments, and will never depart from the principles I avowed in 1769. The present danger, I conceive, we have to apprehend is, that Hunt, Cartwright, and Cobbett, who march in the front, will, if they storm the fortress, take the command of it as the price of their bravery and zeal, and that torrents of blood will flow before a stop can be put to the fury of resentment and the passion of revenge. The question is, will they be allowed to retain the lead? If their combinations are not so compact and riveted as to assure them this authority and annihilate the credit of those who would dispute it, they will be amongst the first victims of a revolution which they better knew how to plan than to conduct, and hence an anarchy, with free quarters to the dissolute and penniless, which may place us in the situation of France under the tyranny of Robespierre.

That we deserve in our turn to taste the evils experienced by others cannot well be doubted. I have it in my power to prove that the British Cabinet is the primary cause of all the calamities which have desolated Europe for the last twenty-five years. I had resolved to prove it by a voluminous publication which must have opened the eyes of every man. I have already charged the King as the author of the war, in my letter addressed to the Prince of Wales in 1808. You have the letter, and I refer you to it. I had it from the man[1] who was to have succeeded Mr. Pitt if Mr. Pitt

[1] The Earl of Moira.

had possessed virtue enough to have remained firm in the opinion he avowed to me in 1790 and 1791 respecting the Revolution, and to the principles to which I fully expected he would adhere when he sent me to Paris. It was in 1791, before France had committed any act of hostility—before any excess had been committed demanding notice, except that of the Parisian populace marching to Versailles, when my friend General Lafayette instantly followed them and saved the lives of the royal family—that his Majesty sent a message by the late Lord Liverpool to Mr. Pitt that he must *war with France* or *resign*. At the time I went to France the Minister was well disposed towards the Revolution; his change of sentiment may be attributed to his love of place and patronage. But what can justify his sacrificing his country and all Europe, as it were, to his avarice of power and the favour of his royal master?[1] All this I had arranged for the press, and transmitted to a confidential friend in England to publish, when the result of the first meeting at Spa Fields, where you had nearly fallen a victim, made me pause. A mere accident a few days afterwards brought me acquainted with the plan of attack resolved upon, with other particulars, which, connected as they were with transactions in 1795, convinced me that I ought to defer the intended publication, and not at such a moment 'spread the compost on the weeds to

---

[1] 'But the main charge against Mr. Pitt is his having suffered himself to be led away by the alarms of the Court and the zeal of his new allies, the Burke and Windham party, from the ardent love of peace, which he professed and undoubtedly felt, to the eager support of the war against France, which might well have been avoided had he but stood firm. The deplorable consequences of this change in his conduct are too well known: they are still too sensibly felt.'—*Historical Sketches of Statesmen who flourished in the Time of George III.*, by Henry, Lord Brougham. London, 1855, i. 280.

make them ranker.' The same mail that conveyed my
first letter to you on this subject was also charged with
a letter to my friend, interdicting for the present the
publication; the notes and documents on which are
too valuable to be lost and shall in due time appear.
When I found that Cartwright, Cobbett, and Hunt
aspired to be *sovereigns* as well as *liberators*, and that
the elective franchise was to extend to the lodgers of
every house in Hedge Lane, Chick Lane, St. Giles's,
Whitechapel, and Wapping—making these gentlemen,
in point of fact, *Returning Officers* for London, Westminster, and the Borough and county of Middlesex—I
really felt the country to be in danger. Every man
has it in his power to be honest, but abilities do not
belong to all mankind; and hence it is evident that,
even as horses must be guided, the great bulk of the
people must be governed. Intellects are to the human
race what vision is to the brute creation, and it
becomes a duty in those who are the best organised to
watch over the interests of their less happily constructed fellow-creatures. This duty is violated when
the former are tyrants over the latter. But I am
alarmed at the popular ferment that everywhere prevails,
and at the consequences of subverting the Government,
as it were, by a *coup de main*.[1] Under such circum-

[1] 'Let us go on to the next of the revolutionary postulates concerning man: its egalitarian doctrine. "Equality," says Bailleul, "which is nothing but strict justice, was the aim of the Revolution from the beginning." But equality is a question-begging word. And it is precisely the opposite of strict justice, as Plato observed two thousand years ago, to dispense equality alike to equals and unequals. Here, again, the new gospel ignores the facts of life. Men are no more absolutely equal than they are absolutely good or absolutely reasonable. Equal in their common nature they are. Equal before the law they ought to be. Equal, in the sense of equivalent in the body politic, they certainly are not, and never will be until doctrinaires succeed in radically transforming mankind. This appears to have been more or less clearly apprehended by one of

stances, ill as I thought and must think of Ministers, I thought it due to my country at large to suspend the work in question, and to recommend their being supported, rather than allow these men to break down all the fences of the constitution, and rush in upon the nation, followed by famished thousands inflamed to madness by reiterated wrongs, and reinforced by a dissolute, ferocious rabble; but anxious as I was to guard against an event so deplorable, I frankly stated in both my letters to you that Ministers must concede —that it was only by concessions they could avoid a revolution, and, from what I have this day been informed, I again repeat that they must yield.

" the giants of 1792," a certain Armand de la Meuse, who is recorded to have demanded the introduction of mental equality. This sage was certainly within his logic. He went to the root of the matter. The great, the perennial source of inequality among men lies in difference of intellectual constitution and of psychic power.'—*Century of Revolutions*, by William S. Lilly, London, 1890, p. 172.

THE END.

PRINTED BY
SPOTTISWOODE AND CO., NEW-STREET SQUARE
LONDON

AUGUST, 1893

A

# CLASSIFIED CATALOGUE

## OF WORKS IN

# GENERAL LITERATURE

| | PAGE |
|---|---|
| BADMINTON LIBRARY (THE) | 9 |
| BIOGRAPHY, PERSONAL MEMOIRS, ETC. | 6 |
| CHILDREN'S BOOKS | 20 |
| CLASSICAL LITERATURE, TRANSLATION, ETC. | 14 |
| COOKERY AND DOMESTIC MANAGEMENT | 22 |
| EVOLUTION, ANTHROPOLOGY, ETC. | 14 |
| FICTION, HUMOUR, ETC. | 16 |
| HISTORY, POLITICS, POLITY, AND POLITICAL MEMOIRS | 3 |
| INDEX OF AUTHORS | 2 |
| LANGUAGE, HISTORY AND SCIENCE OF | 13 |
| MENTAL, MORAL, AND POLITICAL PHILOSOPHY | 10 |
| MISCELLANEOUS AND CRITICAL WORKS | 23 |
| POETRY AND THE DRAMA | 15 |
| POLITICAL ECONOMY AND ECONOMICS | 13 |
| POPULAR SCIENCE | 18 |
| SILVER LIBRARY (THE) | 21 |
| SPORT AND PASTIME | 8 |
| TRAVEL AND ADVENTURE | 7 |
| WORKS OF REFERENCE | 20 |

LONDON

LONGMANS, GREEN, AND CO.

NEW YORK: 15 EAST 16th STREET

# INDEX OF AUTHORS.

| Name | Page | Name | Page | Name | Page |
|---|---|---|---|---|---|
| Abbott (Evelyn) | 3, 14 | Halliwell-Phillipps (J. O.) | 7, 23 | Plato | 14 |
| —— (T. K.) | 10 | Harrison (Mary) | 23 | Pole (W.) | 10 |
| Acland (A. H. D.) | 3 | Harrison (Jane E.) | 14 | Pollock (W. H.) | 9 |
| Acton (Eliza) | 22 | Harte (Bret) | 17 | Poole (W. H. and Mrs.) | 23 |
| Æschylus | 14 | Hartwig (G.) | 18, 19 | Praeger (F.) | 7 |
| Allingham (W.) | 15 | Hassall (A.) | 6 | Pratt (A. E.) | 8 |
| Anstey (F.) | 16 | Hearn (W. E.) | 4, 11 | Prendergast (J. P.) | 5 |
| Aristophanes | 14 | Heathcote (J. M. & C. J.) | 9 | Proctor (Richard A.) | 10, 19, 24 |
| Aristotle | 11 | Helmholtz (Prof.) | 19 | Raine (James) | 4 |
| Armstrong (E.) | 5 | Henry (W.) | 9 | Ransome (Cyril) | 3 |
| —— (G. F. Savage-) | 15 | Hodgson (Shadworth H.) | 11, 24 | Reader (E. E.) | 21 |
| —— (E. J.) | 6, 15, 23 | Hooper (G.) | 6 | Rhoades (J.) | 14, 16 |
| Arnold (Sir Edwin) | 7, 15 | Hopkins (E. P.) | 10 | Ribot (T.) | 12 |
| Arnold (T.) | 3 | Horley (E.) | 4 | Rich (A.) | 14 |
| Ashley (W. J.) | 13 | Howard (B. D.) | 8 | Richardson (Sir B. Ward) | 24 |
| Atelier du Lys (Author of) | 16 | Howitt (William) | 8 | Rickaby (John) | 12 |
| Bacon | 6, 11 | Hullah (John) | 24 | —— (Joseph) | 12 |
| Bagehot (Walter) | 6, 13, 23 | Hume (David) | 11 | —— (A.) | 8 |
| Bagwell (R.) | 3 | Hunt (W.) | 4 | Riley (J. W.) | 16 |
| Bain (Alexander) | 11 | Hutchinson (Horace G.) | 9 | Robertson (A.) | 18 |
| Baker (James) | 16 | Huth (A. H.) | 14 | Roget (John Lewis) | 24 |
| Baker (Sir S. W.) | 7 | Hyne (C. J. C.) | 17 | —— (Peter M.) | 13 |
| Ball (J. T.) | 3 | Ingelow (Jean) | 15, 20 | Romanes (G. J.) | 14 |
| Baring-Gould (S.) | 23 | Jefferies (Richard) | 7 | Ronalds (A.) | 10 |
| Barrow (Sir J. Croker) | 15 | Jewsbury (Geraldine) | 24 | Roosevelt (T.) | 4 |
| Beaconsfield (Earl of) | 16, 17 | Johnson (J. & J. H.) | 24 | Rossetti (M. F.) | 24 |
| Beaufort (Duke of) | 9 | Johnstone (L.) | 11 | Round (J. H.) | 5 |
| Becker (Prof.) | 14 | Jones (E. E. C.) | 11 | Seebohm (F.) | 5, 6 |
| Bell (Mrs. Hugh) | 15 | Jordan (W. L.) | 13 | Sewell (Eliz. M.) | 18 |
| Bent (J. Theodore) | 7 | Joyce (P. W.) | 4 | Shakespeare | 16 |
| Björnsen (B.) | 15 | Justinian | 11 | Shearman (M.) | 9 |
| Boase (C. W.) | 4 | Kant (I.) | 11 | Shirres (L. P.) | 13 |
| Boedder (B.) | 12 | Killick (A. H.) | 11 | Sidgwick (Alfred) | 12 |
| Boyd (A. K. H.) | 6, 23 | Kitchin (G. W.) | 4 | Sinclair (A.) | 9 |
| Brassey (Lady) | 7 | Knight (E. F.) | 8 | Smith (R. Bosworth) | 5 |
| Bray (C. and Mrs.) | 11 | Ladd (G. T.) | 11 | Sophocles | 14 |
| 'Brenda' | 20 | Lang (Andrew) | 4, 10, 14, 15, 17, 20, 24 | Southey (R.) | 24 |
| Buckle (H. T.) | 3 | Lavisse (E.) | 4 | Spedding (J.) | 6 |
| Bull (T.) | 22 | Lear (H. L. Sidney) | 23 | Stanley (Bishop) | 19 |
| Burrows (Montagu) | 4 | Lecky (W. E. H.) | 4, 16 | Steel (A. G.) | 9 |
| Bury (Viscount) | 9 | Lees (J. A.) | 8 | Stephen (Sir James) | 7 |
| Butler (E. A.) | 18 | Leslie (T. E. C.) | 13 | Stephens (H. C.) | 5 |
| —— (Samuel) | 23 | Lewes (G. H.) | 11 | —— (H. Morse) | 5 |
| Campbell-Walker (A.) | 9 | Leyton (F.) | 16 | —— (T.) | 5 |
| Carlyle (Thomas) | 23 | Lodge (H. C.) | 4 | Stevenson (Robert Louis) | 16, 18, 21 |
| Carðe (W. D.) | 5 | Loftie (W. J.) | 4 | Stock (St. George) | 12 |
| Chesney (Sir G.) | 5 | Logeman (W. S.) | 13 | Strong (H. A.) | 13 |
| Chetwynd (Sir G.) | 8 | Longman (F. W.) | 10 | Stubbs (J. W.) | 5 |
| Chilton (E.) | 17 | Longmore (Sir T.) | 7 | Sturgis (Julian) | 18 |
| Cholmondeley-Pennell (H.) | 10 | Lubbock (Sir John) | 14 | Suffolk and Berkshire (Earl of) | 9 |
| Cicero | 14 | Lyall (Edna) | 17 | Sully (James) | 12 |
| Clarke (R. F.) | 12 | Lydekker (R.) | 19 | Suttner (Baron von) | 18 |
| Clerke (Agnes M.) | 11 | Lyttelton (R. H.) | 9 | Swinburne (A. J.) | 12 |
| Clodd (Edward) | 14 | Lytton (Earl of) | 16 | Symes (J. E.) | 13 |
| Clutterbuck (W. J.) | 8 | Macaulay (Lord) | 5, 16 | Thompson (Annie) | 18 |
| Comyn (L. N.) | 17 | Macfarren (Sir G. A.) | 24 | —— (D. G.) | 12 |
| Conington (John) | 14 | Mackail (J. W.) | 14 | Thomson (Archbishop) | 12 |
| Cox (Harding) | 9 | Macleod (H. D.) | 13 | Tirebuck (W.) | 18 |
| Crake (A. D.) | 20 | Maher (M.) | 12 | Todd (A.) | 6 |
| Creighton (Bishop) | 4 | Mannering (G. E.) | 8 | Toynbee (A.) | 13 |
| Crozier (J. B.) | 11 | Marbot (Baron de) | 5 | Trevelyan (Sir G. O.) | 6 |
| Crump (A.) | 3, 13 | Marshman (J. C.) | 6 | Trollope (Anthony) | 18 |
| Curzon (Hon. G. N.) | 8 | Martin (A. P.) | 7 | Tupper (C. L.) | 7 |
| Cutts (E. L.) | 4 | Matthews (Brander) | 17, 24 | Tyrrell (R. Y.) | 14 |
| Dante | 15 | Maunder (S.) | 20 | Verney (Francis P.) | 7 |
| Davidson (W. L.) | 11, 13 | Max Müller (F.) | 11, 13, 24 | Virgil | 14 |
| Deland (Mrs.) | 17 | May (Sir T. Erskine) | 5 | Wade (G. W.) | 13 |
| Dent (C. T.) | 9 | Meath (Earl of) | 13 | Wakeman (H. O.) | 6 |
| De Salis (Mrs.) | 22, 23 | Meade (L. T.) | 20, 21 | Walford (Mrs.) | 7, 18 |
| De Tocqueville (A.) | 3 | Melville (G. J. Whyte) | 17 | Wallaschek (R.) | 24 |
| Devas (C. S.) | 13 | Mendelssohn | 24 | Walpole (Spencer) | 6 |
| Dougall (L.) | 17 | Merivale (Dean) | 5 | Walsingham (Lord) | 9 |
| Dowell (S.) | 13 | Mill (James) | 12 | Walter (J.) | 7 |
| Doyle (A. Conan) | 17 | Mill (John Stuart) | 12, 13 | Watson (A. E. T.) | 9 |
| Falkener (E.) | 10 | Milner (G.) | 24 | Webb (T. E.) | 12 |
| Farnell (G. S.) | 14 | Molesworth (Mrs.) | 21 | Weir (R.) | 9 |
| Farrar (Archdeacon) | 13, 17 | Monck (H. S.) | 12 | West (C.) | 23 |
| Fitzpatrick (W. J.) | 3 | Moore (E.) | 6 | Weyman (Stanley J.) | 18 |
| Ford (H.) | 10 | Nansen (F.) | 8 | Whately (Archbishop) | 12 |
| Francis (Francis) | 10 | Nesbit (E.) | 16 | —— (E. J.) | 13 |
| Freeman (Edward A.) | 3 | Norton (C. L.) | 8 | Wheeler (B. I.) | 13 |
| Froude (James A.) | 4, 6, 8, 17 | O'Brien (W.) | 17 | Whishaw (F. J.) | 8 |
| Furneaux (W.) | 18 | Oliphant (Mrs.) | 18 | Wilcocks (J. C.) | 10 |
| Gardiner (Samuel Rawson) | 4 | Osbourne (L.) | 18 | Wilkin (A.) | 14 |
| Gleig (G. R.) | 7 | Parkes (Sir H.) | 5 | Willich (C. M.) | 20 |
| Goethe | 15 | Parr (Mrs.) | 18 | Wilson (A. J.) | 13 |
| Gordon (E. J. A.) | 8 | Paul (H.) | 13 | Wishart (G.) | 6 |
| Graham (G. F.) | 13 | Payn (James) | 18 | Wolff (H. W.) | 8, 13 |
| Graves (R. P.) | 6 | Payne-Gallwey (Sir R.) | 9, 10 | Woodgate (W. B.) | 9 |
| Green (T. Hill) | 11 | Pembroke (Earl of) | 8 | Wood (J. G.) | 19 |
| Greville (C. C. F.) | 4 | Perring (Sir P.) | 24 | Wordsworth (Bishop Charles) | 7 |
| Haggard (H. Rider) | 17 | Phillipps-Wolley (C.) | 9, 18 | Wylie (J. H.) | 6 |
| —— (Ella) | 15 | Piatt (S. & J. J.) | 16 | Zeller (E.) | 12 |

# MESSRS. LONGMANS, GREEN, & CO.'S
## CLASSIFIED CATALOGUE

OF

# WORKS IN GENERAL LITERATURE.

## History, Politics, Polity, and Political Memoirs.

**Abbott.**—A HISTORY OF GREECE. By EVELYN ABBOTT, M.A., LL.D.
Part I.—From the Earliest Times to the Ionian Revolt. Crown 8vo., 10s. 6d.
Part II.—500-445 B.C. Crown 8vo., 10s. 6d.

**Acland and Ransome.**—A HANDBOOK IN OUTLINE OF THE POLITICAL HISTORY OF ENGLAND TO 1890. Chronologically Arranged. By the Right Hon. A. H. DYKE ACLAND, M.P., and CYRIL RANSOME, M.A. Crown 8vo., 6s.

ANNUAL REGISTER, (THE). A Review of Public Events at Home and Abroad, for the year 1892. 8vo., 18s.

Volumes of the ANNUAL REGISTER for the years 1863-1891 can still be had. 18s. each.

**Armstrong.**—ELIZABETH FARNESE; The Termagant of Spain. By EDWARD ARMSTRONG, M.A., Fellow of Queen's College, Oxford. 8vo., 16s.

**Arnold.**—Works by T. ARNOLD, D.D., formerly Head Master of Rugby School.
INTRODUCTORY LECTURES ON MODERN HISTORY. 8vo., 7s. 6d.
MISCELLANEOUS WORKS. 8vo., 7s. 6d.

**Bagwell.**—IRELAND UNDER THE TUDORS. By RICHARD BAGWELL, LL.D. (3 vols.) Vols. I. and II. From the first invasion of the Northmen to the year 1578. 8vo., 32s. Vol. III. 1578-1603. 8vo. 18s.

**Ball.**—HISTORICAL REVIEW OF THE LEGISLATIVE SYSTEMS OPERATIVE IN IRELAND, from the Invasion of Henry the Second to the Union (1172-1800). By the Rt. Hon. J. T. BALL. 8vo., 6s.

**Buckle.**—HISTORY OF CIVILISATION IN ENGLAND AND FRANCE, SPAIN AND SCOTLAND. By HENRY THOMAS BUCKLE. 3 vols. Crown 8vo., 24s.

**Chesney.**—INDIAN POLITY: a View of the System of Administration in India. By Lieut.-General Sir GEORGE CHESNEY. New Edition, Revised and Enlarged. [In the Press.

**Crump.**—A SHORT ENQUIRY INTO THE FORMATION OF POLITICAL OPINION, from the reign of the Great Families to the advent of Democracy. By ARTHUR CRUMP. 8vo., 7s. 6d.

**De Tocqueville.**—DEMOCRACY IN AMERICA. By ALEXIS DE TOCQUEVILLE. 2 vols. Crown 8vo., 16s.

**Fitzpatrick.**—SECRET SERVICE UNDER PITT. By W. J. FITZPATRICK, F.S.A., Author of 'Correspondence of Daniel O'Connell'. 8vo., 7s. 6d.

**Freeman.**—THE HISTORICAL GEOGRAPHY OF EUROPE. By EDWARD A. FREEMAN. D.C.L., LL.D. With 65 Maps. 2 vols. 8vo., 31s. 6d.

## History, Politics, Polity, and Political Memoirs—*continued*.

**Froude.**—Works by JAMES A. FROUDE, Regius Professor of Modern History in the University of Oxford.

THE HISTORY OF ENGLAND, from the Fall of Wolsey to the Defeat of the Spanish Armada.
Popular Edition. 12 vols. Crown 8vo., 3s. 6d. each.
Silver Library Edition. 12 vols. Crown 8vo. 3s. 6d. each.

THE DIVORCE OF CATHERINE OF ARAGON: the Story as told by the Imperial Ambassadors resident at the Court of Henry VIII. *In usum Laicorum.* Crown 8vo., 6s.

THE SPANISH STORY OF THE ARMADA, and other Essays, Historical and Descriptive. Crown 8vo., 6s.

THE ENGLISH IN IRELAND IN THE EIGHTEENTH CENTURY. 3 vols. Crown 8vo., 18s.

SHORT STUDIES ON GREAT SUBJECTS. Cabinet Edition. 4 vols. Crown 8vo., 24s.
Silver Library Edition. 4 vols. Crown 8vo., 3s. 6d. each.

CÆSAR: a Sketch. Crown 8vo., 3s. 6d.

**Gardiner.**—Works by SAMUEL RAWSON GARDINER, M.A., Hon. LL.D., Edinburgh, Fellow of Merton College, Oxford.

HISTORY OF ENGLAND, from the Accession of James I. to the Outbreak of the Civil War, 1603-1642. 10 vols. Crown 8vo., 6s. each.

A HISTORY OF THE GREAT CIVIL WAR, 1642-1649. 4 vols. Crown 8vo., 6s. each

THE STUDENT'S HISTORY OF ENGLAND. With 378 Illustrations. Crown 8vo., 12s.

*Also in Three Volumes.*

Vol. I. B.C. 55—A.D. 1509. With 173 Illustrations. Crown 8vo. 4s.
Vol. II. 1509-1689. With 96 Illustrations. Crown 8vo. 4s.
Vol. III. 1689-1885. With 109 Illustrations. Crown 8vo. 4s.

**Greville.**—A JOURNAL OF THE REIGNS OF KING GEORGE IV., KING WILLIAM IV., AND QUEEN VICTORIA. By CHARLES C. F. GREVILLE, formerly Clerk of the Council. 8 vols. Crown 8vo., 6s. each.

**Hearn.**—THE GOVERNMENT OF ENGLAND: its Structure and its Development. By W. EDWARD HEARN. 8vo., 16s.

**Historic Towns.**—Edited by E. A. FREEMAN, D.C.L., and Rev. WILLIAM HUNT, M.A. With Maps and Plans. Crown 8vo., 3s. 6d. each.

BRISTOL. By the Rev. W. HUNT.
CARLISLE. By MANDELL CREIGHTON, D.D., Bishop of Peterborough.
CINQUE PORTS. By MONTAGU BURROWS.
COLCHESTER. By Rev. E. L. CUTTS.
EXETER. By E. A. FREEMAN.
LONDON. By Rev. W. J. LOFTIE.
OXFORD. By Rev. C. W. BOASE.
WINCHESTER. By Rev. G. W. KITCHIN, D.D.
YORK. By Rev. JAMES RAINE.
NEW YORK. By THEODORE ROOSEVELT.
BOSTON (U.S.) By HENRY CABOT LODGE.

**Horley.**—SEFTON: A DESCRIPTIVE AND HISTORICAL ACCOUNT. Comprising the Collected Notes and Researches of the late Rev. ENGELBERT HORLEY, M.A., Rector 1871-1883. By W. D. CARÖE, M.A. (Cantab.), Fellow of the Royal Institute of British Architects, and E. J. A. GORDON. With 17 Plates and 32 Illustrations in the Text. Royal 8vo., 31s. 6d.

**Joyce.**—A SHORT HISTORY OF IRELAND, from the Earliest Times to 1608. By P. W. JOYCE, LL.D., Author of 'Irish Names of Places,' 'Old Celtic Romances,' etc. Crown 8vo., 10s. 6d.

**Lang.**—A HISTORY OF ST. ANDREWS. By ANDREW LANG. With Illustrations by J. HODGE. [*In the Press.*

**Lavisse.**—GENERAL VIEW OF THE POLITICAL HISTORY OF EUROPE. By ERNEST LAVISSE, Professor at the Sorbonne. Translated by CHARLES GROSS, Ph. D. Crown 8vo., 5s.

**Lecky.**—Works by WILLIAM EDWARD HARTPOLE LECKY.

HISTORY OF ENGLAND IN THE EIGHTEENTH CENTURY.
Library Edition. 8 vols. 8vo., £7 4s.
Cabinet Edition. ENGLAND. 7 vols. Crown 8vo., 6s. each. IRELAND. 5 vols. Crown 8vo., 6s. each.

HISTORY OF EUROPEAN MORALS FROM AUGUSTUS TO CHARLEMAGNE. 2 vols. Crown 8vo., 16s.

HISTORY OF THE RISE AND INFLUENCE OF THE SPIRIT OF RATIONALISM IN EUROPE. 2 vols. Crown 8vo., 16s.

# History, Politics, Polity, and Political Memoirs—*continued.*

**Macaulay.**—Works by LORD MACAULAY.
COMPLETE WORKS OF LORD MACAULAY.
   Cabinet Edition. 16 vols. Post 8vo., £4 16s.
   Library Edition. 8 vols. 8vo., £5 5s.
HISTORY OF ENGLAND FROM THE ACCESSION OF JAMES THE SECOND.
   Popular Edition. 2 vols. Cr. 8vo., 5s.
   Student's Edition. 2 vols. Cr. 8vo., 12s.
   People's Edition. 4 vols. Cr. 8vo., 16s.
   Cabinet Edition. 8 vols. Post 8vo., 48s.
   Library Edition. 5 vols. 8vo., £4.
CRITICAL AND HISTORICAL ESSAYS, WITH LAYS OF ANCIENT ROME, in 1 volume.
   Popular Edition. Crown 8vo., 2s. 6d.
   Authorised Edition. Crown 8vo., 2s. 6d., or 3s. 6d., gilt edges.
   Silver Library Edition. Cr. 8vo., 3s. 6d.
CRITICAL AND HISTORICAL ESSAYS.
   Student's Edition. 1 volume. Cr. 8vo., 6s.
   People's Edition. 2 vols. Cr. 8vo., 8s.
   Trevelyan Edition. 2 vols. Cr. 8vo., 9s.
   Cabinet Edition. 4 vols. Post 8vo., 24s.
   Library Edition. 3 vols. 8vo., 36s.

ESSAYS which may be had separately price 6d. each sewed, 1s. each cloth.
   Addison and Walpole.
   Frederick the Great.
   Croker's Boswell's Johnson.
   Hallam's Constitutional History.
   Warren Hastings. (3d. sewed, 6d. cloth).
   The Earl of Chatham (Two Essays).
   Ranke and Gladstone.
   Milton and Machiavelli.
   Lord Bacon.
   Lord Clive.
   Lord Byron, and The Comic Dramatists of the Restoration.

SPEECHES. Crown 8vo., 3s. 6d.

MISCELLANEOUS WRITINGS
   People's Edition. 1 vol. Crown 8vo., 4s. 6d.
   Library Edition. 2 vols. 8vo., 21s.

MISCELLANEOUS WRITINGS AND SPEECHES.
   Popular Edition. Crown 8vo., 2s. 6d.
   Student's Edition. Crown 8vo., 6s.
   Cabinet Edition. Including Indian Penal Code, Lays of Ancient Rome, and Miscellaneous Poems. 4 vols. Post 8vo., 24s.

SELECTIONS FROM THE WRITINGS OF LORD MACAULAY. Edited, with Occasional Notes, by the Right Hon. Sir G. O. Trevelyan, Bart. Crown 8vo., 6s.

**May.**—THE CONSTITUTIONAL HISTORY OF ENGLAND since the Accession of George III. 1760-1870. By Sir THOMAS ERSKINE MAY, K.C.B. (Lord Farnborough). 3 vols. Crown 8vo., 18s.

**Merivale.**—Works by the Very Rev. CHARLES MERIVALE, Dean of Ely.
HISTORY OF THE ROMANS UNDER THE EMPIRE.
   Cabinet Edition. 8 vols. Cr. 8vo., 48s.
   Silver Library Edition. 8 vols. Crown 8vo., 3s. 6d. each.
THE FALL OF THE ROMAN REPUBLIC: a Short History of the Last Century of the Commonwealth. 12mo., 7s. 6d.

**Parkes.**—FIFTY YEARS IN THE MAKING OF AUSTRALIAN HISTORY. By Sir HENRY PARKES, G.C.M.G. With 2 Portraits (1854 and 1892). 2 vols. 8vo., 32s.

**Prendergast.**—IRELAND FROM THE RESTORATION TO THE REVOLUTION, 1660-1690. By JOHN P. PRENDERGAST, Author of 'The Cromwellian Settlement in Ireland'. 8vo., 5s.

**Round.**—GEOFFREY DE MANDEVILLE: a Study of the Anarchy. By J. H. ROUND, M.A. 8vo., 16s.

**Seebohm.**—THE ENGLISH VILLAGE COMMUNITY Examined in its Relations to the Manorial and Tribal Systems, &c. By FREDERIC SEEBOHM. With 13 Maps and Plates. 8vo., 16s.

**Smith.**—CARTHAGE AND THE CARTHAGINIANS. By R. BOSWORTH SMITH, M.A., Assistant Master in Harrow School. With Maps, Plans, &c. Crown 8vo., 6s.

**Stephens.**—PAROCHIAL SELF-GOVERNMENT IN RURAL DISTRICTS: Argument and Plan. By HENRY C. STEPHENS, M.P. 4to., 12s. 6d.

**Stephens.**—A HISTORY OF THE FRENCH REVOLUTION. By H. MORSE STEPHENS, Balliol College, Oxford. 3 vols. 8vo. Vols. I. and II. 18s. each.

**Stephens.**—MADOC: An Essay on the Discovery of America, by MADOC AP OWEN GWYNEDD, in the Twelfth Century. By THOMAS STEPHENS, Author of "The Literature of the Kymry'. Edited by LLYWARCH REYNOLDS, B.A. Oxon. 8vo., 7s. 6d.

**Stubbs.**—HISTORY OF THE UNIVERSITY OF DUBLIN, from its Foundation to the End of the Eighteenth Century. By J. W. STUBBS. 8vo., 12s. 6d.

## History, Politics, Polity, and Political Memoirs—*continued*.

**Todd.**—PARLIAMENTARY GOVERNMENT IN THE COLONIES. By ALPHEUS TODD, LL.D. [*In the Press.*

**Tupper.**—OUR INDIAN PROTECTORATE: an Introduction to the Study of the Relations between the British Government and its Indian Feudatories. By CHARLES LEWIS TUPPER, Indian Civil Service. 8vo., 16s.

**Wakeman and Hassall.**—ESSAYS INTRODUCTORY TO THE STUDY OF ENGLISH CONSTITUTIONAL HISTORY. By Resident Members of the University of Oxford. Edited by HENRY OFFLEY WAKEMAN, M.A., and ARTHUR HASSALL, M.A. Crown 8vo., 6s.

**Walpole.**—Works by SPENCER WALPOLE.

HISTORY OF ENGLAND FROM THE CONCLUSION OF THE GREAT WAR IN 1815 TO 1858. 6 vols. Crown 8vo., 6s. each.

THE LAND OF HOME RULE: being an Account of the History and Institutions of the Isle of Man. Crown 8vo., 6s.

**Wylie.**—HISTORY OF ENGLAND UNDER HENRY IV. By JAMES HAMILTON WYLIE, M.A., one of H. M. Inspectors of Schools. 2 vols. Vol. I., 1399-1404. Crown 8vo., 10s. 6d. Vol. II. [*In the press.*

---

## Biography, Personal Memoirs, &c.

**Armstrong.**—THE LIFE AND LETTERS OF EDMUND J. ARMSTRONG. Edited by G. F. ARMSTRONG. Fcp. 8vo., 7s. 6d.

**Bacon.**—LETTERS AND LIFE, INCLUDING ALL HIS OCCASIONAL WORKS. Edited by J. SPEDDING. 7 vols. 8vo., £4 4s.

**Bagehot.**—BIOGRAPHICAL STUDIES. By WALTER BAGEHOT. 8vo., 12s.

**Boyd.**—TWENTY-FIVE YEARS OF ST. ANDREWS, 1865-1890. By A. K. H. BOYD, D.D., Author of 'Recreations of a Country Parson,' &c. 2 vols. 8vo. Vol. I., 12s. Vol. II. 15s.

**Carlyle.**—THOMAS CARLYLE: a History of his Life. By J. A. FROUDE.
1795-1835. 2 vols. Crown 8vo., 7s.
1834-1881. 2 vols. Crown 8vo., 7s.

**Fabert.**—ABRAHAM FABERT: Governor of Sedan and Marshal of France. His Life and Times, 1599-1662. By GEORGE HOOPER, Author of 'Waterloo,' 'Wellington,' &c. With a Portrait. 8vo., 10s. 6d.

**Fox.**—THE EARLY HISTORY OF CHARLES JAMES FOX. By the Right Hon. Sir G. O. TREVELYAN, Bart.
Library Edition. 8vo., 18s.
Cabinet Edition. Crown 8vo., 6s.

**Hamilton.**—LIFE OF SIR WILLIAM HAMILTON. By R. P. GRAVES. 3 vols. 15s. each.
ADDENDUM TO THE LIFE OF SIR WM. ROWAN HAMILTON, LL.D., D.C.L. 8vo., 6d. sewed.

**Havelock.**—MEMOIRS OF SIR HENRY HAVELOCK, K.C.B. By JOHN CLARK MARSHMAN. Crown 8vo., 3s. 6d.

**Macaulay.**—THE LIFE AND LETTERS OF LORD MACAULAY. By the Right Hon. Sir G. O. TREVELYAN, Bart.
Popular Edition. 1 volume. Cr. 8vo., 2s. 6d.
Student's Edition. 1 volume. Cr. 8vo., 6s.
Cabinet Edition. 2 vols. Post 8vo., 12s.
Library Edition. 2 vols. 8vo., 36s.

**Marbot.**—THE MEMOIRS OF THE BARON DE MARBOT. Translated from the French by ARTHUR JOHN BUTLER, M.A. Crown 8vo., 7s. 6d.

**Montrose.**—DEEDS OF MONTROSE: THE MEMOIRS OF JAMES, MARQUIS OF MONTROSE, 1639-1650. By the Rev. GEORGE WISHART, D.D. (Bishop of Edinburgh, 1662-1671). Translated, with Introduction, Notes, &c., and the original Latin (Part II. now first published), by the Rev. ALEXANDER MURDOCH, F.S.A., (Scot.) Canon of St. Mary's Cathedral, Edinburgh, Editor and Translator of the Grameid MS. and H. F. MORELAND SIMPSON, M.A. (Cantab.) F.S.A. (Scot.) Fettes College. 4to., 36s. net.

**Moore.**—DANTE AND HIS EARLY BIOGRAPHERS. By EDWARD MOORE, D.D., Principal of St. Edmund Hall, Oxford. Crown 8vo., 4s. 6d.

**Russell.**—A LIFE OF LORD JOHN RUSSELL (EARL RUSSELL, K.G.) By SPENCER WALPOLE. With 2 Portraits.
Cabinet Edition. 2 vols. Cr. 8vo., 12s.
Library Edition. 2 vols. 8vo., 36s.

**Seebohm.**—THE OXFORD REFORMERS—JOHN COLET, ERASMUS AND THOMAS MORE: a History of their Fellow-Work. By FREDERIC SEEBOHM. 8vo., 14s.

## Biography, Personal Memoirs, &c.—*continued.*

**Shakespeare.**—OUTLINES OF THE LIFE OF SHAKESPEARE. By J. O. HALLIWELL-PHILLIPPS. With numerous Illustrations and Fac-similes. 2 vols. Royal 8vo., £1 1s.

**Shakespeare's** TRUE LIFE. By JAMES WALTER. With 500 Illustrations by GERALD E. MOIRA. Imp. 8vo., 21s.

**Sherbrooke.**—LIFE AND LETTERS OF THE RIGHT HON. ROBERT LOWE, VISCOUNT SHERBROOKE, G.C.B., together with a Memoir of his Kinsman, Sir JOHN COAPE SHERBROOKE, G.C.B. By A. PATCHETT MARTIN. With 5 Portraits. 2 vols. 8vo., 36s.

**Stephen.**—ESSAYS IN ECCLESIASTICAL BIOGRAPHY. By Sir JAMES STEPHEN. Crown 8vo., 7s. 6d.

**Verney.**—MEMOIRS OF THE VERNEY FAMILY DURING THE CIVIL WAR. Compiled from the Letters and Illustrated by the Portraits at Claydon House, Bucks. By FRANCES PARTHENOPE VERNEY. With a Preface by S. R. GARDINER, M.A., LL.D. With 38 Portraits, Woodcuts and Fac-simile. 2 vols. Royal 8vo., 42s.

**Wagner.**—WAGNER AS I KNEW HIM. By FERDINAND PRAEGER. Crown 8vo., 7s. 6d.

**Walford.**—TWELVE ENGLISH AUTHORESSES. By L. B. WALFORD, Author of 'Mischief of Monica,' &c. With Portrait of Hannah More. Crown 8vo., 4s. 6d.

**Wellington.**—LIFE OF THE DUKE OF WELLINGTON. By the Rev. G. R. GLEIG, M.A. Crown 8vo., 3s. 6d.

**Wiseman.**—RICHARD WISEMAN, Surgeon and Sergeant-Surgeon to Charles II.: a Biographical Study. By Surgeon-General Sir T. LONGMORE, C.B., F.R.C.S., &c. With Portrait and Illustrations. 8vo., 10s. 6d.

**Wordsworth.**—Works by CHARLES WORDSWORTH, D.C.L., late Bishop of St. Andrews.

ANNALS OF MY EARLY LIFE, 1806-1846. 8vo., 15s.

ANNALS OF MY LIFE, 1847-1856. 8vo., 10s. 6d.

## Travel and Adventure.

**Arnold.**—SEAS AND LANDS. By Sir EDWIN ARNOLD, K.C.I.E., Author of 'The Light of the World,' &c. Reprinted letters from the 'Daily Telegraph'. With 71 Illustrations. Crown 8vo., 7s. 6d.

**Baker.**—Works by Sir SAMUEL WHITE BAKER.

EIGHT YEARS IN CEYLON. With 6 Illustrations. Crown 8vo., 3s. 6d.

THE RIFLE AND THE HOUND IN CEYLON. 6 Illustrations. Crown 8vo., 3s. 6d.

**Bent.**—THE RUINED CITIES OF MASHONALAND: being a Record of Excavation and Exploration in 1891. By J. THEODORE BENT, F.S.A., F.R.G.S. With a Chapter on the Orientation and Mensuration of the Temples. By R. M. W. SWAN. With Map, 13 Plates, and 104 Illustrations in the Text. Crown 8vo., 7s. 6d.

**Brassey.**—Works by LADY BRASSEY.

THE LAST VOYAGE TO INDIA AND AUSTRALIA IN THE 'SUNBEAM.' With Charts and Maps, and 40 Illustrations in Monotone (20 full-page), and nearly 200 Illustrations in the Text from Drawings by R. T. PRITCHETT. 8vo., 21s.

**Brassey.**—Works by LADY BRASSEY—*cont.*

A VOYAGE IN THE 'SUNBEAM'; OUR HOME ON THE OCEAN FOR ELEVEN MONTHS.

Library Edition. With 8 Maps and Charts, and 118 Illustrations. 8vo. 21s.
Cabinet Edition. With Map and 66 Illustrations. Crown 8vo., 7s. 6d.
Silver Library Edition. With 66 Illustrations. Crown 8vo., 3s. 6d.
Popular Edition. With 60 Illustrations. 4to., 6d. sewed, 1s. cloth.
School Edition. With 37 Illustrations. Fcp., 2s. cloth, or 3s. white parchment.

SUNSHINE AND STORM IN THE EAST.
Library Edition. With 2 Maps and 141 Illustrations. 8vo., 21s.
Cabinet Edition. With 2 Maps and 114 Illustrations. Crown 8vo., 7s. 6d.
Popular Edition. With 103 Illustrations. 4to., 6d. sewed, 1s. cloth.

IN THE TRADES, THE TROPICS, AND THE 'ROARING FORTIES'.
Cabinet Edition. With Map and 220 Illustrations. Crown 8vo., 7s. 6d.
Popular Edition. With 183 Illustrations. 4to., 6d. sewed, 1s. cloth.

THREE VOYAGES IN THE 'SUNBEAM'.
Popular Edition. With 346 Illustrations. 4to., 2s. 6d.

## Travel and Adventure—*continued.*

**Clutterbuck.**—ABOUT CEYLON AND BORNEO: being an Account of Two Visits to Ceylon, one to Borneo, and How We Fell Out on our Homeward Journey. By W. J. CLUTTERBUCK, Joint Author of 'Three in Norway'. With 47 Illustrations. Crown 8vo., 10s. 6d.

**Curzon.**—PERSIA AND THE PERSIAN QUESTION. With 9 Maps, 96 Illustrations, Appendices, and an Index. By the Hon. GEORGE N. CURZON, M.P., late Fellow of All Soul's College, Oxford. 2 vols. 8vo., 42s.

**Froude.**—Works by JAMES A. FROUDE.
OCEANA: or England and her Colonies. With 9 Illustrations. Crown 8vo., 2s. boards, 2s. 6d. cloth.
THE ENGLISH IN THE WEST INDIES; or, the Bow of Ulysses. With 9 Illustrations. Crown 8vo., 2s. boards, 2s. 6d. cloth.

**Howard.**—LIFE WITH TRANS-SIBERIAN SAVAGES. By B. DOUGLAS HOWARD, M.A. Crown 8vo., 6s.
\*\*\* *This work contains a description of the manners, customs, and daily life of the Sakhalin Ainos, and combines an account of native hunting and other adventures with scientific observation.*

**Howitt.**—VISITS TO REMARKABLE PLACES. Old Halls, Battle-Fields, Scenes, illustrative of Striking Passages in English History and Poetry. By WILLIAM HOWITT. With 80 Illustrations. Crown 8vo., 3s. 6d.

**Knight.**—Works by E. F. KNIGHT, author of the Cruise of the 'Falcon'.
THE CRUISE OF THE 'ALERTE': the narrative of a Search for Treasure on the Desert Island of Trinidad. With 2 Maps and 23 Illustrations. Crown 8vo., 3s. 6d.
WHERE THREE EMPIRES MEET: a Narrative of Recent Travel in Kashmir, Western Tibet, Baltistan, Ladak, Gilgit, and the adjoining Countries. With a Map and 54 Illustrations. 8vo. 18s.

**Lees and Clutterbuck.**—B. C. 1887: A RAMBLE IN BRITISH COLUMBIA. By J. A. Lees and W. J. Clutterbuck, Authors of 'Three in Norway'. With Map and 75 Illustrations. Crown 8vo., 3s. 6d.

**Mannering.**—WITH AXE AND ROPE IN THE NEW ZEALAND ALPS. By GEORGE EDWARD MANNERING. With 18 Illustrations and Map. 8vo., 12s. 6d.

**Nansen.**—Works by Dr. FRIDTJOF NANSEN.
THE FIRST CROSSING OF GREENLAND. With numerous Illustrations and a Map. Crown 8vo., 7s. 6d.
ESQUIMAUX LIFE. Translated by WILLIAM ARCHER. [*In the Press.*

**Norton.**—A HANDBOOK OF FLORIDA. By CHARLES L. NORTON. With 49 Maps and Plans. Fcp. 8vo., 5s.

**Pratt.**—TO THE SNOWS OF TIBET THROUGH CHINA. By A. E. PRATT, F.R.G.S. With 33 Illustrations and a Map. 8vo., 18s.

**Riley.**—ATHOS: or, the Mountain of the Monks. By ATHELSTAN RILEY, M.A. With Map and 29 Illustrations. 8vo., 21s.

THREE IN NORWAY. By Two of Them. With a Map and 59 Illustrations. Crown 8vo., 2s. boards, 2s. 6d. cloth.

**Whishaw.**—OUT OF DOORS IN TSARLAND: a Record of the Seeings and Doings of a Wanderer in Russia. By FRED. J. WHISHAW. Crown 8vo., 7s. 6d.

**Wolff.**—Works by HENRY W. WOLFF.
RAMBLES IN THE BLACK FOREST. Crown 8vo., 7s. 6d.
THE WATERING PLACES OF THE VOSGES. Crown 8vo., 4s. 6d.
THE COUNTRY OF THE VOSGES. With a Map. 8vo., 12s.

## Sport and Pastime.

AMERICAN WHIST, Illustrated: containing the Laws and Principles of the Games, the Analysis of the New Play and American Leads, and a series of Hands in Diagram, and combining Whist Universal and American Whist. By G. W. P. Fcp. 8vo. 6s. 6d.

**Campbell-Walker.**—THE CORRECT CARD: or, How to Play at Whist; a Whist Catechism. By Major A. CAMPBELL-WALKER, F.R.G.S. Fcp. 8vo., 2s. 6d.

**Chetwynd.**—RACING REMINISCENCES AND EXPERIENCES OF THE TURF. By Sir GEORGE CHETWYND, Bart. 2 vols. 8vo., 21s.

DEAD SHOT (THE): or, Sportsman's Complete Guide. Being a Treatise on the Use of the Gun, with Rudimentary and Finishing Lessons on the Art of Shooting Game of all kinds, also Game Driving, Wild-Fowl and Pigeon Shooting, Dog Breaking, etc. By MARKSMAN. Crown 8vo., 10s. 6d.

## Sport and Pastime—*continued*.
## THE BADMINTON LIBRARY.
Edited by the DUKE of BEAUFORT, K.G., assisted by ALFRED E. T. WATSON.

ATHLETICS AND FOOTBALL. By MONTAGUE SHEARMAN. With 51 Illustrations. Crown 8vo., 10s. 6d.

BIG GAME SHOOTING. By C. PHILLIPPS-WOLLEY, W. G. LITTLEDALE, Colonel PERCY, FRED. JACKSON, Major H. PERCY, W. C. OSWELL, Sir HENRY POTTINGER, Bart., and the EARL OF KILMOREY. With Contributions by other Writers. With Illustrations by CHARLES WHYMPER and others. 2 vols. [*In the press.*

BOATING. By W. B. WOODGATE. With an Introduction by the Rev. EDMOND WARRE, D.D., and a Chapter on 'Rowing at Eton,' by R. HARVEY MASON. With 49 Illustrations. Crown 8vo., 10s. 6d.

COURSING AND FALCONRY. By HARDING COX and the Hon. GERALD LASCELLES. With 76 Illustrations. Crown 8vo., 10s. 6d.

CRICKET. By A. G. STEEL and the Hon. R. H. LYTTELTON. With Contributions by ANDREW LANG, R. A. H. MITCHELL, W. G. GRACE, and F. GALE. With 63 Illustrations. Crown 8vo., 10s. 6d.

CYCLING. By VISCOUNT BURY (Earl of Albemarle), K.C.M.G., and G. LACY HILLIER. With 89 Illustrations. Crown 8vo., 10s. 6d.

DRIVING. By the DUKE OF BEAUFORT. With 65 Illustrations. Crown 8vo., 10s. 6d.

FENCING, BOXING, AND WRESTLING. By WALTER H. POLLOCK, F. C. GROVE, C. PREVOST, E. B. MITCHELL, and WALTER ARMSTRONG. With 42 Illustrations. Crown 8vo., 10s. 6d.

FISHING. By H. CHOLMONDELEY-PENNELL. With Contributions by the MARQUIS OF EXETER, HENRY R. FRANCIS, Major JOHN P. TRAHERNE, FREDERIC M. HALFORD, G. CHRISTOPHER DAVIES, R. B. MARSTON, &c.

Vol. I. Salmon, Trout, and Grayling. With 158 Illustrations. Crown 8vo., 10s. 6d.

Vol. II. Pike and other Coarse Fish. With 133 Illustrations. Crown 8vo., 10s. 6d.

GOLF. By HORACE G. HUTCHINSON, the Rt. Hon. A. J. BALFOUR, M.P., Sir W. G. SIMPSON, Bart., LORD WELLWOOD, H. S. C. EVERARD, ANDREW LANG, and other Writers. With 91 Illustrations. Crown 8vo., 10s. 6d.

HUNTING. By the DUKE OF BEAUFORT, K.G., and MOWBRAY MORRIS. With Contributions by the EARL OF SUFFOLK AND BERKSHIRE, Rev. E. W. L. DAVIES, DIGBY COLLINS, and ALFRED E. T. WATSON. With 53 Illustrations. Crown 8vo., 10s. 6d.

MOUNTAINEERING. By C. T. DENT, Sir F. POLLOCK, Bart., W. M. CONWAY, DOUGLAS FRESHFIELD, C. E. MATHEWS, C. PILKINGTON, and other Writers. With 108 Illustrations. Crown 8vo., 10s. 6d.

RACING AND STEEPLE-CHASING. *Racing:* By the EARL OF SUFFOLK AND BERKSHIRE and W. G. CRAVEN. With a Contribution by the Hon. F. LAWLEY. *Steeple-chasing:* By ARTHUR COVENTRY and ALFRED E. T. WATSON. With 58 Illustrations. Crown 8vo., 10s. 6d.

RIDING AND POLO. By Captain ROBERT WEIR, J. MORAY BROWN, the DUKE OF BEAUFORT, K.G., the EARL OF SUFFOLK AND BERKSHIRE, &c. With 59 Illustrations. Crown 8vo., 10s. 6d.

SHOOTING. By LORD WALSINGHAM and Sir RALPH PAYNE-GALLWEY, Bart. With Contributions by LORD LOVAT, LORD CHARLES LENNOX KERR, the Hon. G. LASCELLES, and A. J. STUART-WORTLEY.

Vol. I. Field and Covert. With 105 Illustrations. Crown 8vo., 10s. 6d.

Vol. II. Moor and Marsh. With 65 Illustrations. Crown 8vo., 10s. 6d.

SKATING, CURLING, TOBOGGANING, AND OTHER ICE SPORTS. By J. M. HEATHCOTE, C. G. TEBBUTT, T. MAXWELL WITHAM, the Rev. JOHN KERR, ORMOND HAKE, and Colonel BUCK. With 284 Illustrations. Crown 8vo., 10s. 6d.

SWIMMING. By ARCHIBALD SINCLAIR and WILLIAM HENRY, Hon. Secs. of the Life Saving Society. With 119 Illustrations. Crown 8vo., 10s. 6d.

TENNIS, LAWN TENNIS, RACKETS, AND FIVES. By J. M. and C. G. HEATHCOTE, E. O. PLEYDELL-BOUVERIE and A. C. AINGER. With Contributions by the Hon. A. LYTTELTON, W. C. MARSHALL, Miss L. DOD, H. W. W. WILBERFORCE, H. F. LAWFORD, &c. With 79 Illustrations. Crown 8vo., 10s. 6d.

YACHTING. By the EARL OF PEMBROKE, the MARQUIS OF DUFFERIN AND AVA, the EARL OF ONSLOW, LORD BRASSEY, Lieut.-Col. BUCKNILL, LEWIS HERRESHOFF, G. L. WATSON, E. F. KNIGHT, Rev. G. L. BLAKE, R.N., and G. C. DAVIES. With Illustrations by R. T. PRITCHETT, and from Photographs. 2 vols. [*In the press.*

## Sport and Pastime—*continued*.

**Falkener.**—GAMES, ANCIENT AND ORIENTAL, AND HOW TO PLAY THEM. Being the Games of the Ancient Egyptians, the Hiera Gramme of the Greeks, the Ludus Latrunculorum of the Romans, and the Oriental Games of Chess, Draughts, Backgammon, and Magic Squares. By EDWARD FALKENER. With numerous Photographs, Diagrams, &c. 8vo., 21s.

**Ford.**—THE THEORY AND PRACTICE OF ARCHERY. By HORACE FORD. New Edition, thoroughly Revised and Re-written by W. BUTT, M.A. With a Preface by C. J. LONGMAN, M.A. 8vo., 14s.

**Francis.**—A BOOK ON ANGLING: or, Treatise on the Art of Fishing in every Branch; including full Illustrated List of Salmon Flies. By FRANCIS FRANCIS. With Portrait and Coloured Plates. Crown 8vo., 15s.

**Hopkins.**—FISHING REMINISCENCES. By Major E. P. HOPKINS. With Illustrations. Crown 8vo., 6s. 6d.

**Lang.**—ANGLING SKETCHES. By ANDREW LANG. With 20 Illustrations by W. G. BURN MURDOCH. Crown 8vo., 7s. 6d.

**Longman.**—CHESS OPENINGS. By FREDERICK W. LONGMAN. Fcp. 8vo., 2s. 6d.

**Payne-Gallwey.**—Works by Sir RALPH PAYNE-GALLWEY, Bart.

LETTERS TO YOUNG SHOOTERS (First Series). On the Choice and use of a Gun. With Illustrations. Crown 8vo., 7s. 6d.

**Payne-Gallwey.**—Works by SIR RALPH PAYNE-GALLWEY, Bart.—*continued*.

LETTERS TO YOUNG SHOOTERS. (Second Series). On the Production, Preservation, and Killing of Game. With Directions in Shooting Wood-Pigeons and Breaking-in Retrievers. With a Portrait of the Author, and 103 Illustrations. Crown 8vo., 12s. 6d.

**Pole.**—THE THEORY OF THE MODERN SCIENTIFIC GAME OF WHIST. By W. POLE, F.R.S. Fcp. 8vo., 2s. 6d.

**Proctor.**—Works by RICHARD A. PROCTOR.
HOW TO PLAY WHIST: WITH THE LAWS AND ETIQUETTE OF WHIST. Crown 8vo., 3s. 6d.
HOME WHIST: an Easy Guide to Correct Play. 16mo., 1s.

**Ronalds.**—THE FLY-FISHER'S ENTOMOLOGY. By ALFRED RONALDS. With coloured Representations of the Natural and Artificial Insect. With 20 coloured Plates. 8vo., 14s.

WHIST IN DIAGRAMS: a Supplement to American Whist, Illustrated; being a Series of Hands played through, illustrating the American leads, the new play, the forms of Finesse, and celebrated coups of Masters. With Explanation and Analysis. By G. W. P. Fcp. 8vo., 6s. 6d.

**Wilcocks.**—THE SEA FISHERMAN: Comprising the Chief Methods of Hook and Line Fishing in the British and other Seas, and Remarks on Nets, Boats, and Boating. By J. C. WILCOCKS. Illustrated. Crown 8vo., 6s.

## Mental, Moral and Political Philosophy.
### *LOGIC, RHETORIC, PSYCHOLOGY, ETC.*

**Abbott.**—THE ELEMENTS OF LOGIC. By T. K. ABBOTT, B.D. 12mo., 3s.

**Aristotle.**—Works by.

THE POLITICS: G. Bekker's Greek Text of Books I., III., IV. (VII.), with an English Translation by W. E. BOLLAND, M.A.; and short Introductory Essays by A. LANG, M.A. Crown 8vo., 7s. 6d.

THE POLITICS: Introductory Essays. By ANDREW LANG (from Bolland and Lang's 'Politics'). Crown 8vo., 2s. 6d.

THE ETHICS: Greek Text, Illustrated with Essay and Notes. By Sir ALEXANDER GRANT, Bart. 2 vols. 8vo., 32s.

**Aristotle.**—Works by.

THE NICOMACHEAN ETHICS: Newly Translated into English. By ROBERT WILLIAMS. Crown 8vo., 7s. 6d.

AN INTRODUCTION TO ARISTOTLE'S ETHICS. Books I.-IV. (Book X. c. vi.-ix. in an Appendix). With a continuous Analysis and Notes. Intended for the use of Beginners and Junior Students. By the Rev. EDWARD MOORE, D.D., Principal of St. Edmund Hall, and late Fellow and Tutor of Queen's College, Oxford. Crown 8vo. 10s. 6d.

SELECTIONS FROM THE ORGANON. Edited by JOHN R. MAGRATH, D.D., Provost of Queen's College, Oxford. Small 8vo. 3s. 6d.

## Mental, Moral and Political Philosophy—*continued.*

**Bacon.**—Works by.
COMPLETE WORKS. Edited by R. L. ELLIS, J. SPEDDING and D. D. HEATH. 7 vols. 8vo., £3 13s. 6d.

THE ESSAYS: with Annotations. By RICHARD WHATELY, D.D. 8vo., 10s. 6d.

**Bain.**—Works by ALEXANDER BAIN, LL.D.
MENTAL SCIENCE. Crown 8vo. 6s. 6d.
MORAL SCIENCE. Crown 8vo., 4s. 6d.

*The two works as above can be had in one volume, price 10s. 6d.*

SENSES AND THE INTELLECT. 8vo., 15s.
EMOTIONS AND THE WILL. 8vo., 15s.
LOGIC, DEDUCTIVE AND INDUCTIVE. Part I. 4s. Part II. 6s. 6d.
PRACTICAL ESSAYS. Crown 8vo., 2s.

**Bray.**—Works by CHARLES BRAY.
THE PHILOSOPHY OF NECESSITY: or Law in Mind as in Matter. Cr. 8vo., 5s.

THE EDUCATION OF THE FEELINGS: a Moral System for Schools. Cr 8vo., 2s. 6d.

**Bray.**—ELEMENTS OF MORALITY, in Easy Lessons for Home and School Teaching. By Mrs. CHARLES BRAY. Cr. 8vo., 1s. 6d.

**Crozier.**—CIVILISATION AND PROGRESS. By JOHN BEATTIE CROZIER, M.D. With New Preface. More fully explaining the nature of the New Organon used in the solution of its problems. 8vo., 14s.

**Davidson.**—THE LOGIC OF DEFINITION, Explained and Applied. By WILLIAM L. DAVIDSON, M.A. Crown 8vo., 6s.

**Green.**—THE WORKS OF THOMAS HILL GREEN. Edited by R. L. NETTLESHIP. Vols. I. and II. Philosophical Works. 8vo., 16s. each.
Vol. III. Miscellanies. With Index to the three Volumes, and Memoir. 8vo., 21s.

**Hearn.**—THE ARYAN HOUSEHOLD: its Structure and its Development. An Introduction to Comparative Jurisprudence. By W. EDWARD HEARN. 8vo., 16s.

**Hodgson.**—Works by SHADWORTH H. HODGSON.
TIME AND SPACE: a Metaphysical Essay. 8vo., 16s.
THE THEORY OF PRACTICE: an Ethical Inquiry. 2 vols. 8vo., 24s.
THE PHILOSOPHY OF REFLECTION. 2 vols. 8vo., 21s.

**Hume.**—THE PHILOSOPHICAL WORKS OF DAVID HUME. Edited by T. H. GREEN and T. H. GROSE. 4 vols. 8vo., 56s. Or separately, Essays. 2 vols. 28s. Treatise of Human Nature. 2 vols. 28s.

**Johnstone.**—A SHORT INTRODUCTION TO THE STUDY OF LOGIC. By LAURENCE JOHNSTONE. With Questions. Cr. 8vo., 2s. 6d.

**Jones.**—AN INTRODUCTION TO GENERAL LOGIC. By E. E. CONSTANCE JONES, Author of 'Elements of Logic as a Science of Propositions'. Crown 8vo., 4s. 6d.

**Justinian.**—THE INSTITUTES OF JUSTINIAN: Latin Text, chiefly that of Huschke, with English Introduction, Translation, Notes, and Summary. By THOMAS C. SANDARS, M.A. 8vo., 18s.

**Kant.**—Works by IMMANUEL KANT.
CRITIQUE OF PRACTICAL REASON, AND OTHER WORKS ON THE THEORY OF ETHICS. Translated by T. K. ABBOTT, B.D. With Memoir. 8vo., 12s. 6d.
INTRODUCTION TO LOGIC, AND HIS ESSAY ON THE MISTAKEN SUBTILTY OF THE FOUR FIGURES. Translated by T. K. ABBOTT, and with Notes by S. T. COLERIDGE. 8vo., 6s.

**Killick.**—HANDBOOK TO MILL'S SYSTEM OF LOGIC. By Rev. A. H. KILLICK, M.A. Crown 8vo., 3s. 6d.

**Ladd.**—Works by GEORGE TURNBULL LADD.
ELEMENTS OF PHYSIOLOGICAL PSYCHOLOGY. 8vo., 21s.
OUTLINES OF PHYSIOLOGICAL PSYCHOLOGY. A Text-book of Mental Science for Academies and Colleges. 8vo., 12s.

**Lewes.**—THE HISTORY OF PHILOSOPHY, from Thales to Comte. By GEORGE HENRY LEWES. 2 vols. 8vo., 32s.

**Max Müller.**—Works by F. MAX MÜLLER.
THE SCIENCE OF THOUGHT. 8vo., 21s.
THREE INTRODUCTORY LECTURES ON THE SCIENCE OF THOUGHT. 8vo., 2s. 6d.

## Mental, Moral and Political Philosophy—*continued*.

**Mill.**—ANALYSIS OF THE PHENOMENA OF THE HUMAN MIND. By JAMES MILL. 2 vols. 8vo., 28s.

**Mill.**—Works by JOHN STUART MILL.
A SYSTEM OF LOGIC. Crown 8vo., 3s. 6d.
ON LIBERTY. Crown 8vo., 1s. 4d.
ON REPRESENTATIVE GOVERNMENT. Crown 8vo., 2s.
UTILITARIANISM. 8vo., 5s.
EXAMINATION OF SIR WILLIAM HAMILTON'S PHILOSOPHY. 8vo., 16s.
NATURE, THE UTILITY OF RELIGION, AND THEISM. Three Essays. 8vo., 5s.

**Monck.**—INTRODUCTION TO LOGIC. By H. S. MONCK. Crown 8vo., 5s.

**Ribot.**—THE PSYCHOLOGY OF ATTENTION. By TH. RIBOT. Crown 8vo., 3s.

**Sidgwick.**—DISTINCTION: and the Criticism of Belief. By ALFRED SIDGWICK. Crown 8vo., 6s.

**Stock.**—DEDUCTIVE LOGIC. By ST. GEORGE STOCK. Fcp. 8vo., 3s. 6d.

**Sully.**—Works by JAMES SULLY, Grote Professor of Mind and Logic at University College, London.
THE HUMAN MIND: a Text-book of Psychology. 2 vols. 8vo., 21s.
OUTLINES OF PSYCHOLOGY. 8vo., 9s.
THE TEACHER'S HANDBOOK OF PSYCHOLOGY. Crown 8vo., 5s.

**Swinburne.**—PICTURE LOGIC: an Attempt to Popularise the Science of Reasoning. By ALFRED JAMES SWINBURNE, M.A. With 23 Woodcuts. Post 8vo., 5s.

**Thompson.**—Works by DANIEL GREENLEAF THOMPSON.
THE PROBLEM OF EVIL: an Introduction to the Practical Sciences. 8vo., 10s. 6d.
A SYSTEM OF PSYCHOLOGY. 2 vols. 8vo., 36s.
THE RELIGIOUS SENTIMENTS OF THE HUMAN MIND. 8vo., 7s. 6d.
SOCIAL PROGRESS: an Essay. 8vo., 7s. 6d.
THE PHILOSOPHY OF FICTION IN LITERATURE: an Essay. Crown 8vo., 6s.

**Thomson.**—OUTLINES OF THE NECESSARY LAWS OF THOUGHT: a Treatise on Pure and Applied Logic. By WILLIAM THOMSON, D.D., formerly Lord Archbishop of York. Post 8vo., 6s.

**Webb.**—THE VEIL OF ISIS: a Series of Essays on Idealism. By T. E. WEBB. 8vo., 10s. 6d.

**Whately.**—Works by R. WHATELY, formerly Archbishop of Dublin.
BACON'S ESSAYS. With Annotation. By R. WHATELY. 8vo. 10s. 6d.
ELEMENTS OF LOGIC. Crown 8vo., 4s. 6d.
ELEMENTS OF RHETORIC. Crown 8vo., 4s. 6d.
LESSONS ON REASONING. Fcp. 8vo., 1s. 6d.

**Zeller.**—Works by Dr. EDWARD ZELLER, Professor in the University of Berlin.
HISTORY OF ECLECTICISM IN GREEK PHILOSOPHY. Translated by SARAH F. ALLEYNE. Crown 8vo., 10s. 6d.
THE STOICS, EPICUREANS, AND SCEPTICS. Translated by the Rev. O. J. REICHEL, M.A. Crown 8vo., 15s.
OUTLINES OF THE HISTORY OF GREEK PHILOSOPHY. Translated by SARAH F. ALLEYNE and EVELYN ABBOTT. Crown 8vo., 10s. 6d.
PLATO AND THE OLDER ACADEMY. Translated by SARAH F. ALLEYNE and ALFRED GOODWIN, B.A. Crown 8vo., 18s.
SOCRATES AND THE SOCRATIC SCHOOLS. Translated by the Rev. O. J. REICHEL, M.A. Crown 8vo., 10s. 6d.
THE PRE-SOCRATIC SCHOOLS: a History of Greek Philosophy from the Earliest Period to the time of Socrates. Translated by SARAH F. ALLEYNE. 2 vols. Crown 8vo., 30s.

## MANUALS OF CATHOLIC PHILOSOPHY.
*(Stonyhurst Series).*

A MANUAL OF POLITICAL ECONOMY. By C. S. DEVAS, M.A. Crown 8vo., 6s. 6d.

FIRST PRINCIPLES OF KNOWLEDGE. By JOHN RICKABY, S.J. Crown 8vo., 5s.

GENERAL METAPHYSICS. By JOHN RICKABY, S.J. Crown 8vo., 5s.

LOGIC. By RICHARD F. CLARKE, S.J. Crown 8vo., 5s.

MORAL PHILOSOPHY (ETHICS AND NATURAL LAW. By JOSEPH RICKABY, S.J. Crown 8vo., 5s.

NATURAL THEOLOGY. By BERNARD BOEDDER, S.J. Crown 8vo., 6s. 6d.

PSYCHOLOGY. By MICHAEL MAHER, S.J. Crown 8vo., 6s. 6d.

## History and Science of Language, &c.

**Davidson.**—LEADING AND IMPORTANT ENGLISH WORDS: Explained and Exemplified. By WILLIAM L. DAVIDSON, M.A. Fcp. 8vo., 3s. 6d.

**Farrar.**—LANGUAGE AND LANGUAGES: By F. W. FARRAR, D.D., F.R.S. Crown 8vo., 6s.

**Graham.**—ENGLISH SYNONYMS, Classified and Explained: with Practical Exercises. By G. F. GRAHAM. Fcp. 8vo., 6s.

**Max Müller.**—Works by F. MAX MÜLLER.
SELECTED ESSAYS ON LANGUAGE, MYTHOLOGY, AND RELIGION. 2 vols. Crown 8vo., 16s.
THE SCIENCE OF LANGUAGE, Founded on Lectures delivered at the Royal Institution in 1861 and 1863. 2 vols. Crown 8vo., 21s.
BIOGRAPHIES OF WORDS, AND THE HOME OF THE ARYAS. Crown 8vo., 7s. 6d.
THREE LECTURES ON THE SCIENCE OF LANGUAGE, AND ITS PLACE IN GENERAL EDUCATION, delivered at Oxford, 1889. Crown 8vo., 3s.

**Paul.**—PRINCIPLES OF THE HISTORY OF LANGUAGE. By HERMANN PAUL. Translated by H. A. STRONG. 8vo., 10s. 6d.

**Roget.**—THESAURUS OF ENGLISH WORDS AND PHRASES. Classified and Arranged so as to Facilitate the Expression of Ideas and assist in Literary Composition. By PETER MARK ROGET, M.D., F.R.S. Recomposed throughout, enlarged and improved, partly from the Author's Notes, and with a full Index, by the Author's Son, JOHN LEWIS ROGET. Crown 8vo. 10s. 6d.

**Strong, Logeman, and Wheeler.**—INTRODUCTION TO THE STUDY OF THE HISTORY OF LANGUAGE. By HERBERT A. STRONG, M.A., LL.D., WILLEM S. LOGEMAN, and BENJAMIN IDE WHEELER. 8vo., 10s. 6d.

**Wade.**—ELEMENTARY CHAPTERS IN COMPARATIVE PHILOLOGY. By G. WOOSUNG WADE, M.A. Crown 8vo., 2s. 6d.

**Whately.**—ENGLISH SYNONYMS. By E. JANE WHATELY. Fcp. 8vo., 3s.

## Political Economy and Economics.

**Ashley.**—ENGLISH ECONOMIC HISTORY AND THEORY. By W. J. ASHLEY, M.A. Crown 8vo., Part I., 5s. Part II. 10s. 6d.

**Bagehot.**—Works by WALTER BAGEHOT.
ECONOMIC STUDIES. 8vo., 10s. 6d.
THE POSTULATES OF ENGLISH POLITICAL ECONOMY. Crown 8vo., 2s. 6d.

**Crump.**—AN INVESTIGATION INTO THE CAUSES OF THE GREAT FALL IN PRICES which took place coincidently with the Demonetisation of Silver by Germany. By ARTHUR CRUMP. 8vo., 6s.

**Devas.**—A MANUAL OF POLITICAL ECONOMY. By C. S. DEVAS, M.A. Crown 8vo., 6s. 6d. (*Manuals of Catholic Philosophy*.)

**Dowell.**—A HISTORY OF TAXATION AND TAXES IN ENGLAND, from the Earliest Times to the Year 1885. By STEPHEN DOWELL. (4 vols. 8vo.) Vols. I. and II. The History of Taxation, 21s. Vols. III. and IV. The History of Taxes, 21s.

**Jordan.**—THE STANDARD OF VALUE. By WILLIAM LEIGHTON JORDAN. 8vo., 6s.

**Leslie.**—ESSAYS IN POLITICAL ECONOMY. By T. E. CLIFFE LESLIE. 8vo., 10s. 6d.

**Macleod.**—Works by HENRY DUNNING MACLEOD, M.A.
THE ELEMENTS OF BANKING. Crown 8vo., 3s. 6d.
THE THEORY AND PRACTICE OF BANKING. Vol. I. 8vo., 12s. Vol. II. 14s.
THE THEORY OF CREDIT. 8vo. Vol. I. 7s. 6d. Vol. II., Part I., 4s. 6d. Vol. II. Part II., 10s. 6d.

**Meath.**—Works by The EARL OF MEATH.
SOCIAL ARROWS: Reprinted Articles on various Social Subjects. Crown 8vo., 5s.
PROSPERITY OR PAUPERISM? Physical, Industrial, and Technical Training. 8vo., 5s.

**Mill.**—POLITICAL ECONOMY. By JOHN STUART MILL.
Silver Library Edition. Crown 8vo., 3s. 6d.
Library Edition. 2 vols. 8vo., 30s.

**Shirres.**—AN ANALYSIS OF THE IDEAS OF ECONOMICS. By L. P. SHIRRES, B.A., sometime Finance Under-Secretary of the Government of Bengal. Crown 8vo., 6s.

**Symes.**—POLITICAL ECONOMY: a Short Text-book of Political Economy. With Problems for Solution, and Hints for Supplementary Reading. By Professor J. E. SYMES, M.A., of University College, Nottingham. Crown 8vo., 2s. 6d.

**Toynbee.**—LECTURES ON THE INDUSTRIAL REVOLUTION OF THE 18th CENTURY IN ENGLAND. By ARNOLD TOYNBEE. 8vo., 10s. 6d.

**Wilson.**—Works by A. J. WILSON. Chiefly reprinted from *The Investors' Review*.
PRACTICAL HINTS TO SMALL INVESTORS. Crown 8vo., 1s.
PLAIN ADVICE ABOUT LIFE INSURANCE. Crown 8vo., 1s.

**Wolff.**—PEOPLE'S BANKS: a Record of Social and Economic Success. By HENRY W. WOLFF. 8vo., 7s. 6d.

## Evolution, Anthropology, &c.

**Clodd.**—THE STORY OF CREATION: a Plain Account of Evolution. By EDWARD CLODD. With 77 Illustrations. Crown 8vo., 3s. 6d.

**Huth.**—THE MARRIAGE OF NEAR KIN, considered with Respect to the Law of Nations, the Result of Experience, and the Teachings of Biology. By ALFRED HENRY HUTH. Royal 8vo., 21s.

**Lang.**—CUSTOM AND MYTH: Studies of Early Usage and Belief. By ANDREW LANG, M.A. With 15 Illustrations. Crown 8vo., 3s. 6d.

**Lubbock.**—THE ORIGIN OF CIVILISATION and the Primitive Condition of Man. By Sir J. LUBBOCK, Bart., M.P. With 5 Plates and 20 Illustrations in the Text. 8vo., 18s.

**Romanes.**—Works by GEORGE JOHN ROMANES, M.A., LL.D., F.R.S.
 DARWIN, AND AFTER DARWIN: an Exposition of the Darwinian Theory, and a Discussion on Post-Darwinian Questions. Part I. The Darwinian Theory. With Portrait of Darwin and 125 Illustrations. Crown 8vo., 10s. 6d.
 AN EXAMINATION OF WEISMANNISM. Crown 8vo.

## Classical Literature.

**Abbott.**—HELLENICA. A Collection of Essays on Greek Poetry, Philosophy, History, and Religion. Edited by EVELYN ABBOTT, M.A., LL.D. 8vo., 16s.

**Æschylus.**—EUMENIDES OF ÆSCHYLUS. With Metrical English Translation. By J. F. DAVIES. 8vo., 7s.

**Aristophanes.**—THE ACHARNIANS OF ARISTOPHANES, translated into English Verse. By R. Y. TYRRELL. Crown 8vo., 1s.

**Becker.**—Works by Professor BECKER.
 GALLUS: or, Roman Scenes in the Time of Augustus. Illustrated. Post 8vo., 7s. 6d.
 CHARICLES: or, Illustrations of the Private Life of the Ancient Greeks. Illustrated. Post 8vo., 7s. 6d.

**Cicero.**—CICERO'S CORRESPONDENCE. By R. Y. TYRRELL. Vols. I., II., III., 8vo., each 12s.

**Clerke.**—FAMILIAR STUDIES IN HOMER. By AGNES M. CLERKE. Crown 8vo., 7s. 6d.

**Farnell.**—GREEK LYRIC POETRY: a Complete Collection of the Surviving Passages from the Greek Song-Writting. Arranged with Prefatory Articles, Introductory Matter and Commentary. By GEORGE S. FARNELL, M.A. With 5 Plates. 8vo., 16s.

**Harrison.**—MYTHS OF THE ODYSSEY IN ART AND LITERATURE. By JANE E. HARRISON. Illustrated with Outline Drawings. 8vo., 18s.

**Lang.**—HOMER AND THE EPIC. By ANDREW LANG. Crown 8vo., 9s. net.

**Mackail.**—SELECT EPIGRAMS FROM THE GREEK ANTHOLOGY. By J. W. MACKAIL, Fellow of Balliol College, Oxford. Edited with a Revised Text, Introduction, Translation, and Notes. 8vo., 16s.

**Plato.**—PARMENIDES OF PLATO, Text, with Introduction, Analysis, &c. By T. MAGUIRE. 8vo., 7s. 6d.

**Rich.**—A DICTIONARY OF ROMAN AND GREEK ANTIQUITIES. By A. RICH, B.A. With 2000 Woodcuts. Crown 8vo., 7s. 6d.

**Sophocles.**—Translated into English Verse. By ROBERT WHITELAW, M.A., Assistant Master in Rugby School; late Fellow of Trinity College, Cambridge. Crown 8vo., 8s. 6d.

**Tyrrell.**—TRANSLATIONS INTO GREEK AND LATIN VERSE. Edited by R. Y. TYRRELL. 8vo., 6s.

**Virgil.**—THE ÆNEID OF VIRGIL. Translated into English Verse by JOHN CONINGTON. Crown 8vo., 6s.
 THE POEMS OF VIRGIL. Translated into English Prose by JOHN CONINGTON. Crown 8vo., 6s.
 THE ÆNEID OF VIRGIL, freely translated into English Blank Verse. By W. J. THORNHILL. Crown 8vo., 7s. 6d.
 THE ÆNEID OF VIRGIL. Books I. to VI. Translated into English Verse by JAMES RHOADES. Crown 8vo., 5s.
 THE ECLOGUES AND GEORGICS OF VIRGIL. Translated from the Latin by J. W. MACKAIL, M.A., Fellow of Balliol College, Oxford. Printed on Dutch Handmade Paper. Royal 16mo., 5s.

**Wilkin.**—THE GROWTH OF THE HOMERIC POEMS. By G. WILKIN. 8vo., 6s.

## Poetry and the Drama.

**Allingham.**—Works by WILLIAM ALLINGHAM.
IRISH SONGS AND POEMS. With Frontis- of the Waterfall of Asaroe. Fcp. 8vo., 6s.
LAURENCE BLOOMFIELD. With Portrait of the Author. Fcp. 8vo., 3s. 6d.
FLOWER PIECES; DAY AND NIGHT SONGS; BALLADS. With 2 Designs by D. G. ROSETTI. Fcp. 8vo., 6s.; large paper edition, 12s.
LIFE AND PHANTASY: with Frontispiece by Sir J. E. MILLAIS, Bart., and Design by ARTHUR HUGHES. Fcp. 8vo., 6s.; large paper edition, 12s.
THOUGHT AND WORD, AND ASHBY MANOR: a Play. With Portrait of the Author (1865), and four Theatrical Scenes drawn by Mr. Allingham. Fcp. 8vo., 6s.; large paper edition, 12s.
BLACKBERRIES. Imperial 16mo., 6s.
*Sets of the above 6 vols. may be had in uniform Half-parchment binding, price 30s.*

**Armstrong.**—Works by G. F. SAVAGE-ARMSTRONG.
POEMS: Lyrical and Dramatic. Fcp. 8vo., 6s.
KING SAUL. (The Tragedy of Israel, Part I.) Fcp. 8vo., 5s.
KING DAVID. (The Tragedy of Israel, Part II.) Fcp. 8vo., 6s.
KING SOLOMON. (The Tragedy of Israel, Part III.) Fcp. 8vo., 6s.
UGONE: a Tragedy. Fcp. 8vo., 6s.
A GARLAND FROM GREECE: Poems. Fcp. 8vo., 7s. 6d.
STORIES OF WICKLOW: Poems. Fcp. 8vo., 7s. 6d.
MEPHISTOPHELES IN BROADCLOTH: a Satire. Fcp. 8vo., 4s.
ONE IN THE INFINITE: a Poem. Crown 8vo., 7s. 6d.

**Armstrong.**—THE POETICAL WORKS OF EDMUND J. ARMSTRONG. Fcp. 8vo., 5s.

**Arnold.**—Works by Sir EDWIN ARNOLD, K.C.I.E., Author of 'The Light of Asia,' &c.
THE LIGHT OF THE WORLD: or the Great Consummation. A Poem. Crown 8vo., 7s. 6d. net.
Presentation Edition. With Illustrations by W. HOLMAN HUNT, &c. 4to., 20s. net.
POTIPHAR'S WIFE, and other Poems. Crown 8vo., 5s. net.
ADZUMA: or the Japanese Wife. A Play. Crown 8vo., 6s. 6d. net.

**Barrow.**—THE SEVEN CITIES OF THE DEAD, and other Poems. By Sir JOHN CROKER BARROW, Bart. Fcp. 8vo., 5s.

**Bell.**—Works by Mrs HUGH BELL.
CHAMBER COMEDIES: a Collection of Plays and Monologues for the Drawing Room. Crown 8vo., 6s.
NURSERY COMEDIES: Twelve Tiny Plays for Children. Fcp. 8vo., 1s. 6d.

**Björnsen.**—PASTOR LANG: A PLAY. By BJÖRNSTJERNE BJÖRNSEN. Translated by WILLIAM WILSON.

**Dante.**—LA COMMEDIA DI DANTE. A New Text, carefully Revised with the aid of the most recent Editions and Collations. Small 8vo., 6s.

**Goethe.**
FAUST, Part I., the German Text, with Introduction and Notes. By ALBERT M. SELSS, Ph.D., M.A. Crown 8vo., 5s.
FAUST. Translated, with Notes. By T. E. WEBB. 8vo., 12s. 6d.
FAUST. The First Part. A New Translation, chiefly in Blank Verse; with Introduction and Notes. By JAMES ADEY BIRDS. Crown 8vo., 6s.
FAUST. The Second Part. A New Translation in Verse. By JAMES ADEY BIRDS. Crown 8vo., 6s.

**Haggard.**—LIFE AND ITS AUTHOR: an Essay in Verse. By ELLA HAGGARD. With a Memoir by H. RIDER HAGGARD, and Portrait. Fcp. 8vo., 3s. 6d.

**Ingelow.**—Works by JEAN INGELOW.
POETICAL WORKS. 2 vols. Fcp. 8vo., 12s.
LYRICAL AND OTHER POEMS. Selected from the Writings of JEAN INGELOW. Fcp. 8vo., 2s. 6d. cloth plain, 3s. cloth gilt.

**Lang.**—Works by ANDREW LANG.
GRASS OF PARNASSUS. Fcp. 8vo., 2s. 6d. net.
BALLADS OF BOOKS. Edited by ANDREW LANG. Fcp. 8vo., 6s.
THE BLUE POETRY BOOK. Edited by ANDREW LANG. Special Edition, printed on Indian paper. With Notes, but without Illustrations. Crown 8vo., 7s. 6d.

## Poetry and the Drama—*continued*.

**Lecky.**—POEMS. By W. E. H. LECKY. Fcp. 8vo., 5s.

**Leyton.**—Works by FRANK LEYTON.
THE SHADOWS OF THE LAKE, and other Poems. Crown 8vo., 7s. 6d. Cheap Edition. Crown 8vo., 3s. 6d.
SKELETON LEAVES: Poems. Crown 8vo. 6s.

**Lytton.**—Works by THE EARL OF LYTTON (OWEN MEREDITH).
MARAH. Fcp. 8vo., 6s. 6d.
KING POPPY: a Fantasia. With 1 Plate and Design on Title-Page by ED. BURNE-JONES, A.R.A. Crown 8vo., 10s. 6d.
THE WANDERER. Crown 8vo., 10s. 6d.

**Macaulay.**—LAYS OF ANCIENT ROME, &c. By Lord MACAULAY.
Illustrated by G. SCHARF. Fcp. 4to., 10s. 6d.
——————— Bijou Edition. 18mo., 2s. 6d. gilt top.
——————— Popular Edition. Fcp. 4to., 6d. sewed, 1s. cloth.
Illustrated by J. R. WEGUELIN. Crown 8vo., 3s. 6d.
Annotated Edition. Fcp. 8vo., 1s. sewed, 1s. 6d. cloth.

**Nesbit.**—Works by E. NESBIT (Mrs. HUBERT BLAND).
LEAVES OF LIFE: Verses. Cr. 8vo., 5s.
LAYS AND LEGENDS. First Series. Crown 8vo., 3s. 6d. Second Series. With Portrait. Crown 8vo., 5s.

**Piatt.**—AN ENCHANTED CASTLE, AND OTHER POEMS: Pictures, Portraits, and People in Ireland. By SARAH PIATT. Crown 8vo. 3s. 6d.

**Piatt.**—Works by JOHN JAMES PIATT.
IDYLS AND LYRICS OF THE OHIO VALLEY. Crown 8vo., 5s.
LITTLE NEW WORLD IDYLS. Cr. 8vo.

**Rhoades.**—TERESA AND OTHER POEMS. By JAMES RHOADES. Crown 8vo., 3s. 6d.

**Riley.**—OLD FASHIONED ROSES: Poems. By JAMES WHITCOMB RILEY. 12mo., 5s.

**Shakespeare.** — BOWDLER'S FAMILY SHAKESPEARE. With 36 Woodcuts. 1 vol. 8vo., 14s. Or in 6 vols. Fcp. 8vo., 21s.
THE SHAKESPEARE BIRTHDAY BOOK. By MARY F. DUNBAR. 32mo., 1s. 6d. Drawing Room Edition, with Photographs. Fcp. 8vo., 10s. 6d.

**Stevenson.** — A CHILD'S GARDEN OF VERSES. By ROBERT LOUIS STEVENSON. Small Fcp. 8vo., 5s.

## Works of Fiction, Humour, &c.

ATELIER (THE) DU LYS: or, an Art Student in the Reign of Terror. Crown 8vo., 2s. 6d.

BY THE SAME AUTHOR.

MADEMOISELLE MORI: a Tale of Modern Rome. Crown 8vo., 2s. 6d.
THAT CHILD. Illustrated by GORDON BROWNE. Crown 8vo., 2s. 6d.
UNDER A CLOUD. Crown 8vo., 2s. 6d.
THE FIDDLER OF LUGAU. With Illustrations by W. RALSTON, Crown 8vo., 2s. 6d.
A CHILD OF THE REVOLUTION. With Illustrations by C. J. STANILAND. Crown 8vo., 2s. 6d.
HESTER'S VENTURE: a Novel. Crown 8vo., 2s. 6d.
IN THE OLDEN TIME: a Tale of the Peasant War in Germany. Crown 8vo., 2s. 6d.
THE YOUNGER SISTER: a Tale. Cr. 8vo., 6s.

**Anstey.**—Works by F. ANSTEY, Author of 'Vice Versa'.
THE BLACK POODLE, and other Stories. Crown 8vo., 2s. boards, 2s. 6d. cloth.
VOCES POPULI. Reprinted from 'Punch'. With Illustrations by J. BERNARD PARTRIDGE. First Series. Fcp. 4to., 5s. Second Series. Fcp. 4to., 6s.
THE TRAVELLING COMPANIONS. Reprinted from 'Punch'. With Illustrations by J. BERNARD PARTRIDGE. Post 4to., 5s.
THE MAN FROM BLANKLEY'S: a Story in Scenes, and other Sketches. With Illustrations by J. BERNARD PARTRIDGE. Fcp. 4to., 6s.

**Baker.**—BY THE WESTERN SEA. By JAMES BAKER, Author of 'John Westacott'. Crown 8vo., 3s. 6d.

**Beaconsfield.**—Works by the Earl of BEACONSFIELD.
NOVELS AND TALES. Cheap Edition. Complete in 11 vols. Cr. 8vo., 1s. 6d. each.

| | |
|---|---|
| Vivian Grey. | Henrietta Temple. |
| The Young Duke, &c. | Venetia. Tancred. |
| Alroy, Ixion, &c. | Coningsby. Sybil. |
| Contarini Fleming, &c. | Lothair. Endymion. |

## Works of Fiction, Humour, &c.—*continued.*

**Beaconsfield.**—Works by the Earl of BEACONSFIELD.

NOVELS AND TALES. The Hughenden Edition. With 2 Portraits and 11 Vignettes. 11 vols. Crown 8vo., 42s.

**Chilton.**—THE HISTORY OF A FAILURE, and other Tales. By E. CHILTON. Fcp. 8vo., 3s. 6d.

**Comyn.**—ATHERSTONE PRIORY: a Tale. By L. N. COMYN. Crown 8vo., 2s. 6d.

**Deland.**—Works by MARGARET DELAND, Author of 'John Ward'.
THE STORY OF A CHILD. Cr. 8vo., 5s.
MR. TOMMY DOVE, and other Stories. Crown 8vo. 6s.

DOROTHY WALLIS: an Autobiography. With Preface by WALTER BESANT. Crown 8vo., 6s.

**Dougall.**—Works by L. DOUGALL.
BEGGARS ALL Crown 8vo., 3s. 6d.
WHAT NECESSITY KNOWS. 3 vols. Crown 8vo.

**Doyle.**—Works by A. CONAN DOYLE.
MICAH CLARKE: A Tale of Monmouth's Rebellion. With Frontispiece and Vignette. Cr. 8vo., 3s. 6d.
THE CAPTAIN OF THE POLESTAR, and other Tales. Cr. 8vo., 3s. 6d.
THE REFUGEES: A Tale of Two Continents. Cr. 8vo., 6s.

**Farrar.**—DARKNESS AND DAWN: or, Scenes in the Days of Nero. An Historic Tale. By Archdeacon FARRAR. Cr. 8vo., 7s. 6d.

**Froude.**—THE TWO CHIEFS OF DUNBOY: an Irish Romance of the Last Century. by J. A. FROUDE. Cr. 8vo., 3s. 6d.

**Haggard.**—Works by H. RIDER HAGGARD.
SHE. With 32 Illustrations by M. GREIFFENHAGEN and C. H. M. KERR. Cr. 8vo., 3s. 6d.
ALLAN QUATERMAIN. With 31 Illustrations by C. H. M. KERR. Cr. 8vo., 3s. 6d.
MAIWA'S REVENGE: or, The War of the Little Hand. Cr. 8vo., 1s. boards, 1s. 6d. cloth.
COLONEL QUARITCH, V.C. Cr. 8vo. 3s. 6d.

**Haggard.**—Works by H. RIDER HAGGARD. —*continued.*

CLEOPATRA. With 29 Full-page Illustrations by M. GREIFFENHAGEN and R. CATON WOODVILLE. Cr. 8vo., 3s. 6d.
BEATRICE. Cr. 8vo., 3s. 6d.
ERIC BRIGHTEYES. With 17 Plates and 34 Illustrations in the Text by LANCELOT SPEED. Cr. 8vo., 3s. 6d.
NADA THE LILY. With 23 Illustrations by C. H. M. KERR. Cr. 8vo., 6s.
MONTEZUMA'S DAUGHTER. Cr. 8vo., 6s.

**Haggard and Lang.**—THE WORLD'S DESIRE. By H. RIDER HAGGARD and ANDREW LANG. Cr. 8vo. 6s.

**Harte.**—Works by BRET HARTE.
IN THE CARQUINEZ WOODS. Fcp. 8vo. 1s. 6d.
ON THE FRONTIER, &c. 16mo., 1s.
BY SHORE AND SEDGE. 16mo., 1s.
\*\*\* Three Works complete in one Volume. Cr. 8vo., 3s. 6d.

**Hyne.**—THE NEW EDEN: a Story. By C. J. Cutcliffe Hyne. With Frontispiece and Vignette. Cr. 8vo., 2s. 6d.

KEITH DERAMORE: a Novel. By the Author of 'Miss Molly'. Cr. 8vo., 6s.

**Lyall.**—THE AUTOBIOGRAPHY OF A SLANDER. By EDNA LYALL, Author of 'Donovan,' &c. Fcp. 8vo., 1s. sewed.
Presentation Edition. With 20 Illustrations by LANCELOT SPEED. Cr. 8vo., 5s.

**Matthews.**—Works by BRANDER MATTHEWS.
A FAMILY TREE, and other Stories. Cr. 8vo., 6s.
WITH MY FRIENDS: Tales told in Partnership. With an Introductory Essay on the Art and Mystery of Collaboration. Cr. 8vo., 6s.

**Melville.**—Works by G. J. WHYTE MELVILLE.

| The Gladiators. | Holmby House. |
| The Interpreter. | Kate Coventry. |
| Good for Nothing. | Digby Grand. |
| The Queen's Maries. | General Bounce. |
| Cr. 8vo., 1s. 6d. each. | |

**O'Brien.**—WHEN WE WERE BOYS: a Novel. By WILLIAM O'BRIEN. Cr. 8vo., 2s. 6d.

## Works of Fiction, Humour, &c.—*continued.*

**Oliphant.**—Works by Mrs. OLIPHANT.
MADAM. Cr. 8vo., 1s. 6d.
IN TRUST. Cr. 8vo., 1s. 6d.

**Parr.**—CAN THIS BE LOVE? By Mrs. PARR, Author of 'Dorothy Fox'. Crown 8vo. 6s.

**Payn.**—Works by JAMES PAYN.
THE LUCK OF THE DARRELLS. Cr. 8vo., 1s. 6d.
THICKER THAN WATER. Cr. 8vo., 1s. 6d.

**Phillipps-Wolley.**—SNAP: a Legend of the Lone Mountain. By C. PHILLIPPS-WOLLEY. With 13 Illustrations by H. G. WILLINK. Cr. 8vo., 3s. 6d.

**Robertson.**—THE KIDNAPPED SQUATTER, and other Australian Tales. By. A. ROBERTSON. Cr. 8vo., 6s.

**Sewell.**—Works by ELIZABETH M. SEWELL.
A Glimpse of the World.   Amy Herbert.
Laneton Parsonage.        Cleve Hall.
Margaret Percival.        Gertrude.
Katharine Ashton.         Home Life.
The Earl's Daughter.      After Life.
The Experience of Life.   Ursula. Ivors.
Cr. 8vo., 1s. 6d. each cloth plain. 2s. 6d. each cloth extra, gilt edges.

**Stevenson.**—Works by ROBERT LOUIS STEVENSON.
STRANGE CASE OF DR. JEKYLL AND MR. HYDE. Fcp. 8vo., 1s. sewed. 1s. 6d. cloth.
THE DYNAMITER. Fcp. 8vo., 1s. sewed, 1s. 6d. cloth.

**Stevenson and Osbourne.**—THE WRONG BOX. By ROBERT LOUIS STEVENSON and LLOYD OSBOURNE. Cr. 8vo., 3s. 6d.

**Sturgis.**—AFTER TWENTY YEARS, another Stories. By JULIAN STURGIS Cr. 8vo., 6s.

**Suttner.**—LAY DOWN YOUR ARMS (*Di Waffen Nieder*): The Autobiography of Martha Tilling. By BERTHA VON SUTTNER. Translated by T. HOLMES. C: 8vo., 7s. 6d.

**Thompson.**—A MORAL DILEMMA: Novel. By ANNIE THOMPSON. Crow 8vo., 6s.

**Tirebuck.**—Works by WILLIAM TIREBUCK
DORRIE. Crown 8vo. 6s.
SWEETHEART GWEN. Crown 8vo., 6s.

**Trollope.**—Works by ANTHONY TROLLOPE.
THE WARDEN. Cr. 8vo., 1s. 6d.
BARCHESTER TOWERS. Cr. 8vo., 1s 6d.

**Walford.**—Works by L. B. WALFORD Author of 'Mr. Smith'.
THE MISCHIEF OF MONICA: a Novel Cr. 8vo., 2s. 6d.
THE ONE GOOD GUEST: a Story. C: 8vo., 6s.

**West.**—HALF-HOURS WITH THE MILLIONAIRES: Showing how much harder it to spend a million than to make i Edited by B. B. WEST. Cr. 8vo., 6s.

**Weyman.**—Works by STANLEY J. WEYMAN.
THE HOUSE OF THE WOLF: a Romance Cr. 8vo., 3s. 6d.
A GENTLEMAN OF FRANCE. 3 vols Cr. 8vo.              [*In the Pres.*

## Popular Science (Natural History, &c.).

**Butler.**—OUR HOUSEHOLD INSECTS. By E. A. BUTLER. With numerous Illustrations.                    [*In the Press.*

**Furneaux.**—THE OUTDOOR WORLD; or The Young Collector's Handbook. By W. FURNEAUX, F.R.G.S. With numerous Illustrations including 6 Plates in Colours. Crown 8vo., 7s. 6d.

**Hartwig.**—Works by Dr. GEORGE HARTWIG.
THE SEA AND ITS LIVING WONDERS With 12 Plates and 303 Woodcuts. 8vo 7s. net.
THE TROPICAL WORLD. With 8 Plate and 172 Woodcuts. 8vo., 7s. net.
THE POLAR WORLD. With 3 Maps, Plates and 85 Woodcuts. 8vo., 7s. net.

## Popular Science (Natural History, &c.)—*continued.*

**Hartwig.**—Works by Dr. GEORGE HARTWIG—*continued.*

THE SUBTERRANEAN WORLD. With 3 Maps and 80 Woodcuts. 8vo., 7s. net.

THE AERIAL WORLD. With Map, 8 Plates and 60 Woodcuts. 8vo., 7s. net.

HEROES OF THE POLAR WORLD. 19 Illustrations. Cr. 8vo., 2s.

WONDERS OF THE TROPICAL FORESTS. 40 Illustrations. Cr. 8vo., 2s.

WORKERS UNDER THE GROUND. 29 Illustrations. Cr. 8vo., 2s.

MARVELS OVER OUR HEADS. 29 Illustrations. Cr. 8vo., 2s.

SEA MONSTERS AND SEA BIRDS. 75 Illustrations. Cr. 8vo., 2s. 6d.

DENIZENS OF THE DEEP. 117 Illustrations. Cr. 8vo., 2s. 6d.

VOLCANOES AND EARTHQUAKES. 30 Illustrations. Cr. 8vo., 2s. 6d.

WILD ANIMALS OF THE TROPICS. 66 Illustrations. Cr. 8vo., 3s. 6d.

**Helmholtz.**— POPULAR LECTURES ON SCIENTIFIC SUBJECTS. By Professor HELMHOLTZ. With 68 Woodcuts. 2 vols. Cr. 8vo., 3s. 6d. each.

**Lydekker.**—PHASES OF ANIMAL LIFE, PAST AND PRESENT. By. R. LYDEKKER, B.A. With 82 Illustrations. Cr. 8vo., 6s.

**Proctor.**—Works by RICHARD A. PROCTOR. *And see Messrs. Longmans & Co.'s Catalogue of Scientific Works.*

LIGHT SCIENCE FOR LEISURE HOURS. Familiar Essays on Scientific Subjects. 3 vols. Cr. 8vo., 5s. each.

CHANCE AND LUCK: a Discussion of the Laws of Luck, Coincidence, Wagers, Lotteries and the Fallacies of Gambling, &c. Cr. 8vo., 2s. boards. 2s. 6d. cloth.

ROUGH WAYS MADE SMOOTH. Familiar Essays on Scientific Subjects. Cr. 8vo., 5s. Silver Library Edition. Cr. 8vo., 3s. 6d.

PLEASANT WAYS IN SCIENCE. Cr. 8vo., 5s. Silver Library Edition. Cr. 8vo., 3s. 6d.

THE GREAT PYRAMID, OBSERVATORY, TOMB AND TEMPLE. With Illustrations. Cr. 8vo., 5s.

NATURE STUDIES. By R. A. PROCTOR, GRANT ALLEN, A. WILSON, T. FOSTER and E. CLODD. Cr. 8vo., 5s. Silver Library Edition. Crown 8vo., 3s. 6d.

**Proctor.**—Works by RICHARD A. PROCTOR. —*continued.*

LEISURE READINGS. By R. A. PROCTOR, E. CLODD, A. WILSON, T. FOSTER and A. C. RANYARD. Cr. 8vo., 5s.

**Stanley.**—A FAMILIAR HISTORY OF BIRDS. By E. STANLEY, D.D., formerly Bishop of Norwich. With Illustrations. Cr. 8vo., 3s. 6d.

**Wood.**—Works by the Rev. J. G. WOOD.

HOMES WITHOUT HANDS: a Description of the Habitation of Animals, classed according to the Principle of Construction. With 140 Illustrations. 8vo., 7s., net.

INSECTS AT HOME: a Popular Account of British Insects, their Structure, Habits and Transformations. With 700 Illustrations. 8vo., 7s. net.

INSECTS ABROAD: a Popular Account of Foreign Insects, their Structure, Habits and Transformations. With 600 Illustrations. 8vo., 7s. net.

BIBLE ANIMALS: a Description of every Living Creatures mentioned in the Scriptures. With 112 Illustrations. 8vo., 7s. net.

PETLAND REVISITED. With 33 Illustrations. Cr. 8vo., 3s. 6d.

OUT OF DOORS; a Selection of Original Articles on Practical Natural History. With 11 Illustrations. Cr. 8vo., 3s. 6d.

STRANGE DWELLINGS: a Description of the Habitations of Animals, abridged from 'Homes without Hands'. With 60 Illustrations. Cr. 8vo., 3s. 6d.

BIRD LIFE OF THE BIBLE. 32 Illustrations. Cr. 8vo., 3s. 6d.

WONDERFUL NESTS. 30 Illustrations. Cr. 8vo., 3s. 6d.

HOMES UNDER THE GROUND. 28 Illustrations. Cr. 8vo., 3s. 6d.

WILD ANIMALS OF THE BIBLE. 29 Illustrations. Cr. 8vo., 3s. 6d.

DOMESTIC ANIMALS OF THE BIBLE. 23 Illustrations. Cr. 8vo., 3s. 6d.

THE BRANCH BUILDERS. 28 Illustrations. Cr. 8vo., 2s. 6d.

SOCIAL HABITATIONS AND PARASITIC NESTS. 18 Illustrations. Cr. 8vo., 2s.

## Works of Reference.

**Maunder's (Samuel) Treasuries.**
  BIOGRAPHICAL TREASURY. With Supplement brought down to 1889. By Rev. JAMES WOOD. Fcp. 8vo., 6s.
  TREASURY OF NATURAL HISTORY; or, Popular Dictionary of Zoology. With 900 Woodcuts. Fcp. 8vo., 6s.
  TREASURY OF GEOGRAPHY, Physical, Historical, Descriptive, and Political. With 7 Maps and 16 Plates. Fcp. 8vo., 6s.
  THE TREASURY OF BIBLE KNOWLEDGE. By the Rev. J. AYRE, M.A. With 5 Maps, 15 Plates, and 300 Woodcuts. Fcp. 8vo., 6s.
  HISTORICAL TREASURY: Outlines of Universal History, Separate Histories of all Nations. Fcp. 8vo., 6s.
  TREASURY OF KNOWLEDGE AND LIBRARY OF REFERENCE. Comprising an English Dictionary and Grammar, Universal Gazeteer, Classical Dictionary, Chronology, Law Dictionary, &c. Fcp. 8vo., 6s.

**Maunder's (Samuel) Treasuries**—*continued.*
  SCIENTIFIC AND LITERARY TREASURY. Fcp. 8vo., 6s.
  THE TREASURY OF BOTANY. Edited by J. LINDLEY, F.R.S., and T. MOORE, F.L.S. With 274 Woodcuts and 20 Steel Plates. 2 vols. Fcp. 8vo., 12s.

**Roget.**—THESAURUS OF ENGLISH WORDS AND PHRASES. Classified and Arranged so as to Facilitate the Expression of Ideas and assist in Literary Composition. By PETER MARK ROGET, M.D., F.R.S. Recomposed throughout, enlarged and improved, partly from the Author's Notes, and with a full Index, by the Author's Son, JOHN LEWIS ROGET. Crown 8vo., 10s. 6d.

**Willich.**—POPULAR TABLES for giving information for ascertaining the value of Lifehold, Leasehold, and Church Property, the Public Funds, &c. By CHARLES M. WILLICH. Edited by H. BENCE JONES. Crown 8vo., 10s. 6d.

## Children's Books.

**"Brenda."**—Works by "BRENDA".
  OLD ENGLAND'S STORY IN LITTLE WORDS FOR LITTLE CHILDREN. With 29 Illustrations. Imp. 16mo., 3s. 6d.
  WITHOUT A REFERENCE. A Story. Cr. 8vo., 3s. 6d.

**Crake.**—Works by Rev. A. D. CRAKE.
  EDWY THE FAIR; or, The First Chronicle of Æscendune. Crown 8vo., 2s. 6d.
  ALFGAR THE DANE: or, the Second Chronicle of Æscendune. Cr. 8vo. 2s. 6d.
  THE RIVAL HEIRS: being the Third and Last Chronicle of Æscendune. Cr. 8vo., 2s. 6d.
  THE HOUSE OF WALDERNE. A Tale of the Cloister and the Forest in the Days of the Barons' Wars. Crown 8vo., 2s. 6d.
  BRIAN FITZ-COUNT. A Story of Wallingford Castle and Dorchester Abbey. Cr. 8vo., 2s. 6d.

**Ingelow.**—VERY YOUNG, and QUITE ANOTHER STORY. Two Stories. By JEAN INGELOW. Crown 8vo., 6s.

**Lang.**—Works edited by ANDREW LANG.
  THE BLUE FAIRY BOOK. With 8 Plates and 130 Illustrations in the Text by H. J. FORD and G. P. JACOMB HOOD. Crown 8vo., 6s.

**Lang.**—Works edited by ANDREW LANG. —*continued.*
  THE RED FAIRY BOOK. With 4 Plates and 96 Illustrations in the Text by H. J. FORD and LANCELOT SPEED. Crown 8vo., 6s.
  THE GREEN FAIRY BOOK. With 11 Plates and 88 Illustrations in the Text by H. J. FORD and L. BOGLE. Cr. 8vo., 6s.
  THE BLUE POETRY BOOK. With 12 Plates and 88 Illustrations in the Text by H. J. FORD and LANCELOT SPEED. Cr. 8vo., 6s.
  THE BLUE POETRY BOOK. School Edition, without Illustrations. Fcp. 8vo., 2s. 6d.
  THE TRUE STORY BOOK. With Plates and Illustrations in the Text, by H. J. FORD, LUCIEN DAVIS, LANCELOT SPEED, and L. BOGLE. Crown 8vo., 6s.

**Meade.**—Works by L. T. MEADE.
  DADDY'S BOY. With Illustrations. Crown 8vo., 3s. 6d.
  DEB AND THE DUCHESS. With Illustrations by M. E. EDWARDS. Crown 8vo., 3s. 6d.

## Children's Books—*continued.*

**Meade.**—Works by L. T. MEADE—*continued.*
THE BERESFORD PRIZE. With Illustrations by M. E. EDWARDS. Cr. 8vo., 5*s.*

**Molesworth.**—Works by Mrs. MOLESWORTH.
SILVERTHORNS. Illustrated. Crown 8vo., 5*s.*
THE PALACE IN THE GARDEN. Illustrated. Crown 8vo., 5*s.*
THE THIRD MISS ST. QUENTIN. Crown 8vo., 6*s.*
NEIGHBOURS. Illustrated. Crown 8vo., 6*s.*
THE STORY OF A SPRING MORNING, &c. Illustrated. Crown 8vo., 5*s.*

**Reader.**—VOICES FROM FLOWER-LAND: a Birthday Book and Language of Flowers. By EMILY E. READER. Illustrated by ADA BROOKE. Royal 16mo., cloth, 2*s.* 6*d.*; vegetable vellum, 3*s.* 6*d.*

**Stevenson.**—Works by ROBERT LOUIS STEVENSON.
A CHILD'S GARDEN OF VERSES. Small Fcp. 8vo., 5*s.*
A CHILD'S GARLAND OF SONGS, Gathered from 'A Child's Garden of Verses'. Set to Music by C. VILLIERS STANFORD, Mus. Doc. 4to., 2*s.* sewed; 3*s.* 6*d.*, cloth gilt.

## The Silver Library.

CROWN 8VO. 3*s.* 6*d.* EACH VOLUME.

**Baker's (Sir S. W.) Eight Years in Ceylon.** With 6 Illustrations. 3*s.* 6*d.*

**Baker's (Sir S. W.) Rifle and Hound in Ceylon.** With 6 Illustrations. 3*s.* 6*d.*

**Baring-Gould's (Rev. S.) Curious Myths of the Middle Ages.** 3*s.* 6*d.*

**Baring-Gould's (Rev. S.) Origin and Development of Religious Belief.** 2 vols. 3*s.* 6*d.* each.

**Brassey's (Lady) A Voyage in the 'Sunbeam'.** With 66 Illustrations. 3*s.* 6*d.*

**Clodd's (E.) Story of Creation:** a Plain Account of Evolution. With 77 Illustrations. 3*s.* 6*d.*

**Conybeare (Rev. W. J.) and Howson's (Very Rev. J. S.) Life and Epistles of St. Paul.** 46 Illustrations. 3*s.* 6*d.*

**Dougall's (L.) Beggars All:** a Novel. 3*s.* 6*d.*

**Doyle's (A. Conan) Micah Clarke.** A Tale of Monmouth's Rebellion. 3*s.* 6*d.*

**Doyle's (A. Conan) The Captain of the Polestar, and other Tales.** 3*s.* 6*d.*

**Froude's (J. A.) Short Studies on Great Subjects.** 4 vols. 3*s.* 6*d.* each.

**Froude's (J. A.) Cæsar:** a Sketch. 3*s.* 6*d.*

**Froude's (J. A.) Thomas Carlyle:** a History of his Life.
1795-1835. 2 vols. 7*s.*
1834-1881. 2 vols. 7*s.*

**Froude's (J. A.) The Two Chiefs of Dunboy:** an Irish Romance of the Last Century. 3*s.* 6*d.*

**Froude's (J. A.) The History of England,** from the Fall of Wolsey to the Defeat of the Spanish Armada. 12 vols. 3*s.* 6*d.* each.

**Gleig's (Rev. G. R.) Life of the Duke of Wellington.** With Portrait. 3*s.* 6*d.*

**Haggard's (H. R.) She:** A History of Adventure. 32 Illustrations. 3*s.* 6*d.*

**Haggard's (H. R.) Allan Quatermain.** With 20 Illustrations. 3*s.* 6*d.*

**Haggard's (H. R.) Colonel Quaritch, V.C.:** a Tale of Country Life. 3*s.* 6*d.*

**Haggard's (H. R.) Cleopatra.** With 29 Full-page Illustrations. 3*s.* 6*d.*

**Haggard's (H. R.) Eric Brighteyes.** With 51 Illustrations. 3*s.* 6*d.*

**Haggard's (H. R.) Beatrice.** 3*s.* 6*d.*

**Harte's (Bret) In the Carquinez Woods and other Stories.** 3*s.* 6*d.*

**Helmholtz's (Professor) Popular Lectures on Scientific Subjects.** With 68 Woodcuts. 2 vols. 3*s.* 6*d.* each.

**Howitt's (W.) Visits to Remarkable Places.** 80 Illustrations. 3*s.* 6*d.*

**Jefferies' (R.) The Story of My Heart:** My Autobiography. With Portrait. 3*s.* 6*d.*

**Jefferies' (R.) Field and Hedgerow.** Last Essays of. With Portrait. 3*s.* 6*d.*

**Jefferies' (R.) Red Deer.** With 17 Illustrations by J. CHARLTON and H. TUNALY. 3*s.* 6*d.*

**Jefferies' (R.) Wood Magic:** a Fable. With Frontispiece and Vignette by E. V. B. 3*s.* 6*d.*

**Knight's (E. F.) The Cruise of the 'Alerte':** the Narrative of a Search for Treasure on the Desert Island of Trinidad. With 2 Maps and 23 Illustrations. 3*s.* 6*d.*

**Lang's (A.) Custom and Myth:** Studies of Early Usage and Belief. 3*s.* 6*d.*

**Lees (J. A.) and Clutterbuck's (W. J.) B. C. 1887, A Ramble in British Columbia.** With Maps and 75 Illustrations. 3*s.* 6*d.*

**Macaulay's (Lord) Essays and Lays of Ancient Rome.** With Portrait and Illustration. 3*s.* 6*d.*

**Macleod's (H. D.) The Elements of Banking.** 3*s.* 6*d.*

**Marshman's (J. C.) Memoirs of Sir Henry Havelock.** 3*s.* 6*d.*

www.ingramcontent.com/pod-product-compliance
Lightning Source LLC
Chambersburg PA
CBHW031959300426
44117CB00008B/836